MEDIA OF REASON

NEW DIRECTIONS IN CRITICAL THEORY
Amy Allen, General Editor

New Directions in Critical Theory presents outstanding classic and contemporary texts in the tradition of critical social theory, broadly construed. The series aims to renew and advance the program of critical social theory, with a particular focus on theorizing contemporary struggles around gender, race, sexuality, class, and globalization and their complex interconnections.

Narrating Evil: A Postmetaphysical Theory of Reflective Judgment, María Pía Lara
The Politics of Our Selves: Power, Autonomy, and Gender in Contemporary Critical Theory, Amy Allen
Democracy and the Political Unconscious, Noëlle McAfee
The Force of the Example: Explorations in the Paradigm of Judgment, Alessandro Ferrara
Horrorism: Naming Contemporary Violence, Adriana Cavarero
Scales of Justice: Reimagining Political Space in a Globalizing World, Nancy Fraser
Pathologies of Reason: On the Legacy of Critical Theory, Axel Honneth
States Without Nations: Citizenship for Mortals, Jacqueline Stevens
The Racial Discourses of Life Philosophy: Négritude, Vitalism, and Modernity, Donna V. Jones
Democracy in What State? Giorgio Agamben, Alain Badiou, Daniel Bensaïd, Wendy Brown, Jean-Luc Nancy, Jacques Rancière, Kristin Ross, Slavoj Žižek
Politics of Culture and the Spirit of Critique: Dialogues, edited by Gabriel Rockhill and Alfredo Gomez-Muller
The Right to Justification: Elements of Constructivist Theory of Justice, Rainer Forst
The Scandal of Reason: A Critical Theory of Political Judgment, Albena Azmanova
The Wrath of Capital: Neoliberalism and Climate Change Politics, Adrian Parr

MEDIA OF REASON

A Theory of Rationality

MATTHIAS VOGEL

Translated by Darrell P. Arnold

Columbia University Press *New York*

Columbia University Press
Publishers Since 1893
New York   Chichester, West Sussex
cup.columbia.edu
Copyright © Suhrkamp Verlag, Frankfurt
Translation copyright © 2012 Columbia University Press
All rights reserved

Library of Congress Cataloging-in-Publication Data

Vogel, Matthias.
 [Medien der Vernunft. English]
 Media of reason : a theory of rationality / Matthias Vogel ; translated by Darrell P. Arnold.
   p. cm. — (New directions in critical theory)
 Includes bibliographical references and index.
 ISBN 978-0-231-15058-3 (cloth : alk. paper) — ISBN 978-0-231-52775-0 (e-book)
 1. Rationalism. 2. Mass media—Philosophy. I. Arnold, Darrell (Darrell P.) II. Title.
 B833.V6412 2012
 128'.33—dc23

2012021327

∞ Columbia University Press books are printed on permanent and durable acid-free paper.
This book is printed on paper with recycled content.
Printed in the United States of America

c 10 9 8 7 6 5 4 3 2 1

References to websites were accurate at the time of writing. Neither the author nor Columbia University Press is responsible for URLs that may have expired or changed since the manuscript was prepared.

CONTENTS

Foreword   vii
Translator's Preface   xv

1 / INTRODUCTION   1

    1.1. On the Situation of the Project of the Enlightenment   1
    1.2. What Is Enlightenment?   8
    1.3. How to Achieve the Enlightenment   15
    1.4. Orienting Reflections on the Theory of Rationality   24
    1.5. Why a Theory of Rationality as a Theory of Media?   75

2 / WHAT ARE MEDIA?   78

    2.1. Sociological Theory of Media   80
    2.2. Media and Technology   93
    2.3. Dewey's Action-Theoretic Conception of Media   96

3 / TOWARD A GENERAL THEORY OF MEDIA   114

    3.1. Introduction   114
    3.2. An Interpretationism Expanded by Media Theory   119
    3.3. Further Theoretical Foundations of Media Theory   240

4 / THE CONSEQUENCES FOR A CONCEPT OF RATIONALITY   267

    4.1. The Explicative Benefits   268
    4.2. The Normative Returns   298

Notes   307
Bibliography   341
Index   365

FOREWORD

In our century hardly a basic philosophical concept has been reconstructed and assessed in such irreconcilable ways as the concept of rationality. While some—who are obliged to the tradition of the Enlightenment— place the development of a stable concept of rationality at the center of their theoretical efforts, indeed even maintain "that philosophy in its postmetaphysical, post-Hegelian currents is converging toward the point of a *theory of rationality*,"[1] others are working to dismantle it, are busy debunking and demonizing it. A third group of philosophers has become suspicious of these efforts, whether of one group or the other. They have already left reflections on reason behind and turned away from disputes about the concept of rationality, despite the fact that the attempt to specify reason has been one of the central issues of European philosophy since its beginnings.

Against the background of these diverging tendencies, in this book I want to make a proposal that, on the one hand, adheres to the perspective of the Enlightenment, but that, on the other, attempts to accommodate reservations about the typical reconstructions of reason. I will do so by offering a view of rationality that is not guilty of the one-sidedness that motivates the attempts of the postmoderns and their predecessors to debunk it. Even if many of the existing reservations about reason can only be taken seriously as symptoms of a discomfort, which is often only able to be articulated at the cost of a pragmatic self-contradiction, and it is not rare that arguments are lacking that could be dealt with in detail, the tradition of the Enlightenment is obliged to a sensitivity that attempts to consider every reservation appropriately. To demand that these reservations assume the form of arguments may not appear to be an inappropriate expectation in the context of philosophy; nevertheless, to make this a condition for a self-critical withdrawal from the process of the Enlightenment appears to me to be too demanding of a requirement. Here I would like *Enlightenment* to be understood as an open learning process, which need not be viewed as a closed or an incorrigibly "violent" process, yet to which, moreover, in my view, no acceptable alternatives exist. For as beings that are what we are because we interpret ourselves, we are dependent on articulated self-understandings. And if the self-understandings prove to be too simple or distorted, then we have no alternative, as learning beings, but to revise them in the process of Enlightenment. However, introducing the concept of a "learning process" already raises difficulties for any rational-theoretical-based Enlightenment project. For if by learning one means more than a physicalistically or functionalistically interpreted behavior-changing process, then it appears that, for its part, explicating what a learning process consists in is already dependent on a concept of rationality. For a learning process with steps that we should be able to assume a critical stance toward presupposes a concept of rationality, which codevelops in the learning process: with the help of this concept of rationality, we are able to assess and justify the alternatives generated in the learning process. The problem of circular reference contexts depicted here is characteristic of the difficulties that are found in the framework of a theory of rationality with normative claims. And yet we have no alternative to a procedure in which we precalculate the costs of each existing explication of rationality and then, in the case of a negative balance, replace the costly explication as we place a *constructive* vote of no confidence.

My reflections are based on the intuition that the theory of rationality should be developed in reference to a more *fundamental* and simultaneously *more general* perspective than is possible within the framework of any of the influential traditions that are centered on the analysis of instrumental or linguistic competencies. The plausibility of this intuition can initially be shown with the help of two simple caveats regarding the established rational-theoretic paradigms of *instrumental work* and *linguistic communication*.

The *instrumental* paradigm is problematic, and indeed not so much because it entails a certain inherent "violence," but because it entails too many presuppositions to be able to play a fundamental explanative role in a theory of rationality. For we can only determine what work or instrumental action is if we already possess a theory of the actors' preferences, plans, and descriptions of the reality—in short, if we possess a theory of the intentional states that a theory of rationality, formulated with instrumental concepts, remains dependent on. However, if the concept of work remains dependent on a theory of mental states, then some theory that can explain the existence of such states, for example, using the concepts of an interpretation or the concepts of one's (self-)understanding, is better suited to serve as the foundation for a theory of rationality.

The *linguistic* paradigm, which makes processes of comprehension or of understanding the focal point, appears to have comparatively good chances of being fundamental enough to be able to serve as a conceptually independent foundation for a theory of rationality. However, the linguistic paradigm presents problems because it is too specific. For if it is correct (as I am convinced it is) that a theory of rationality should be laid out with concepts of a theory of understanding, it (still) remains questionable why this theory should deal solely with *linguistic* understanding. Naturally, proponents of the linguistic paradigm do not deny that, besides the linguistically conveyed communications processes, there are also those in which nonlinguistic means are used; however, it appears they do not have confidence that the analysis of nonlinguistic communication processes is able to make a relevant contribution to the project of explicating rationality. In light of the enormous difference regarding the theoretical means that are available to us for analyzing linguistic and nonlinguistic communication processes, this may not be so remarkable; yet still, within the parameters of the linguistic paradigm, when faced with the efforts to describe art as a dimension in which reason unfolds, one cannot shake the suspicion that the linguistic paradigm does not provide conceptual resources suited to meet this requirement.

To put it clearly: the conception offered here shares with the adherents of the linguistic paradigm the belief that the core of our rationality can be laid open by an analysis of our competencies of understanding, but it attempts to free itself from the fixation on the concept of linguistic understanding in order to gain a basis general enough to allow an explication of the theory of rationality—a basis of explication that includes the processes of nonlinguistic understanding as they appear in exemplary form in the context of art. Of course, it is possible to accommodate the fact that there is something like nonlinguistic understanding without wanting to draw conclusions of a rational-theoretic nature, but it is not clear how we can ensure that a suitable and comprehensive portrayal of rationality is provided if we exclude certain forms of understanding from the explanative basis. Instead of searching for arguments to justify this exclusion, which show that nonlinguistic understanding is a derived, deficient, or parasitic form of understanding, it appears to me to be theoretically more productive to attempt to characterize linguistic expressions as a special case of *medial action* and to interpret language as one (in various respects exceptional) *medium* among *others*. For if we speak of understanding in the case of nonlinguistic—as in the case of linguistic—expressions, it initially seems obvious that we should identify those characteristics that linguistic and nonlinguistic expressions share in order to specify the basis of these shared characteristics, which accounts for the special status of linguistic expressions. To presume that the shared characteristics have nothing to do with reason would then require a stronger argument. However, in order to be able to do theoretical justice to the common characteristics of linguistic and nonlinguistic expressions, we need a concept that itself is more general than the concept of language and considerably more specific than concepts that aim at perceptible characteristics of expressions. What we need, I would like to suggest, is the concept of the medium.

A proposal that amounts to placing the media concept in a central theoretical position has to contend with the fact that we do not possess a general and robust concept of the medium, and every media concept that plays a role—above all, in the context of media studies, but also in the domain of cultural-diagnostic approaches—is more likely to lastingly damage the reputation of the media concept. Above all, those who view the appearance of computers and global nets as an occasion to present a cultural diagnosis founded on media theory are to be thanked for the fact that the media concept has not yet been exposed to the light rays of fallibilism. Nor can the attempt to develop a productive media concept within another tradition in which the media concept has gained some popularity be met with good cheer; for the acceptance of the concept in system theory has left us with a media concept that suffers from all the ills that plague system theory itself. In connection with a rather schematic reconstruction of the existing media concepts, I will thus attempt to meet the risk-filled task of developing a robust and theoretically homogeneous concept of the medium that can withstand the pressure of rationality theory.

The focus of this book is on the attempt to better understand what rationality is. Hereby, I am attempting to develop conceptual means that can accommodate the fact that there are good reasons that the development of (modern) art is also understood to constitute a dimension in the development of rationality. The view of rationality developed here attempts to argue that a moment of productivity is inherent in rationality that does not depend on having language at one's disposal, a moment of playful productivity that simply is incapable of ceding to the paper tiger of the postmodern critique of reason. However, if it can be plausibly shown that the roots of rationality reach into *nonlinguistic intentional states*, philosophy must at the same time develop a new view of the human mind, which is more complex than the meager one that describes it as an inferentially organized network of propositional attitudes. Even if one accepts the development as an achievement in the philosophy of mind—among other things, because it allows us to explicate the irreducible specifications of the mental in a way that is not immersed in the conceptually dark introspection theories—one will have to admit that it has moved quite some distance from the widespread intuitions, above all because of its alternative conception to that of a thoroughly linguistically constituted mind.

Because this book can be read with very different interests, I would like to provide a cursory overview of what is going on in the following chapters.

Chapter 1 situates my reflections in the context of the debates about the concept of the Enlightenment and the normative core of a theory of Enlightenment rationality. In this chapter I attempt to show that it is plausible to maintain a normative concept of Enlightenment that is worthwhile and rich in content. Because a concept of the Enlightenment is dependent on a concept of rationality insofar as learning theories are only able to be differentiated from processes of mere transformation with the help of normative criteria, I subsequently comment on a series of paradigmatic theories of rationality while sketching out a *minimal view of Enlightenment*. Here I presume that the reflections on rationality theory aim to analyze the competencies that are basic for our capacity of understanding. Following Habermas and Davidson, I am of the view that the theory of rationality should be based in a theory of understanding, but I am not able to see why this analysis should remain limited to processes of linguistic understanding.

A comprehensive concept of rationality must rather be able to accommodate the fact that we do not only rightfully view ourselves as the only beings on this planet that are in any demanding sense *rational*, but also that we are the only beings that are capable of artistic action and aesthetic experience, indeed that the last two characteristics are not mere by-products of our rationality but, for their part, are essential dimensions of our rationality. A comprehensive view of rationality must correspondingly be capable of coping with these dimensions and their interrelationships, and in my view it is precisely the lack of a systematic analysis of this context that makes our view of rationality so susceptible to the suspicions to which it is subjected in the conceptually fixated radical critique of reason. I attempt to counter these dangers by not limiting the theory of rationality that is developed here to processes of understanding that are achieved by linguistic means, but by viewing language as one—admittedly privileged—medium of understanding among others. At the end of chapter 1, the following assessment is thus offered: if rationality is interpreted in essence as a competence, then a concept of rationality must be established that is sufficiently universal to include an analysis of *all* the competencies of understanding, consequently also of those competencies of a nonlinguistic understanding. Because understanding, however, initially is an intersubjective process, it must include a comprehensive theory of rational competencies, especially of the means that make nonlinguistic communication possible. Then, however, we need a close analysis of those means that I, in conformity with influential theories, view as nonlinguistic analogues to language, which is the means to linguistic communication. In short, we need a theory of media.

Chapter 2 presents the compressed results of a critical analysis of established media theories; this turns out to be somewhat depressing since none of the existing theories provides a robust theory of media that one can accept in good conscience. While the media concept of McLuhan and his students is not nearly developed enough and—because of the frightening lack of depth both in regard to theory and terminology—is not able to be molded into the needed form, the media concepts of the sociological tradition (Parsons, Habermas, Luhmann) suffer above all because, as a result of preliminary decisions regarding the architectonics of the theory, they are very heterogeneous; in addition, their link to the perspective of system theory makes it difficult to refer them back to the processes of understanding. Only in Dewey's little-examined, and unfortunately also hardly detailed, media-theoretic reflections can we, in my view, find points of contact for a robust concept of the medium.

Chapter 3 is in various respects the heart of this book. There I attempt, in the face of the deficiencies and incongruities of the established media theories, to lay bare a structure that underlies all media and that makes it possible to formulate a general and resilient concept of the medium and to make it fecund for understanding nonlinguistic action. I above all analyze the processes of understanding in reference to the understanding of works of art. Here I view artwork as the means of a form of communication that is deeply rooted in fundamental processes of interaction through which we become beings with minds. From this point, language can be plausibly shown to be a specific form of media communication: it is erected on the nonlinguistic structure of mind and is developed in more basic communicative relations.

In chapter 4 I return to the problems set out at the beginning by attempting to make the theory of media fecund for a new view of rationality and for the further development of the project of the Enlightenment.

I would like to thank all those who have supported me with critique and encouragement during the nearly endless time in which this book was developed, especially Alexander Becker, Hauke Brunkhorst, Dieter Burdorf, Kai-Uwe Bux, Simone Dietz, Carolin Emcke, Rainer Forst, Aki Hockerts, Axel Honneth, Gertrud Koch, Michael Kohler, and Lutz Wingert. Many discussions about the visual arts, music, film, and photography with Theodor Buhl, Steffi Hartel, Udo Koch, Michael Maierhof, Christian Ofenbauer, Bernhard Schreiner, and Susa Templin have helped me develop and more precisely formulate my thoughts in contact with real artistic thinking and not merely in reference to philosophical fantasies about it. I would like to thank Bernd Stiegler, from Suhrkamp Verlag, whose committed and critical editing helped render the German edition of this book more readable, clearer, and, gratefully, considerably shorter. Further thanks are extended to the Graduiertenförderung der Freien und Hansestadt Hamburg, which supported the early research on the theory presented here with a stipend.

I owe Wolfgang Detel and Eva Gilmer thanks that exceed what can be expressed in the parameters of this foreword. The book is dedicated to Eva Gilmer.

I am very pleased that this book, a good ten years after the first edition of its publication, is now available to English language readers. I would first of all like to thank Jürgen Habermas, who advocated to include it in the publishing series of Columbia University Press, and of course the press, which accepted the recommendation. I am very grateful to Darrell Arnold for his commitment, his always-constructive collaboration, and the extremely successful translation. I would like to thank Christian Heilbronn for his precise and critical editing of an early version of the translation. I am thankful to my parents for their diverse support over the past few years.

TRANSLATOR'S PREFACE

In *Media of Reason*, Matthias Vogel offers a critical appraisal of the recent discussion of the Enlightenment tradition, a penetrating analysis of contemporary writings on reason in the German, French, and Anglo-American literature, and an overview of theories of media as expressed especially in social theory and media studies. While Vogel joins Habermas in proposing the continuation of the Enlightenment project and views the postmodern attempts to merely deconstruct reason, then cast it aside, as involving postmodern theorists in what Habermas has famously called a "performative contradiction," he is also critical of what he views as Habermas's over-identification of reason with linguistic-based competencies. In fact, Vogel levels a stinging critique of the major Continental views of reason since the "linguistic turn," arguing that they offer truncated views of reason, unsuited to account for the understanding that occurs through nonlinguistic media such as music and the plastic arts.

Yet the razor's edge of Vogel's critique cuts two ways: Both those who accept reason and those who reject it have an inadequate understanding of what it is. While Vogel is critical of Habermas's view for failing to account for nonlinguistic forms of understanding, he does not for that accept that some forms of understanding (for example, in music and art) transcend reason since they are nonlinguistic. Instead, he argues that it is simply false to limit our understanding of what is rational to that which is discursive. Setting out from the rather Kantian view that a comprehensive conception of reason must account for all the competencies of understanding, in part through thorough reflections on competencies for nonlinguistic communication, Vogel develops a comprehensive theory of media that serves as the basis for a theory of rationality. In putting forward that view he argues that besides the media of language, further media of reason exist.

Further, while Vogel is critical of the views of reason proposed since the linguistic turn, he does not suggest a return to a simple philosophy of consciousness. Rather, he views the various media of reason, like language, as embodied in social practices and as socially mediated. In alignment with Dewey's view of media, Vogel does view media in the arts, and elsewhere, as "specific possibilities for action" (p. 115). And while action and social practices are to be understood against these possibilities, the possibilities are also mediated in social interaction and embodied in social institutions, whether in music lessons or forms of interaction with infants and toddlers who have not yet acquired language.

Given that critical theory has always understood itself as engaged in a reason-based critique of society, and it is vital for critical theorists to clearly apprehend what reason is and how its forms become embodied in social practices in multifarious ways, the reflections on reason offered here do make a valuable contribution to that tradition. Indeed, Vogel's views may well facilitate a better understanding of the forms of "intramundane transcendence" so vital to the historically situated critique that is central to much of critical theory.

Still, given the work's broad contribution to views of reason and media, the book should also appeal to many who are not interested in critical theory at all. The book offers an introduction to some recent German thought on reason that is not well known to English-speaking philosophers. It provides profitable overviews of the views of media found in Parsons, Habermas, Luhmann, and McLuhan, as well as an important reconstruction of Dewey's media concept. It also contains insights relevant to John Searle's and Donald Davidson's work of potential interest to those working on philosophy of mind.

TECHNICAL POINTS

Because a few quotes in the original German edition of this text were not referenced in the footnotes, the note numbers in the English translation do not correspond fully with the numbering in the German version. It was necessary to add the following notes, with corresponding references: in chapter 1, notes 35 and 121 were added; in chapter 2, notes 89 and 98; in chapter 3, notes 20, 53, and 56; no notes were added to chapter 4. The chapter numbers also differ in the original and the translated versions of the book. In the German edition, the foreword is counted as chapter 1. In this translation, however, chapter 1 is the introduction.

TRANSLATOR'S ACKNOWLEDGMENTS

In this translation I have attempted to remain faithful to the German while rendering a translation accommodating to English language readers. In this, I benefited enormously from Christian Heilbronn's very critical reading and from consultation with Matthias Vogel. I am also indebted to Elisabeth Jütten for her generous help in working through some of the particularly difficult passages of the German version of the book, as well as Christina Lustig for work on the notes and bibliography.

MEDIA OF REASON

1 / INTRODUCTION

1.1. ON THE SITUATION OF THE PROJECT OF THE ENLIGHTENMENT

The illustrious project of the Enlightenment, once the heart of European philosophy, has, in our day, a bad reputation. Those who commit themselves to the Enlightenment quickly meet with distanced reactions. For don't we owe the destruction of nature to the Enlightenment? Isn't the Enlightenment, with its demand to bring societal process under the control of rational planning, the project that is responsible for the societal systems of coercion? And isn't the Enlightenment the project that set free processes of technical innovation, the consequences of which we cannot even begin to estimate? And isn't a reason at work behind all of these processes that the Enlightenment thinkers promised would bring a release from our self-imposed immaturity?

Even if this diagnosis paints too bleak a picture, the discourse of modernity appears to be characterized by the development of aporias that overbid one another whereby each encompasses the other. These have condensed into an opaque, interwoven nexus, constituting a general crisis of the Enlightenment, which has recently increasingly been mistaken for the end of the Enlightenment. However, such a bleak view of the Enlightenment is hardly one that has only been offered by our contemporaries. Long before it had become the fashion to skirt problems by attempting to withdraw into a new era with the help of the prefix "post," Adorno, for example, attempted to depict a violence of the Enlightenment impulse, which he had traced back to the very capillaries of conceptuality itself. This sort of attempt, for which Adorno is initially only to serve as an example, has always been connected with the problem that the diagnosis of the violent structure of the Enlightenment remained dependent on a medium that, for its part, belonged on the continuum of the Enlightenment, and thus could not be exempted from the scope of the critique. Thus, any self-critical process like this also entails the danger that the critique will rob itself of its own normative foundations. In this aporetic structure, however, only one motif reappears, albeit in a radicalized form, that was already connected to the earliest formulations of the concept of the modern, as found initially in Hegel. The process known as the Enlightenment has been subject to increasingly radical critique since its beginnings, and it has attempted, even in the development of aporetic structures, to strike a learning pose to critique. Precalculating the costs of the dominant concept of reason has always been an element of the Enlightenment.

In the wake of the end of the Enlightenment and the modern, the context needed for a self-critically developing Enlightenment threatens to unravel. Reaching back to the example of Nietzsche's generalized—heuristically explosive, but methodologically implosive—suspicion[1] that reason is intrinsically empty and thus only an instrument of the will to power, demasking critique has been established as the form for the fundamental critique of the program and process of the Enlightenment. There are essentially four possible reactions characterizing how this type of critique has been taken up by theories of the Enlightenment.

If the demands of such a demasking critique are *accepted*, there remain possibilities: *First*, defensive immunization is possible; this can be done, for example, by ratcheting down the theoretical claims. *Second*, it is possible to integrate the perspective of demasking critique into the Enlightenment concept; here, however, the theoretical attempts become increasingly aporetic. If the demands of the critique are *rejected*, then there are further possibilities: either *third*, a basis must be developed that grounds the critique of the critique and that, for its part, cannot be (completely) encompassed by the critique that has been rejected, or *fourth*, the critique must be reconstructed within broadened parameters that are able to maintain the connection with the project of the Enlightenment. Irrespective of whether one is of the view that each of these four theoretically possible reactions leads to intelligible viewpoints, in any case critique would generate a development that, as a whole, can be understood precisely as Enlightenment. In such a perspective it appears to be irrelevant whether the critique develops within the parameters of Enlightenment theories or outside the parameters of such theories.

In the 1980s, however, it appears that this scenario fundamentally changes. It no longer presents *the situation* of the project of the Enlightenment, but only *one perspective* of the situation: for many, the case recently brought against the Enlightenment has, in its final appeal, now been closed. Others think that it is a process that is no longer relevant because foundations for such a process, in their immanent violence, have become a clear sign of the guilt of the accused.[2] Hereby, the perspectives centered around the Enlightenment appear to have become mere variations among other possible perspectives; and with this change in the point of view, images shift abruptly between perspectives of the Enlightenment as an incomplete project (Habermas), as a *grand récit* (Lyotard), as a catastrophic dynamic[3] (Baudrillard), as a historical program with exaggerated foundationalist demands (Rorty), or as a bankrupt host of old European thought (Luhmann). Today it no longer appears possible to once again reorient the kaleidoscope of perspectives, redirecting them to the Enlightenment, simply by understanding the Enlightenment as a learning process and interpreting all critiques of this learning process, for their part, *as a part* of the learning process. For a more basic cause of the diagnosed decentering of the Enlightenment is the *in*ability of the program to learn. Radical critics of the Enlightenment find this above all at two levels, which can be labeled "theory and violence" and "theory and self-reference."

a. The motif showing the project of the Enlightenment to entail an implicit moment of violence is widespread, irrespective of the cleft between critics and defenders of the Enlightenment. The diagnoses motivating the basic skepticism toward or the turn away from the project of the Enlightenment range from an emphasis on the "will to power" to an emphasis on the preponderance of the general over the individual,[4] the claim of ostensive metadiscourse to hegemony,[5] and the structural power of the code.[6] If, however, on the basis of such diagnoses, the medium of the Enlightenment is conceived as intrinsically connected to violence, then the (refined or sublimated) continuance of the project of the Enlightenment can only be feared; so theoretical work has to be joined to powers external to the Enlightenment. To this end every topos that is opposed to the alleged structures of the Enlightenment is offered: in opposition to the terror of the concept of unity, the other of reason stands as the "nonidentical,"[7] the "incommensurable," the "heterogeneous," or the degraded;[8] and art, ecstasy, deconstruction, and catastrophe are called to its aid.

b. The second, in a certain sense unavoidable, reproach to the tradition of the Enlightenment is that of self-referentiality, which in normative and legitimating contexts is sharpened to an allegation that it involves a circular self-presupposition. Theories of the Enlightenment appear to be dependent on presupposing something that they are precisely intending to portray. According to this diagnosis, the specific scientific knowledge of the Enlightenment "cannot know and make known that it is the true knowledge without resorting to the other, narrative, kind of knowledge, which from its point of view is no knowledge at all. Without such recourse it would be in the position of presupposing its own validity and would be stooping to what it condemns: begging the question, proceeding on prejudice. But does it not fall into the same trap by using narrative as its authority?"[9]

Aside from the implied crude identification of "scientific knowledge" and "true knowledge," which is foreign to most (modern) philosophies of science, and aside from the fact that the diagnosis that the Enlightenment is involved in a self-presupposition is among the recurring forms of critique of an enlightened Enlightenment, the fact that something is a self-presupposition is a problem only in a certain sense, a sense that comes into purview if we turn our attention to the ability to subject theoretical constructions to criticism. If the self-presupposition is no longer able to be criticized in an explicative or normative context without at the same time accepting the theory in which this structure is generated, then a theory program exists to which there are apparently no alternatives as long as one adheres to the criticism. This situation can be described more precisely as follows: if the *presuppositions* of a theory are joined with the *explanatory claim* of this theory such that the relationship between the presupposition and the claim can no longer be criticized without presupposing that this relationship is valid, then the theory forms more or less its own environment and loses every external reference. Even criticism of the theory would be nothing more than an "externalized" self-reflection of this theory. Such a parthenogenic concept of reason, however, that indiscriminately includes the critique of itself, and that because of its totalizing self-referentiality must develop everything out of itself, belongs in essence among the fossils of the history of philosophy; only with great effort could it be restored as an adversary to be taken seriously today. In connection with problems of self-presupposition, what "remains is a formal peculiarity that one finds in the concept of rationality and perhaps nowhere else: The concept of rationality must be subsumed autologically, must be formed rationally."[10] This, however, by no means prevents concepts of rationality from being established in different ways, and thereby the avoidance of structures that solidify in self-reference.

The theoretical approaches that, in the marketplace of ideas, not long ago found (and still find) their customers under the marketing label "postmodern" and that in many cases, with their critique of the violence and self-reference of the Enlightenment, refer more to a caricature of the current conceptions of the Enlightenment[11] than to systematic problems, require this distorted background in order to plausibly show that they have somehow escaped the continuum of the Enlightenment learning process. But even the fact that theories that are included as part of the radical critique of the Enlightenment by no means stand in a consistent relationship to the Enlightenment, but oscillate between the "revision of the modern" and the discrediting of the medium of the modern—discourse[12]—does not restore a connection between making suggestions and critique, which is prescribed in the development of a robust concept of the Enlightenment. For precisely this concept—understood as a narrative of legitimation—has not only lost its credibility,[13] but, by being "demasked" as a narrative, has forfeited the status that secured the conditions for its immanent critique. If one presupposes, like Lyotard, that scientific knowledge "requires that one language game, denotation, be retained and all others excluded"[14] and that it legitimizes itself only by recourse to narrative forms of knowledge,[15] which for their part are "never subject to argumentation or proof,"[16] then the validity of the critique of science and thus of the Enlightenment would be disconnected from argumentation and would thereby leave the realm of reason-supported intersubjective argumentation. A critique conceived in this way has to face up to the charge that it itself is nothing more than a metanarrative. To fail to see a problem even in this is to begin the transformation from philosophy to entertainment.

The question that arises in the face of the above considerations is how, in this situation, an examination of forms of the radical critique of reason, the subject, and the Enlightenment can be established without degenerating into a witless exchange of opinions. It appears to me that what is necessary in order to do this is, first of all, a hard breach:

1. Some of the postmodern approaches repeat mistakes of the radical critique of the Enlightenment that have long been identified, and they presume rationality concepts and theoretical claims—undoubtedly also for reasons of rhetorical enhancement—that are seldom defended today in the ways that would suit the postmodern critique.[17] Habermas, who is stylized as a hydra of rationality theory,[18] years ago wrote:

> Just as it always has, philosophy understands itself as the defender [of rationality] in the sense of the claim of reason endogenous to our form of life. In its work, however, it prefers a combination of strong propositions with weak status claims; so little is this totalitarian, that there is no call for a totalizing critique of reason against it.[19]

2. Such a radical critique of reason is only able to be brought to its recipients at the cost of performative contradictions, because, if it is to be an intelligible and correct analysis, for its part, it must raise claims of validity that it purports to demask as violent impertinencies:[20]

> Is legitimacy to be found in consensus obtained through discussion, as Jürgen Habermas thinks? Such consensus does violence to the heterogeneity of language games.[21]

In light of the grave problems associated with this type of critique, we can hardly expect the dispute with it to be the linchpin of a philosophical theory that is concerned with a broadened concept of rationality. Rather, the radical critique of reason constitutes only a part of the background against which this attempt will be made, whereas precisely those theories that are the object of postmodern critique constitute the real—and to put it clearly, the only—sensible links.

3. It is certainly also clear that, against the background of the evident weaknesses of the postmodern critique, it is not possible simply to speak of the affirmation of the Enlightenment. Rather, the attempt to break from the continuum of the learning process must be taken seriously as a *symptom* that even the most developed conceptions of the project of

the Enlightenment may display grave weaknesses. What may be gained from the reception of the postmodern variations of the critique of reason and the Enlightenment is not a foundation for critically examining the theories of rationality or modernity. Rather, it is an increased sensitivity to the costs of those theories that today represent the tradition of the Enlightenment. If "postmodern knowledge" were limited to this sensibilizing function, then the following formulation from Lyotard could nearly be accepted without qualification: "Postmodern knowledge is not simply a tool of the authorities; it refines our sensitivity to differences and reinforces our ability to tolerate the incommensurable."[22] Luhmann, who here should be taken as a representative of the functionalist distance to the emphatic project of the Enlightenment, also accentuates this sensitivity to differences. Developing his thought against the background of the concept of difference, Luhmann shares Lyotard's diagnosis that there is no *métarécit*, indeed "because there are no external observers." As he continues, "Whenever we use communication [!]—and how could it be otherwise—we are already operating within society."[23] But in Luhmann's view as well, the benefits of the postmodern are limited to the diagnostic:

> The proclamation of the "postmodern" has at least one virtue. It has clarified that contemporary society has lost faith in the correctness of its self-description[s]. . . . They, too, have become contingent. . . .[24] What is important here is not the emancipation of reason but emancipation from reason. This emancipation need not be anticipated; it has already happened.[25]

However, Luhmann's distance, especially from the utopian moments of the Enlightenment process, does not go so far as to abrogate cooperation with the project of the Enlightenment: For "even this 'bifurcation' [of the process of modernity in spontaneous decomposition and utopian renewal] can be understood as unity, namely as applying the process of learning to the little understood phenomenon of modern society."[26]

A similarly supported view has by now also become widespread among prominent theoreticians of the postmodern, namely that "postmodernity is not a new age, it is the re-writing of some features modernity had tried or pretended to gain, particularly in founding its legitimation upon the purpose of the general emancipation of mankind. But such a re-writing, as has already been said, was *for a long time active in modernity itself.*"[27]

Regardless of what comes into purview from a postmodern perspective, the most developed theories of the Enlightenment and of rationality entail problems that provide occasion enough for dissatisfaction with mere justification. These theories deserve a fundamental and detailed critique precisely because they have taken it on themselves to develop robust and criticizable basic principles of critical social-theoretical reflection that go beyond the best-known, but most effective, forms of totalizing critique. Insofar as the bleak picture sketched out at the beginning presents only a murky variation of the view of a situation in which, if we remove the postmodern visors, we can find a link for continuing the project of the Enlightenment.

1.2. WHAT IS ENLIGHTENMENT?

The question "What is Enlightenment?" appears antiquated in a climate of declining theoretical weightiness and inflationary declarations of its obituary. Given the lack of prospects of theories that believe they are able to do without this concept, I believe there are nevertheless no alternatives to proposing a clear, contoured concept of the Enlightenment and to checking whether this is able to hold out against critical objections that are developed in the context of a critique of reason.

Agreement about the meaning of the concept of Enlightenment is limited essentially to the characterization of it as a societal process. However, far-reaching differences become apparent as soon as an assessment of this process is at issue. Besides the pessimistic assessment of postmodern concepts sketched out above, two different basic conceptions can be differentiated.

When using the word *enlightenment* in a rather descriptive way, it characterizes a process that has developed (contingently) within the parameters of a certain culture. In contrast with this distanced observer perspective, concepts that normatively charge the idea assume an internal perspective, which is a result of their participatory partiality. Odo Marquard, for example, whom I would like to mention as an exemplary representative of the distanced description of the process, characterizes the Enlightenment as the development of a de-emotionalized, epistemic stance: "The Enlightenment is the tradition of the routinized courage to an unagitated sobriety."[28]

"Sobriety," as the stance that arises in the Enlightenment process, which is to secure both a distance from possible goals of action as well as a distance from emotional attachment to them, simultaneously has the function of easing the weight of the goals of the tradition, which has been passed on, and the objective of making these goals themselves the object of passionless reflection: "In short, Enlightenment sobriety, that is, the usance of modernity, is the exoneration of the absolute."[29] This antiutopian impulse is sharpened in Luhmann's descriptive concept of the Enlightenment. Luhmann radicalizes the process of exonerating the absolute, and it becomes a process of generating contingency. With the internal differentiation of modern societies, the impossibility of privileged perspectives becomes increasingly prominent; for anything that can be seen can also be seen differently. The emancipatory impulse, which is intrinsic to the Enlightenment until then, loses the character of a goal that is to be sought and is transformed into a process that unavoidably arises as an epiphenomenon of technical modernization.

> Technology, in its broader sense, is *functional simplification*, that is, a form of the reduction of complexity that can be constructed and realized even though the world and the society where this takes place is unknown. It is self-assessing. The emancipation of individuals, even irrational individuals, is an unavoidable side effect of this technologizing.[30]

However, as already said, here this is no longer a matter of "the emancipation of reason but emancipation from reason. This emancipation need not be anticipated; it has already happened."[31] In this perspective, too, the Enlightenment remains a learning process. From the perspective of the observer, however, it is one in which, as binding descriptions of the world are unrelentingly deconstructed, any knowledge thought to be secure or any goal thought to be justified is again shown to be contingent. But within this learning process, strong intuitions and normative ideas are no longer stable foundations of the Enlightenment concept; they—like everything else—are subject to observations from standpoints that can be freely chosen, and they consequently lose their status as foundational points of orientation. Orientation on any of the kernel ideas on which the observations can be centered is only one of many possibilities.

Privileged standpoints, which could function as starting points for theories of the Enlightenment, can only be taken up at the price of an antecedent narrowing of one's perspective. When asked about the problem of a lack of a certain standpoint of his theory or an intuition that stood behind it, in a 1985 interview, Luhmann answered:

> I would say that the structure of my theory is rather open for very diverse areas of society, rather open to both the positive and the negative sides of modern society. Habermas' problem is that his thinking is organized in reference to a moral duty of social theory. That lends this theory indeed a special attraction, but at the same time also indicates it boundaries. From the point of view of such a position, for example, one cannot see the money economy, law, or political machinery critically or can only view these with negative, critical depreciation.[32]

Luhmann further specifies the openness of his theoretical perspective while denigrating Habermas's concept, which is centered on the intuition of undistorted intersubjectivity and is committed to a "utopian perspective of reconciliation and freedom."[33] He does so by indicating the different starting point of his theory and its primarily descriptive tasks:

> I, for example, think it is more fruitful, not to begin theories with unity, but with difference, and not to allow them to end in unity (in the sense of reconciliation), but, how should I say this, with a better difference.... As a stance for research, the idea behind this is that one could do it all much better than any of the interpretations so far. So, one must withhold moral judgment or critique until one sees how it is possible to think about modern society.[34]

Understood against this background, the Enlightenment is not a committed and normatively grounded intervention. Rather, it is an observation that abstains from moral judgments, descriptively accompanying the societal processes, which generate ever-new configurations. It is an observation that is prepared to reflect the reduction of complexity that is intrinsic to any observation and, by introducing new differentiations, to construct it more complexly.

Richard Rorty, to introduce a final distinguished advocate of a primarily descriptive view of the Enlightenment—starting from a pragmatic deconstruction of central values of Western rationalism (e.g., "objective truth")—also maintains a distance from the normative claims of the Enlightenment and describes it as a historically contingent process. He is convinced that in the wake of a pragmatic deconstruction, philosophy ought to leave unproductive theoretical debates behind and accept the view that philosophical beliefs are not the cause of societal processes, and that, beyond their contextual usefulness, theories cannot be shown to be true. Against this background, Rorty pleads for a "light-minded aestheticism . . . toward traditional philosophical questions," which should serve the same end "as does the encouragement of light-mindedness about traditional theological topics":[35]

> Like the rise of large market economies, the increase in literacy, the proliferation of artistic genres, and the insouciant pluralism of contemporary culture, such philosophical superficiality and light-mindedness helps along the disenchantment of the world. It helps make the world's inhabitants more pragmatic, more tolerant, more liberal, more receptive to the appeal of instrumental rationality.[36]

Only if we put aside the pathos of philosophy and accede to a perspective of purposively rational reflection—in accord with which we evaluate the use value of theories, institutions, and social practices, oriented toward praxis—will we escape the danger of becoming entangled in irrelevant academic questions. What is relevant—leaving aside entertainment value—are in any case the practical consequences of theoretical proposals, not their abstract claims to validity.

> For the pragmatist, by contrast, "knowledge" is, like "truth," simply a compliment paid to the beliefs which we think so well justified that, for the moment, further justification is not needed.[37]

As a result of the radical cut in the breadth of validity claims to concrete cases, both a concept of universal transcultural rationality[38] and a concept of an encompassing project of the Enlightenment have become superfluous. In the final analysis, only concrete individuals in their respective life situations can decide whether the societal condition in which they live offers suitable tools for satisfying their needs or not. Here it seems to me to be problematic that, after the abandonment of the philosophical critique of social practices, the theory maintains only an elevated stance with view to liberal society, which, for its part, represents the milieu of evolutionary change and, against the background of our needs, is either retained or not. Individuals can learn from failure, "but they will not learn a philosophical truth, any more than they will learn a religious one. They will simply get some hints about what to watch out for when setting up their next experiment."[39]

Beyond both the cool distance of Rorty and the sobriety of Marquard, as well as Luhmann's theory, which is oriented on an exact description of societal processes, in the debate that centers around the concept of the Enlightenment there are normatively constructed theories, which, while not basing their concept of the Enlightenment on transhistorical or "objective" norms, do, however, argue with norms that assume a prominent position within the theoretical framework. The works of Mittelstraß and Habermas provide exemplary cases of such views.

Mittelstraß characterizes the Enlightenment as a process of confronting the existing conditions with normative criteria. In the examination of the culturalist concept of rationality, as it has been developed by Kambartel in connection with the concept of a form of life found in Wittgenstein,[40] he emphasizes the intervening character of critical reason that is engaged and that realizes itself in the process of the Enlightenment.

> In contrast to the specific *affirmative* character of a culture of reason, in accordance with Kambartel, I maintain that reason can in principle only become real as a form of resistance, as a critique of existing circumstances and as a projection of different circumstances, as *enlightenment*. The differentiation between rational and irrational circumstances, which we cannot get around if our talk of reason is not to become empty and vacuous, is a distinction *that we bring into the world*.[41]

Mittelstraß worries that by redirecting the Enlightenment project toward descriptive tasks and by focusing on the implications of the rationality for societal reality, the critical distance of the Enlightenment to the existent reality and to what is described will be lost. For "if the culture of reason as a universal culture is itself *normative*, as it is now called, precisely then is the appeal to its *reality* affirmative."[42] Consequently, he insists "that reason cannot be *extracted* from the circumstances, but rather must always be *asserted against* them."[43] As the *form* of the Enlightenment, critique remains dependent on the basic principles of a normative concept of reason, for "reason is an *idea*. And ideas are not defined. They are rather determined in reference to *ideal demands*, postulates."[44] The "Enlightenment idea of reason" that Mittelstraß is concerned with counters the existing conditions in a culture with a judgment about its existing practices that can be reformulated into demands on the participating subjects. "Reason is not an *attribute* of bourgeois culture or some other culture, but a form of evaluation of these cultures."[45]

Against this background, the Enlightenment is a process that—based on the suggestions of individuals[46]—aids in the development of rational conditions, and these conditions, which are to be created, must be able to achieve general acceptance. They must "prove themselves to be developed in comparison to the existing conditions and as suited to serve as the basis for future justified developments."[47]

Habermas surely is the most prominent advocate of a normatively constructed theory of the Enlightenment. His Enlightenment perspective is fully connected to the intersubjective sphere of linguistic communication, and in two senses: on the one hand, linguistic communication is the medium in which the process of the Enlightenment is carried out; on the other hand, the conditions that must be achieved in order for understanding to occur simultaneously serve as the basis for the normative criteria on which the Enlightenment, as a learning process, can orient itself. Socioculturally, the process of the Enlightenment is carried out through a process in which a medium of reflection is socially implemented that makes possible the intersubjective examination of validity claims that are raised in linguistic action. Here, at the level of collective imagination, the process sets out from the "linguistification of the sacred."[48] In the course of this, the traditional and unproblematic presuppositions lose their self-evident status and become the objects of critical debate, the objects of argumentation. The reflexive problematizing of traditional models of integration and orientation at the collective level corresponds to a process of decentralizing one's egocentric understanding of the world at the individual level.[49] In this process, discursive socialization yields to an ability to change perspectives and exchange roles.[50] A linguistic understanding or even more specifically the "communicative sociation"[51] of the individual is essential for both forms of learning that are basic to the Enlightenment; and the differentiating of the further development of linguistic interaction into forms of communicative action that are solely committed to examining validity claims that are made, i.e., to discourses, is at the same time also the moving force of a dynamic of rationalization that is characteristic of the Enlightenment process.

In comparison to Mittelstraß's view that the rational stands in a constitutive opposition to existing conditions, the normative aspects of the Habermasian Enlightenment concept are subtly interwoven into the existing conditions; for noncoercive discourse, as the medium for thematizing and critical examination, is an idealized construction whose basis—action oriented toward understanding—underlies linguistic interaction even in its most contorted forms. Enlightenment thus does not appear at an abstract distance from what exists; rather, as an advocate of noncoercive understanding, it can assure itself of the normative implications even of everyday communication by pointing to the conditions that make understanding possible at all. A communicative rationality that unfolds in the process of the Enlightenment can, supported by the analysis of the conditions of communicative action, rely on the fact that, whatever the accidental limitations the process of understanding may be subject to, an irreducible telos of mutual understanding is inherent to linguistic communication.[52]

> Communicative reason, too, treats almost everything as contingent, even the conditions for the emergence of its own linguistic medium. But for everything that claims validity *within* linguistically structured forms of life, the structures of possible mutual understanding in language constitute something that cannot be gotten around.[53]

The final authority in the process of the Enlightenment here remains solely argumentative discourse, to which those involved in the process of the Enlightenment are to unreservedly submit, allowing their hypotheses and theories to be examined by others.

> The vindicating superiority of those who do the enlightening over those who are enlightened is theoretically unavoidable, but at the same time it is fictive and requires self-correction: in a process of enlightenment there can only be participants.[54]

1.3. HOW TO ACHIEVE THE ENLIGHTENMENT

As a participant in the Enlightenment in this sense, in the following reflections I want to contribute to the understanding of the concept of the Enlightenment, which while not attributing too much weight to utopian elements, does not exhaust itself in the sobriety of an epistemic attitude. I attempt to develop an Enlightenment concept, which tries not to settle for a "levity in dealing with philosophical topics"; for doing so leads all too easily to the elimination of the presuppositions for that very levity. Rather, I attempt to hold fast to the perspective of intersubjective learning, responsive to suggestions and critique. To this end I assume the following preliminary provision:

(A1) The Enlightenment is the social process in which we develop and learn to understand our ability to understand.

At the center of this proposition lies the idea that the process of the Enlightenment should be characterized on the basis of competencies that are so fundamental that any possible self-understanding of social actors is connected to these competencies. It is clear that (A1) is initially nothing more than a thesis that stands in need of further justification; it appears to be especially questionable how (A1) stands in relation to those conceptions of the Enlightenment that place the process of the Enlightenment in an intimate relationship to the realization of rational structures, be they rationalizable beliefs, effective problem solving, just social structures, or what have you. For the justification of their proposals, normatively committed Enlightenment positions are dependent on theories of rationality, with the help of which it can first be shown what we can view as a rational belief, problem solving, or social structure. However, Enlightenment, understood in this way, is then a process that is dependent on an explicit theory of rationality. Viewed more closely, it becomes clear, however, that (A1) is not a noncommittal thesis, for irrespective of which conception underlies the characterization of the rational, thesis (A1) yields restrictions that are authoritative for all conceptions of rationality. These restrictions come to light if we attempt to characterize a minimal conception of the Enlightenment that is compatible with (A1).

1.3.1. A Minimal Conception of the Project of the Enlightenment

If the process of the Enlightenment is understood as the social implementation of competencies of understanding, then, by characterizing requirements for social processes of understanding that cannot be undercut, we can determine basic aspects of the process of the Enlightenment more precisely; on the basis of such a minimal conception it will not be necessary to center the project of the Enlightenment on wide-reaching and specific objectives. Such requirements are:

(A2) Any theory of the Enlightenment

1. must, as a *normative* theory, be normatively *consistent*;
2. cannot, as a theory with implied descriptions of human competencies, make decisions in advance about specific competencies that might limit self-understanding; in short, it must be anthropologically open;
3. must, on the one hand, be able to place the conception of its own theory of understanding in the context of historical conceptions of understanding (*tradition/historical competence*) and, on the other hand, must not consist of a mere reformulation of these (*progressiveness*);
4. must be *universal* insofar as it must include any possible form of understanding.

It may not be so obvious that precisely these—not exactly weak—demands be considered the *minimal* criteria of a concept of the Enlightenment. Thus in what follows I will comment on and attempt to justify the specific criteria. The general strategy here is to eliminate those theories of rationality that do not meet the restrictions following from (A1) from being considered a normative basis for the Enlightenment process.

1.3.1.1. On Normative Consistency

Under the keyword of *normative consistency* I want to thematize problems of normative logic that are connected to the constitutive normative character of all rationality theories. Insofar as all rationality theories make evaluative standards available, they are at the same time faced with the problem that the means that they use in their construction must not contradict the evaluative standards to which they owe their normative content. On closer examination, problems of normative consistency are posed at two levels.

If the Enlightenment is dependent on normative theories of rationality, then the critique based on rationality theory must be precluded from contradicting the very normative basis to which it owes its normative justification, i.e., Enlightenment critique must be protected from self-application that is autodestructive.[55] If, for example, the medium of the critique itself cannot be viewed as anything other than an instantiation of that which is to be criticized, then the critical status of an intervention employing this medium collapses. If a conception of the Enlightenment exhibits a normative inconsistency of this sort, this does not merely mean that the critical enterprise is up against particular difficulties, which are to be supported once it is finally specified what the Enlightenment is; rather, the result is that a conception like this is itself no longer rational. For good reasons cannot be provided for engaging in a practice that inevitably reproduces the very thing that the practice counters. In other words: *it is incomprehensible what orienting oneself on a theory of rationality like this would mean.*

However, it is just as clear that the problem of autodestructive self-reference cannot be solved simply by removing the normative basis from the scope of those things that can be criticized on its basis. For in this way the normative foundation would in principle be immunized and above all disconnected from further learning processes. However, if a concept of rationality requires that its normative basis be immunized, it limits the process of learning by bracketing certain objects from criticism. Then, however, it implies two incompatible postulates: the postulate of justifying normative foundations, which consists of nothing other than dealing with anticipated criticism, and the postulate of exempting the normative basis from justification. However, one cannot rationally (*verstehend*) adhere to postulates that are so incompatible. Between the autodestructive character of the critique and the immunization of its normative foundation, for a theory whose basis falls prey to its own critical potential, the possibility of self-criticism must be secured by developing a follow-up theory whose normative basis falls within the scope of the criticism, and yet whereby the criticism is held at bay. On the other hand—and that is the second aspect of normative consistency—on the basis of a desire to make the normative basis comprehensible, circular structures must not be built into the conception that end up being identified with the presuppositions and the performance.

1.3.1.2. On Anthropological Openness

The criterion of anthropological openness ought to raise awareness of the implications of theoretical concepts: beyond having a design value for the theory, basic concepts also have consequences for the openness of the anthropological design. For if the contribution of a theoretical construct comes at the cost of the possibilities available to people in developing images of themselves, then the possibilities for self-interpretation are sacrificed to the more primary need for stable theories. A theory of rationality that is to satisfy the criterion of anthropological openness thus must not secure its epistemological stability by constituting itself or its components in a way that predetermines the possible scope of self-conception.

The problem that I am attempting to address with the criterion of anthropological openness becomes clearer if we keep in mind that anthropological considerations and theoretical considerations about rationality are interwoven in a peculiar and often intimate way. For, on the one hand, the emphasis on specific abilities, with the help of which, from an anthropological perspective, we attempt to differentiate the human species from others, almost always also forms the basis for the exemplification and explication of rationality; on the other hand, theoretical considerations of rationality have anthropological implications. Reference is made to these in the attempt to provide evidence of the suitability of conceptions of reason in species-specific dispositions or practices. For example, the function that the ability for planned labor[56] or that the availability of language[57] take on in anthropological contexts when determining criteria for the species is complemented in each respective case by a corresponding concept of rationality (*Vernünftigkeit*); they become a prescriptive amalgam that runs the danger of becoming dead weight in the process of the Enlightenment. The criterion of anthropological openness thus has the function of testing whether rationality concepts are *sufficiently general* and do not owe their plausibility to the fixation of anthropologically prominent species competencies. For the type of beings we understand ourselves to be and the type of beings we consequently partially are should continually be able to be newly determined in the course of the Enlightenment process.[58]

1.3.1.3. On Historical Competence and Progressiveness

The criterion of historical competence and progressiveness is meant to ensure that a concept of reason, like every other idea that has made a contribution in the continuum of Enlightenment ideas, is placed in relationship to the work that has already been performed and the breadth of ideas that have been developed; against this background, its specific contribution is to be elucidated. To put it technically, the criterion requires, on the one hand, that new concepts be compatible with the old ones. This functions to make access to proposed concepts more probable by conjoining them to known ones. On the other hand, it expresses the expectation that a contribution proceed beyond the stand of the discussion thus far reached as long as the issue at hand remains problematic. There is a simple reason that the criterion of historical competence is a necessary criterion for rationality theories. For the resources that are available to us for understanding any possible *new* rationality theory can by definition only originate from already understood, known theories. Insofar, the criterion of historical competence should only secure conditions for the possibility of understanding theories, which are fundamental for the process of the Enlightenment.[59]

The criterion of progressiveness prohibits the mere citation of existing theories, thus reformulations that are not interpretations. For we demand of interpretations that are to document the understanding of a contribution to the process of the Enlightenment that they be informative by showing, in their own formulations, that it is plausible that this contribution can be made comprehensible with the help of reasons.

1.3.1.1. On Universality

The most suspect of the criteria of a theory of rationality is certainly the claim to universality, precisely in the context of a conception of Enlightenment processes. Against the background of the now widely propagated view that demands that are supposed to be connected with philosophical theories ought to be abnegated, the criterion of universality surely awakens the impression of a search for new masterly thinking. In the following I would thus like to illustrate more clearly why I think such a criterion belongs to the minimal criteria needed for the concept of rationality. Concerns about constructing a universalistic concept of rationality are primarily based on two caveats.

If "universalistic" is supposed to mean "culturally invariant," then it is objected that, hidden behind the well-intended requirements of a universalistic concept are nothing more than ethnocentric or cultural-centric overgeneralizations of standards that are in fact relativistic, and that, in the wake of these, there is a leveling of the specifics of cultural developments. In this criticism—which is motivated, or at least supported, by the obvious economic dominance of the centers of Western capitalism and the destruction of traditional ways of life in other political economies, which are subdued and have compatibility forced on them—the Western and merely allegedly universal concept of rationality is reproached for having an element of violence immanent to it that extinguishes what is foreign, and the source of the evil is perceived precisely in the demand for universality. From this perspective, the alleged universality of the rationality concept becomes the theoretical background for a cultural imperialism that subjects what is foreign to its own models.

A further caveat against the universalistic conception of rationality views a rationality concept that is allegedly universal as imperialistically imposing itself on differing spheres of human activity. In accord with this caveat, it is questionable whether all areas, thus whether all types of action or cultural spheres also within a culture, may be viewed similarly from the standpoint of a unified concept of rationality. Put more precisely, in accord with this perspective, it is questionable, first, whether all of the object areas are accessible by reason, and second, should this be affirmed, it remains unclear whether we here are dealing with *one* reason or different types of rationality, each of which is to be assigned to a specific object area.

At the basis of both of these elements of suspicion is the common motive to contrast the diversity of types of action, social practices, institutions, traditions, and cultures with the alleged hybrid demand of universalistic rationality theories, whose grasp of the factual plurality of phenomena leads to a homogenization that levels the differences under the aegis of a monomaniacal concept of reason. However, in view of this critical perspective, it is questionable what it could mean to *learn* from it. For if we are supposed to be able to learn something from this perspective, then it is only under the presupposition that we can *understand* what the arguments of critical intervention mean and what changes in our practices they suggest. However, apart from the reconstruction of possible motives, there are serious obstacles precisely to understanding this.

The alleged homogenizing universalism is most radically opposed by a *relativist* interpretation. In the light of this often-criticized variation, we are faced with the alternative either of interpreting statements that claim the relativism of all propositions as statements with truth-value, which are self-refuting, or of describing such statements not primarily as expressing truth claims, but as having expressive goals, which, however, then certainly remain deficient with a view to theoretical demands.

Because of the methodological lethality of radical relativistic positions, to be able to ensure a continued hearing of the caveats about universalism that arise, a *contextualist* reformulation is needed, such as the one Rorty, borrowing from Wittgensteinian motifs, has in mind; it emphasizes the need to save the antifundamentalist impulse of relativism in the process of disarming it.[60] Rorty rebuffs two untenable interpretations of relativism as being self-contradictory or "overstretched"; namely, those that assert the indifference to all standards and those that assent to a plurality of standards that correspond to the diversity of procedures for justification. He then, however, characterizes an acceptable interpretation of the relativistic caveat as one that insists that, beyond describing the procedures for justification established in (our) society, there is nothing sensible about truth and rationality that can be said. This interpretation, which is contextualistic since it is ethnocentric, does not view itself as epistemologically secured, but expects evaluative expressions to be context dependent in a way that is supposed to be comparable to indexical expressions.

However, even if, against the background of this analysis, which has taken leave of inconsistent incommensurability theses, we grant that the formulation of context-transcending standards is connected with a God's-eye perspective that we cannot assume, we cannot avoid the question regarding the perspective from which the *differences* can be diagnosed. For even a modest, context-sensitive theory of rationality must aim at differences in its diagnosis of cultural differentiations that are initially differences from the perspectives of those doing the diagnosis, and thus stated from their own cultural perspective; beyond this, however, the act of stating differences presupposes that they are related to an object that is in some way comparable. For otherwise it would not be at all clear whether the matter of concern was a (completely?) different kind of entity or process, or something that simply is not one of this specific type of entity or process. If, however, the diagnosis of allegedly essential differences is part of the kernel of contextualist relativism, this more moderate relativism implies the universalistic hypothesis that differences concern something comparable as well.[61]

The argumentation strategies sketched out at the beginning can only be sensibly understood as a critique *of certain formulations* of a universalistic concept of reason. For, on the one hand, a congruous methodic relativism is a methodologically self-contradictory position, from which nothing follows but the unacceptability of this position.[62] On the other hand, positions that insist on a basic divergence of cultural developments or human spheres of activity, and thus reject universalistic concepts of rationality, themselves lay claim to a latent form of universalism insofar as the divergence that they advocate can only be considered valid against the background of a universalizing hypothesis that can secure the comparability of what is divergent. However, if this latent universalism is itself a necessary condition for the diagnosis of culturally and ethnically significant differences, then the real problem connected with universalistic conceptions of rationality is not to be found in their universalistic claims or implications, but in the specific characteristics of the concepts of rationality themselves, which only more or less meet the universalistic claims.

The task, then, that presents itself in connection with the universalistic implications of conceptions of rationality consists in designing the concept of rationality so that it can avoid being unmasked as, in fact, particular. This demand is compatible with a theory of rationality aiming for universality as a regulative idea and the failure of every concrete formulation of a rationality concept in reference to this demand. But that can only be shown from the perspective of a rationality concept that is more universal than what is criticized.

The universality criterion should thus here be understood as indicating that it allows the criticism of the particularity of a concept of rationality that is propagated as a real universality; this can be done without necessarily being oriented immanently on the normative structure of what is criticized. This criterion makes a distance from (one's own) standards possible; it is analogous to ideology critique, but does not share its presuppositions, which require that the normative basis for the critique be adopted from its objects.[63] Recalling the fact that one's own standards are a product of a process that is subject to contingent influences, a self-distancing is possible that is guided by the criterion of universality. For this, the concept of universality must be designed to be supported by necessary presuppositions of critique and the generation of arbitrary alternatives to what is being criticized.

Both of the preceding considerations can be connected to the following argument and radicalized. For it can be shown that universalism is in a certain sense necessary, and indeed necessary for dealing with what is other—and probably endangered by the universal—or what is allegedly "completely other." If we want to understand activities or practices that we are not familiar with, we must initially impute the standards *we* use for orientation to *those whose behavior we want to understand*.[64] It is clearly inevitable that we start with the differences that we are familiar with and on which our familiar concepts are based; for initially we simply have nothing else to work with. If, on the basis of these standards, we fail to understand activities that we are not familiar with, we can modify our schemes for differentiating things (our differentiational sets) and base these on other hypothetical standards. But even these types of standards, which there have been reasons to modify, remain *our* standards, and they *have to* remain ours if they are to assume their function in our process of interpreting and understanding. For if the set of modified standards were (normatively) completely incompatible with the set of standards that we started out with, then it would not be possible to provide any reasons that would be able to explain the transition from set A to set B. For every hypothetically modified set of standards, the following criteria thus must apply:

   a. In order to secure its status as a set of *standards*, we must be convinced that we are able to explain our own actions with its help.
   b. We reservedly assume that the hypothetical standard is universal. Our reservation, however, is *limited*: we cannot allow the reservation about our standards to be all-encompassing, because doing so would deprive us of the possibility of understanding (ourselves *and* others or the other).

In the face of these conditions, it is clear that every concept of rationality must prove its worth for *two* perspectives *at the same time*. Confronted with the phenomena that we are attempting to understand, it must hypothetically allow modification, and it must retain the ability to be connected to the standards with the help of which we explain our own actions as rational.

This weak concept of universalism—weak because it is necessary—is not to be confused with cultural imperialism, because this universalism is reciprocal and because every formulation of a hypothetical-universalistic standard counts on its own provisional character—not in the form of a global suspicion, but with the consciousness of the partial fallibility of every single formulation of rational standards. What the theory of rationality can adopt from the relativistic or contextual critiques of reason thus does not take the form of an argument, but the form of a gesture, a gesture that says essentially: "Do not hold the formulations of the standards of rationality that you are assuming to be valid under all conditions and for all time." And "learn to achieve a reflexive distance from your standards by viewing them from the perspective of alternative interpretations!" Yet the only form in which this gesture can be taken into account is as the insight that each and every assumption of universality is fallible. But an assumption of universality can only be falsified with the aid of a better position—that is to say with a *constructive* vote of no confidence.[65]

If we presume with the normatively laden views of the Enlightenment that it is only possible to determine the process of the Enlightenment with the help of normative criteria, which, for their part, are capable of being justified, then it is clear that a theory of such criteria moves directly toward a theory of rationality. With provisions (A1) and (A2) I have specified a perspective that makes it possible to consult different and competing theories of rationality with a view to which conceptual resources they make available for an adequate, comprehensive concept of understanding.

Because the outline of my study is anything but obvious, in the following section, after offering a relatively schematic historical overview, I want to again take up those systematic demands that rationality theories can raise.

1.4. ORIENTING REFLECTIONS ON THE THEORY OF RATIONALITY

Beyond the path of a totalizing critique of reason, Habermas's assessment "that philosophy in its postmetaphysical, post-Hegelian currents is converging toward the point of a theory of rationality"[66] seems to have found broad acceptance.[67] Even at first glance, however, it is clear that the rediscovery of the topic of rationality is not connected with a movement toward a common concept of rationality. So, as in connection with the concepts of the Enlightenment, rationality theories with normative claims can initially be differentiated from those that reject the normative implications of the rationality concept or that at least consider implicit (*vernunftinterne*) normative determinations of the rationality concept to be unsustainable.

In order to examine the group of views that lie between emphatic normative theories and normatively disinterested theories, in the following reflections I would first like to cover the systematic possibilities that exist regarding the basic conception of rationality theories. To simultaneously embed these aspects of theory construction in a historical context and in this way to depict strands of development that are taken up by current works in this area, I will—leaning on the work of Herbert Schnädelbach[68]—draw out some lines along which the discourse about the definition of rationality has developed. In connection with this, I will situate some paradigmatic conceptions of our day against the background of the historical development and discuss systematic problems of rationality theory.

The history of the concept of rationality can—following Schnädelbach—be described as a history of the *subjectivizing* of reason, which converges with the history of the decentering of reason and rendering it less normatively potent.[69] Schnädelbach describes the steps involved in the history of the subjectivizing of reason as follows.

Following the *objective logos* of antique metaphysics comes the first step of the subjectivizing; this is *objective subjectivizing*, which is found in Christianity when the objective *logos* is implemented as a characteristic of a personal (*personenhaften*) God. This process passes into the phase of *subjective subjectivizing*, which is raised by Descartes's reconstitution of what is objective in his methodic, subjective doubt and that continues through Kant's reconstruction of reason as a subjective capability. In this process, Hegel's absolutizing of reason seems like a final rebellion of the objective view of reason, centered on a reformulated *logos*, undercut by the tradition of an "*empirical* interpretation of the aprioris of reason" that prepares the setting for the post-Hegelian decentering.

> What comes after idealism is no longer a philosophy of reason, but a *metaphysics of the irrational* . . . , existential thinking and then naturalism

and objectivism in all its forms. What they have in common: reason is not denied or rejected out of hand. It is pushed into secondary ranking; it is no longer the core or the essence, but . . . a function of something which in essence is not reason.[70]

The results of this latter phase of the decentering process, which simultaneously serves as a preparation for the preceding[71] described forms of postmodern demasking critique, can be illustrated in reference to positions that subordinate reason to specific authorities external to reason. Schopenhauer, for example, views reason as a subordinate tool of the will. Nietzsche and Freud follow him in this. Naturalism views reason as a natural fact, as a product of evolution. Sociologizing, in contrast, views it as a social fact. And, finally, existential philosophy (Kierkegaard, Heidegger) understands reason to be a phenomenon that is subordinate to the specifics of people, namely, existence and decisions.[72] In all of these cases, reason is defined by its *function*, as an instrument of authorities external to it. Rationality is, in a manner of speaking, a competence for solving problems that reason-extrinsic authorities use in an attempt to solve problems according to their own goal-setting standards.

According to Schnädelbach, the rationality at the gate of this decentering process, which is still going on today, has remained a philosophical topic because of nineteenth-century neo-Kantianism, which insisted that reason is "not simply one object among the other objects of the sciences, because it has something to do with what makes scientific objectivity possible in the first place."[73] With the concept of reflection, which has been connected with the resistance to a voluntarist and emotivist neutralization strategy since Kant, *procedures* become the focal point of considerations about rationality theory.[74] If, namely, judgments about the status or the function of reason itself always rely on reason, then the explication of what reason is can orient itself on the procedures of justification. *Procedural* concepts of reason thus do not rely on authorities external to rationality, whose importance in contexts of justification itself has to be justified; rather, the procedures of justification themselves become a normative foundation. The kernel of such approaches is, as Schnädelbach plastically notes, the idea "to use reason, which is the *medium* of critique, at the same time as its *standard*."[75] This is the enormous advantage of procedural conceptions. Reason need not be brought into play as a static capability, but, as the very process of critique, it is open, and it is in this way to be connected to learning processes and Enlightenment. Committed to this insight, today above all Habermas has once again taken up this central element of Kant's critical philosophy and reconstructed it in his theory of communicative reason in the concept of discourse as a procedure for the intersubjective examination of truth claims that are raised.[76]

Today if we once again want to place rationality at the center of philosophical reflection, on the one hand—and here I decisively agree with Schnädelbach—this must occur with a consciousness of the results of the "demythologizing history of reason."[77] As a result of this, we view reason as a concrete human capability: "Without the realization of the human disposition, 'rationality,' there is nothing rational in the world; everything else is bad metaphysics or misleading metaphorics."[78]

On the other hand, however, simultaneous with the subjectivizing—which the approaches that subordinate reason to authorities external to it make clear—the process in which it loses normative potency occurs:

> Insofar as we can survey the history of reason, it can be described as a history of the normative neutralizing of reason, which, in the end, offers pure functionalist rationality conceptions; the transition from a substantive conception of reason to a functional conception, which has only really been carried out today, has a long prehistory.[79]

Procedural concepts, which share with the functional concept a temporal aspect and a tendency to dynamization, but not normative vacuousness, thus initially appear to be the only means by which to develop a rationality concept with normative ambitions today. Indeed, in connection with the normative neutralization of rationality, Schnädelbach has drawn attention to a striking convergence between functional and procedural conceptions of reason:

> The borders between a purely procedural and a functionalist rationality concept can no longer be drawn if the procedural concept no longer includes an element of substantialist rationality, i.e., if the rules that establish the procedures of norm justification themselves are normatively neutral.[80]

If, in the development of my project, I adhere to a procedural rationality concept, then a goal of this project must also consist in identifying rules that, in a manner to be more precisely determined, are not arbitrary.

The preliminary results of the development of rationality concepts are summarized in figure 1.1.[81] However, here it is necessary to point to one aspect of the project of providing a foundation to a rationality concept that relies on elements external to reason that Schnädelbach does not illuminate in his presentation of the process by which the normative element of reason loses potency. For there is a methodological problem connected with the strategy of generating a form of reason that is internally normatively laden and is simultaneously able to be reconstructed as a motif of functionalistic concepts. That is to say, if substantialist concepts of reason—be they objective, subjective, or procedural in nature—are not able to fall back on authorities external to reason for a normative definition of the concept, then the only remaining possibility is to conceive of rationality such that the concept functions simultaneously as the basis of norms as well as the concept for their justification. In opposition to this inevitable circularity of substantialist concepts of reason, it is possible to call on the intuition that only authorities external to reason are able to break through the circle of self-sufficient self-justification. Reason must, as it were, be brought into connection with something other than itself. For "the process of reason, if left to its own devices, resembles a self-regulated machine whose functioning is no longer controlled by a particular end."[82]

The versatile forms of the problem with such "sui-sufficient" conceptions of rationality can be detected in the decentering history of rationality. Here, two forms of self-sufficiency are to be distinguished. The problem of connecting reason to *purposes* or *goals* must be differentiated from the question of which *requirements* external to reason rationality has. It is possible, for example, to point out that, for its part, rationality has historical requirements that are not themselves rational.

> What we consider to be our reason did not always exist. Our individual and collective capacity to think and to act reasonably obviously was generated, and it has changed—whether in the wake of natural or cultural evolution of the development of language and communication, interaction and production. As something generated and changing, it has a history.[83]

Even this admittedly rough sketch sensitizes us to an alternative that each theory of rationality that is to be developed must address: on the one hand, if we decide on the substantialist-procedural interpretation, then an authority must be found that makes it possible to break through

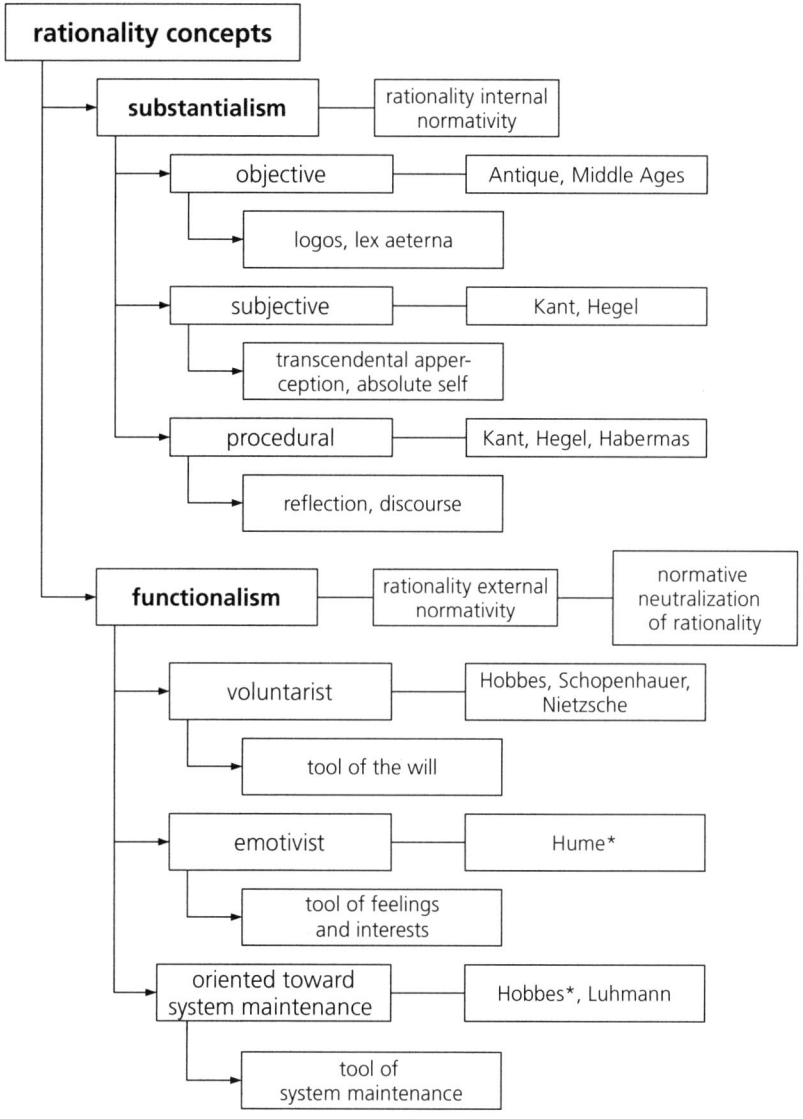

FIGURE 1.1 Concepts of rationality according to Schnädelbach (with additions)

the circular nexus of relations of justification internal to reason and to provide reason with a task that points beyond the justification of justifications. On the other hand, if we take a functionalist path, then it is necessary to avert the danger of reducing reason to a loose-leaf collection of hypothetical imperatives.

1.4.1. Positions in the Current Debate on Rationality

Calling to mind the positions in the current debate on rationality, one discovers a complex field with fault lines along which it is possible to make out relativistic, culturalistic, universalistic, normatively ambitious, normatively mitigated, more reconstructive, and more constructivist positions.[84] In what follows, in proceeding through some paradigmatic positions, I attempt to sort through the field of argumentation to gain an idea about which form a theory of rationality *ought to* take, which normative claims it ought to make, and what its explanative basis ought to consist in.

Initially we can presume that we ourselves—in contrast to what philosophical reflection about rationality suggests—actually are quite able to decide what is rational and what is not, and that we can do this without having well-worked-out criteria of rationality. We have obviously not acquired this familiarity with reason by memorizing systems of rules for rational action (otherwise the philosophical question of the kernel of rationality would hardly be so pressing), but because of the fact that we are practically incorporated into a more or less rational social practice. In his concept of reason as an aspect of our orientation practice, Friedrich Kambartel proceeds on this intuition.

1.4.1.1. Rationality as an Aspect of Our Orientation Practice

On the basis of the analysis of two different principles of rationality (rational self-interest and rational discourse), Kambartel reconstructs a cultural practice of judgment in order to show that reason cannot be understood as a criterion, a general principle, or a set of rules. If, in the face of concrete problems, we "are in a position as learned rational beings to deliberatively judge a series of different criteria, albeit connected to one another, in diverse ways," that is, we are in a position to weigh the suitability of the criteria for the problematic situation, in doing so we are not able to refer to higher criteria in compliance with which we might be able to secure the adequacy of our judgment regarding the suitability of the criteria of judgment.[85] In short: we have to get by without universal standards of adequacy. Thus "reason is dependent upon our power of judgment and upon the life experience that in general underlies it."[86]

As a proponent of the concept of rationality that attempts to accommodate the view that, with the lack of general criteria of adequacy, life experience is at the basis of reason, Kambartel reconstructs culture as the framework within which we—as participants in a common, not individual, practice—educate ourselves to become rational beings. As we begin to participate in cultural practices, we become acquainted with the "various definitions of the rational" that are at work *within* a culture of reason and that, under the presupposition of "'local' suitability," belong to the "*grammatical network* of this culture."[87] In this, the various definitions of rationality illustrate the diversity of the "grammatical forms for overcoming a particular (individual, subjective) orientating practice."[88]

The obvious advantage of such argumentation consists in the fact that rationality, with the help of a culturalistic reconstruction, need not be presented to the societal practice from a problematic external perspective, but can be viewed as already existing in the social world. However, this advantage—if one agrees with Mittelstraß—comes at a high price: "If the culture of reason as a universal culture is itself *normative*, as it is now called, precisely then the appeal to its *reality* is affirmative."[89] The rejection of a normative interpretation of the rationality concept, which could be explicated criteriologically, "makes reason into an attribute of relationships (*Verhältnissen*) rather than understanding it as a medium of critique."[90]

Beyond these costs, which were calculated by Mittelstraß, there are further ones that are caused by the soft contextualism of Kambartel's concept. For what precisely does it mean to speak of different definitions of the rational (in different contexts)? In any case, the step beyond a particular orientating practice alone cannot serve as a sufficient criterion for categorizing an orientation as rational, for transindividual orientation practices, like orienting important decisions on the basis of horoscopes, can eventually be irrational. Criteria are thus needed with the help of which it is possible to characterize a general orientation practice as rational.

With a view to the argument that insofar as it is not possible to find general criteria of the rational, because "definitions of the rational" are really only meaningful in their respective contextual relationships, it is necessary to ask how it is possible to speak of a reason that transcends specific contexts if the contextual interpretation is not compatible with more basic criteria of the rational. In other words: if we admit that acting beings act rationally in specific contexts, then we impute *elementary* rationality principles to the actors, principles that can never be contradicted in their contextual specification. Otherwise talk of reason simply would be disparate. Any specification of criteria of rationality that aims to be adequate must be understood as a process that, technically speaking, maintains downward compatibility to fundamental criteria of rationality. The contextualization of reason that is required is thus not a *diversification* but a *specification*. Let us then once again take up the idea that Mittelstraß places at the center of his critique of Kambartel.

1.4.1.2. Reason as an Ideal

Mittelstraß understands criteria of rationality as criteria that are developed in *opposition* to existing affairs and thus cannot be reconstructed from them: "Reason is an *idea*. And ideas are not defined. They are rather determined in reference to *ideal demands*, postulates."[91] Mittelstraß does not refer back to sociocultural practices as the source of reason, but confronts these with outlines of rational affairs. His concept is not determined in a reconstruction of what exists but in contrast to it.

> Reason is thus not something that is everywhere to be found, but—according to the Enlightenment thinkers—something that can always be awakened, in every *head* and in every *life*. In any case, reason is always an achievement.[92]

This procedure is connected to an experimental character of normative rational postulates that by no means require that reason be exhaustively defined or that a principle of rationality be formulated. However, in Mittelstraß's view, beyond the particularity of the postulate of reason, there is an "idea of the unity of reason," which can be articulated in "developments that (increasingly) bring about a rational life, that is, in rational developments."[93] As criteria for affairs that are to be directed to rational developments, Mittelstraß mentions general reasonableness and the possibility for consent to the affairs, their level of development in contrast to naturally emerging affairs, and their suitability to serve as a *"basis for future justified developments."*[94]

However, it remains problematic that, for their part, the criteria for rational development cannot be criteriologically justified. Like the particular rationality postulates, the criteria of general reasonableness and of the possibility for consent retain an obvious contingent character. Conditions for justified consent—for example, as in Habermas's attempts to depict them on the basis of indissoluble connections between meaning and validity, which are consequently to be differentiated from contingent suggestions—are not, however, joined to procedures with the help of which suggestions can be reliably verified.

A more interesting impulse is contained in these reflections, namely, the impulse toward a criterion of development; this can be read as a demand to assess suggestions in reference to their consequences for the possibility of shaping future affairs. So, rationality can be understood as a criterion that prescribes the possibility of future action under conditions where there are an abundant number of alternatives. Here too, however, a strong justification of the criterion is lacking.

The reflections so far contrast two different ways of viewing reason, each of which is poignantly debunked in the respective work of Kambartel and Mittelstraß. While Kambartel, in a rather reconstructive perspective, insists that reason is not something that we have to be lectured about from a position independent of our practices, Mittelstraß emphasizes the idea that, for the sake of its critical function, reason must be something that, of necessity, retains a certain distance from our de facto practices. From his rather constructivist perspective, he emphasizes that if we view reason as something that is, in a manner of speaking, inherent to our practices, then the normative character of reason gives way. Both positions appear to capture something correct, but given their incompatibility, they cannot both be simultaneously correct. However, we must thus be able to expect from a more developed theory of rationality that, in the process of a more or less complex mediation, it does justice to both the *normative character* of reason and also to the fact that we—as potential addressees of the norms of rationality—view ourselves as beings who are *in fact* at least partially already reasonable. Habermas's theory of communicative action can be viewed as an attempt to do justice equally to both of these elements.

1.4.1.3. Rationality and Reaching Understanding

Habermas's attempt "to secure a concept of reason by means of formal pragmatics, that is, by means of an analysis of the general characteristics of a communication-oriented action"[95] is certainly one of the most ambitious conceptions of a reconstructive rationality concept. Here, too, in his universal pragmatic construction, Habermas refers to a social practice, but this case is more complex.

First, Habermas constructs his rationality concept cognitively: "When we use the expression 'rational' we suppose that there is a close relation between rationality and knowledge."[96] Here rationality describes a disposition of individuals, who, on the basis of their knowledge, attempt to successfully achieve their objectives. A decisive differentiation of the mode for applying the propositional knowledge can be added to this first characterization, which defines rationality in reference to its application in descriptive knowledge.[97] According to whether this knowledge finds application in goal-oriented action or in communicative action, which is oriented on processes of uncoerced agreement in the medium of argumentative speech, we can distinguish a form of *cognitive instrumental reason* from a form of *communicative reason*.[98] As a consequence of the reference to knowledge—underlying both types of action is "fallible knowledge"[99]—rationality is simultaneously placed in a context of justification and critique. This is why Habermas's reflections lead "in the direction of basing the rationality of an expression on its being susceptible of criticism and grounding."[100] For we judge the rationality of actions with regard to the possibilities for justifying the claims that are raised by them. The ability to connect such claims with actions is doubtless a competence of subjects who have communicative and action competencies. If we understand the concept of rationality as a competence of subjects, that is, we use the term dispositionally, then individuals who act with instrumental rationality must be imputed with other competencies than individuals who act oriented toward understanding.

Before these competencies are more precisely investigated, Habermas first broadens the parameters of actions oriented toward understanding; against the background of our way of applying the predicate "rational," the earlier introduced example of truth—as a claim that is raised in communicative action—proves insufficient. For "*normatively regulated actions* and *expressive self-presentations* have, like assertions or constative speech acts, the character of meaningful expressions, understandable in their context, which are connected with criticizable validity claims. Their reference is to norms and subjective experiences rather than to facts."[101]

It is now possible to connect the view of the expanded cognitive concept of rationality to a reconstructive procedure that investigates the competencies that must be attributed to actors oriented toward understanding. Habermas calls the research program that takes up this task universal pragmatics. In analyzing the necessary conditions for communicative competence, universal pragmatics concerns itself with the reconstruction of a "pre-theoretical knowledge,"[102] which underlies the ability to linguistically communicate. What is fundamental here is that communicative competence is differentiated into an ability that underlies the generation of grammatically correct propositions and the competence that, based on this communicative competence to follow rules (or *communicative rule competence*), puts the speaker in a position to use propositions "as elements of speech, that is, for representational, expressive, and interpersonal functions."[103] Only on the basis of this *communicative rule competence* are speakers in the position "to embed" their speech in "a well-formed sentence in relation to reality."[104] To do this, a speaker must refer to an object; that is, she must determine some propositional content that reproduces a fact or experience; she must express herself by expressing her intentions; and she must express herself in such a way that an interaction arises between those involved in the communication, which has a form acceptable to the participants and thus conforms to recognized norms and self-understandings.[105]

This means, however, that beyond fulfilling the demand for comprehensibility, "a successful utterance must satisfy three additional validity claims: it must count as true for the participants insofar as it represents something in the world; it must count as truthful insofar as it expresses something intended by the speaker; and it must count as right insofar as it conforms to socially recognized expectations."[106] A possible agreement among those involved in the communication "is measured against exactly three criticizable validity claims; in coming to an understanding about something with one another and thus making themselves understandable, actors cannot avoid embedding their speech acts in precisely three world-relations and claiming validity for them under these aspects."[107] The validity claim of truth that is raised in constative speech acts, with which the cognitive concept of rationality began, is thus only one special kind of validity claim that can be raised in speech acts.[108]

As a result of the universal pragmatic reconstruction the concepts of *understanding* and *meaning*, on the one hand, and the concept of *validity*, on the other, complement one another. The core idea of truth semantics—that "to understand a sentence means to know the conditions under which it is true," as this was developed by Davidson and Dummett in connection with the early Wittgenstein[109]—is transformed. This is done as the dimensions of validity are now broadened to include the "variety of illocutionary powers" and as a result of the speech act theoretical transition from the analytical unity of a "sentence" to the unity of a "speech act." The transformation is to the following formulation:[110] "We understand a speech act when we know what makes it acceptable."[111] And "a speech act may be called 'acceptable' if it satisfies the conditions that are necessary in order that the hearer be allowed to take a 'yes' position on the claim raised by the speaker."[112]

In this way Habermas gains a pragmatically reconstructed concept of communication that includes not only the exchange of information, but also aspects of action coordination; this concept is at the same time connected to a normatively laden theory of meaning, which connects meaning to justifiable (*einlösbar*) validity claims and thus establishes "an inseverable composite of the meaning and validity of speech acts."[113] Herewith, the possibility of understanding speech acts is connected to the fact that criticizable validity claims are raised in speech acts; in contrast, speech acts to which this does not apply cannot be understood.

> Not all illocutionary acts are constitutive for communicative action, but only those with which speakers connect criticizable validity claims.[114]

As a result of the outlined transformational steps, the explication of what constitutes rationality can draw on the competence of communicatively active subjects to use language with communicative intent, a competence that speakers realize by making sense on the basis of criticizable validity claims. If the connection between meaning and validity that communicative actors draw on in interaction oriented toward understanding is to be made the basis of a concept of rationality, it must, however, be shown that communicative action is the *basic* form of linguistic action. So, it must be shown in the next step "that the use of language with an orientation to reaching understanding is the *original mode* of language use, upon which indirect understanding, giving something to understand or letting something be understood, and the instrumental use of language in general, are parasitic."[115]

In order to show this, Habermas ties into Austin's speech act theoretical differentiation between locutionary, illocutionary, and perlocutionary acts; here, for Habermas, besides the locutionary act, with which speakers express matters of fact, the difference between illocutionary and perlocutionary acts is of special relevance. While the speaker expresses her intention with the help of illocutionary acts by determining the specific use she makes of a proposition, the perlocutionary acts serve to generate effects from the hearer, which the speaker attempts to elicit through a goal-oriented attitude. Figure 1.2 presents an overview of the internal differentiation of the speech act.[116]

By means of speech act theory, in a further step, the illocutionary element of the performative speech act can now be identified as a component of a speech act that is constitutive for action oriented toward understanding insofar as it is used to help characterize the modi of the speech act—i.e., to characterize it as maintaining, promising, suggesting, etc.—that relate the communicative meaning of a proposition to the intentions of the speaker.

While the "illocutionary aim a speaker pursues with an utterance follows from the very meaning of what is said," the perlocutionary aim of the speaker "does not follow from the manifest content of the speech act; this aim can be identified only through the agent's intention."[117] As in the case of teleological action in general, to reconstruct the perlocutionary

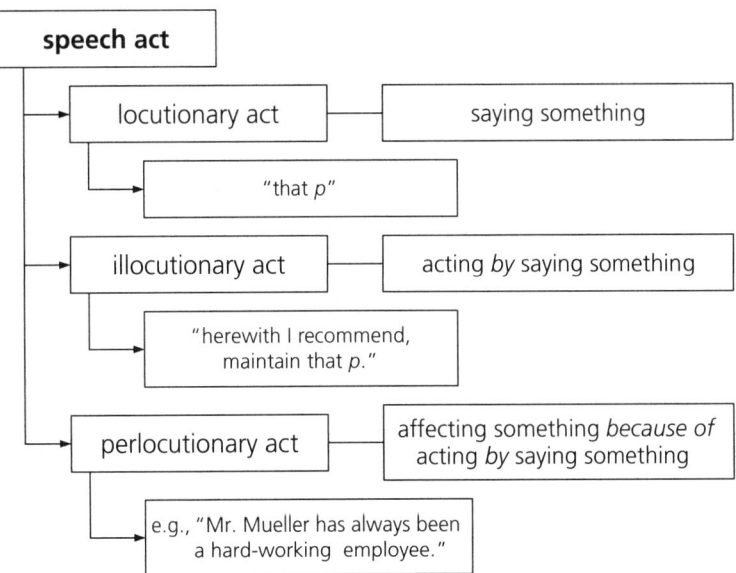

FIGURE 1.2 Aspects of speech acts

intention of a speaker, we must "refer to a context of teleological action that *goes beyond* the speech act."[118] For perlocutionary effects can only be made out in relation to descriptions of states of affairs in the world,[119] that is, in relation to descriptions that transcend the parameters of interpersonal relationships. However, a condition for the success of perlocutionary action is that at the same time the speaker hides her strategic intention behind an illocution.

Social action that is aimed at perlocutionary effects thus already presupposes the parameters of communicative action whereby it is shown that the modus of speech action that is oriented toward understanding is "the original modus" of language use. Hereby the intuition "that a telos of mutual understanding is built into linguistic communication"[120] is given a firm foundation with the help of universal pragmatics. Habermas only uses the term *communicative action* for the type of interaction that remains free of such strategic components and "in which *all* participants harmonize their individual plans of action with one another and thus pursue their illocutionary aims *without reservation.*"[121] Figure 1.3[122] situates communicative action in relation to other types of action and the intentions or validity claims that correspond to them.

In connection with the rational theoretical considerations, the following aspects are of decisive importance:

1. The view of a rationality concept can no longer be explicated by drawing on the instrumentality of problem-solving action, but is rather to be developed against the richer background of communicative action, which spans the dimensions of comprehensibility, truth, rightness, and sincerity.[123]

2. If meaning and validity are brought into such a close relationship to one another that the constitutive meaning of a speech act is connected to an inherent claim to validity, then the judgment of the rationality of a person who formulates an expression can be joined to a monitoring procedure that tests the justification of the validity claim raised. Habermas views discourse as one such procedure. What is decisive here is that discourse is constitutively connected to the sphere of intersubjective understanding; for only in the framework in which action is oriented toward understanding, thus in which meaning can emerge, can validity claims constitutive for meaning be verified. Speech acts can be considered justified if their validity claims achieve intersubjective, shared recognition in a process of undistorted argumentative debate.

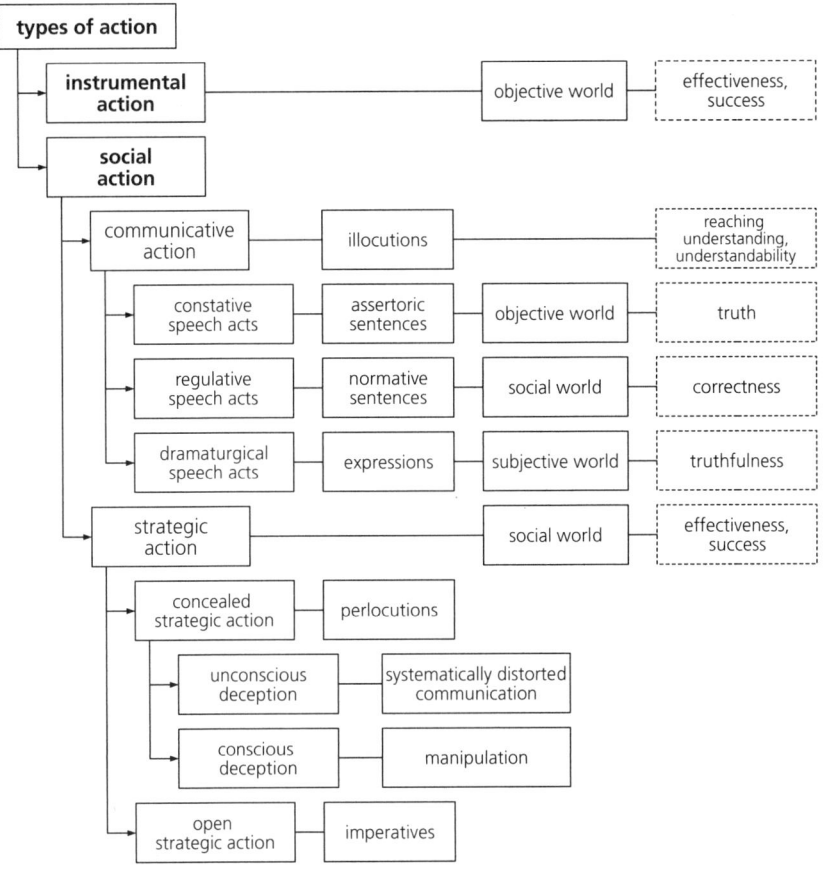

FIGURE 1.3 Types of action in Habermas

> Every consensus rests on an intersubjective recognition of criticizable validity claims; it is thereby presupposed that those acting communicatively are *capable of mutual criticism*.[124]

Rationality, we can infer, is the ability of competent speakers to generate speech acts that are criticizable. For achieving the conditions of criticizability secures the meaning of the speech act and the possibility of learning. The intrinsic normativity of the concept of meaning thus refers to discourse as a procedure for verifying validity claims; and it can be connected to processes of societal learning. The concept of rationality is thus, on the one hand, related to a universal pragmatic core of necessary conditions, which avoids historicizing reason; on the other hand, it is coupled to a procedure of critical testing that can both avoid the reproach of being affirmative and be open to processes of historical evolution.[125]

3. At the same time, the concept of rationality is not abstractly contrasted to the societal conditions, but can draw on the analysis of processes of understanding in which, even under contingent conditions, traces of reason can be made out that, simply as a result of the meaningful content of speech acts, can be related to an intersubjective procedure for critically testing validity claims. At the same time, here the necessary implications of such a procedure can, as normative instances, be mobilized against the existing forms of understanding (*Verständigungsverhältnisse*).[126] Philosophy, which is essentially a theory of rationality, can thus appear "as the defender of rationality in the sense of the *claim* of reason *endogenous to our form of life.*"[127]

The advantage of this conception is that a critique based on the normative concept of rationality need not accept the accusation that it is affirmative, nor that it merely differs abstractly from what exists; rather it can draw on potentials that dwell within the existing practice. In contrast to the theoreticians of the old Frankfurt School, Habermas need not view the societal institutions as emptied of all traces of reason,[128] such that points of connection for societal learning processes are fruitless from the outset.

The obvious advantages of this conception, however, also entail problems. Here I would just like to single out four central difficulties. I would like to go into (1) the problem of the unity of the concept of reason, (2) the problem of universality, (3) the problem related to normativity, and (4) the problem concerning the foundations for theoretical considerations of meaning.

1. Among the central impulses of the Habermasian rationality theory is a differentiation between the dimensions of rationality that arises as the concept of action is differentiated. While concepts that are oriented on an (allegedly) homogeneous type of action can be reproached for giving rise to a concept of reason that is one-sided and overly simplified because of this orientation, it must be possible to question an internally differentiated concept of rationality with respect to its internal homogeneity. Habermas established a formal connection between the specific elements of reason that correspond to validity claims: "Between the differentiated

moments of reason there is now only a formal connection, namely the procedural unity of argumentative grounding."[129] Because reason, which in "metaphysical worldviews . . . was projected as a substantial unity," could not be divested from the process of differentiating spheres of validity, "the concept of an objective reason itself fell prey in the end to the rationalization of worldviews."[130] Habermas contrasts this historically disavowed substantial unity with a procedural one: "In principle, when substantive reason comes apart into its different moments, reason can retain its unity in the form of procedural rationality."[131]

The kernel of this procedural unity is the process of argumentative justification. If we follow this view, however, we meet with difficulties; Habermas himself has called attention to the fact that validity claims of sincerity that are raised in expressive action are not accessible to argumentative justification:

> The sincerity of expressions cannot be *grounded* but only *shown*; insincerity can be *revealed* by the lack of consistency between an utterance and the past or future actions internally connected with it.[132]

And despite the prospect of the procedural unity of reason, Habermas does not hesitate to admit that *solely* "the truth of propositions and the rightness of moral norms and the comprehensibility or well-formedness of symbolic expressions are . . . universal validity claims that can be tested in discourse."[133] Even if this difference can be softened terminologically, given that such expressions are viewed as open to criticism, but not as open to discourse,[134] it is still questionable what the repercussions of these qualifications are for the procedural unity of reason. For this unity would lose sight of specifically modern elements of aesthetic expressivity that Habermas had announced are to be appropriately considered for a nondistorted view of reason.[135] The kernel of the Habermasian concept of reason, it must be assumed, is so tailored to processes of intersubjective *linguistic* understanding that, in those places where the subjective sphere is not linguistically related to the process of intersubjective processes of understanding, it becomes nontransparent for a theory of rationality.

2. In my view it thus also remains questionable whether the rationality concept, despite its internal differentiation, is not *too narrowly* applied; for its basis—the connection between meaning and validity—is developed solely in the context of linguistic understanding. The problem

connected with the methodological decision to analyze rationality in the context of linguistic action is that forms of action that cannot easily be reduced to linguistic action are relegated outside the scope of the rational.

3. Rationality, as a disposition of subjects capable of action, can be explained as the ability to raise criticizable validity claims. Here rationality is not initially connected to successful justification, but to speech acts being understandable, that is, that they fulfill the condition of being criticizable. Beyond this basic ability, which Habermas understands itself to be a validity claim,[136] rationality also consists in the ability to *de facto* justify validity claims that are raised. Rationality, in this narrower sense, is expressed in types of behavior (*Verhaltensweisen*) for which there are good reasons. At the same time, however, the existence of good reasons is dependent on a procedure for verifying them. We cannot know whether reasons are good reasons before we have verified the reasons on the basis of justified procedures. In addition, however, such justification procedures must be amenable to verification processes.

Habermas has indeed referred to ideal conditions of intersubjective verification procedures, but he rejects, for good reasons, an ultimate justification of verification procedures such as Karl-Otto Apel has attempted to carry out.[137] The cost of this decision is that the procedure he uses must itself be viewed as fallible, and it is only with difficulty that such a view, to which alternatives might be conceived at any time, can, for its part, be plausibly made an unshakable normative foundation.[138] In addition, Schnädelbach has rightly drawn attention to the fact that a procedural concept that disallows any form of fundamentalism and thus waives substantial characterizations of reason can no longer be differentiated from functionalist procedures.

4. In my view, among the most problematic decisions that Habermas makes about theory construction is the decision to make theoretical considerations of competence the groundwork for the theory of meaning. Initially the specific achievement of universal pragmatics consists in the reconstruction of those competencies of competent speakers that enable them to use linguistic entities in order to say something. And Habermas was faced with two sorts of competencies in his reconstruction, namely, linguistic and communicative competencies.[139] Here, the first competence consists in being able to generate well-formed linguistic entities; the second consists in embedding grammatically well-formed entities in relationships with reality and in using them in this way for purposes of

representation. For my reservations about relying on a theory of competencies to conceptualize the theory of meaning, what is decisive is that an ability to follow rules underlies both aforementioned competencies: namely, those rules that must be followed in order to generate well-formed linguistic entities and those that must be followed in order to successfully engage in communicative action within an intersubjectively shared context of norms of action, values, and conventions. However, the concept of rule competence that is taken up here raises the question of whether a strategy based in theoretical issues of competence, which makes explanatory use of rules, does not presuppose far too much in order to avoid an infinite regress in the theory of meaning. For after all, those who not only have a causal disposition to behave in a certain way in certain situations, but also can follow rules, must already have means to understand the rules, must already master an (interpretation) language in order to be able to follow rules. Should the mastery of the (interpretation) language, for its part, be based on a rule competence, then the regress would be inevitable; consequently, the function of the theory of meaning as a normative basis for the theory of rationality would be jeopardized.

Regarding this problem of regress, however, Habermas seems to be hopeful that a developmental pattern—analogous to the moral development—in which the rule competence evolves as a product of an "evolutionary succession of stages of communication" can end the regress.[140] But to me it seems questionable how such an evolutionary succession can be shown to be plausible if a step has to be constructed within the succession to indicate the transition from a speech practice that is stochastic to one that is constituted by rule competence. For this step would presuppose that, at the preceding stage, a language had to be developed with the help of which the rules of the developed stage could be formulated and interpreted. In short: at the evolutionarily lower stage, the language would already be presupposed; without its help, the conventions of meaning and the rules of the next, higher stage could not be agreed on. If, for the sake of testing this, one here assumes the perspective of an evolutionary paradigm, then, in reference to Chomsky's reflections, it will be possible to clarify what the problem of an evolutionary transition consists in. As is well known, Chomsky supposes that behind the diversity of natural languages there is a species-specific generative capacity, and the grammars of natural languages ought to be understood as individuating manifestations of this. He does not hesitate to characterize the structures that provide this generative capacity as a "mental organ."[141] In a perspective like this it is no surprise if the biological structure of organisms and—by virtue of their reproductive history—their organs are viewed within the framework of evolutionary theoretic explanations as a substrate of evolutionary processes. It is only questionable how we are able to move from a structural-functional description of these organs to a description of a rule-integrated practice. No clarity is gained regarding the problem of regress by introducing an oxymoron like a "mental organ." The elegant connection of the mental and the functional or of the physicalistic vocabulary ignores the explanatory deficiency; it does not overcome it. For if we assume that actors follow rules when acting, we implicitly always presuppose that, in principle, actors always have the possibility not only of explicating rules that guide action, but also of breaking them. The language in which actors formulate the rules that they follow provides for the possibility of changing, suspending, or breaking rules. However, the research specifically in the area of generative grammar points out that this is not the case for the assumed species competencies. The "mental structure" innate to humans, which Chomsky irritatingly characterizes as *rule* systems,[142] only makes the development of individual grammars possible *within certain boundaries*. But these fundamental programs need not be understood in order to be effective; nor is it possible to elude them when developing a language.[143]

If my argumentation is solid and it is not unproblematic to use the rule concept for a theory of meaning, yet at the same time it is also impossible to defuse it with evolutionary theory, then it remains to be considered whether it is possible within the framework of Habermasian theory to substitute another, less problematic concept for it. However, this strategy is not simply there for the taking; for the close connection between the Habermasian theory of meaning and the concept of a rule is not due to a theoretical confusion. It is rather the result of a decision to join understanding, and consequently the theory of meaning, to conditions for acceptability, which for their part are connected to intersubjective normative contexts integrated by rules.[144] If strategies from evolutionary theory do not provide a plausible way to end the regress, and substituting the rule concept is not an option because of the intimate connection between meaning and validity, then the task arises of developing a "theory of meaning without a (presupposed) meaning," and consequently a theory of meaning that is able to explain meaning without taking up a vocabulary that implicitly presupposes a concept of meaning, be that in the concept of meaning something in particular, of intending, or of rule following. Donald Davidson posed this task with an impressive radicality. Before I attempt to extract from his texts a concept of rationality that is based on a thinner theory of meaning than exists in Habermas's view, I want to give voice to another objection to Habermas's ambitious theory of communicative action, namely, to one that is based on Stefan Gosepath's theory. Gosepath thinks especially that Habermas's attempt to wrench moral norms from the conditions for understanding is exorbitant; he contrasts it with a view of instrumental reason reminiscent of Hume's.

1.4.1.4. Rationality as Reflected Smartness (Klugheit)

In his detailed and extremely precise work, *Aufgeklärtes Eigeninteresse*—which I would like to introduce here as an example of a theory of rational interest—Gosepath[145] combines a reconstructive procedure that secures intersubjectively shared ideas by analyzing our use of the concept of what is "rational" with a constructivist element regarding the characterization of rules, which if followed, ought to guarantee rational action. The delineated rules take on the character of a normative construction insofar as the definition of rational action does not emerge solely from the analysis of our use of the concept, but relies on systematizations and reductions that prepare the ground for a criteriological interpretation of rational action. Gosepath emphatically argues for a concept that explains rationality in reference to justification. In doing so he advocates the internalist thesis that we can only judge the rationality of an activity in reference to the process of generating the activity and in reference to a person's motives, goals, and state of knowledge.

Gosepath pursues his project of developing a robust concept of rationality in two steps: first, he is led by the presupposition that "the question of the meaning of the term 'rationality' . . . can only be answered by analyzing the way the word 'rational' is used."[146] In connection with this analysis, he attempts to show "that there is a uniform meaning of the word rational or reasonable" that can be pronounced "well-grounded" for all situations in which it is used.[147] In a second step he then evaluates whether the concept of being "well-grounded" allows for the formulation of a robust rationality concept.[148] Gosepath hopes to find the answer to this question in a procedure that is sketched out as follows. As candidates for *x* in a predication of the type "*x* is rational," he first tests beliefs, actions, desires, goals, norms, and expressions, whereby beliefs and actions are the main candidates; at the same time a differentiation between theoretical and practical rationality is achieved.[149] If *x* represents persons, institutions, and so on, then one is speaking of rationality in a derivative sense, which can be referred back to the rationality of actions. For both theoretical and practical rationality, rationality is understood as "the following of internal production rules (for one, for beliefs; for another, for actions), with results that are internally justified."[150] The result of the research aimed specifically at beliefs and actions is, on the one hand, a *rule principle of theoretical rationality*, which operationally defines rational beliefs on the basis of requirements for belief formation:

> It is rational for S to hold the belief that *p*, at time *t*, if and only if this belief emerges from or is maintained by particular rules for the formation of beliefs.[151]

On the other hand, it is a *rule principle of practical rationality* that formulates requirements for a rational choice among alternative actions:

> An action is rational for S at time *t* if and only if the action is carried out on the basis of a practical consideration of S regarding *t* concerning what the best thing to do is in the situation in which the person involved finds herself, and this consideration is made according to the rules of practical rationality.[152]

The content of these models of justification can now be specified using rules of rational belief formation. For *theoretical rationality*, Gosepath provides rules of theoretical rationality that I would like to characterize as smartness rules (*Klugheitsregeln*). Besides demanding the maximization of true beliefs and the minimization of false and irrelevant beliefs, these rules require the consideration of all sensible hypotheses, the cautious weighting of the evidence, and the choice of the best hypothesis with reference both to the intentions of the person reflecting on the matters and to the expected epistemic uses.[153] Against the background of these smartness rules, the judgment about the rationality of beliefs can nonetheless come to differing results. All rules remain relative, for example, regarding background presuppositions. This limitation initially corresponds to the conditions to which we connect the evaluation of the rationality of beliefs; for we would not allow beliefs based on views that the believers are not epistemically accountable for to be drawn on in judging their rationality. Because of this, the question is whether, beyond the relative sense of rationality, a stronger "absolute concept of rationality" can be developed. To clarify this question, Gosepath first differentiates the relativity of the rationality of processes of belief formation: he posits a relativity regarding the *cognitive starting point* of a person and a relativity regarding the *rules* of rationality. However, on the basis of the investigation of the relativity of the existing beliefs, it is necessary to analyze the relativity of rules; for "the cognitive starting point that, with regard to beliefs, is considered rational, i.e., justified, can . . . only be legitimated relative to the validity of certain rules, methods, laws, and goals."[154] But regarding the relativity of rules, three versions are possible. Under the presupposition of a starting point, we can judge the rationality of belief formation with reference to

a. the rules accepted by a person (the radically subjective variation);
b. general rules (the radically objective variation); or
c. rules that the person has accepted after careful consideration (the reflective subjective variation).

If we apply one of these variations to our judgment, then at the next step the problem of substantiating the rules poses itself: if it is assumed—as in the radically subjective variation—that the rules are in principle dependent on the subject or the context, then a relativistic stance is taken that, however, itself would have to be relativized; consequently, it is hardly possible to explicate precisely what the position says. If, in the face of the performative contradiction that radical relativism becomes entangled with, it is pointed out that relativism is also subject to the laws of logic, then the objective variation comes into view. However, with recourse to the rules of logic (the principle of contradiction), only a subset of rules—namely, pure formal rules—are determined. Gosepath thus suggests taking the reflective subjective rules as the basis.

On the basis of an anthropological constancy—that all people have goals[155]—theories, and thus systems of beliefs, can be judged as contributions to the solution of problems. The criterion that Gosepath thus proposes is once again a comparative one. It states "that those standards are rational that . . . more successfully solve problems than competing standards."[156] With this proposal, three things are able to be achieved: *First*, it can be maintained that the critique of a concrete problem-solving attitude takes up a motive of the actor—namely, her interest in solving the problem; and this interest must, *second*, at the same time also include an interest in improving the standard. This also ensures that the standards are open for learning and critique so that the historical development of standards of rationality is compatible with the criterion. With problem solving, as a *tertium comparationis*, it is possible in a cautious manner, *third*, to provide for cultural invariances in the standards of rationality, and to avert the danger of radical relativism. Nonetheless, "rational reasons . . . thus remain subjective reasons, which, however, must be criticizable, but internally, that is from the standpoint of the person that is being criticized."[157] In summary, the following can be maintained:

> The rationally formed belief is, after careful consideration by the subject, the most effective means by which to reach the chosen goal.[158]

Insofar as Gosepath's proposal in the area of theoretical rationality connects the rationality of beliefs to goals that are chosen, the problem of justifying standards of rationality is now transferred to the possibility of justifying goals, desires, and interests. Gosepath devotes himself to the investigation of goals, desires, and interests in his considerations of *practical rationality*; it, analogously to theoretical rationality, is differentiated into a relative practical rationality, which presumes the given goals, and an absolute rationality, which could serve to justify goals, desires, and interests. For Gosepath's internalist concept of rational action, two aspects connected to Davidson's work are central:

> There are two ideas that are implicit in the concept of acting on reasons: the idea of a cause and the idea of a justification. A reason for action is a justified cause.[159]

This conception of rational action presupposed, a person (*P*) acts rationally, according to Gosepath:

1. If, on the basis of the belief that her goal Z can be reached by means M, P chooses that action that employs M to achieve Z.[160]
2. If, in a situation in which the means to achieving a goal are otherwise of equal value, P chooses the action that achieves the goal to the greatest degree by the least difficult means.[161]
3. If, in the case where the unintended disadvantages of an action surpass its expected uses, P refrains from the action.[162]
4. If, from among all the means to reaching a goal that come under consideration, P chooses the one "that infringes on other goals (in quality and quantity) least—above all if those are higher goals—and that fosters other goals most or fulfills them at the same time."[163]
5. If, when there are incompatible goals, P chooses the means that make it possible to reach the greatest number of P's goals "in line with how desirable they are."[164]
6. If P orders the goals hierarchically in such a way that they are "complete and consistent."[165]
7. If, in her attempt to organize the goals in a certain time period, P chooses the plan that achieves her highest goals or the same ones to the greatest degree by the least difficult means, and where if P has another plan that can achieve all the goals of the earlier plan and at least one further goal, P prefers that plan.[166]
8. If, when goals are roughly of equal value, P carries out those actions or pursues those plans that maximize the probability of success, and when there is the same probability of success, the result will be more highly valued.[167]
9. If, when there is lack of surety about her goals and the way they are to be achieved, P initially makes plans such that all the possibilities remain open, but in doing so only reflects on the matter as long as the use of the consideration is worth the trouble.[168]

Relative practical rationality can thus be understood as compliance with smartness rules, which, for given goals, guarantee the most effective, most useful, least disadvantageous, and most conflict-free realization of interests, and, where there is lack of surety about the goals, attempt to prevent the chances for achieving interests from being limited.

Subsequent to the investigation of instrumental (or goal-relative) rationality, the question is whether, beyond justifying actions relative to the desires and objectives of the actors, it is also possible to justify desires and objectives themselves. Reflection of this kind is in a certain sense already connected with every practical decision insofar as the actors have to choose between competing goals.[169] However, because the criteria that can be used for such reflections must in the final analysis always be found by the individual actors, and in this respect they remain goal relative, for Gosepath norms have only hypothetical validity. For: "The final authority for justification consists in the freedom and the interests of the individual."[170]

According to the internalist interpretation, it is only rational for an actor to follow a norm if she has a reason to follow the norm, namely, the desire to follow the norm. Because Gosepath interprets norm-compatible action as a special case of teleological action, the relationship between the individual and the norm is in the final analysis subject to the rules of relative practical rationality; thus, rational action conforming to rules cannot be traced back to structures of duty but solely to the interests of the individual that affect motivation. Rationality is thus the instrumental ability to orient decisions on the effective realization of goals.

> Every type of rationality consists in the decision about the most effective means to reaching certain goals. That also applies to the goals themselves, which can only be justified in reference to higher ones.[171]

Indeed, Gosepath's argumentation entails a weighty presupposition, namely, *individual freedom*; one can ask whether this freedom has presuppositions of its own that might serve as the basis for justifying categorical norms. For if we understand freedom as the possibility of individuals to choose between alternatives,[172] then the existence of such alternatives could be viewed as a value that takes a particular position in reference to the freedom of the individual, a position, namely, that is characterized both by the fact that the existence of choice is a general *constitutive condition* of rational action and that it is also a *result of realizing rational competencies*. Because these action alternatives are of necessity alternatives *for* the acting persons, these alternatives do not exist independently of the competencies to individually specify the possibilities; consequently, we can postulate that, independently of the interests of individuals, it is necessary to maximize the possibilities for action and description. One can object that in the last analysis the number of these possibilities only measures the factual interests of individuals. However, insofar as the interests only come into purview from the perspective of the competencies of persons to individually individuate these in a process of self-interpretation, it is possible, relying on rational conditions of autonomy, to incorporate processes for generating the means for self-interpretation into the characterization of rationality and to understand the development of these as a norm that is independent of interests. We could thus investigate the *conditions for the possibility of choice* and connect a substantive concept of rationality, rich in content, to the ability to maintain or extend the conditions for choice. Gosepath, however, does not pursue this course. He ends his reflections with a rather sobering assessment:

> I . . . do not see how the concept of rationality can be coupled with a conception of the good life by recognizing certain substantial claims about the choice of human goals and the right form of cooperative life together. Because we are, in my view, forced to reject such more substantial conceptions, there remains only a rationality concept that resembles the Humean one and that is so formal that it does not allow the rational or irrational ordering of norms and values, societies, and worldviews.[173]

Even if one shares this assessment in reference to the "true goal of humankind," Gosepath may draw consequences that are too broad insofar as he decouples certain forms of social interaction and consequently, in a broad sense, forms of cooperative life that are necessary for the development of the competence of self-understanding, from the concept of rationality. However, it would at the very least be strange if the rationality concept was neutral about the conditions for the possibility of self-understanding, even if we must assume that these conditions must be assumed to be at least partially fulfilled in order to speak of rationality.

If, as Gosepath himself maintains, rationality is connected with autonomy insofar as it is the final authority for justification, then the question emerges regarding how this connection can be made plausible with the help of a rationality concept empty of substance. For if the procedural norms that explain and ground rationality have the character of hypothetical imperatives, there would only be a connection if the individuals have an interest in autonomy. At the same time it appears that we can only speak of actions if we presume that the actors are at least partially autonomous; with this, however, a conceptual and not merely contingent connection between rationality and autonomy seems to emerge. Rationality is not simply an instrument of autonomous persons, but a condition for their autonomy because self-determination requires a relationship to the self that can only be fulfilled by actualizing rational competencies. In short: rationality is not only an instrument relative to the interests and the autonomy of individuals; rather, it is a set of competencies that allows this autonomy and the interests to be individually specified in the first place. However, on the basis of Gosepath's reflections, it is not possible to theoretically secure these views. Because Gosepath views the predicate "rational" as coextensive with the predicate "well-grounded," he cannot interpret competencies that are initially competencies of (self-) understanding, and not competencies for justification, as an aspect of rationality.

After these, in part, rather tentative remarks, in closing I would like to point to a difficulty related to the explanative structure of Gosepath's theory. Because Gosepath explains rationality in all nonderivative contexts as being well-grounded, it is not clear offhand how it is possible to avoid a circular explanation of what it is to be *well*-grounded by simply reverting to rationality. Amazingly, Gosepath treats this objection, which Schnädelbach had formulated in the context of the discussion of justification-centered rationality concepts, in a footnote in which he gives one pause to think that being "well-grounded" can be explained with recourse to procedural rules; moreover, explanations that draw on the rationality that they explain do not make the content of the explanation circular.[174] His reply thus looks more like a defense against an argument about self-application than a reaction to the diagnosis of circularity. Because the suspicion of circularity does not only apply to Gosepath's theory and is of systemic interest, in the following remarks I will deal with it in more detail.

1.4.1.5. Intermediate Remarks: Rationality and Justification

The intimate relationship between rationality and justification that is drawn on by nearly all of the rationality theories outlined here—especially, however, by the theories of Habermas and Gosepath—was subject to critical examination by Schnädelbach in his article "Rationalität und Begründung." Schnädelbach first shows that "fixating on the justification model of rationality leads [to] holding everything to be irrational as long as it is not fully argumentatively or discursively justified."[175] With this, however, the "scope of the irrational would be broadened to gigantic proportions,"[176] and, in addition, such an explication of rationality promotes a scientistic view of reason. To counter this truncation of the concept of rationality, which identifies rationality with the ability to know or act for reasons, Schnädelbach brings three arguments to bear.

First, it can be objected that reason is not exhausted by the ability to answer why-questions. Besides the ability to justify knowledge or action, there are also rational abilities that are not mere justifications. Schnädelbach mentions the ability to engage in reality testing, as discussed in Freud; the ability to learn from mistakes and errors, as discussed in Popper; the ability to solve problems in nexuses of action that contain feedback processes, as discussed in Gehlen; and the goal-oriented choice of means, as discussed in Weber.[177] *Second*, rationality concepts oriented on justification must proceed from a pre-understanding that, for its part, "is much too complex to be fully exhausted by a justification concept."[178] In relation to this pre-understanding, the explication of rationality with the help of a justification concept is just one among various alternatives, and it must show itself to be the most preferable alternative.

Whether these objections are strong objections can be rightfully doubted, for the competencies that Freud, Popper, Gehlen, and Weber bring into play may not completely be worked into justification competencies, but it does not seem very plausible that competencies for reality testing, learning, and (instrumental) problem solving could be characterized as these competencies without relating these to justifications; a preunderstanding is not sacrosanct.

More serious than these rather bland objections is, however, the *third* objection, namely, that rationality and justification stand in a circular relationship to one another in a rather strict sense insofar as justifications "themselves [must] be qualified as rational in order to be able to exemplify rationality."[179] If we are confronted with the fact that someone has reasons for a rationality concept that is based on justification, this by no means implies that those reasons are good ones. But what good reasons are depends on the criteria used to characterize good reasons, typically on criteria as they are developed in a theory of rationality. If one now investigates possible reasons for a concept, it is possible to differentiate between material and formal reasons. Here it immediately becomes clear that material reasons that may be true, suitable, cogent, plausible, etc., are not sufficient, suitable candidates for justifying a concept of rationality or even for comprehensively characterizing rationality; for irrationality does not result from material falsity.

> What is false is not irrational, because only something rational can be false; otherwise it is simply senseless. Those who are mistaken are thus not irrational; but only rational beings can err.[180]

So after the recourse to material "qualities of reasons" has failed, because what is to be determined with their help "itself already must be rational in a broader sense of the word,"[181] there remains only the examination of the formal characteristics of reasons. The formal qualities of reasons, such as correctness and stringency, that pertain to the relationship between reasons and justifications, remain—excluding material reasons—related to the framework of hypothetical validity. Formally good justifications are then those that satisfy the particular procedures of formal justification, as they are developed in formal logic or by discursively satisfying the validity claims raised. With regard to discourse theory, however, it can be shown that the rules and procedures according to which validity claims can be examined themselves could become the object of a rational discussion according to rules and procedures. We must thus, in connection with the attempt to determine rationality in reference to formal qualities of justification, "be satisfied with a *procedural* explication of reason, which, in addition, is itself in principle fallible."[182] According to Schnädelbach, there is no way to bypass the circular consequence that the explication of what is rational on the basis of the formal qualities of justifications presupposes rules and procedures that are fit for the task precisely because they are rational. In short:

> Explications of "rationality" with "justification" are . . . thus necessarily circular because justifications themselves must always already raise a rationality claim in order to be identifiable as justifications.[183]

In light of the fact that the discussion here is not about some tolerable form of circularity,[184] but it is claimed that this is a basic objection to an explanative strategy, it is irritating that Gosepath, for example, who must be directly vulnerable to the argumentation, does not appear to be particularly impressed by these considerations. And perhaps it is in fact not really completely clear how Schnädelbach's text should be understood. Two interpretations are conceivable. One interpretation could be called a "self-imputing argument"; another could be characterized as a "strong circularity argument." The self-imputing argument essentially means that if P wants to characterize rationality in reference to justification procedures J, then P must impute to himself that this explication itself is sufficient for J. Gosepath appears to understand the circularity argument in this or some similar sense, and in this form it in fact is more of a diagnosis of a peculiarity of any explanation of rationality than a fundamental problem. Schnädelbach could, however, also have the following much stronger argument in mind:

(P1) Any nonderived case of the predicate "is rational" can be replaced by the predicate "is well-grounded."[185]

(P2) Sentences of the type "X is well-grounded" are true if and only if there is a good justification for X.

(P3) Good justifications are based either on

   a. *material* reasons for X or
   b. *formal* reasons for X,
   c. and there are no other kinds of reasons.

(P4) If reasons that are drawn on to justify X are materially false, it follows that X is not well-grounded, but it does not follow—in contrast to (P1)—that X is irrational.[186]

(K1) Therefore: (in order to be able to accept [P1]) it is necessary to determine good justifications with the aid of formal reasons.

(P5) Formally good reasons are reasons that satisfy certain procedures of formal justification.

(P6) Procedures of formal justification are fallible.

(K2) Therefore: to characterize good procedures of formal justification, rationality criteria are needed—which amounts to saying that (P1) is *circular*.

This argument is not based on self-application, but it shows that the explanative resources that are drawn on to define rationality are precisely the resources that have to be characterized with the aid of the rationality concept; it is not a diagnosis of normative, but of explanative circularity. Something is explained with the aid of something else that can only be identified by presupposing the explanation. On the other hand, because it can hardly be disputed that there is a relevant connection between rationality and justification, the question arises as to how one should react to the argument. It is clear that one cannot avoid this circularity by exempting the particular instance of explication from all assumptions of rationality; for if we want to explain rationality, we must impute rationality to ourselves. Here, however, there is a significant limitation: we must not *identify* the particular instance of explication with rationality, because if we do there is no explicans independent of the explicandum.[187] The elucidation of what rationality is must not presume a *comprehensive* definition of rationality, but must limit itself to presuming rationality in some contingent *pre-understanding*:

> It is not rationality in general, but rationality in a finally contingent interpretation that is the a priori that we encounter in the first person perspective as the highest or deepest point of our philosophical self-assurance.[188]

Schnädelbach attempts to avoid the narrowness of a concept of rationality based solely on justification and its entanglement in circularity by interpreting rationality as an "open concept" that "cannot be completely explained for all contexts,"[189] because each thematization of rationality, for its part, can also be thematized without thereby constituting a threshold for self-reference. This, in my view, defensive approach appears strategically to be motivated, among other things, by the attempt to deal with the radical critique of reason, which aspires to unmask a concept of rationality that is oriented on justification as a scientific truncation of reason.[190] A danger of this procedure consists in the fact that this "openness" passes over into indetermination and then implies that we accept something as rational that is incompatible with our respective standards of rationality; for nothing can appear to us to be rationally demanded that is simply incompatible with our de facto rationality standards. If, in addition, the openness is characterized with reference to the view that reason cannot be *explained* completely "for all contexts," that is, by characterizing it in a manner somehow related to Kambartel's skepticism about general criteria of reason, then one has to allow the question how it is possible to *identify* reason in the various contexts.

Schnädelbach makes it clear that "rational" must not be identified with "well-grounded" and that, instead of that, we should be on the lookout for an explanation of rationality that does not lead to explanative circularity. Because we are nonetheless to maintain the close connection between justification and rationality, rationality must be interpreted as something that is more comprehensive than justification competencies. Along with Schnädelbach, I thus conclude from the previous argument:

(K3) Therefore: there are rational competencies that are not justification competencies.

Schnädelbach, however, only implies what these comprehensive rational competencies might consist in, and, in particular, the problem remains whether we could accept the idea that these competencies, which, taken together, are supposed to explain the concept of rationality, constitute a collection of the most varied abilities; for if we accepted this idea, we would not be able to say why precisely *these* competencies, taken together, ought to characterize reason. I would now like to suggest that we count among the postulated competencies of (K3) all of those that make understanding possible and, among these, especially competencies for understanding that are not characterized by reasons. In my view these are forms of understanding that occur at a nonpropositional level; understanding of this sort need not be accounted for by recourse to reasons. Schnädelbach has also affirmed that if we explain rational competencies as the individuation of mental states with content, then competencies of nonlinguistic articulation are among the things that a sufficiently refined theory of rationality has to explain.[191] In chapter 3 I will make an emphatic attempt to show the validity of this view on the basis of a theory of media and nonlinguistic understanding. First, however, on the basis of Davidson's reflections, I will attempt to clearly portray what it means to explain rationality against the background of processes of understanding.

1.4.1.6. Rationality and Understanding

Donald Davidson's thoughts about the theory of rationality start, like Habermas's investigations, from problems of the theory of meaning, but the basic concept that Davidson's thoughts center on is not the concept of communication (in German, *Verständigung*, which is variously translated as communication, comprehension, or reaching a mutual understanding)[192] but that of *understanding* (in German, *Verstehen*). Davidson, unlike Habermas, does not presume antecedent instances of a symbolically mediated lifeworld, but sets out from the "original setting (*Ursituation*) of the more recent analytic philosophy,"[193] which became well known through Quine's *Word and Object* as the situation of radical translation.

To put oneself in this position means first of all to base the problems of understanding on considerably slimmer premises, for Davidson is not concerned, like Wittgenstein or Habermas,[194] with explaining "understanding" within the framework of an existing rule-bound communicative practice, but with making it plausible that understanding is possible under more adverse conditions in which neither language nor a form of life in the stricter sense need to be shared by speakers and interpreters. However, in contrast to Quine's empirical student of language, who is entrusted with compiling a handbook of translation for the "translation of the language of a hitherto untouched people," in which "all help of interpreters is excluded,"[195] Davidson starts from a situation in which the interpreter is no longer able to trust the "ordering power of language," which is supposed to enable him to access what is meant.[196] In this situation of radical *interpretation*, the concern is not with producing a network of lexical relations between expressions of different languages that are already understood as ordered systems, but with *simultaneously* unlocking what the speaker believes and the meaning of his expressions.

From the analysis of this situation, Davidson hopes to be able to track *all* the presuppositions that must be fulfilled so that interpretation, i.e., understanding, is possible,[197] and one of his central insights is that a universal assumption of rationality is among these inevitable presuppositions; this has achieved renown as the *principle of charity*.

Before I more precisely present the situation of radical interpretation, as well as the consequences for interpretation and rationality theory that Davidson draws from his analysis, I would like to make it clear that Davidson's strategy is not simply a result of the preference of analytic philosophy to work off of artificial situations that are tailored to one's purposes—precise but irrelevant. It does not result from a philosophical style, but from his wide-reaching diagnosis that most relevant interpretive strategies are bound to fail. According to Davidson's analysis, the basic problem, which cannot be solved within the framework of established theories of meaning, consists in the fact that, in order to formulate the theory, all of these theories have to make use of a concept of meaning that is only available as a result of these theories. According to Davidson, this includes any theory that bases its explication of the concept of meaning on *specific* intentions of the speaker, be these in the form of direct reference to communicative intentions (Grice) or in the form of an analysis of the research on social action contexts (Wittgenstein, Austin); for the reference to realistically interpreted specific intentions of speakers assumes that the theory of meaning is not needed in order to introduce the semantic vocabulary theoretically. However, if one presumes that actors or speakers have intentions independent of their self-interpretations and independent of the interpretations of others, then one makes use of semantic relations such as believing and interpreting as basic concepts of the theory of meaning, which are supposed to explain these semantic concepts in the first place. Davidson finds three basic maneuvers to be promising in this situation.

1. He advances an *antirealistic theory of meaning*, which avoids bringing intentional vocabulary into play when identifying what is understandable. The starting point of the theory of meaning, which in Davidson's view is a subdiscipline of action theory, is expressive *events*, consequently sounds caused by (human) organisms that are physically describable, which are then described in the theory of meaning as a specific type of *action*. Davidson thus does not expect expressive actions to disclose themselves in the horizon of a lifeworld, but views expressive actions as products of a descriptive and interpretative perspective, which makes expressive events part of an intentional description. In the framework of this antirealist perspective, meanings have the same ontological status as interpretations; they are nothing other than products of the (self-)interpretation of expressions that can be reconstructed within the framework of a nominalist ontology.

2. He gives the theory of meaning the character of an empirical theory, which, on the basis of the elementary characterization of the concept of

meaning, as a product of interpretation, applies the concept of meaning as a theoretical concept and does not attempt further elucidation from more conceptual analysis. As a result of the empirical status of the theory of meaning, the following questions play a fundamental role in this:

a. Which knowledge would enable the interpreter to understand expressions of the speaker of a language completely foreign to the interpreter?
b. How can an interpreter acquire the knowledge necessary for the interpretation?

A Davidsonian theory of meaning thus has the task of explaining how finite beings are in the position to understand a potentially infinite number of expressions; it has the task of identifying *finite* knowledge that places speakers and interpreters in the position to understand an infinite number of expressions. Davidson entrusts formal semantics with the task of identifying this knowledge.

3. According to Davidson, formal semantics offers a theoretical framework, with the help of which the knowledge needed by speakers and interpreters is able to be represented as a form of finite knowledge; for in connection with the work of Frege and Tarski, by means of formal semantics, it can, for one, be shown that the meaning of all possible expressions is dependent on a finite number of attributes of the constituents that are used in expressions, and, for another, it can be shown how the meaning of expressions can be determined with a view to the contribution of the expressions to the meaning of the propositions that they form. In Davidson's view, to understand expressions as sentences that are formed by units and correspondingly to determine the meaning of components of sentences with recourse to their function for the meaning of a sentence both hinge on the assumption of truth-conditional semantics, that sentences can be described as truth functions.

In order to more precisely determine the place of the Davidsonian rationality theory, it is first of all necessary to bring to light the central implications of the above orientation and to reconstruct their systematic links with one another.

From what has been said, it follows that Davidson understands a theory of meaning of a language L to be an empirical theory that provides the truth conditions for sentences and expressions in L. This theory is formulated in a metalanguage whose objects are the sentences and expressions of the object language that is to be explained. With a view to the issue of whether something is able to be learned, the theory of meaning must present the truth conditions of expressions in L in a finite form. Davidson meets this demand by structuring the theory of meaning axiomatically. A theory of meaning for a language L first of all consists in

(TM)

  a. a finite number of axioms that provide the semantic function of the expressions of the object language in which they, for example, determine their extensions;
  b. a finite number of rules for combining expressions; and
  c. a finite number of rules, with the help of which theorems can be deduced that provide the truth conditions of object-language sentences.

This is made more precise if, against the background of Davidson's nominalism and his diagnosis of the implicit circularity of established theories of meaning, one asks which form the theorems may assume. It is first of all clear that the typical form for the specification of meaning

(Th_1) *s* means *m*

cannot be the form of the theorems for the theory of meaning because it is incompatible with Davidson's nominalism, the view that truth has theoretical primacy over meaning, as well as the diagnosis of circularity. For (Th_1) allows, for one, that we treat meanings like entities, for example, if we replace *m* with singular terms, which are supposed to refer to meanings; however, for another, it does not make it possible to relate meaning to truth conditions, nor can it be formulated without the two-place predicate "meaning," which is what one is supposed to be explaining with a theory of meaning in the first place. It is clear that the criticism applies both to theories of communicative intentions (Grice) and to pragmatic theories of meaning (of Wittgensteinian or Habermasian provenance); for specifications of meaning within the framework of these theories take on the form of (Th$_1$). Therefore, as a form for the specification of meaning in an intentionalist theory of meaning,

(Th$_{1i}$) s means m because A means m if A expresses s

must also be precluded from being a candidate for the theorem of a Davidsonian theory of meaning, and

(Th$_{1p}$) s means m because there is a rule in the speech community to which A belongs that says that s, in the situation in which A expresses s, means m

must be precluded as a form for specifying the meaning in a pragmatic theory of meaning. As a further candidate, Davidson thus also tests the theorem schema

(Th$_2$) s means that p,

which at least has the advantage of containing something like an implicit relation to truth conditions. The problem with (Th$_2$), however, consists in the fact that implementing it would involve us in "intensional springs";[198] for the sentence-forming sentential operator "means that" spans an intensional context in which coextensional expressions cannot be exchanged *salva veritate*. If, however, as a result, the truth-value of the theorem of the theory of meaning can be false just because an intensional predicate is used, then (Th$_2$) cannot be the suitable form for the theorem of the theory of meaning without having consequences for the empirical status of the theory of meaning. Davidson's own suggestion thus must do without intensional predicates, and it must simultaneously bring into play a systematic connection to truth conditions. His suggestion is:

(T) s is true if and only if p.

This results, first of all, in the following advantage: a T-theorem is formed with the aid of the pure *extensional* sentential operator "if and only if," and a T-theorem produces a relation between two sentences that are capable of truth-value, namely, the sentence that is formed from the metalinguistic name "s" for a sentence in the object language and the predicate "is true," as well as the sentence *p*, and it is thus in a form that satisfies the core requirement of truth conditional semantics. However, if a theory of meaning consisted solely in T-theorems, this would immediately result in a difficulty, namely, that the schema (T) produces an infinite number of theorems, which would conflict with the demand that the theory of meaning is to specify finite knowledge that must be available to the speaker in order for him or her to be able to speak and understand a language *L*. In view of the necessity that interpreters must be in a position to deal with a potentially infinite number of expressions, this characteristic of the schema (T) cannot be waived. The demand for finitude must be reconciled with other components of the theory of meaning. Davidson complies with this demand by designing the theory of meaning in a form corresponding to (TM), which shows for a language *L* "'how the meanings of sentences depend upon the meanings of words' if it contains a recursive definition of truth-in-*L*."[199] In Davidson's view, the model of such a theory can be found in Tarski's theory of an extensional truth definition for formal languages. Tarski solved the problem for *finite axiomatization* by applying the method of *recursive definition*, i.e., by specifying all operations with the help of which complex sentences are formed from simple ones and indicating the way that the truth-values of the complex sentences are dependent on those of the simple ones. However, because halfway interesting languages contain not only sentences, but also open sentences (thus a bit of quantificational logic), a procedure is also needed that brings the truth-value of quantified sentences into connection with open sentences, which by virtue of the quantification become closed sentences. Tarski provides for this procedure by a recursive definition of "true-in-*L*," which, for quantified sentences, makes use of a recursive definition of the relation of *satisfaction* (which can exist between open sentences and objects or a series of objects).[200] However, while Tarski's efforts aimed to provide an extensional definition of truth, Davidson assumes the concept of truth as an undefined basic concept in order to initiate an extensional theory of meaning.

The next step must now consist in clarifying whether the form of Tarski's theory, which was developed for formal languages, can serve as a suitable model for the development of a theory of meaning for natural languages. In that case it would eventually be necessary to come to terms with the following difficulties: a procedure has to be found that copes with the particularity of natural languages, namely, that natural languages contain indicators or deictic expressions. Here, however, the truth-values of expressions containing indicators vary with the temporal and spatial coordinates of the expression. However, it is possible to accommodate this peculiarity of natural languages by reformulating the schema for T-sentences (with the aid of a three-place truth predicate) in the following way:

(T') *s* is true in *L* for the speaker of *s* under the conditions of its utterance (i.e., at time *t*, at place *o*) if and only if *p*.

Besides these difficulties, which are easy to defuse, natural languages exhibit a series of further peculiarities such as unreal conditionals, adverbs, mass terms, belief sentences, imperatives, optatives, questions, and normative and modal sentences; for each of these, as Davidson himself sees,[201] it must be shown in detail how T-propositions can contribute to their comprehension. With a view to some of these particularities, Davidson's theory of meaning must thus be seen as an open research project.[202]

An important characteristic of a theory of meaning, as an empirical theory, is that the T-theorems are empirically testable. For it is clear that a theory of meaning can only be a theory for the interpretation of the linguistic behavior of real speakers if there are criteria for testing the T-theorems. Davidson thus requires that the correctness of T-theorems is able to be confirmed by *evidence* that is accessible to interpreters with no previous knowledge of the language that is to be interpreted and that the way the T-theorems are *interpretive*, thus the way the expressions of real speakers can be interpreted with their aid, can be shown. For with a view to the problem of the interpretability of T-theorems, it must first of all be recognized that *individual* T-theorems are obviously too weak a basis for suitable interpretations insofar as a mere truth-value agreement between the object-language expression and the metalinguistic sentence provides too few restrictions for appropriate interpretations.[203] With respect to the problem of evidence, Davidson admits that the truth of T-theorems cannot be solved independently of the problem of interpretation; for the evidence for T-theorems is evidence that the metalinguistic translation of an object-language sentence is correct. However, it is first of all clear that situations in which speakers express their sentences must serve as evidence for a T-theorem.

For both problems, however, there are solutions that have become known under the catch phrases of *radical interpretation* and *holism*. This is first defused by the fact that Davidson views T-theorems as lawlike sentences, thus as sentences that formulate *causal law hypotheses*. Here it is presumed that speakers think occasion sentences are true because there are causes in the world that affect (*bewirken*) whether speakers accept these sentences as true. However, insofar as the concern is with lawlike connections, it can be precluded that expressions are connected with expressive situations in a contingent unique way, and interpretations are not subject to chance evidence.

The theory of radical interpretation, which starts out from a situation in which we cannot resort to knowledge of the language of the speaker or the help of a dictionary or translator, confronts the fact that for T-theorems of type (T') we do not have independent access to the beliefs of the speaker and to the meanings of the expressions that she uses. In contrast, in order to determine those beliefs, we need assumptions about the meaning of the expressions, and, in order to determine the meaning of the expressions, we need assumptions about the beliefs. In order to cut through the knots of this reciprocal dependency, Davidson proposes that we set out from the *content-unspecified* assumption that the speakers think their sentences are true.[204]

With a view to mental states, holism asserts that these can only be individuated in a network of inferential relationships; and with a view to language it asserts that T-theorems are only interpretive relative to a net of linguistic expressions, i.e., in the context of a language and in the context of expressive situations. A theory of meaning must, however, also prove itself in that T-theorems must be deducible from it that are also true for sentences that contain indexical expressions.[205]

However, holism and radical interpretation also entail new problems; for against the background of the interdependence of meanings and beliefs, we now need criteria that allow us to make reasonable choices between competing interpretations. The *principle of charity* (PC), which Davidson views as a necessary presupposition for interpretation, is supposed to throw light on this problem. The (PC) requires that interpreters not ascribe absurd beliefs to the speakers, but rather ascribe beliefs that maximize the rationality of the speakers.

Why should we do that? In contrast, aren't people often irrational? Perhaps, however, if we assumed that, we would not be able to understand them; for understanding presumes that we assume the conditions for understandability are fulfilled by what is to be understood. However, this amounts to saying that we assume that what is to be understood is that which we ourselves think is rational. For, otherwise, we could not integrate an interpretation into our system of beliefs. In short: what we ascribe to those we are trying to interpret must be a possible thought for us—something rational. So, what does the (PC) demand of us? In Davidson's view, the following:

(PC)

> (COH) Principle of Coherence: If you are interpreting a speaker, assume that he has the least possible number of contradictory beliefs (i.e., beliefs that you think are contradictory).
> (COR) Principle of Correspondence: If you are interpreting a speaker, assume that the majority of his beliefs (according to your own standards) are true.

(COR) must be explained against the background of holism in the following way: Although holism asserts that the meaning of sentences depends on the entire system of beliefs, it is still necessary to preclude the possibility that such a system, while being coherent, is entirely empirically false. Occasion sentences thus are a suitable starting point for explaining the (COR). For they offer the only possibility that interpreters in the situation of radical interpretation can ascribe the speaker beliefs in a way that is intersubjectively accessible, namely, by referring to a causal relation to the world.

With the reference to the world Davidson brings the causal theory of reference of meaning into play in a way that he connected with an elementary learning situation in the later triangulation model. The triangulation model has, on the one hand, an antiskeptical function, which makes it possible for two beings in an intersubjectively accessible world to observe the correlation between expressions and the conditions for making expressions, and, on the other hand, the function of joining the theory of meaning to a process of language acquisition that is to be achieved intersubjectively. The language acquisition of a student is explained by the triangulation such that the student can create a relation between his reaction to an observable event in the world and the (linguistic) reaction of the teacher to this event.[206] It is "a matter of two private perspectives converging to mark a position in intersubjective space"[207] such that that in which the perspectives converge can be understood as a cause of a linguistic reaction. In the triangulation model Davidson attempts in a fruitful way to expand interpretationism, which in a situation of radical interpretation requires that the interpreter already have a metalanguage available with the help of which he can formulate T-theorems and evidence so as to suitably reconstruct processes of language acquisition. Here the *social* conditions clearly emerge through which beings develop mind.

> Hence I believe there could not be thoughts in one mind if there were no other thoughtful creatures with which the first mind shared a natural world.[208]

With the triangulation model Davidson appears to have managed in a radical sense to connect the ability to think to social conditions; strikingly, he manages to do this without presuming that the ability to speak, which is the basis on which thinking is possible, can only be explained with recourse to a set of shared rules. Even though I do not think that the triangulation model accomplishes what it sets out to accomplish, namely, because its presuppositions are also far too excessive,[209] I share with Davidson the belief that thinking is an ability that is acquired by internalizing *social processes of interpretation*.[210] In the place of rules there is, in the interpretationist perspective, a sufficiently stable linguistic practice of a speaker who is to be understood, on the basis of which hypotheses can be formed and tested. Thus for Davidson—in contrast to Habermas—knowledge of rules is not ascribed an elemental function for the possibility of understanding, but rather at best an economic one; for in general our willingness to continually produce complex analyses of linguistic behavior from scratch is quickly exhausted if it does not concern interpretations of things that we have a great interest in understanding.

The foregoing explanations should, in any case, have made it clear that an understanding of linguistic action is, in Davidson's view, a process in which we ascribe intentional states to the beings that we interpret, which we understand as causes of linguistic action. Here, we presume that these states are propositional states and as such can only be individuated in a network of further propositional states. Because this network of propositional states is constituted by inferential relationships, the attempt to ascribe to a being a propositional attitude, which can function as a reason, implies that we ascribe *rational* organization to the network.

Thoughts, like propositions, have logical relations. Since the identity of a thought cannot be divorced from its place in the logical network of other thoughts, it cannot be relocated in the network without becoming a different thought. Radical incoherence in belief is therefore impossible. To have a single propositional attitude is to have a largely correct logic, in the sense of having a pattern of beliefs that logically cohere. *This is one reason why to have propositional attitudes is to be a rational creature.*[211]

In a manner of speaking, rationality is constitutive for having a mind. Herewith Davidson explicates a dimension of rationality that, for example, is misapplied in Gosepath's instrumental conception, although it is among the necessary presuppositions of a mind that is supposed to be capable of instrumental considerations in the first place. If it is additionally supposed to be correct that having an individual propositional attitude implies the existence of a network of propositional attitudes and networks of propositional attitudes imply the implementation of rational relations, then it is possible to maintain that rationality in this sense is not something that can be demanded of a being. Rationality is rather a *condition for the possibility* of having propositional attitudes and—insofar as an antirealistic interpretation of propositional attitudes is our basis— for interpreting whatsoever.

In what follows I would like to more precisely investigate what it means for the concept of rationality to follow these thoughts. Here I would like to orient myself on the following questions: (1) If rationality is a presupposition for having propositional attitudes, to what degree and in what sense is rationality then still a normative concept, and what presuppositions must a being really fulfill so that it can really still be understood? (2) How is irrationality possible?

1. Davidson's texts leave no doubt that successfully imputing rationality is a *condition* sine qua non for understanding. So, for example, he notes in "Radical Interpretation":

> If we cannot find a way to interpret the utterances and other behavior of a creature as revealing a set of beliefs largely consistent and true by our own standards, we have no reason to count that creature as rational, as having beliefs, or as saying anything.[212]

However, how does one examine whether it is right to impute rationality? What are the detailed determinations of content or the criteria for rationality? By mentioning freedom from contradiction and truth, the quote indeed provides two criteria, but it is still not clear precisely which criteria a being must fulfill in order to be intelligible as a rational being. One may be suspicious of the circularity, above all, of the reference to the fact that an intelligible being must be *largely* free of contradiction, for if "largely" means more or less "sufficiently," then it appears that it is not possible at all to explain freedom from contradiction independently of interpretability:

(RD) A being, B, acts rationally if and only if B's action A is understandable, and A is understandable if an interpreter of the activity that constitutes A can describe it as an activity that B carries out for (largely good) reasons (intentions and beliefs).

This circularity, however, is not by chance, for a being acts rationally and is only understandable insofar as she acts in accord with *our* standards of rationality. However, are these the standards that Davidson notes in his articles? That is, standards like the following:

(RD′)

  a. The *principle of the requirement of total evidence*: "give your credence to the hypothesis supported by all available relevant evidence."[213]
  b. The *principle of self-control or the principle of continence*: "Perform the action judged best on the basis of all available relevant reasons."[214]
  c. The *principle of conservation*: change as few expectations as possible if, under the condition of the constancy of some things, you begin to integrate recalcitrant things.[215]
  d. The elementary *principles of decision theory* (e.g., the transitivity of preferences).[216]
  e. The *logic* of sentence structure.

Hardly, for then could we not understand beings who, confused by the fact that some things in their surroundings are not as they expect, act pretty clumsy and draw on explanatory hypotheses that do not exactly correspond to the *principle of conservation*? After all, it is Davidson who tells us the (fictive) story of how he, after walking into his neighbor's house, lost in his thoughts, attempted, with the help of numerous improbable assumptions, to explain why the furniture was so mad and why the neighbor was mixing a drink in his living room.[217] Through this or merely thereby is Davidson a being that we can no longer understand and thus who is also no longer rational? In the case of the continence principle, things may be different, for in a certain sense, part of the concept of best action is that one carries it out if one is ready to act. However, it is questionable even in such cases whether a being that does not follow, or only seldom follows, the continence principle is correspondingly incomprehensible.

The suspicion arises that, for Davidson, at least two levels of rationality are in play. On the fundamental level, rationality in a strong sense in fact characterizes the *conditions* for understanding; this appears to demand weaker criteria than those that are expressed in Davidson's principles. Thus Alexander Becker has shown that in understanding language on the basis of a truth-conditional semantics, one can only assume the ability to follow modus ponens as a universal principle of fundamental rationality.[218] Rationalizing interpretations thus meet up against a limit of understanding if an interpreter is not able to suggest an interpretation of a being's behavior that describes it as having intentional states that are largely organized in conformity to modus ponens. Only if this point is reached is it no longer necessary that we attribute the interpretation that a being is not fundamentally rational and that its action is consequently incomprehensible to the inability to rationalize the action.

2. Even if it is questionable whether Davidson in fact articulates fundamental conditions of understanding with the suggested principles (RD'), it is still clear that his reconstructive efforts are aimed at a constitutive dimension of rationality. However, against the background of these mentally constitutive conditions, the question of how irrationality is possible becomes all the more virulent.[219] Consequently, for Davidson the problem arises regarding how it is possible to ascribe something like irrationality at all in dealing with actors who are ascribed with propositional attitudes.

> To explain irrationality we must find a way to keep what is essential to the character of the mental—which requires preserving a background of ratio-

nality—while allowing forms of causality that depart from the norms of rationality. What is needed to explain irrationality is a mental cause of an attitude, but where the cause is not a reason for the attitude it explains.[220]

Among the costs of Davidson's philosophy of mind is thus that in cases in which we are confronted with genuine forms of irrationality—for example, when individuals carry on and knowingly act against their own preferences—we must presume the division of mind into two subnets that are further rationally structured internally. This consequence hardly appears plausible, for after all, the mental states of the subnets—according to interpretationist premises—can only be given content by the rational self-interpretation of the person who harbors these subnets. How then can the mind of a person be divided if the existence of the subnets, for their part, presumes a rational interpreter?

Under the premises of a thin theory of meaning, Davidson makes available a theory that promotes, with impressive radicality, the attempt to spell out rationality using the concepts of a theory of understanding. Even if his theory poses questions that, for example, in the case of genuine irrationality, suggest that, besides propositional attitudes, other mental states with content (other than perceptions, etc.) are also brought into play with content that is not dependent on interpretations, in the following reflections I would like to pursue the interpretationist perspective that Davidson was important in inaugurating. Because I do not see why such a perspective should remain limited to the analysis of linguistic behavior and the ascription of propositional attitudes, I will attempt to open it up to nonlinguistic communication processes in order to include dimensions for a theory of rationality that usually fall victim to the linguistic paradigm.

1.4.2. Summary

The passage through some paradigmatic contemporary theories of rationality has shown that rationality is defined as

1. the culturally conveyed competence of actors to orient themselves with the help of transindividual but context-varying standards in situations of action (Kambartel);

2. a set of normative demands, which, if followed, should promote the production of forms of life that find general agreement, are generally perceived to be acceptable and are thought to present a suitable basis for justified developments (Mittelstraß);
3. the competence of communicative actors to subject their communicative actions to universal validity claims and thus to fulfill the conditions required to criticize and, hence, understand them (Habermas);
4. the competence of actors to optimize their actions and beliefs relative to their well-understood individual interests (Gosepath);
5. a set of normative demands that are directed to interpreters who want to describe and understand the behavior of beings as actions and, to that end, ascribe a mental organization to those beings that substantially fulfills the individuating conditions for propositional states (Davidson, Dennett);
6. a competence of systems to reduce the complexity of their environment under conditions of self-maintenance and to assume a perspective that relates the selectivity of the system to the improbability of its existence—whatever that means (Luhmann).

Habermas's concept allows us to solve the problem that we first of all have to view rationality as something that we ascribe to ourselves and that, to this degree, as Kambartel claims, is inherent in our practices; at the same time, as Mittelstraß emphasizes, it must be interpreted as something with a normative character and that can counter our practices. For Habermas's anchoring of rationality theory in a pragmatic theory of meaning allows rationality to be described as a capability to generate and understand criticizable expressions. Inherent to our practices oriented toward understanding is thus simultaneously a capacity to fulfill rational competencies; so, too, there is an inherent possibility that each contribution to these practices will be an object of critique that measures the validity *claim* raised by the contribution in reference to its factual fulfillment. Habermas's theory is problematic in the first instance because his theory of meaning is too ambitious insofar as its concept of rule following brings competencies into play that in my view can only be shown to be plausible if one presumes that the beings whose communicative competencies we want to elucidate with the concepts of rule following already possess a language that makes it possible for them to formulate, understand, and break rules.

Davidson's considerations of rationality theory, like those of Habermas, are rooted in the theory of meaning, but Davidson's theory of meaning can be understood as a theory that attempts to get by with minimal assumptions. Here, however, a strange shift in the normative perspective occurs. For in Davidson's analytical perspective, rationality is first of all that which an interpreter must impute to a being so that it is understandable. However, what the interpreter here imputes to this being cannot establish a demand on the being that is to be understood, for it is only a possible addressee of normative criteria if it already fulfills these criteria in accord with the interpreter's interpretation. In this sense, rationality, as a necessary assumption that makes understanding possible, has no normative function in the stricter sense, but a constitutive one. However, at the same time, Davidson also presents criteria for rationality that indeed have a normative character, but without it being clear how these criteria are related to the criteria that are constitutive for understanding and are directed at the interpreter. Although this ambivalence can be understood to be a result of the interpretationist composition of Davidson's theory, in which self-interpretation is the anticipated interpretation of the other, in the face of this problem, one should manage to differentiate *various levels* of rationality that throw light on the question of the relationship between self-assumption and the normative demand, which Schnädelbach discussed under the catchword of necessary pre-understanding.

I thus would like to suggest differentiating the following levels of explication in the theory of rationality:

1. *Basal* rationality is that rationality that must be presupposed in order to be able to describe a being's activity or behavior *as an action*. Basal rationality is thus introduced via an explicitly circular procedure: a being is minimally rational if it behaves in such a way that its behavior can be understood to fulfill the norms of minimal rationality—its behavior thus can be described as action. We decide whether minimal rationality exists with the aid of an *all-or-nothing* criterion; minimal rationality thus does *not* come in degrees. Four short remarks about that:

   1. If the criterion for minimal rationality is not fulfilled, the behavior that is to be explained loses the status of action.
   2. It is not easy to precisely determine the content of the criterion of basal rationality insofar as basal rationality is in a fundamental

sense *relative to the interpreter*. However, perhaps it is possible to say that the attempt to understand an activity as an action has limits that can be specified by the fact that actions are activities that are based on reasons and that the existence of reasons has transindividual preconditions that come into play via the *holism* of the mental and of language. It is possible to specify the content of the requirements for basal rationality if one asks which principles must be presumed to be fulfilled so that it is possible to ascribe a being with intentions and beliefs that can take on the role of reasons for the actor. The holism of the mental now claims that it is not possible to ascribe to a being solely one intentional state insofar as the relational identity of the ascribed state is dependent on its inferential position in a network of further intentional states. Admittedly the restrictions for the inferential relations that are supposed to integrate such additional, necessarily ascribed intentional states into the system do not appear to be very comprehensive; rather, they appear essentially to be exhausted in that a being acts so that the network of intentional states that is ascribed to it is reconcilable with modus ponens.
3. The criterion for basal rationality is normative only in the special sense that fulfilling it *legitimizes a way of speaking* about a being. It cannot be required that a being fulfill the criterion. In short: the criterion has a different *direction of fit* than normal normative criteria.
4. It is possible to keep the ascription of basal rationality *local* in the sense that, for the purposes of explaining action, no assumptions about the entire network of the intentional states of a being must be made, and partial coherence may be sufficient for explanations of action.

2. *Habitual* rationality, in contrast to basal rationality, can be ascribed to those beings that participate in a social practice of interpretation and thus necessarily fulfill the criterion of basal rationality. If we, as outsiders to this practice of interpretation, gain the impression that this practice of interpretation is successful with a view to the ascribed problems of action coordination, then we are justified in the assumption that the participants in this contribute something: such beings follow factual norms that see to it that they are more often interpreted correctly (in relation to their interests). Norms that are generally followed by habitually rational

beings—habitual rationality comes in degrees—cannot be specified in a canonical list with a claim to completeness. However, as a rule, habitually rational beings follow the principles named under (RD′).[221]

3. *Optional* rationality is a form of second-order rationality. It assumes that the criterion of basal rationality and most principles of habitual rationality are usually or always fulfilled. Optional rationality makes the order of the network of intentional states itself the content of intentional states. It contrasts with habitual rationality, which indeed has consequences for the ordering of the network of intentional states insofar as it, in the interest of facilitating interpretation by others, adjusts the order of the network to mechanisms for successful understanding. The object of optional rationality, in contrast, is the optimization of the network with a view to coherence and comprehensiveness. The maximization of optional rationality is the basis for *learning processes in the stricter sense* and the development of a *scientific attitude*.

The criteria for optional rationality are normative insofar as achieving optional rationality requires that strategies are followed and beings are able to make the fulfillment of such criteria the object of their own intentional states, or not. Such norms require that the addressees

1. minimize episodic irrationality;
2. actively increase the overall coherence of the system of their intentional states;
3. increase the number of coherently correlated intentional states; and
4. expand their competencies for understanding.

The last-mentioned criteria for optional rationality of course articulate precisely those demands on learning processes that are Enlightenment processes in the sense that I have characterized them.[222] The only questionable matter is why these competencies for understanding should remain limited to competencies of linguistic (self-)interpretation.

1.5. WHY A THEORY OF RATIONALITY AS A THEORY OF MEDIA?

The theory of rationality converges to a theory of understanding. This is especially clear for thinkers like Habermas and Davidson, who operate within the framework of the linguistic paradigm and place the analysis of linguistic processes of understanding at the center of their work. However, in light of the fact that we possess highly developed forms of nonlinguistic communication, with art being in my view the exemplary case, this limitation is a restriction of the analysis of processes of understanding, which requires its own justification. At the same time, it is the reason that it is still necessary to achieve Habermas's central goal of establishing a *comprehensive* concept of rationality that is *not one-sided*.

A first step in this direction could consist in establishing a concept of rationality that goes *deeper* than the level of linguistically communicative action. Habermas, who is skeptical of such "sub-surface migrations" of communication theory, has armed his theory against such attempts, which he views as threatening to relapse into mentalism. I attempt to contrast this with a theory of nonlinguistic understanding that nonetheless does not abandon the framework of the interactionist paradigm and to that degree does not think it is necessary to fear mentalism.

Habermas orients his work explicitly on the "conviction that language forms the medium for the historical and cultural embodiments of the human mind, and that a methodologically reliable analysis of mental activity must therefore begin with the *linguistic* expressions of intentional phenomena, instead of immediately with the latter."[223] The project I am following here, however, only shares one impulse of this belief: namely, that the study of the activity of mind is not directly accessible to a methodologically robust analysis. In contrast, restricting the analysis solely to the linguistic medium of the embodiment of mind seems questionable to me. I thus think it is sensible to search for an analogue to language that allows, *first*, the analysis of nonlinguistic forms of understanding within the framework of the interactionist paradigm of philosophy with which, *second*, it is possible to explain to what degree nonlinguistic forms of communication are processes of *understanding* and with which, *third*, it is possible to check and see whether these processes are based in something that is to be penetrated by a broadened concept of rationality. In agreement with some influential theories, I view *media* as such an analogue. In other words: without falling back into the immediacy of the philosophy of consciousness, with a study of media theory, I attempt to gain a view of the entire range of media through which the activity of mind can be expressed.

Given the lack of a comprehensive body of research such as that which has been developed since the beginning of the linguistic turn, a project of this type confronts disproportionately greater methodological difficulties than linguistically oriented analysis. An analysis aimed at all media must first secure its methodological basis, but in doing this it is not able to draw on presuppositions comparable to those that have been developed in over one hundred years of the philosophy of language. As I will show in the next chapter, it must indeed first develop a concept of media that can withstand the pressure of the demands of a theory with normative ambitions.

2 / WHAT ARE MEDIA?

Hardly any concept has been circulated with such numerous and often dramatically underspecified meanings as that of media. While academic reference works[1] have been rather hesitant to list the concept and have only recently begun to do so—with a largely semiotic understanding—in everyday language, as well as theoretical contexts, it is used in varied ways. In social theory contexts alone the collection of explications characterizing media yields an astoundingly heterogeneous composite. On the basis of his study of the concepts of the media theory of Parsons, Luhmann, and Habermas, Jan Künzler has compiled the following list:

> Languages, symbolic meaning, the definition of a situation, affect, intelligence, performance capacity, value-commitment, influence, power, money, law, truth, love, joy, art, belief, reputation, the formation of transcendental order, health, the formation of empirical order: all that is supposed to be media.[2]

If one extends the study beyond the parameters of sociology and social theory, the compilation can be extended beyond nearly all limits. So in the area of so-called media studies, a discipline that has been struggling to specify its field of research since its emergence at the beginning of the 1960s and that has been searching for a *conception* of medium,[3] heterogeneous concepts of media have arisen, above all as a result of diverse attempts to link up with the varied vocabularies of established disciplines. Such concepts show clear traces of the theoretical contexts to which they are closely related. One can clearly differentiate between the conceptual views from public relations, information theory, and communication sociology, but also literature and theater studies.[4] Alongside, and at times transverse to, these media concepts, which are closely connected with the need to provide media studies with an orientation, there is also research that refers to individual "media" such as radio or film.[5] It seems to me that this situation of media studies is characterized by two features: on the one hand, by discussions that—in light of the low degree of institutionalization of the young discipline, as well as the lack of specification of the discipline that may be responsible for this—threaten to prevent developments in a discipline that merely engages in confident reassertions of its ambiguous conceptualization; on the other hand, by a marked lack of sovereignty in dealing with media concepts that are not part of media theory in the narrow sense.[6] As a consequence, the chances that they provide for specifying the basic conceptuality of the field largely remain untapped.

Standing in complete contrast to this rather halfhearted approach is the chutzpa with which the venerated Marshall McLuhan, who is viewed by some as the father of media theory, sets about his work. Among the things he adds to the above list are writing, script characters, television, language, electric lighting, electric power, radio, telegraph, film, book printing, books, and paper; he believes he has found the theoretical basis that allows for the formulation of a media concept in the concept of the "extensions of man."[7]

To push a concept that from outside appears to be a theoretical jack-of-all-trades to the center of one's own reflections entails obvious dangers and might only be considered harmless if one attempts to define the concept against the background of influential conceptions, not least of all in order to avoid simply reproducing their conceptual difficulties. It is in any case clear that, regarding the diversity of the "concept of" medium, one can hardly attempt to console oneself with reference to the openness of the word *medium*, or take refuge in the systematization of the translation of the word into English or another language (mediator, mediated, medium) in order to make this the starting point for one's systematic efforts; for this type of a procedure would entail presuppositions that can no longer be shared by those with a post-representational understanding of language.

Notwithstanding, I would like to spare readers the exercise of a detailed reconstruction of the developments of media theory and limit myself to a rather schematic overview of it in order to clearly show that neither the serious nor the influential theories provide us with a concept of medium that we might be content to place at the center of a general theory of media.[8]

2.1. SOCIOLOGICAL THEORY OF MEDIA

In sociology and social theory, the media concept has had a striking career, connected closely with the rise of the conceptuality of system theory. Parsons, as well as Habermas and Luhmann, introduces the concept within a theoretical framework that system theory entrusts to special competencies for dealing with the complex research object, society. Here the media concept gains—in various ways unawares—a central position within social theory insofar as media theory in all of these theories is entrusted not only with solving explanative tasks, but also with dealing with basic problems of theoretical structure. Because a media theory that is not related to three of the most influential media theories of our day is subject to reproach for ignorance, in the following I want to at least show the plausibility that the wide-reaching conceptual tensions in the various concepts of media are caused not only by the problems of the vocabulary of system theory, but especially by the architectonic tasks of the theory.

2.1.1. Media in Parsons

Parsons was the first social theoretician to formulate a comprehensive media concept, and he at the same time staked out the bigger part of the framework within which Habermas and Luhmann developed their media theories—indeed, in a certain sense Parsons bequeaths to his successors the use of the media concept for dealing with problems of theoretical structure. Parsons's media concept is here characterized by an idiosyncratic intermediary position insofar as it is systematically linked both with (1) the system-theoretic reconstruction of society and with (2) the analysis of social interaction at the level of interpersonal relationships. In line with Parsons, (3) these levels can be integrated under the umbrella concept, code.

1. While at the beginning of his development, Parsons only spoke of systems as theoretical instruments[9] whose function was to theoretically integrate the various constitutive components of social action, in the course of his attempt to differentiate and schematize these components, he developed a conception of systems that allowed him to explain the possibility of social order—which he viewed as the fundamental problem—as one of four general system problems. Systems, *as systems*, need to solve the following problems: They must adapt their inner order under the conditions of a changing environment (A), which they at the same time must use as a resource for their own reproduction (G). Here they must coordinate their internal dynamic by integrating their constitutive elements (I) without endangering their basic structure (L). These four basic problems, which Parsons outlines in his famous four-function schema (AGIL),[10] are faced by all living systems "from the unicellular organism to the highest human civilization."[11]

If one now understands a society as a social system in the sense outlined and presumes that it, as a system, differentiates itself into subsystems that are specialized to deal with the four system problems, then the question arises as to how these subsystems remain in contact with each other in evolutionarily differentiated societies and achieve intersystematic exchange, thereby at the same time guaranteeing the integrity of the social system as a whole. To solve this problem Parsons first introduces four *media* (money, power, influence, and value commitment) that make available for the social system in general the specific performances of the subsystems of the social system, namely, the economic system (A), the political system (G), the societal community system (I), as well as the cultural fiduciary system (L). The *media* ought to be able to take on this special system-integrative task, which is determined from a macrosociological perspective, because they allow the subsystem performances to be converted on the basis of a *coding* that places the products and resources of the subsystems into relationship with symbolic units that are, for their part, quantifiable and that, as a result of the lack of an intrinsic use value, do not resist effective exchange processes. Herewith, the media disencumber the exchange processes between the systems from specific translation performances—related to particular occasions—insofar as these have already been provided beforehand in the construction of the medial codes. If one views the social system as a subsystem of the general system of action with which Parsons would like to theoretically

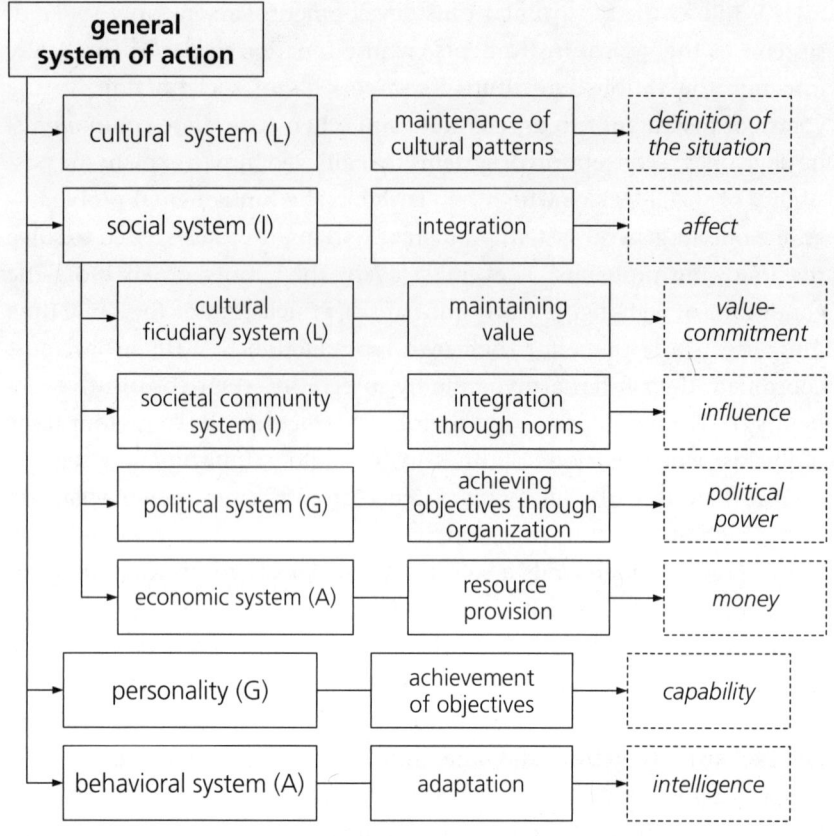

FIGURE 2.1 Subsystems of the action system

apprehend the constitutive elements of social action, figure 2.1 results as a schematic overview.[12]

2. Besides the exchange function at the level of macrosociology, the media also ought to function from the microsociological perspective as "special languages" with the help of which those addressed by social action can be motivated to accept an offer, an order, or an appeal. At the intersubjective level, media thus take on the function of making the successful coordination of action more probable so that they make a contribution to solving the problem from which Parsons's action-theoretic foundation of sociology set forth: the problem, namely, of how the free action of social individuals and the possibility of social order are theoreti-

cally to be integrated.¹³ To deal with the action-coordinating function of media, the following characteristics are of foundational importance:

1. In relation to the orientation of the actors, the media take on a *structuring* function in which they, in a move to standardize the *articulation of interests*, define situations.
2. So that the media can be sufficiently generally accepted in interaction contexts as means of coordinating action, they have to be *institutionalized*, as this is the basis of the trust of the social actors, required to use symbolic medial coordination mechanisms.
3. In order for the media to be effective means for coordinating action, they must be understood as *motivationally effective* mechanisms with the help of which it is possible to formulate offers in relation to the interests of interaction partners, whereby the medium itself, as a symbolic representation of an *intrinsic satisfier*, serves as a reason to take up an offer or, in the expectation of negative sanctions, not to reject it.

If a medium, for example, money, is institutionalized, then, with its help, it is possible to formulate standardized offers[14] that those who are addressed have the alternative of accepting or rejecting; at the same time, this opens the possibility that the person making an offer will link her own preferences with the contingent preferences of the person addressed through positive incentives or negative sanctions. In this respect money is a medium with the help of which it is possible to formulate, by the use of positive incentives, offers of advantages; in contrast, power activates obligations "to comply with collectively binding decisions,"[15] whereby the refusal of those addressed to cooperate is sanctioned with disadvantages. In contrast to offers supported by power and money, the media of influence and value commitment do not aim at the situations of those addressed but at their intentions. While with the help of influence, as the medium for shaping generalized opinion, that can act on the definition of interests of the persons addressed by positively influencing them to orient their interests toward collective goals or to be led to such goals or to integrate their interests into such goals, the medium of value commitment—supported by moral sanctions, thus under threat of feelings of guilt—acts on the value orientations of those addressed.[16]

3. Parsons was obviously optimistic that under the umbrella of the code concept he could theoretically integrate two different models—namely, the model of interpersonal action coordination and the model of exchange—the latter of which initially serves to explain intersystematic exchange processes insofar as these processes have to be carried out by actors but also play a role at the interpersonal level. So he describes, on the one hand, money (like the other media) as a specialized language that "expresses and communicates messages having meanings with reference to a code—that is, a set of rules for the use, transformation, and combination of symbols."[17] On the other hand, however, he attempts to reformulate exchange processes with the help of the code concept in reference to information science. "The circulation of money is the 'sending' of messages which give the recipient capacity to command goods and services through market channels."[18] The differences appear to disappear entirely if one is prepared to view "financial transactions" as "a certain type of 'conversation.'"[19] It remains unclear, however, not only how the scarcity condition for means of exchange is to be made compatible with the limitless character of the tokens of symbolic expressions, but also how communicative situations are to be described as exchange situations; for in contrast to a payment, a communicative exchange is not accompanied by a decrease of the symbolic token of a speaker. Expressions simply are not divestitures.

Beyond calling into the question the code concept, however, the generalization procedure—with the help of which Parsons attempts to define the structural characteristics of media in general in accord with the exemplary medium of money—must be called into question. Here doubt about this procedure concerns not only the functional definition of money, with the help of which—granting the above-noted trade-offs—it is easiest to plausibly show that it can function as a means of exchange between actors, as an action-coordinating means of communication between actors, as a means of exchange between subsystems, and as a means of integration for systems. It also concerns the structural characteristics that the media allegedly share: so it is especially questionable what the specific *symbolic* inventory for the media of power, influence, and value commitment is supposed to consist in, where specifically influence and value commitment are so dependent on linguistic communication that a special symbolism is virtually superfluous. And it is also questionable whether one can sensibly speak, for example, of influence needing to be *capable of circulation*, because precisely influence is largely connected to persons. It also remains questionable what it might mean that media other than money can play the role of *standards of value* that can be used to measure those values "in terms of a continuous linear variable"[20] that are symbolized by the media; for while power can perhaps still be measured with the help of "ordinal variables,"[21] it is not clear how one might measure influence or normative authority.

Once again: Parsons was originally driven by the question of how social order is possible under conditions in which the preferences of social actors are contingent. Because he thinks the socially binding force of language clearly appears to be too weak, he conceives of media as a *means of communication* that, in the move to symbolically standardize situations of interaction, ought to increase the willingness of social actors to cooperate. However, because Parsons reformulates the original question also with the help of the concepts of system maintenance under conditions of evolutionary transformation, media simultaneously acquire the character of system-constitutive, intersystemic *exchange mechanisms*. However, the concept of code that is supposed to integrate both conceptions proves itself to be hopelessly overtaxed.

2.1.2. Media in Habermas

As in Parsons's work, in Habermas's work the media concept stands in close connection with problems of social theory design. However, Habermas, who develops his concept of the media in critical dialogue with Parsons, explicitly proposes conceptually integrating elements of action theory and system theory—which, in his view, no sufficiently complex social theory can dispense with—with the help of a media theory.

Here Habermas follows a theoretical strategy in which *explanative* and *critical* claims of social theory are entangled with one another in a complex way: at the *explanative level* the concern is to explain how modern societies solve their steering problems after the evolutionary shift from traditional forms of action coordination to post-traditional forms of action coordination has raised a new steering problem insofar as, with the social realization of the model of discursive action coordination, the danger increases that processes of balancing interests will fail.[22] In order to compensate for the risk of dissent, which also increases as a result of the declining ability to generate consensus in the lifeworld, newer mechanisms are needed that ease action coordination, and Habermas names these mechanisms *media*. At the explanative level, in doing this, these have a dual function: on the one hand, they explain the possibility of successful action coordination in that they relieve the interaction from the risk of dissent of action oriented toward understanding; on the other hand, however, they also explain how differentiation processes can occur at the level of societal subsystems insofar as they make possible the formation of action contexts oriented toward effectiveness and centered around media. Here the interaction conveyed by media within the functional subsystems makes it possible for the subsystems to achieve independence from the context, which they have differentiated themselves from with the help of the media. To that extent, the media have a "system-building effect."[23]

At the same time, however—and this can be diagnosed from the perspective of a *critical* social theory—hereby these subsystems achieve independence; they are "decoupled" from the lifeworld.[24] And to the degree to which the media effectively compensate for the loss of the ability to generate consensus in the lifeworld, they enable action coordination to be made independent of the lifeworld contexts; here the rationalization dynamic and the imperative to maintain the subsystems are increasingly dominant and colonize the lifeworld.[25]

If one traces the function that the media have in their explanative and critical perspective back to their function in the theoretical architectonic, then Habermasian media theory is presented with the task of dealing with the conceptual act of balancing the theory of lifeworld interactions, based on action theory, and the theory of all subsystems when examined from the perspective of system theory, which are specifically decoupled from the rationality of social actors and are steered by their own systems logic. However, because the societal subsystems in this way become opaque to action theory,[26] the media that hold "the economic and the administrative action system together"[27] are supposed to ensure that it is possible to structurally describe the system.

Admittedly, Habermas constructs his media concept so that both the effectiveness-centered interaction modus specific to the subsystems and the interaction modus oriented toward understanding that is specific to the lifeworld are mirrored in it and the homogeneity of the media concept is threatened. In connection with Parsons's differentiation between rational and empirically motivating media, Habermas distinguishes between *"symbolically generalized communication media,"* which substitute for linguistic understanding (which he later calls steering media) and *"media of generalized communication,* which functionally specify and simplify the mechanism of linguistic understanding."[28] While money and power, in the attempt to substitute for linguistic communication, may decrease the costs of the act of interpretation and contribute to a decrease in the risk of dissent, and thus permit a decoupling of action coordination from processes of reaching understanding based in the lifeworld that expands "the degrees of freedom of success-oriented action,"[29] (for their part) influence and value commitment remain dependent on a lifeworld "reserve" (*Deckungsreserve*) and thus on a mode of action coordination oriented toward understanding, which they merely facilitate. Thus while influence and value commitment can still be understood according to Parsons's model of special languages, "steering media may not be understood as a functional specification of language; rather they are a *substitute* for special functions of language."[30] Leaning on Parsons, Habermas understands steering media here as mechanisms that ought to lead those addressed in standard situations to an empirically motivated willingness to accept the offers, while media of generalized communication generate a rationally motivated willingness to accept offers. In the *Theory of Communicative Action*, Habermas expands the two families of media, adding one member to each. As media of generalized communication, he adds mass media to influence and value commitment. These "free communication processes from the provinciality of spatiotemporally restricted contexts and permit public spheres to emerge, through establishing the abstract simultaneity of a virtually present network of communication contents far removed in space and time and through keeping messages available for manifold contexts."[31] In addition to the media of money and power, on the other hand, positive law is added as a further steering medium. In cases, namely, "where the law serves as a means for organizing media-controlled subsystems, . . . the *law* is combined with the media of power and money in such a way that it takes on *the role of a steering medium* itself."[32] Admittedly the case of law is more complex than, for instance, money and power, because, as an institution, the medium of law remains rooted in lifeworld contexts (see figure 2.2).[33]

Even if this differentiation, which results in a "media dualism," yields a theoretical position with a view to the structural characteristics that is

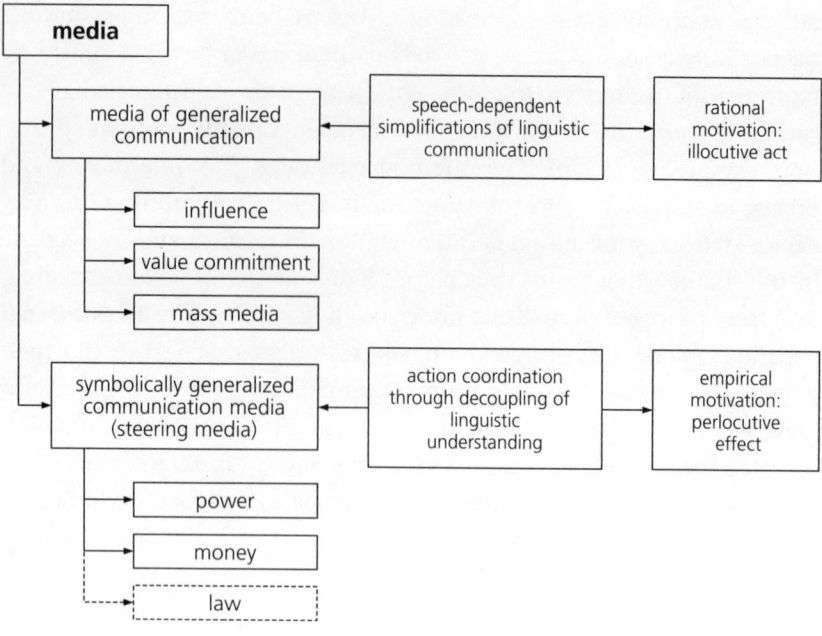

FIGURE 2.2 Media in Habermas

more relaxed than Parsons's view, because the characteristics for symbolizing value, for institutionalization, for measurability, and for the ability to be circulated and stored must be fulfilled by the steering media alone, it can now hardly be seen how systems theory and action theory are to be integrated by means of media theory if media theory itself is bifurcated.[34]

However, even if one, in agreement with this differentiation, limits the structural characteristics of the steering media, one still has to come to terms with differences: differences with a view to the measurability of money and power, which Habermas himself grants, and differences regarding circularity, which Habermas plays down when he characterizes power as a media that does not circulate "from home."[35] If, in the face of these difficulties, one can only quell one's doubts with great effort, then, in the case of law, reassurances that play things down remain ineffective. For law does not fulfill the necessary qualitative criteria for steering media, because here one can neither sensibly speak of measurability nor of an ability to be circulated.[36]

Habermas indeed announced a critique of the process of generalization, with the help of which Parsons had attempted to specify the structural characteristics of media in accord with the paradigm of the prototypical medium of money, but even the relief lent to the problem of determining such characteristics that comes from differentiating the media concept does not fully mitigate it. As a consequence of the media dualism, the criteriological definition of media takes a *disjunctive* form that can only be related to *functional* attributes: media are social mechanisms that ease action coordination either by simplifying linguistic coordination processes, whereby they provide reasons for a certain behavior to those addressed, *or* by making linguistic coordination processes superfluous by confronting those addressed symbolically with different outcome scenarios.

2.1.3. Media in Luhmann

In Luhmann's theory of social systems—at least until 1986—in order to show the plausibility of the existence of social systems that reproduce themselves through communication, media had the function of reducing the improbability of the occurrence of the constitutive basic operation of social systems—namely, communication—under conditions of double contingency. Here Luhmann views systems not as theoretical tools or as subsystems with their own logic, integrated into society, but as existing entities.[37] Together with epistemic-instrumental understanding, Luhmann eliminates all the strong teleological implications of the system concept with the help of which Parsons had schematized system *problems*. Systems have no inherent telos to maintain continued existence; they exist as long as they can reproduce themselves.

As a result of this far-reaching restructuring, in Luhmann's theory of social systems, media theory is given a decisive role in clarifying the conditions for all processes that first and foremost constitute the object of social theory, that is, society.[38] Because, according to Luhmann's perspective, communications are nothing other than coordinated selections, and all selections of communicating unities occur under conditions of double contingency, mechanisms are needed that make it more probable that communications, which are highly improbable, will come to pass. Luhmann calls such mechanisms *media*. Luhmann differentiates three respects in which it is improbable that communications will occur, each of which corresponds to a type of media. Here, the improbability of understanding is mitigated by the *medium of language*; the improbability of

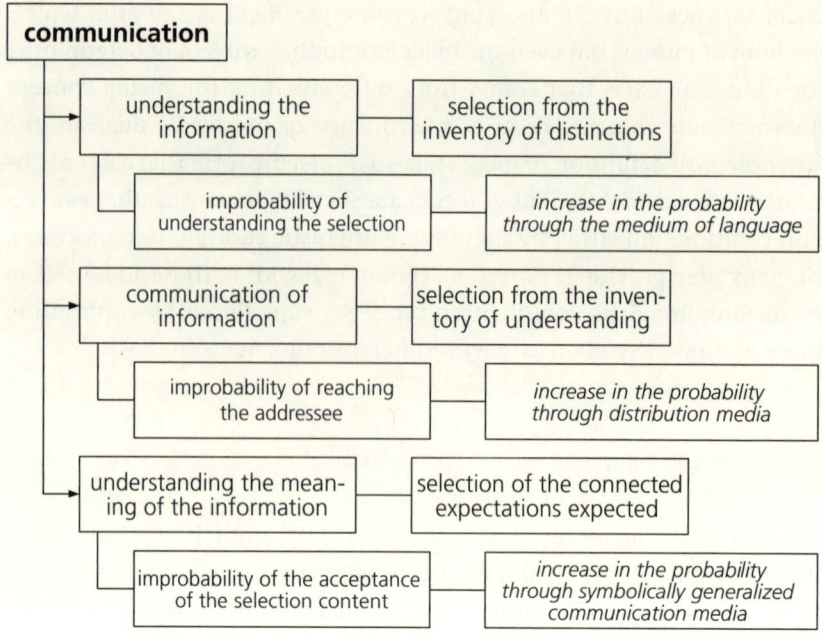

FIGURE 2.3 Media and communication in Luhmann

reaching those addressed by a communication through *distribution media* such as writing, funk, etc.; and the improbability of successfully communicating through the adoption of *symbolically generalized media* that motivate choice such as money, power, love, art, and belief (see figure 2.3).[39]

In order to free the theory of communication media from its dependency on the problems of evolutionary differentiation and integration, which are at the center of Parsons's media theory, Luhmann generalizes at three basic levels. *First*, he generalizes the *concept of contingency*—which he unhinges from the alleged close connection with system differentiation, within which it was related to the description of contingent relationships between differentiated subsystems, in the sense of reciprocal relationships of dependence—drawing on a "general modal-theoretical concept of contingency, which also characterizes the 'other possible existence' of the existent being."[40] *Second*, he generalizes the concept of *exchange media*, which is oriented on exchange relationships and the reciprocal satisfaction of one's needs, making it a concept of *communication media* oriented on general communication processes.[41] And *third*,

Luhmann generalizes the *concept of code* in order to use it to differentiate the structure of media more precisely from language, as "we do not see codes as values or as series of symbols plain and simple, but with a specific abstraction as disjunctions, as 'yes or no,' 'having or not having,' 'truth or falsity,' 'just or unjust,' 'beauty or ugliness.'"[42] Against this background, media can now be *defined* functionally through their contribution to reducing the improbability of communication:

> We would like to call media the evolutionary achievements that enter at those possible breaks in communication and that serve in a functionally adequate way to transform what is improbable into what is probable.[43]

If, beyond this global specification, it is to be able to explain *how* media effect the increase in probability, a mechanism must be identified with the help of which it is possible to explain how the contingent selections of communicating actors can be adjusted. Precisely in order to address this problem, Luhmann takes up the concept of the *code*, which had already been closely connected with probabilistic problems of communication within the framework of the semiotic tradition.[44] However, because Luhmann, under the auspices of the generalized code concept, brings together a mixture of such heterogeneous concepts, it remains largely unclear which structural characteristics are to serve as the basis for counting social means of interaction as media.

Initially Luhmann understands "code" only to include "a structure which is in a position to *look for and attribute a different complementary item to any item whatever within its field of reference*."[45] On the basis of the classification structure that Luhmann calls the "duplication rule," it must now be possible to explain how media, on the basis of their code structures, wield influence over the possibilities for selection in communication processes, and how, in this process, the improbability can be decreased at the three levels of communication; namely, of the understanding of selection, the transfer of information, and the understanding of the meaning of a selection that is communicated. And indeed Luhmann finds a duplication rule at each of these three levels:

1. At the level of the medium of language, its "negation potential" takes on the function of a duplication rule "by making two settings available for all the existing information: a position and a nega-

tive."[46] Then the relata used in the duplication rule "negation" are bits of information (or propositions?) (for example, p, $\neg p$).

2. At the level of the distribution media, the concept of the duplication rule is used as a classifying relation between selections and signs or between (phonetic) signs and other (for example, written) signs, that is, between sets of symbolic relata. Here an item from set A is classified with an item from set B (for example: $a = $ ⁞; $b = $ ⁞; $c = $ ⁞).

3. At the level of communication media that affect motivation, as a duplication rule, a "binary schematism," in turn, organizes its items, which are positive values, to the negation of those values (for example, legal/illegal in the case of the medium of law, loves me/love me not in the case of the medium of love).

However, the differences between the relations that Luhmann includes under the concept of the duplication rule are obvious: while propositions and the negation of them—both relative to truth and relative to the possibility of understanding—are of equal value but are not equivalent, and the relation is not symmetrical, for the binary schematism of the positive–negative value dichotomy it is of decisive importance that the symmetry is overcome. A completely different relation is found, in turn, in the classification of symbols from different symbol systems; the types of symbols that are classified together indeed are equivalent because of the rule of classification.

The inconsistencies in a code concept that is utilized at all levels of communication may be one reason that, since 1986, Luhmann has continually weakened the aspect of preference coding,[47] which was initially supposed to plausibly show how symbolically generalized media play a motivating role in the selection of positive values.[48] He has replaced this with the difference between codes and programs. Now he no longer speaks of a preference for one of the values of a media code or of an asymmetry between the poles of the difference. The successor to the concept of preference coding is now the concept of the "program," which Luhmann sharply distinguishes from the "criterion" of the code. While the criteria produce binary coding, the programs define "given conditions for the suitability of the selection of operations."[49]

In this situation, there is the option either of giving up on the concept of the media of generalized communication or of limiting the activity of the media such that, with their help, communications are centered on value disjunctions. As a result of such limitations, media would only simplify the understanding of selections, while the choice of certain affiliated actions (namely, of those related to positively interpreted values) would be made more probable by programs. Admittedly, in this case, from a functional point of view, the positive–negative value dichotomization would no longer be distinguished from the duplication rule "negation." Herewith, however, there is a threat that the concept of media has been hollowed out. Künzler is fully correct to note: "If the code of the medium is no longer coding preferences, the definiens is no longer applicable, the specific differentia of the media gets lost: the emblematization of the unity of selection and motivation."[50]

2.2. MEDIA AND TECHNOLOGY

While sociological media theory proposes media concepts that only have a distant connection to the prominent everyday understanding of media as technical means of communication, it is precisely this (latter) understanding that constitutes the focal point of McLuhan's work. McLuhan, whom Gadamer correctly characterized as the apostle of the end of the Gutenberg age, is thus astonishingly influential even today because the generalizing impulse of his views promises to systematically take into consideration every means that we use in order to communicate with one another. Here, McLuhan is especially interested in the effects of the use of media on those who use them, and he attempts to employ these fruitfully in a cultural diagnostic.

In this perspective, which shows a certain affinity to historical materialism, McLuhan interprets the historical development of societal forms as consequences of a dynamic that results from the use of media that become influential throughout history. Here, despite his often imprecise writing style, McLuhan does not maintain that the development of societal structures is immediately determined by the media;[51] rather, he assumes and he underlines this later in *Laws of Media*[52]—that the use of certain media brings about changes in those who use them, which for their part lead to transformations of the societal structures. In McLuhan's view, media analysis does not aim at a syntax of media; rather, it is directed to the study of the consequences of using media.

Against the background of the Popperean differentiation between open and closed societies, which McLuhan draws on,[53] the process of societal revolutions, induced by media use, which McLuhan has in mind, can be described as a three-phase development process.[54]

Here the first phase of the development can be viewed as a closed society whose members are integrated by the presence of means of communication that are simultaneously sensuously complex and lack sensory specialization. Societies in which this oral integration modus is disrupted by the dominant use of the alphabetic medium and in which, as a consequence of sensory specialization (through reading), individualized perspectives are possible, constitute, in contrast, open societies; these are characteristic of the second phase of the transformation process. Against the background of this description, the consequences of the current technological (i.e., medial) developments can be described as the entrance into a third phase, which shares with the first phase the instantaneous distribution of information dependent on presence and "resembles the old tribal society in as much as the ears again acquire great significance and the awareness of the reciprocal dependency of all people and folk groups grows."[55] The entrance to this third phase, which is heralded with the advent of the electronic media, is the centerpiece of McLuhan's most influential book, *Understanding Media*, in which the slogan "the medium is the message"[56] was raised to a platitude.

Here McLuhan now presents a wide-reaching generalization and broadens his approach. The media concept is dramatically expanded to integrate means of communication, tools in general, and forms of energy; and the media in general are understood as "extensions of man."[57] These extensions of the human body, which, according to McLuhan, culminate in the technical reconstruction of the nervous system and the brain, are available, on the one hand, to their users; on the other hand, they have an influence on the organization of the senses and on attentiveness, which differs, depending on the medium. For example, "hot media" (like radio, film, photography, and paper) "that extend . . . one single sense in 'high definition' [where] high definition is the state of being well filled with data,"[58] only require a little interpreting, while "cool media" (like the telephone, television, money, and electric light) are thought to stand in need of a high level of integration by the recipients. In this view, the slogan "the medium is the message" acquires the meaning that the message of the medium consists precisely in the epiphenomena of its individual and collective use, that is, in the reorganization of patterns of attentiveness and reception.

In contrast to this, however, McLuhan clearly also thinks that medial communication will at times have common content: "[A] characteristic of all media [is] that the 'content' of any medium is always another medium. The content of writing is speech, just as the written word is the content of print, and print is the content of the telegraph."[59] However, precisely such graded relationships of content illustrate the reason for McLuhan's crude materialism, which in the later *Laws of Media* is clad as biologism and does not wince at pursuing the chain of content relationships back to the level of cerebral processes: "If it is asked, 'What is the content of speech?' it is necessary to say, 'It is an actual process of thought, which is in itself nonverbal.'"[60]

This leveling of the difference between the content and those actualizing (*Realisatoren*) the mental content, however, illustrates only a further high point in the process of de-differentiation, for the identification of media with artifacts also entails an equation of artifacts and linguistic expressions: "each of man's artifacts is in fact a kind of word, a metaphor that translates experience from one form to another."[61] So the generalizing impulse, which at the beginning perhaps still was connected with the hope of a comprehensive theory of the means of communication, in fact marks the end of McLuhanean thought, for given the lack of criteria, the concept of medium is equated with the concept of the artifact, and thus made theoretically superfluous.

Even if, in the context of this cursory overview of some of the available pertinent media theories, I have not been able to show in detail that the available media concepts are burdened with grave deficiencies, I hope that I at least have thrown doubt on the view that a robust concept of media is available to us. The causes of this deficiency, in the case of sociological theories, are the shaky or inconsistent criteriological definitions of the media concept, which are due to a wide-reaching use of the media concept to solve antecedent problems in theory construction. Beyond that, however, the affinity of the sociological concepts of media to the system-theoretic vocabulary presents a difficulty, if one thinks (as I do) that every reconstruction of communication processes from a system-theoretic standpoint is derivative from its description in intentionalist language. These difficulties can only be averted if one attempts to develop the concept of media consistently within the framework of action theory.

As one of the few linkages to such a project, I will thus attempt in what follows to reconstruct Dewey's theory of aesthetic experience somewhat more fully.

2.3. DEWEY'S ACTION-THEORETIC CONCEPTION OF MEDIA

2.3.1. Introduction

John Dewey, known as one of the founders of pragmatism, is not prominent in media theory, and the concept of media that he develops as a part of his aesthetics has hardly even been noted by any of the so-called media theoreticians. This fact is indeed surprising, not least of all because of the grave theoretical weaknesses of the influential McLuhan school. For as a result of the various theoretical tasks that the concept is to take on in Dewey's theory of aesthetics, Dewey's media concept has acquired a relative sophistication that cultural diagnosticians in media theory could often only dream of.

Dewey's media theoretic ambitions are of special interest because, besides the fact that he developed his media concept in the context of aesthetic reflections and not within the framework of the analysis of system theory or the philosophy of technique, his views are also an example of a contribution to media theory developed in explicit reference to *action theory*. A reconstruction of this concept thus promises a significant contrast to the theories sketched out so far; at the same time, his concept shows an affinity to my concern to make a view of understanding conceived with a broadened media theory the basis of a theory of rationality, which should prove itself up to the task of exhibiting the dimension of aesthetic rationalization processes in modernity. However, the attempt to develop a reconstruction faces an obstacle, namely, that the text in which Dewey developed his media concept is today characterized by a rather strange enthusiasm rather than by sparse analytic precision. The following proposal for a reconstruction, which is not meant to be a detailed contribution to Dewey exegesis, thus takes as its basis the slightly mimetic attempt to work out the kernel of Dewey's media concept from the characteristic mixture of Hegelian and pragmatistic motifs, along with those of *Lebensphilosophie*, which is typical of many of Dewey's texts.

Setting out from an ordinary concept of experience, in *Art as Experience*, from 1934, Dewey specifies a concept of aesthetic experience that he attempts to make plastic in a complex web of relationships. In this network the media concept serves to help reconstruct essential concepts of aesthetic reflection on the basis of a holistic concept of experience; with its help, the vague foundation of everyday experiences is specified so that it is possible to characterize objects and the specifics of aesthetic experience.[62] Thus the media concept plays a decisive role in differentiating art from merely purposive action, in the constitution of expressions and artwork, in the characterization of the objectives of art, in the construction of the ability to understand art, and not least of all in the reconstruction of art as a dimension of intersubjective communication.

Dewey's aesthetic perspective is oriented, first of all, on the procedure of reception aesthetics, developed in Kant, to explain the phenomenon of art through the analysis of specific experiences that we have with works of art. At the same time, however, Dewey attempts to expand the theoretic framework of a primarily individualist reception aesthetic[63] under the assumption of a Hegelian motif with a view to the social contextuality of aesthetic experience. His study thus begins, in accord with reception-aesthetic maxims, not from the specifics of entities known as "works of art" but from the specifics of aesthetic experience, which are prepared both by the recipients and the producers. In accord with pragmatic maxims, in explaining aesthetic experience, Dewey emphasizes its similarities to characteristics of everyday experience. Such experiences integrate moments of perception and sensation, but also of reflection and of interpretation in the context of social life practices. In the sense intended by this integration, experiences are psychic episodes that we remember as unities; here they thus encompass both passive and active elements. Against this background, aesthetic experiences thus can be defined as a subset of experiences that include precisely the experiences that, as an active element, involve a relationship to the productive processes that have led to the generation of the phenomenon experienced. Analogously to the recipients' analysis of aesthetic experience, artistic actions can be understood as a subset of everyday problem solving actions, and indeed precisely as those in which the actors orient themselves on the attributes of their actions or of products that are able to be experienced (by others).[64] If we cross the passive and the active aspects of experience with the views that we can adopt toward works of art, namely, the perspectives of producing a work of art or of being a recipient of one, the following relations result, which structure Dewey's developed concept of aesthetic experience:[65]

1. The aesthetic experience of the producer (P_1) encompasses
   a. an active element insofar as P_1 *frames* an object K;
   b. a passive element insofar as P_1 has *to allow* impulses from K *to have an effect* in order to frame K according to the forms of perception that P_n has imputed to it.

2. The aesthetic experience of the recipient (P_2) encompasses
   a. an active element insofar as P_2 *interprets* an object K;
   b. a passive element insofar as P_2 *has to absorb* impulses from K in order to interpret K according to the intentions that P_2 has imputed to P_1.

The basic situation of aesthetic experience is decidedly *communicative*: P_1 produces a perceptible phenomenon K with a view to the reception of K by other people P_n ($n \geq 1$), and a person P_2 receives K with a view to its having been intentionally produced by P_1.[66]

Against the background of this conception, the interface for Dewey's thoughts on media theory can now be clearly made out. For the view of the recipient to the alleged perspective of the producer and the view of the producer to the possible perspectives of the recipients, and thus the communicative dimension of aesthetic experience, are dependent on mediating elements if these views are not to be lost in pure contingency. It is these mediating elements that Dewey refers to as *media*. A "medium is a mediator. It is a go-between of artist and perceiver."[67] This mediation is concerned—as is clear from the preceding considerations—neither with solving a mere technically understood transport problem nor with problems of social action coordination in the narrower sense. It is rather concerned with providing the aesthetically communicating with means that facilitate the receptive comprehension (*Nachvollzug*) as well as the prospective orientation for the production with respect to the intended effects of the potential recipients; they thus open possibilities for interpreting understanding, on the one hand, and the possibility for the anticipated offering of something to understand (*Zu-verstehen-geben*),[68] on the other.

Media, it can be assumed, provide the recipients of art with mechanisms that allow a certain relief from the situation of radical interpretation, a relief that is necessary because works of art are almost always isolated from their contexts of production such that the recipient, on the basis of a causal theory of references—lacking the observability of context-embedded behavior patterns—could hardly acquire evidence that might be used as the basis for interpretations. Media ease the process by which recipients develop interpretive hypotheses, because we can describe the specifics of a work of art against the background of socially shared matrixes of possibility. For example, we might say a composer chose his notes from the *known* inventory of notes and none of the other possible ones. From the perspective of the artist, this interpretation-supporting function for the recipient stands in contrast to the function of more reliably anticipating interpretations insofar as the potential recipients will describe the works within the shared matrix of possibilities and make comparisons with other works within this matrix. In this respect, media can be understood as schema with the help of which recipients are able to achieve promising interpretive hypotheses insofar as they are able to describe an action as a choice from a known inventory of possibilities, and producers are able to arrive at promising anticipations of the recipients' interpretations because they can describe their own actions as choices from the inventory of a medium that the recipients are acquainted with.

The context in which Dewey first mentions the concept of the medium clearly shows that he analyzes media within the framework of actions, thus within the framework of conscious intentional activities. If one accepts his comments about the role of media for the producers, then, first of all, criteria can be acquired with the help of which the media concept can be specified. In connection with the criteriological reconstruction of the media concept, it can now be shown that the interpretive perspective, which was opened up above, does not need to be imposed on Dewey's media theory, but stands in harmony with its central purposes.

2.3.2. The Development of Media Theory

As was already noted, the first mention of the media concept is in the context of a differentiation between nonintentional action and intentional action:

> An act of discharge or mere exhibition lacks a medium. Instinctive crying and smiling no more require a medium than do sneezing and winking.[69]

Crying, sneezing, and perhaps the winking of an eye are, on the one hand, examples of activities that are usually not done intentionally; however, on the other hand, they are also examples of activities that need no other means than the bodies of the "actors." The point that Dewey is concerned about, however, is not the use of means external to the body, but the conscious purposive use of something that requires further specification. First of all, it appears to me to be central that the body in the activities mentioned is usually not consciously employed as a means. In order that a means can be viewed as a medium, it is necessary that

(1) the means is consciously used purposively.

It is clear that the purposive use of means cannot be a sufficient characteristic for defining media, for otherwise the concept would be equivalent to that of a tool, a consequence that should be avoided in light of its consequences for McLuhan's views. Greater clarification can still be gained by further differentiating the set of consciously used means internally, namely, by drawing on their possible relations to the goal of the action. Media are contrasted with tools: tools must be used consciously and intentionally if they are to meet the criterion of being used *as* tools, but they find themselves in an external, i.e., exchangeable, relationship with the results of their use. In contrast, according to Dewey, media become a part of the products that are created with their aid. With a view to examples such as the use of gasoline as fuel in the context of problems of transportation, he writes:

> Such external or *mere* means, as we properly term them, are usually of such a sort that others can be substituted for them; the particular ones employed are determined by some extraneous consideration, like cheapness. But the moment we say "media" we refer to means that are incorporated in the outcome.[70]

Though a more precise definition of the connection between means and ends initially remains open, as a further criterion for media, the following can provisionally be maintained:

> (2) Within the framework of action, media are means that stand in an intrinsic relationship with the goal of the respective action.

The following remarks by Dewey confirm that he views intentionality and the connection of media to goals as criteria; however, these remarks are irritating given the views sketched out at the beginning, that media stand in a communicative relationship.

> Even bricks and mortar become part of the house they are employed to build; they are not mere means to its erection. Colors *are* the painting, tones *are* the music.[71]

The conjunction of both conditions—intentionality and a connection to goals—can initially provide a necessary criterion for the concept of media, but it remains questionable whether it provides a sufficient one. For it is not clear whether Dewey in all seriousness wants to understand bricks as media. While color and notes stand in an evidently intrinsic relationship with the communicative objective of a work of art, as constitutive parts, the example of bricks suggests, on the one hand, that the construction of a house should be understood primarily as instrumental, rather than communicative; on the other hand, the example does not clearly convey the criterion of the connection to goals either. For although a particular finished house consists of bricks, from which it was built—so the house is identical with the configuration of bricks—it is only in reference to the goal of building *a* house that bricks are exchangeable means (with lime and straw, wood or concrete).[72] Only when the goal consists in building a certain house, namely, a brick one, is it possible to speak with assurance in reference to this example of a connection to goals in a sufficiently precise sense. For example:

> (2a) Media are means that stand in an intrinsic connection with the goal of the respective action in which they are employed as means, and indeed such that the goal can*not* be reached *without* these means.

With a view to this criterion, however, the following objection promises success: although at a certain historical point in time there may only be precisely one tool to solve a problem, for example, boron-carbon blades to mechanically process diamonds, it can at any time be thought that with technical development, alternatives will be established that undermine this necessary condition and make it possible to exchange the tool. Dewey must thus have something else in mind. Maybe:

> (2b) Media are means that stand in an intrinsic relationship to the goal of the respective action, and indeed such that the goal is a product that consists in essence of the means.

Formulation (2b), however, remains problematic insofar as one naturally needs vinegar for vinaigrette and the vinegar is both irreplaceable and a constitutive element of the vinaigrette, but it remains questionable what might be gained by characterizing vinegar as a medium.

An alternative that allows us to avert the equating of media and tools in (2a) and the broadening of the media concept in (2b) only comes to light if we differentiate the goals that media contribute to the realization from those that can be reached with the help of tools or mere means. With a view to the communicative aspect of Deweyan aesthetics, a criterion that offers itself here would characterize media as means with which the users connect communicative goals. However, insofar as bricks contribute in a specific way to the achievement of articulated architectural intentions and houses can be possible objects of aesthetic experience,[73] the apparent ricochet can be stopped and the catalogue of criteria can be broadened to include the following entry:

> (3) Media are means that are used with expressive, communicatory intention.

"What makes a material a medium is that it is used to express a meaning which is other than that which it is in virtue of its bare physical existence: the meaning not of what it physically is, but of what it expresses."[74] Now Dewey does not view this medium merely in relation to those who employ media, thus it is not like the resistant material that Hegel's slave works on, thereby experiencing himself as independent and realizing his own goals;[75] rather, he views it as an intrinsic social material that stands in the service not only of the expression, but also of communication. "A medium as distinct from raw material," Dewey writes, "is always a mode of *language* and thus of expression and *communication*."[76]

The difference from raw material does not yet explain much, but it is interesting how Dewey believes he can more precisely specify this difference. Like Parsons, who characterizes media at the level of interaction among actors as special languages, Dewey sees occasion to place media in relationship to language. In order to be able to use the comparison with language fruitfully as a characterization of media, more must be meant than that media, like language, are means for achieving understanding. If the comparison is limited to this conclusion, then we do not get beyond the characterization provided in (3). However, if one follows Dewey's suggestions in the text, two further characteristics of media can be garnered from the comparison with language: (1) Similarly to language, media are not drawn on ad hoc, but are *established* means of reaching understanding. (2) In contrast to language, media, above all in art, are accorded a function in light of which linguistic communication appears utterly deficient, namely, the function of facilitating the production of objects of collective experience for communicative purposes.

1. The fact that media are *established* means of reaching understanding needs further explication. For one, it is necessary to clarify which mechanisms establish them; for another, however, it is necessary to specify the relationship of media to language (the established means of understanding par excellence), as Dewey continually draws on this relationship in order to show the plausibility of the media concept by characterizing media as "a type of language."[77]

Dewey's text does not clearly indicate the mechanism for establishing this. Instead, various by no means arbitrary but rather systematically relevant elements can be prepared; one of the numerous tasks of a developed media theory is to systematically integrate these. An initial element that I provisionally would like to refer to as the element of the *performative proliferation* of media shows that media emerge when communicative acts are carried out and that successful communication is the mechanism by which they are established. The concept of the performative proliferation initially assumes one implication of the communicative function of media, namely, that the products of medial acts of articulation are publicly accessible, i.e., that they must in a broad sense be observable. The starting point for establishing a medium can thus initially simply consist in a person bringing about an observable condition in the world with a communicative intention. The next step, in accord with Dewey's views, which in any case presupposes that at least one person reacts (with an interpretation), appears to consist in the conversion of the natural substrates of the acts of articulation, "through selection and organization, into an intensified and concentrated medium."[78] It may be that such selection and organization processes in turn take place solely within the framework of attempts to articulate something with the help of material selected and organized in an act of articulation. Here one can further presume that social reactions sanction certain forms of organization and in this way wield influence over the organization of media.

The advantage of this reconstruction in the context of aesthetic reflection is obvious; for with its help the process of the development of artistic means of communication can be explained largely independently of linguistic agreements, and this can be done in such a way that it is possible to fundamentally secure the autonomy of artistic articulation. Indications that Dewey had a sense of this problem are found in formulations in which he emphasizes that artists cannot simply orient themselves on existing rules when producing works of art:

> Since the physical material used in production of a work of art is not itself a medium, no rules can be laid down *a priori* for its proper use. The limits of its esthetic potentialities can be determined only experimentally and by what artists make out of it in practice.[79]

Formulations, like the one quoted, that underline the importance of the performative implementation in the process of medial articulation and that take up the Kantian motif of talent, which does not follow a certain rule, as well as the function of the exemplary for the further development of artistic practice,[80] however, also contrast with formulations that make reference to another procedure for creating and establishing media in which rules obviously play an important role. Yet comments in which Dewey freely acquiesces that media can never be fully determined are completely aligned with the theory of performative proliferation. He admits that "the exact limits of the efficacy of any medium cannot be determined by any *a priori* rule, and that every great initiator in art breaks down some barrier that had previously been supposed to be inherent. If . . . we establish the discussion on the basis of the media, we recognize that they form a continuum, a spectrum, and that while we may distinguish arts as we distinguish the so-called seven primary colors, there is no attempt to tell exactly where one begins and the other ends."[81] In light of the vagueness of the media concept in the McLuhan school, I think it is advisable to emphasize that the fact that media in principle cannot be fully specified should not be confused with a lack of conceptual precision; rather, it is a price that must be paid once a conscious theoretical decision is made to establish media on the basis of performative and not "deliberative" processes.

Besides this strand, a competing motif can be developed that attempts to explain the process of socially establishing media with recourse to the social adherence to rules, and indeed with recourse to rules that constitute media by ascribing certain types of actions a certain status. Searle,[82] drawing on Rawls's "rules of practice,"[83] has defined such *constitutive rules* as those rules without the knowledge of which behavior guided by those rules cannot be adequately described. In contrast to *regulative rules*, which influence an activity that exists independently of these rules, constitutive rules are needed to make some type of action possible, which they regulate. Such rules have the following form: X serves (in context K) as Y!.

In *Art as Experience* there are indications that Dewey had in mind rules that are only established and verified as a criterion for media in intersubjective practice. Thus, in the context of first mentioning the media concept, he offers the example of taboo proscriptions, that is, an exemplary case of a set of constitutive rules, as a condition for the semantization of media:

> Only where material is employed as media is there expression and art. Savage taboos that look to the outsider like mere prohibitions and inhibitions externally imposed may be to those who experience them media of expressing social status, dignity, and honor. Everything depends on the way in which material is used when it operates as medium.[84]

Obviously, Dewey wants to say that media are characteristically established in a specific social way. For media often only fulfill the communicative function on the basis of a shared practice, or, more precisely, on the basis of a shared preknowledge and indeed a preknowledge based on the fact that those who are acting within the framework of the practice under question know that X, which they deal with in the framework of this practice, has a status that it owes to the collective ascription of an attribute or a function. In order to be able to understand the range of the artistic forms of communication on offer, one must be familiar with the rules that constitute the means of the production: "The language of art has to be acquired."[85]

However, it is questionable whether a strong interpretation of the establishment mechanism—for example, on the basis of constitutive rules—lives up to Dewey's intuitions and, beyond that, whether it is sensible.[86] For a consequence of such an interpretation is, first of all, that something is only a medium if it *is considered* a medium, and, second, it contains a problematic implication, namely, that the social existence of media then falls into a fundamental dependency on language, which is the required medium for formulating constitutive rules. With these questions, however, one finds oneself having traversed beyond the questions that Dewey's text might reasonably clearly answer, and at the same time one is in the context of debates about the theory of meaning in which one is confronted with fundamental alternatives—alternatives with respect to which a media theory must assume a position. I would like to mention at least some of the issues in these debates, here not least of all in order to clearly show that Dewey's concept faces difficulties that the philosophical tools of his time hardly allowed him to deal with. The strongest rival view to an interpretation that bases the establishment of the media for understanding on socially established rules is certainly Davidson's concept of *radical interpretation*; in connection with the view that, for purposes of the theory of meaning, recourse to the rule-view is circular insofar as the formulation of explicit rules already (necessarily) presupposes a language that is understood, it is prepared to grant rules only an economic, not a constitutive, function in the process of understanding. The concept of *implicit rules* may allow objections of this sort to be averted, but it is questionable whether such a concept can be plausibly elucidated. After all, it is necessary to explain how it is possible that an actor follows a rule, and that he has the possibility of not following the rule or of consciously breaching it even if he lacks an explicit understanding of the rule at the time. More recent pragmatic views may offer a way out of this situation—for example, Brandom's attempt to trace processes of understanding back to social *sanctioning practices*, in order, in this way, to explain the process of establishing the "rule-bound" medium of language in a noncircular manner. In the framework of offering a pertinent reconstruction of Dewey's media theory, I thus formulate a further criterion in the form of an alternative.

> (4) Media are means of expression that are socially established in the process of stabilizing a performative practice or by constitutive rules.

However, today, as in Dewey's time, the set of constitutive rules in the area of art is seldom specified, but is open to permanent revision by artwork itself. Indeed, one might say that the interpretations of works of art are, inter alia, precisely taking up the *modifications* of the set of known constitutive rules, but that they still are able to orient themselves on deviations from *known* rules. Perhaps we should say that a reconstruction of art, such as is yielded by the application of the Deweyan media concept, assigns the meaning of works of art a place within a system that oscillates between a rule-based concept of meaning with recourse to validity and a concept of meaning that results from radical interpretation on the basis of a causal theory of reference. On the one hand, we could certainly say that the dimensions of meaning in art are due to a framework that is based on a view of socially shared rules. On the other hand, precisely the imperative to expand the scope of what can be experienced with the senses continually threatens this framework so that rules are only suggested after successful threats, that is, a posteriori, in the constitution of the media, which for their part remain connected to productive performative acts of artistic articulation.

2. Reading though the text passages in which Dewey characterizes processes of media-supported artistic communication—often bracketing language—it is striking that Dewey connects them with a nearly unbounded optimism:

> Expression strikes below the barriers that separate human beings from one another. Since art is the most universal form of language, since it is constituted, even apart from literature, by the common qualities of the public world, it is the most universal and freest form of communication.[87]

But how precisely is this communication structured, which Dewey entrusts with so much, and what role do the media play in his optimism about communication? Why is "art . . . the most effective mode of communication that exists"?[88]

A first indication of Dewey's answer to the question is provided by Dewey's estimate that "art is a more universal mode of language than is the speech that exists in a multitude of mutually unintelligible forms."[89] One must indeed also appropriate the "language of art." "But the language of art is not affected by the accidents of history that mark off different modes of human speech."[90] In contrast to this emphatic way of speaking, it is necessary, first of all, to remember that the energy that must be expended to appropriate the "language of art" of other traditions is often underestimated. That is amazing insofar as aesthetic communication after all runs considerably greater risks of failure because its material is already continually subject to broad revisions and new discoveries, which are presented performatively, but usually are not explained (in any case, not in the mode of aesthetic communication).

However, a robust difference between aesthetic communication and linguistic communication in a narrower sense comes into view if we call to mind that we also have experiences with "foreign" or unfamiliar art, and in this process, the artistic artifacts with which we are faced confront us differently than a speech act formulated in a language that we do not know. In contrast to the case of a linguistic expression that we initially do not understand, the work of art confronts us as an object of experience that we can directly relate to those evaluations and interpretations that are available for our experience. According to Dewey, here the genuine power of a work of art consists in readying and externalizing a perception, a feeling, a thought, in short, a mental state such that it can be an object of experience for the recipient. The production of a work of art, which is a process of formation in the space of medial possibilities, aims to generate this experienceability:

> Through selection and organization those features that make any experience worth having as an experience are prepared by art for commensurate perception.[91]

Thus what can be secured at a fundamental communicative level by the reception of works of art, in contrast to language, is the possibility that recipients apprehend a work of art as an object of an *integrated* experience, and indeed even if they do not manage to reach an interpretation of the work of art in the context of the traditions from which it originates. Dewey thinks that the communication process between artists and recipients is distinctive because artists and recipients—with a view to their respective potential to generate experiences—have access to a shared (natural) endowment:

> It is not necessary that communication should be part of the deliberate intent of an artist, although he can never escape the thought of a potential audience. But its function and consequence are to effect communication, and this not by external accident, but from the nature he shares with others.[92]

However, at the same time, in this fundamental relation of communication, which is based on the shared and structurally similar ability to generate experience, we find the foundation for the process, on which art, in successful communication, is oriented, namely, the expansion of these possibilities for experience: "*'Revelation'* in art is the quickened expansion of experience."[93]

> Men associate in many ways. But the only form of association that is truly human, . . . is the participation in meanings and goods that is effected by communication. The expressions that constitute art are communication in its pure and undefiled form.[94]

Even if it is not clear what justifies emphatically characterizing the artistic form more broadly than in my rather technical analysis, it is nonetheless clear that art, as a form of conveying experiences by creating objects that are supposed to be experienced, is a genuine form of communication. Insofar as the social existence of media is a necessary condition for artistic forms of expression, media is accorded central significance for those communicative acts, which, alongside language, and potentially independent from it, make a process possible that conveys and broadens experience.

In summary, the construction of the media concept employed by Dewey can be reconstructed criteriologically as follows:

(MD) M is a medium if the following applies:

1. M is used intentionally;
2. M is employed with an expressive, communicatory intention;

110 / WHAT ARE MEDIA?

    3. *M* becomes a constitutive part of the acts or products which it is drawn on to create;

    4. *M* is

        a. within the framework of a stabilized performative practice;
        b. socially established by constitutive rules;

    5. *M* allows expressive acts or expressive products to be brought about that are publicly perceptible by their recipients and that can be an object of experience, as an integrated episode.

2.3.3. Problems and Links

The reconstructive and systematizing look at Dewey's *Art as Experience* has unearthed an interesting and in many respects plausible view, which largely overcomes both the conceptual vagueness of the McLuhan school's media theory as well as the difficulties of system-theoretic media theories. In my view, these virtues are, on the one hand, a result of the fact that Dewey's view bases the media concept consistently in action theory; on the other hand, they are also perhaps due to the fact that the context for addressing the problem has been limited to aesthetic communication. Nonetheless, the reconstruction attempt also runs up against its limits. For the text is largely dependent on a very charitable reading, and the text provides no sufficient answers to the questions that it raises:

    1. It remains largely unclear what precisely is supposed to characterize the intrinsic connection that Dewey posits between media and the goals that are to be reached with their help. After the discussion of some characteristics of this relation, the reconstruction had to retract that it is only to be secured by the determinations of the goal of medial action. Yet one would like to assume that Dewey had more in mind, for example, an intrinsic connection between a medium and the goal of an action, indicating that the goal (that is, the expressive act) cannot be reached *subjectively* except by the use of the medium. If the expressive act then *consists in* the realization of the possibilities of the medium, then there would be a context allowing the sense of the term "intrinsically" to be specified. Of course, the price of this advantage would be that the criterion for determining the intrinsic connection would no longer be publicly

verifiable, and there would be a suspicion that media are a particular form of private language.

A further problem with the Deweyan talk of an intrinsic connection consists in the fact that his focus on communicative goals may not be sufficient if communication is explained with a view to artistic communication either as carrying out acts or as creating objects that aim to render something that can be experienced by another person. That is to say, if this construct is faced with the test case of the art of cooking, the cook is caught unawares with media. For if we test the ingredients for a dish under the criteria provided for mediality, we must admit that the ingredients that make the experience possible, i.e., that lend the dish a certain taste, stand in an intrinsic relationship with the object of experience, namely, the food. The dish can only be made with these ingredients, not with any others, and the ingredients, which are hardly ever raw material but are selected and organized, constitute the dish; they are its elements. The criterion of communicative use can also be easily met if one assumes that one person wants to acquaint another with an experience of a certain taste by creating an object that will probably bring about a certain experience in the recipient. If one wants to avoid the emerging consequence of a growth in the number of arts and of media, it appears to me that the process of constituting media must be related to conditions that systematically account for the role of intersubjective processes. However, Dewey's work does not systematically specify the role of intersubjectivity for the media clearly enough, despite his remark that media are "neither subjective nor objective."[95]

2. Dewey's view of the media as a means of communication is clear. In contrast, it is irritating that Dewey's conception of aesthetic communication entrusts art with very much indeed. As a matter of course, he summarizes: "In the end works of art are the only media of complete and unhindered communication between man and man that can occur in a world full of gulfs and walls that limit community of experience."[96] However, it is questionable whether artistic communication attempts might not also fail. In contrast, doesn't the historical experience that many fundamental innovations in art over the decades have had to await a fitting reception suggest that artistic communication is hardly robust but it is rather a fragile form of communication, burdened with considerable risks of being misunderstood?

In what I have written above, I have tried to clearly indicate how Dewey's optimism about communication with a view to art can be shown to be plausible within an understanding of artistic communication that is centered around the concept of experience. But in the face of concert scandals and other examples that display a large-scale rejection of art, I do not see how this optimism can justifiably be maintained. In opposition to such examples of failed artistic communication, what Dewey may have in mind—and this is similar to the positions of Cassirer and his successor, Langer[97]—is an instance of *collective* experience that art owes to its origin in ritual and myth. Then, however, it is questionable to what extent ritual and other community-shaping processes are in fact processes of understanding, processes that transcend procedures of identification that are describable with psychology, that increase the feeling of belonging. To what degree is art, which is "the expansion of power from rites and ceremonies, in order to connect people, through an artistic ceremony that all participate in, with a view to all situations of life,"[98] more than a mechanism for generating community?[99] How is this idea—that is aimed at creating unity—to be related to distancing and individuating impulses, which are certainly inherent in art? What are the conditions for the success or failure of communication conveyed by media, and can these conditions be generally formulated such that media play a systematic role within the framework of such explanations?

3. As a result of his interest in aesthetic questions, Dewey unfortunately does not ever put concepts that stem from other contexts (such as economics) in the place of the medium and test their suitability under his criteria, and he consequently does not face the problems associated with the need to develop a concept for purposes of analyzing the internal structure of media; instead he only analyzes particular media. So it is indeed clear that media in some respect present ordered material or ways of acting, which the artists use with a communicative intention. However, as a result of the principle of performative proliferation, it is not clear whether there are structural restrictions that means of expression must fulfill in order to acquire the status of media. Consequently, it is not clear whether someone who threatens another with his walking stick makes that stick into a medium. With the exception of (4)(a) criteria (1)–(5) appear to be fulfilled. It is questionable, in other words, whether criterion (4) is really sufficient as a disjunctive condition.

Besides these ambiguities and questions, however, there are numerous interesting ideas that can be taken up in a developed, autonomous media theory. In conclusion, I would like to highlight one point: in contrast to Habermas, who often argues with a view to the costs of media, Dewey—in any case with a view to the costs of the steering media that arise insofar as they permit action coordination to be disconnected from processes of understanding—links the media concept with processes of learning and with the expansion of our scope of action and perception. And he links these thoughts with a normative dimension by obligating art—for which the interaction with the respective specific media is constitutive—to use the scope of possibilities to its full potential.

> "Medium" in fine art denotes the fact that this specialization and individualization of a particular organ of experience is carried to the point wherein all its possibilities are exploited.[100]

Dewey obviously attempts to draw on the media concept in ways fruitful for the normative questions about reasons that can be appealed to in differentiating worse from better works of art or about the standards that can be used to differentiate between successful or failed artistic experiments. One such standard that he proposes is the ability of a work of art to expand our medial communicated potential for experience beyond its existing level. In connection with these views, art can be characterized as consisting in those kinds of experiments that are aimed at developing and communicating possibilities for aesthetic experience.[101]

It is obvious that Dewey's idea of anchoring a process that serves the development of our possibilities for experience in media is of considerable interest for the project of grounding a theory of rationality in media theory. For, on the one hand, it is clear that the *possibilities for experience* for (both) the artists and the recipients correspond to *possibilities for action* on the part of the artists, which only arise under the conditions in which media are socially established. On the other hand, however, these views of Dewey are connected with a *normative component*, the view, namely, that developing scopes for aesthetic action is a value that needs no external justification. Whether and possibly how these thoughts can be suitably reconstructed and generalized within the framework of a general media theory must be taken up in chapter 4, after an attempt is made in the following chapter to develop a general vocabulary for media theory.

3 / TOWARD A GENERAL THEORY OF MEDIA

There is no media theory.
—J. Baudrillard[1]

3.1. INTRODUCTION

The previous reflections on the media concept should have shown three things. *First*, in all of the theories presented, the respective concept of the media played a prominent role. Except for McLuhan's theory, which fashions itself as a media theory, the media concepts, however, largely owe this role to necessities of theory design. The media theories primarily have a subsidiary function within the framework of the antecedent theoretical intentions; hereby they take on a role that they cannot just shake off, for none of the theoreticians introduces the concept of the medium on the basis of a conceptually independent media theory.

Second, because of the lack of a general media theory with basic conceptual autonomy, the media concepts presented are so influenced by the characteristics of concrete, prototypically introduced media that in the course of their implementation theoretical frictions are established that are more suited to ensure the disavowal of the media concept than to secure it new theoretical attention. In order to develop a robust media concept, it thus appears to me to be necessary to take up the risky task of developing an independent media concept on the basis of fundamental principles; here the concept will not be acquired by generalizing characteristics of the concrete media (e.g., money, language, writing), for this procedure entails the risk that the specifics of such examples in each case will preform the concept that is to be developed in inappropriate ways, and where numerous paradigmatic media are used, a conglomerate of incompatible models may become the basis of media theory. In order to avert the danger of distorting the concept from the outset by systematically orienting it in reference to particularities or inner heterogeneity that tends to develop as methodological inconsistencies, a sufficiently general concept must be chosen as the basis of a conceptual definition of media. Where the conceptual language of a media concept cannot be tailored to specific media—and it thus serves to specify an individual medium—in order to be robust, that language must be so general that the specific individual media can be described by further specifying the general concept.

In my view, a further result of the previous chapter lies, *third*, in the diagnosis that media theories converge by assigning specific scopes of behavior. In each of the presented theories—and the theories converge in this—the media concept serves to characterize specific scopes of possibility that are available in the form of media. Parsons, Habermas, and Luhmann conceive of media as mechanisms that *open up* new possibilities for interaction against the background of the open, nonspecified horizon of language; they achieve this by *limiting* the scope of linguistic action coordination in their specific way. Through the exoneration of the risks of the action coordination, which arise due to the unlimited horizon of language, scopes of possibility emerge that can be understood as specifications (Parsons, Luhmann) or as specifications or substitutions (Habermas) of linguistic interactions. Also from the action-theoretic perspective in accord with which Dewey develops his media concept, media appear to be sets of specific possibilities for action, which Dewey obligates art to develop. And even McLuhan's vaguer media concept achieves its diagnostic power solely against the background of media-dependent possibilities for perception and interaction.

In light of the convergence, finally a connection can be made out between the display of the scope of action that emerges in the framework of media-integrated interaction and the possibility for *understanding* actions and social processes against the background of these possibilities for action. Before a precise analysis of this connection can reap the rational-theoretic reward of a general media theory, first, we are faced with the task of developing the foundation for such a theory. The first section of this chapter is thus dedicated to the sober task of formulating elementary concepts of a media theory.

Bracketing the system-theoretical approach, the short version of the background thesis of the diagnosis of convergence is:

(M1) Every medium presents a specific number of possibilities for action that arise for the actors.

Before I begin the foundational conceptual work, however, I would like to clarify which theoretical perspective I think is capable of solving these conceptual groundwork problems. This perspective comes to light when a more basic dimension of the convergence thesis is viewed than the ability to propose a concept of medium that can serve as the lowest common denominator for the (intelligible) media concepts in their various theoretical contexts. If one more specifically calls to mind the implications of the convergence thesis, it soon becomes clear that the convergence thesis provides a *meta*theoretical diagnosis. It maintains that the media concept plays a central role in attempts to *understand processes of social interaction*. The thesis is not primarily supported by material kinship relationships that exist among the media concepts; rather, it views the function that the media concept has in the respective theories as something that connects the conceptions. The theoreticians introduce the concept of the medium in each case in order to facilitate the understanding of interaction processes *as* processes of understanding. With the help of the media concept, social interaction processes are intelligible *as* communication processes. The media concept makes it possible to describe forms of interactive *behavior* as forms of interactive *action* and indeed by means of the assumption that acting social individuals understand each other reciprocally as beings that *choose* behavior patterns (or sequences of behavior patterns) from a *shared* stock of types of behavior patterns.

Because chosen types of behavior patterns such as these owe their status as (proto-)actions to the interpretations of this behavior, the theoretical perspective that I use in the attempt to develop a basic concept of media theory is an *interpretationist* perspective; however, as I will show, it is a variation of interpretationism that considerably loosens its connection to the linguistic paradigm. The starting point for the development of media theory is, first, the assumption that the concept of the media plays a role in the attempt to understand those social interaction processes in which language plays no role at the surface level of the interaction. Hereby there is no principal difference between the role that the media *concept* plays *for understanding* in theoretical contexts and the role that the *media* play *for those interacting* in the social processes that are to be understood: just as the social theoreticians, from their interpretive perspectives, understand the observed interaction processes against the background of a hypothetical medium, so too, those interacting socially understand the behavior of their counterparts as actions against the background of assumed behavioral alternatives, that is, against the background of medial possibilities.

If I attempt to develop media theory as an *independent* theory in what follows, then, in light of the interpretationist perspective, this attempt must assume a form in which it is possible to show the plausibility of increasingly decoupling understanding from language. If one begins with the familiar concept of radical interpretation in which an interpreter correlates expressions in an object language with metalinguistically articulated truth conditions and in this way formulates empirically testable T-theorems, then a procedure emerges that successively reduces the linguistic preconditions for radical interpretations so that each theoretical element that the foundational vocabulary of an independent media theory must relate to can be identified. I attempt to achieve this process in three steps:

1. In the first step I confront *interpreters who are fully able to use language* with *nonlinguistic expressions* of producers who are able to use language. In order to do this, I will revisit the context in which Dewey developed his view of media—that is, the context of communication at the level of aesthetic experience—and investigate the understanding of nonlinguistic expressions that we commonly refer to as works of art. Here I am above all concerned with showing that the understanding of works of art can be viewed as an *exemplary* case of the understanding of nonlinguistic expressions. Under observance of an important and in my view rightly widespread intuition, namely, the view that works of art *cannot be translated* linguistically, this can nevertheless be reconstructed with the tools of media theory as a genuine case of understanding, and indeed as a case of radical interpretation in which the interpreter makes use of hypothetically assumed media. Within the framework of this scenario I start with the familiar assumption: I examine a case in which art is understood and in which both the interpreter and the one that is supposed to be interpreted can use a natural language. The goal of my analysis is to show that media play a mostly unarticulated role in the inter-

preter's interpretation language, but also in the aesthetic production of those who are supposed to be interpreted (pp. 143–220).
2. In the second step I want to further loosen the linguistically bound prerequisites of the first scenario by assuming a more radical situation of interpretation, a situation in which it is not clear whether *those who are supposed to be interpreted even speak a language*. For this purpose, I introduce a situation from field research in which two competing interpreters who are able to use a fully developed interpretive language investigate members of a fictitious ethnicity in order to find out whether those being interpreted even speak a language and which of their observable means of behavior are linguistic or nonlinguistic (perhaps artistic) expressions. In the framework of this scenario it is not only presupposed that those being interpreted do not use a language for those expressions that the interpreters are trying to understand, but it is even imagined that those being interpreted may not speak any language whatsoever. The goal of the investigation at this level is to specify the role of the media concept against the background of the problem of providing a suitable conceptual reconstruction of a situation in which the interpretation of beings who do not speak a language is carried out by interpreters who do speak one (pp. 220–233).
3. In the third step, a level should finally be reached from which we investigate interactions between beings who we presume do not use anything that we would call a language, but whom we nevertheless view as beings that communicate with one another. The question that is to be raised here is whether the tools of media theory are able to characterize a level of sublinguistic communication that can be understood as an evolutionary–theoretic link between the level of completely developed linguistic communication and mere causal interaction processes. In the framework of this scenario, media theory has to prove that it is able to avoid the circular implications of the established interpretationism; for with a view to the question of how the primacy of the interpretation for the development of language, meaning, and mind can be reconciled to assumptions of evolutionary theory, interpretationism appeases itself with the answer that all speaking beings have parents, consequently parents that possess an in-

terpretation language. However, this raises the question whether we should assume that in the evolutionary history of humans, which must include a transition from a species that does not speak a natural language to humans who do speak one, there were parents who—in contradiction to the interpretationistic assumption—by virtue of their genetic disposition, were interpreters of their children. On the other hand, it is not easy to see how this transition can be construed as gradual, because the rationality that is imputed by the interpreters has a constitutive all-or-nothing character that eludes reconstruction as something that can become established gradually (pp. 233–240).

In contrast to Parsons and Habermas, I thus do not attempt to develop the media concept in a social context in which a language is present as a medium from the outset, which social actors can use to make agreements—for example, to treat something as money—in order, in this way, to institutionalize media, whose specific behavioral possibilities may indeed facilitate special economic forms of interaction, but that *in principle* do not go beyond the linguistically individualizable behavioral possibilities. In the framework of the outlined three-step process, I would like rather to show that media can be understood as sets of behavioral possibilities that do not necessarily depend on the individuating power of language.

3.2. AN INTERPRETATIONISM EXPANDED BY MEDIA THEORY

3.2.1. What Does It Mean to Understand a Work of Art?

As a first step toward expanding interpretationism with the aid of media theory, I want to show the plausibility of the view that artistic media provide behavioral possibilities, which, under certain conditions, can also serve as possible ways of individuating thoughts that cannot be individuated by means of language. Setting out from basic and widespread intuitions regarding that which is expressed by works of art, I want to show how the resources of media theory allow us to develop a view of the production of works of art and their *interpretive* reception that makes it possible to rationally reconstruct these intuitions. In doing this, I will attempt to develop a vocabulary of media theory, in debate with the genuine nonlinguistic, communicative forms of art, that is nonetheless sufficiently general to allow the apprehension of nonlinguistic forms of communication beyond the domain of art.

3.2.1.1. Difficulties with Intuitions

In developing our own interpretationist perspective with a view to the understanding of works of art, we are confronted with the following difficulty: the established interpretationism, which is influenced by Davidson, conceives of understanding as a process in which we correlate the statements that are to be interpreted with (metalinguistic) sentences. However, insofar as these interpreting sentences are meta*linguistic*, a linguistic structure is read into what is interpreted; it is initially at least questionable whether, with a view to the understanding of nonlinguistic works of art, this consequence is appropriate. For besides the theoretical questions regarding whether works of art possess a predicative structure and which role the concept of truth plays in connection with the understanding of works of art, it is not clear how an interpretationist theory can accommodate the intuition that works of art articulate thoughts that cannot be linguistically articulated.[2]

Yet, if with regard to this difficulty, we bear in mind, for example, the basic models that we employ to speak about music,[3] then it is apparent that the model of language exercises an enormous influence even on those artists and theoreticians who insist on the irreducibility of music as an independent form of expression. Strangely, these advocates of the autonomy of musical expression often fail to elude the analogy between music and language; thus, they are forced to take refuge in paradoxical formulations that maintain the independence of music from language precisely with the help of the analogy of language. For example, in addressing the question "What is music?" in 1932 Anton Webern answered:

> Music is language. A human being wants to express ideas in this language, but not ideas that can be translated into concepts—*musical* ideas.[4]

Like Webern, Adorno is also convinced that music is based on a form of quasi-linguistic thinking, which however cannot be transcribed into language; but Adorno does not want to allow the analogy between music and language without further ado. Because language is also the medium of a subsuming form of thinking, a form of violence that Adorno had traced back to the fibers of conceptuality, music is not to be an accomplice to it. Yet, because he cannot bring himself to abandon the language analogy, he must attempt to state the putative linguistic character of music and its (simultaneous) distance from language paradoxically: "It is by distancing itself from language that its resemblance to language finds its fulfillment."[5] A glance at a dictum of Eduard Hanslick, who is associated with the autonomy of music like no other, clearly indicates that it is not first in the twentieth century that music is deemed a language. Hanslick writes:

> Music has sense and logic—but musical sense and logic. It is a language which we speak and understand yet *cannot translate*.[6]

Whatever allure the formulations of Adorno, Webern, and Hanslick may appear to have on a cursory reading, the notion of an untranslatable language raises the suspicion that, in the end, the formulations are attractive solely by virtue of their unintelligibility. For, does it make any sense whatsoever to speak of something as a language if what is supposed to be expressed with its help is not translatable into another language? On the contrary, isn't it basic to our view of languages that they can be translated into one another? Can we view sounds that members of a culture that is foreign—for us—exchange among one another as a language without at the same time believing that they are in principle translatable into our language?[7]

The attempt to follow the intuition that music is an expression of an independent form of thought (and to that extent requires an independent concept of understanding) by trying to secure the independence of music through the employment of the analogy of language appears to me to result in one of two equally unattractive consequences: either we compromise our concept of language by allowing *untranslatable languages* (music being among them) or we understand music—in flagrant contradiction to the intuition that it is independent—as a type of *deficient* language, the status of which can only be clarified by relying on the earlier dignity of language. Even if the analogy to language is inappropriate and, in the cited texts, appears rather inept at plausibly showing the independence of music, the intuition that it is supposed to help express is still clear:

(I_1) Like language, music (along with other arts) provides a resource with the help of which it is possible to articulate (musical) *thoughts*;

   a. consequently it is appropriate to believe that we can *understand* musical works of art; and
   b. if we understand musical works of art, then we understand thoughts that cannot be expressed in language.

This intuition (I_1) expresses to a certain extent that music is not an instrument that, solely on the basis of our knowledge of the human organism, is applied to produce causally describable effects. (I_1) does not view music as a (legal) drug or psychopharmaceutical, and it insists that music has nothing to do with either Kant's[8] or Dr. Rueger's[9] medicine chest, because the mere pharmacological use sterilizes its capacities for interpretation.[10]

On the other hand, despite the capacity of music to articulate thoughts, it is not a language, for music has no predicative structure, and the endeavor to develop a grammar of music on the basis of an analogy to Chomsky's generative grammar, such as Lerdahl and Jackendoff have attempted, creates many more problems than it is able to solve.[11]

3.2.1.2. Works of Art as Products of Ordinary Action

The scarcely plausible consequence of reading a linguistic structure into nonlinguistic works of art can indeed be avoided within the framework of interpretationism, but only at a price: works of art are understood against the pattern of common instrumental explanations of action, and (hereby) as actions or consequences of actions that actors have carried out because they believe that the works of art are appropriate means for achieving certain (for example, expressive) goals. An analysis of this sort does not in fact structure the work of art as a linguistic expression, but it ascribes thoughts to the producers of works of art—specifically, beliefs and preferences—that exhibit the common structure of thoughts composed by language and that present the reasons for the production of the works of art. According to this perspective, understanding a work of art thus consists in nothing but identifying those beliefs and intentions that allow us to rationalize the production of a work of art.

An instrumentalist analysis of artistic action, however, clashes with the further widespread intuition that artistic action concerns a special form of intentionality. According to this intuition, artistic intuitions are indeed intentional in the sense that works of art are not involuntary expressions; but they are not expressions of intentions that those who create them have independently of works of art. (I_2) attempts to articulate some of the motifs that lie behind this often only vaguely formulated intuition.

(I_2) Works of art are intentional products of those who produce them, but:

a. The *type* of intentionality does not appropriately come into purview if works of art are merely understood as *instruments for realizing the intentions* of those who produce them; for in some way unintentionality and happenstance play a role in the production of works of art.
b. A work of art is not adequately understood if we can say "what the artist wanted to say with its help"; understanding works of art does not consist in identifying the intentions that the artist may have had. In any case, this does not exhaust it.
c. If we could *say* without reservation what a work of art is supposed to express, then we would not need the specific form of the work of art in order to articulate what the work of art does express. Works of art are forms of expression of thoughts that require the specific form of the respective work of art for their individuation. That is the reason works of art are not related to intentions the way means are related to ends.

(I_2) insists that works of art are indeed intentional products, but they cannot be understood according to the model used to rationalize common behavior. However, insofar as my analysis is based on an action-theoretic perspective for analyzing nonlinguistic communicative acts, the systematic problem consists in developing an understanding of such acts that is able to accommodate the mentioned intuitions. Before taking this up, however, I would like to clearly explicate the difficulties that arise if works of art are understood in accord with the common action-theoretic perspective.

In adopting the action-theoretic perspective that I have accepted in developing a media theory, one runs up against a problem: how is it possible to introduce a concept of medial action without making media theory conceptually dependent on the general analysis of action? This is problematic because the standard general theory of action conjoins actions with propositional attitudes; so in using the model to explain media theory, it appears to make the possibility of (medial) action dependent on the speech competencies of the actors. In attempting to characterize medial action as a genuine form of action, the media theory being developed here is not just an affront to system theory, but it also stands in a strained relationship to the standard analysis of action, which casts action in terms of propositional attitudes.

If, with the help of the standard analysis, we view a behavior as an action, then we start with a description of the behavior that uses intentional vocabulary, i.e., we position the observable behavior of a person P (a) in relation to her mental conditions, (b) in relation to some meaning that the activities of P have for P, and (c) in relation to the observable consequences of the activities that P performs. The practical syllogism integrates these three presuppositions of an intentional explanation in the form of an argument in which (a) and (b) function as premises and (c) as the conclusion:

(H1)

a. *P intends* to achieve Y;
b. *P believes* that X is a means to achieving Y;
c. (ergo) P does X.[12]

In the context of my reflections, two problems are connected with (H1). For one, (H1) is not suited for the analysis of artistic action because it is irreconcilable with intuition (I_2); for another, (H1) poses a metatheoretical problem, for the problem that arises with a view to the independence of the basic concepts of media theory consists in the fact that, in accord with the perspective of the *linguistic turn*, intentions and beliefs must be described as propositional attitudes, thus the concept of action is made conditional on the existence of the actors' propositional attitudes.[13] However, were we to proceed from such a conception of action, then the main reason for developing the media concept here—namely, to contribute to a concept of understanding and rationality that is not based exclusively on language—would be illegitimate from the outset; for the basic motivation for incorporating media theory into the debate on the conception of rationality as a possible fundament consists precisely in expanding that fundament beyond language.

If, in order to sketch out a concept of action that brings us closer to solving both the problem of the specific intentionality of artistic action and the metatheoretical problem, we now attempt to show that it is plausible to develop a concept of action that does not entail constitutive linguistic presuppositions, then two strategies emerge. For one, it is questionable whether the fact that intentions and desires assume the form of propositions *in intentional explanations* necessarily means that the intentions and desires of the actor must be present as propositions. In line with this strategy, it would have to be claimed that the rationalizing interpretation of the behavior of individuals works with ascriptions that, as linguistically articulated, can only assume the form of propositions, but this does not allow any inferences about the form in which actors represent intentions and desires. In any case, I question whether it is promising to give much weight to an argument that emphasizes the "artifact character" of linguistic reconstruction that a rationalization from the perspective of an interpreter inevitably adopts, because it is not clear how strong a potential difference there is between the form of external rationalizations, on the one hand, and the internal conditions of action, on the other. Within the framework of this strategy, it is still a problem, for example, to explain how the actor, from his or her internal perspective, is supposed to be in a position to individuate different intentions and beliefs without being able to refer back to a medium for individuating the constituents of action, thus intentional states.

Within the framework of a second strategy, I would thus like to attempt to show that there are actions that are *not* connected with the existence of the actors' propositional attitudes, but that can be understood with the help of the assumption that there are other media besides language that allow the ascription of intentions. To begin with, the view that the existence of intentions is fundamental for action is not controversial. However, it is characteristic for a position that strictly adheres to the linguistic turn that the intention that the actors link to their action is dependent on an ability of the actor, namely to articulate it (at least potentially) in a sentence like: "I desire p," or "I believe p," and so on. So this second strategy attempts to loosen up the tight connection between intentionality and language. In a first step (1) I will initially attempt to screen the arguments, above all developed by Davidson, that intentionality is dependent on language. In a second step (2) I will contrast these arguments with Searle's reconstruction of the connection between intentionality and language; because this reconstruction depicts intentionality as a more basic phenomenon than language, it may be able to contribute to solving the two mentioned problems. On the basis of the various difficulties in Davidson's and Searle's positions, I will attempt in two further steps (3) to refine the view of intentionality and (4) to specify the idea of an expanded form of interpretationism.

1. LANGUAGE AS A CONDITION FOR INTENTIONALITY

In the arguments that are meant to support the thesis that intentionality is dependent on language, language plays the role of an instrument for individuating intentional states, which are only able to acquire identity within a network of other intentional states, a network whose inferential relations can only be determined by language. In an interpretationist perspective such as Davidson's, in ascribing intentional states, language functions initially as nothing more than a behavioral pattern that is sufficiently complex to allow the correct inferences to the propositional attitudes of the speaker as long as there is sufficient information about the behavior and which actions are possible.[14] Language thus presents itself as a behavioral pattern, the interpretation of which enables us to make inferences regarding how propositional attitudes can be individuated in a (necessarily) largely coherent network of logical relations. We can thus ascribe the propositional attitudes to the being whose behavior we want to interpret. Certainly, for Davidson this analysis does not have the character of a conclusive argument, with the help of which it can be shown that intentional attitudes are dependent on the possession of language. In order to provide such an argument, it would have to be shown that language is the *only* possible medium for a sufficiently complex behavioral pattern. Because Davidson is in fact convinced that this interrelation is correct,[15] but he cannot prove it to be necessary, the thesis that there is no alternative to language being the medium for individuating intentional attitudes must continue to be viewed as an assumption.

The interpretationist perspective must now, however, face the fact that we, as interpreters, also manage to successfully explain and predict the behavior of nonspeaking animals by, in some manner, ascribing beliefs, desires, and intentions to them. However, because the reason for making allegations of this sort is not mere fad, but because we lack really good alternatives, the thesis of language dependence suffers a further loss of plausibility for the time being. However, Davidson's cited article contains a further and weightier argument for the dependence of intentionality on speech.

On the basis of the holistic assumption that all propositional attitudes (and thus intentions) are dependent on a network of *beliefs*, Davidson claims that only beings with a *concept* of belief can have beliefs and that only those beings with a language can have a concept of a belief.[16] If we accept that beliefs are a fundamental condition for the possibility of intentions, then, following Davidson, we must also accept that only a being that can refer to the fact that it believes *p*—that is, that can form *second-order beliefs*—can develop beliefs about anything at all. For only if a being can draw a distinction between (subjective) beliefs and objective truth with the aid of second-order beliefs does it make any sense to ascribe an ability to have beliefs to this being. From the interpretationist perspective, however, we can only ascribe this ability to a being if we can interpret its behavior in the context of linguistic communication such that it masters the difference between subjective belief and objective truth. In short, only those beings that are able to contrast their subjective beliefs with others' beliefs in an intersubjective speech practice, and in doing so refer to something like an intersubjective truth, have the ability to refer to their own beliefs.[17]

This argument seems much stronger than the earlier one if we can preclude that, on the basis of the assumption that all propositional attitudes are dependent on a context of believing, it begs the question by implying from the outset that the scope of possibilities only includes linguistic entities. Yet, it seems to me to be a stronger claim that all mental states that are relevant for acting depend on states whose propositional equivalents are capable of being true. In other words, it is plausible to maintain that the ability to have *beliefs* is necessarily dependent on the concept of belief, a concept that can only be had by one who possesses a language. But, in order to be able to have a *thought*, is it also necessary to have a concept of a thought? Indeed, according to Davidson, all propositional attitudes are thoughts, but are all thoughts also propositional attitudes?

So, even Davidson's second, stronger argument is only a conclusive argument for the dependence of intentionality on language if it can be shown that a concept of intersubjective truth is the *only* possible way to establish the difference between subjective believing and objective validity, and that it thus presents the only possibility for second-order thoughts. However, a vigorous reconstruction of the argument provides important indications of how the thesis of language dependence can be contested. For as far as I can tell, it leaves only two options: either it can be shown that intentionality always has to be presupposed in order to explain how something like a language can develop (section 2), or it can be successfully shown that the concept of second-order thoughts is not tied to language (section 3). Within the framework of the second strategy it is necessary to show that the concept of second-order thoughts can also be introduced with a view to non-truth-conditional intentional attitudes; consequently, beliefs cannot be necessary conditions for actions.

2. INTENTIONALITY AS THE BASIS OF LANGUAGE

A prominent position that denies a necessary connection between the existence of propositional attitudes and actions is the naturalistic conception that John Searle presents in his work *Intentionality*.[18] According to Searle, actions are not connected to existing propositional attitudes but to "intentional states," which, for their part, are prelinguistic. Searle thus reverses the relationship between intentionality and language proposed by the propositionalists: "Language is derived from Intentionality and not conversely."[19] Searle shows that we must presuppose intentionality as a basic phenomenon in order to explain that mind is able to "impose intentionality on entities that are not intrinsically intentional"[20] by ensuring that these entities deal with something or are related to something. In other words: if mind can relate entities that are not in themselves intentional to something—if, for example, it can use them for purposes of representation—then intentionality cannot be explained with recourse to relations between these entities but is the basis of the possibility of such relations.

In the evolutionary theoretic framework in which Searle develops his theory, it is clear that language must be reconstructed as a late product of evolution on the basis of species competencies. But independently of the evolutionary-theoretic perspective, which, on the basis of prelinguistic forms of intentionality, explains what would be necessary for the development of language,[21] Searle explicitly maintains the logical primacy of intentionality before language because "certain fundamental semantic notions such as meaning are analyzable in terms of even more fundamental psychological notions such as belief, desire, and intention."[22] With recourse to these "more primitive" forms of intentionality, which possess an intrinsic relationship to *conditions of satisfaction*, it is possible to explain how entities that do not have their own intrinsic intentionality are taken up in the service of mind. The intrinsic relationship of primitive intentional states to conditions of satisfaction is, in a manner of speaking, the model that is broadened in the development of language, imposing the same conditions of satisfaction on a speech act as those that the mental state has that is to be expressed with the utterance in the speech act.[23]

It is clear that this concept entails a series of problems, problems that are primarily a result of the inverted relationship between language and intentionality. For it is of course questionable whether a being can draw on one of its intentional states without identifying this state with the means by which it draws on the state. However, it remains an open question whether language is the only means that can assume this function.

Searle appears to think the following idea can serve as a solution to the problem of individuation: while a verificationist theory of meaning only has truth-functional propositions at its disposal with which to individuate beliefs as elements of a network that facilitates the individuation of intentions, Searle attempts to individuate the intentional states *directly* with reference to conditions of satisfaction. Accordingly, an intentional state is a state that is characterized by states of affairs in the world that correspond to its satisfaction. That implies that for "any intentional state with a direction of fit, a being that has that state must be able to distinguish the satisfaction from the frustration of that state,"[24] and we must assume that this differentiation is possible without language if we want to maintain the primacy of intentionality over language. Otherwise Searle's meaning-theoretic program, which he clearly sketches out in the following lines, would be pointless.

> The fact that the conditions of satisfaction of the expressed intentional state and the conditions of satisfaction of the speech act are identical suggests that the key to the problem of meaning is to see that in the performance of the speech act the mind intentionally imposes the same conditions of satisfaction on the physical expression of the expressed mental state, as the mental state has itself.[25]

The attempt to contrast the propositional reconstruction of intentionality with a naturalistic perspective in the interpretation suggested here leaves us initially with a tattered view: from a propositionalist perspective it cannot be clearly shown how we end up with a situation in which there are beings that make intentional use of non-intrinsic-intentional entities if intentions can only be identified by means of such entities; from the naturalistic-intentional perspective, it remains questionable how mind can draw on its intentional states if it lacks the means that can only be generated if individuated intentional states are already presumed.

3. TWO FORMS OF INTENTIONALITY

However, a productive way out of this dilemma does seem to me to be possible if we differentiate at least two forms of intentionality, one that I initially only characterize negatively and describe as a form dependent on language and one linguistically independent form.

Setting out from the broad interpretation that Searle gives to his view of intentionality—namely, to characterize those mental states that are about something or that are directed toward something as intentional states—for the time being, it appears to be neither counterintuitive nor problematic, for example, to ascribe intentional states to small children, who do not yet speak a (propositionally refined) language. Nor does there appear to be a problem with sufficiently individuating these states: in a situation in which a small child stretches his hand out toward an object x, which is in close spatial proximity to a second object y, we are hardly surprised if handing the child x is noted with satisfaction, while handing the child y is protested loudly. In such cases we do not ask how it was possible for the child to find itself in a certain intentional state, but we assume that the child has access to criteria for the conditions of satisfaction of the intentional state that it has, and is thus able to differentiate this intentional state from others without being able to speak a language. So I do not see a problem in initially following Searle and presuming an elementary form of intentionality (which I would like to call A-intentionality), with states that are sufficiently individuated without language.[26]

However, it is questionable whether the child can also behave with reference to the intentional state in which it, according to this analysis, finds itself. In other words, it is questionable whether the child chose the state or could choose it, or whether the A-intentional state befalls the child. It is reasonable to assume with Davidson that the possibility of choosing intentional states or *of intentionally individuating* such states is connected to the ability to draw on these states with the help of a medium like language. A theory of developed intentionality, understood in this way, would now have to show which conditions have to be fulfilled in order, on the basis of A-intentionality, to allow the determination of the competencies and instruments that are needed to develop higher-level intentionality, which includes the possibility of being able to (arbitrarily) produce intentional states.[27]

In view of these thoughts, a preliminary criterion for A-intentional states could, for example, be as follows:

(A1) A mental state I_a of a being B is an A-intentional state if and only if

a. through I_a, B is disposed to differentially respond to its environment; and
b. I_a is individuated in a way (e.g., causally) that precludes it from being steered by B as long as B only has A-intentional states; and
c. the identity of I_a, i.e., the content of I_a, is determined as long as the conditions of satisfaction of I_a are sensuously present to B.

Ascribing A-intentional states is legitimized from the viewpoint of an interpreter if the interpreter's explanation of the behavior must assume that the being that is to be interpreted (B) possesses nonlinguistic *representations* of existing and not-existing states of affairs, and these representations steer the being's activity. Thus, among the linguistically independent states, these states are the ones that we ascribe to beings because we can only plausibly explain their behavior by maintaining that they are able to differentiate states of affairs in reference to whether they are conditions of satisfaction for their intentional states or not. Here, however, A-intentional states are *intrinsically intentional*. They are not intentional by virtue of being self-interpretations. They have content that does not require an interpretation in order to be individuated. Instead, in the context of environmental conditions, it requires a functional role.[28] A-intentional states are thus states that *befall* the being that has them. We must assume that beings with A-intentional states possess a representational machinery that is indeed able to produce representations from states of affairs, but that does not produce representations of such representations. A being whose most developed mental states are A-intentional states thus does not possess the ability to refer to these states; for the content of A-intentional states is never another intentional state. Along with Dretske and Millikan, one can suppose that A-intentional states function to show something, be it inner states or states of affairs, but the fact that a being, because of its history of interaction with its social environment, makes use of suitable means does not result from knowledge *that* these means are suitable, a knowledge that would be accessible to the being as explicit knowledge. Rather, it is warranted by functional mechanisms. If a being finds itself in an A-intentional state, I_{a1}, there are no reasons for the change to a state I_{a2}, but only causes. Here it is not precluded that these causes play a weak normative role that can be completely explained with functionalist concepts, and that have something of the status of needs. In that, A-intentional states occupy a position *between* those mental states that we call perceptions and those mental states that we call thoughts. Like perceptions, they have an intrinsic relationship to content that we can imagine being conveyed via functional mechanisms; like thoughts, they are individuated in normative relations, however, in normative relations that can be completely naturalized.

But even if one accepts this characterization of basic intentional states and in doing so agrees with Searle insofar as one is ready to accept that there is a foundational level of intentionality that is independent of language, it is clear that, on the basis of intrinsic intentionality, complex phenomena like artistic action cannot be reconstructed. For artists work precisely against the background of alternatives that are alternatives *for them*; in a way that is to be more precisely explained, they have *reasons* for developing a work of art in one way and not another.[29]

If one wants to accommodate this fact in a theoretically suitable manner—that means in a way that makes it possible to maintain intuitions (I_1) and (I_2)—then it is necessary to provide a reconstruction of higher-level intentionality that does not imply that this higher-level intentionality can only be achieved if beings acquire linguistic competencies. The higher-level form of intentionality must rather be construed such that the ability of a being to relate to its own mental states becomes plausible; here one can assume that Davidson's demand for a second-order *concept* indicates the specific form by which the higher-level intentional states are reached by linguistic means. Intentional states that are independent of specific linguistic means must thus be characterized as *second-order* intentional states; because of this attribute, they can be actively adopted. In order to be higher-level intentional states, mental states that can fulfill this demand thus must certainly fulfill the following criteria:

(HI) A mental state I_h of a being B is a higher-level intentional state if and only if

1. I_h is individuated in such a way that it can be steered by B; and
2. the identity of I_h, i.e., the content of I_h, is determined as long as
   a. B draws on an A-intentional state with the help of I_h; or
   b. B assigns I_h a position in a network of higher-level intentional states, some of which refer to A-intentional states.

Schema (HI) expresses in a very general form what we think of thoughts; thoughts are products of thinking. Thinking is (in any case, largely) a conscious, active activity; its products have an identity because of the fact that they are related to inner representations or stand in certain relations to other thoughts.

If we provisionally accept that Searle's suspicion is correct, i.e., that the concept of meaning can be analyzed in more basic psychological concepts like the concept of desire, and we adopt this analysis for the construction of the level of A-intentionality, then we are faced with a problem, namely, of how to make the transition from the level of a causal reconstruction on the level of A-intentionality to the level of reasons that integrate the sphere of higher-level intentionality. If it is appropriate to speak of two levels of intentionality, and we assume that only the basic one is a biological phenomenon, then how, precisely, do the two levels connect, and how can we explain the transition between them that linguistic beings have obviously achieved? In principle, the way that I initially imagine this is as follows.[30]

In the above-described situation, the child finds itself in an A-intentional state ($I_a[have\ x]$), which is related to the possession of an object x; here the state is indicated by the outstretched arm and the noises the child produces. The desire that we, from the interpreter's perspective, ascribe to the child is fulfilled if the child, for example, can put x in its mouth. If we assume that the child in the situation interacts with people who possess a form of language, and that in situations like those above accompany the passing of *x* or *y* with gestures and noises that the child itself can produce, then the child can correlate his A-intentional state with these activities and adapt these as instruments to articulate desires. The A-intentional state is hereby broadened to include a linguistic behavior that, in a benevolent social environment, serves as a relatively successful instrument for satisfying desires. For the construction of the higher-level intentionality, it is important that the linguistic activity ("*x*") does not belong to the conditions of satisfaction of the A-intentional desire. Because the expression "*x*" has an instrumental character, and does not intrinsically satisfy the desire, it can be used for a correlation that can exist alongside the world-to-world direction of fit of the articulated desire: an inner-world-to-world direction of fit. If, in conformity with Searle's theory of meaning, we at least assume that "*x*" can be provided with the same conditions of satisfaction as the A-intentional state, then "*x*" can be placed in a double correlation, namely, one to empirically having-*x*, and one to the desire to have *x* ($I_a[\text{have } x]$).

Among the obvious preconditions for expanding A-intentional states via intrinsically non-desire-fulfilling occurrences are the interpreters of the behavior of a child, who continually form hypotheses about which intentional state the child is now in. Another precondition is the sufficient constancy of those linguistic occurrences that the child is supposed to link to its respective states; those occurrences must be sufficient for the child and allow frequently correct ascriptions of its intentional states. If these preconditions are fulfilled, we can assume that the child will stabilize a number of relations between A-intentional states, acts of articulation, and desire fulfillment ($I_a[\text{have } x] \leftrightarrow$ "*x*" $\leftrightarrow$ having-*x*, $I_a[\text{have } y] \leftrightarrow$ "*y*" $\leftrightarrow$ having-*y*, etc.).

In order to plausibly develop higher-level intentionality, it is now imperative that the child not only brings the acts of articulation into an (instrumental) relation to its A-intentions, but also—as noted—that the interpreters react with sufficient constancy to expressions of "*x*," as if the intention exists, $I_a(\text{have } x)$. By virtue of the fact that the interpreters hold constant the relation between relata 2 and 3, they offer the child the possibility to observe the relations of the first two relata based on the expression. What exactly does that mean?

By expanding the relation between A-intentional states and their conditions of satisfaction to include nonintrinsic desire-fulfilling activities, an element is introduced to this relation that is sufficient for A-intentionality, which, since this is aimed at satisfying desire, initially has a primarily instrumental character. From the perspective of the interpreters, however, it takes on the character of a (quite reliable) indication of the existence of certain intentional states. If we assume that children expand their articulations spontaneously by varying or combining modifications, and we further assume that in the social environment of children, certain of these expressions are taken as an occasion to treat children as if they had intentions that correspond to the interpretations of expressions by adults, then the relations are stabilized between varied expressions and the states of affairs that the social environment brings about in reaction to the expressions. Because children behave in a manner that indicates they evaluate these states of affairs, as described above, one can assume that they balance these with their A-intentional intentions.

If we now expand the possibilities for expression so that the children's practices of varying articulations are subject to limitations by virtue of the fact that the adults only accept a subset of the variants, and in this way something like rules of composition are stabilized, then a plausible case can be made that, with dependency on the differentiation of the levels of articulation, the ascription of refined intentional states becomes possible. Now, if expressions, by virtue of their interpretation in a social environment, lead to children being treated as if they had the intention that the interpretation is based on, then any expression of a person that fulfills criteria that are to be more precisely explained can also come to indicate the corresponding intentional state of that person. However, the person does not have this intentional state in the same way as she has an A-intentional state. For people who can achieve that scope of the medium of articulation which is able to be linked to an established practice of interpretation can individuate intentional states that they do not simply adapt, but that they in a certain sense create. But how?

I initially assume that at the level of articulation another form of contingency is possible than at the level of A-intentional states, one that arises from the compositional structure of the articulation. Here nothing more is meant than that the tokens of the established practice of articulation can be described as composites of a finite number of articulation types. Further, I assume that the interpretation practice achieves this contingency for the level of ascribed intentional states as the interpreters ascribe intentional states to the articulating individuals; here the degree of differentiation is correlated with that of the expression, and the person is treated in accordance with this interpretation. With a view to the person being interpreted, I assume, third, that the person learns to understand her own (spontaneous) articulations by the interpretation practices of others; that means she learns to understand them as a symptom of an intentional state that she herself has (in agreement with the interpretation practices of others). To the degree to which the articulation practice is oriented on experiences of ascribing intentions, the medium of articulation becomes a medium for individuating intentional states, which the articulating person learns to ascribe to herself. Here, A-intentional states take on the function of a screen, against the background of which the higher-level intentional states gain relevance as compatible or incompatible with the A-intentional states.

Higher-level intentional states are then, however, only able to be individuated through the differentiations that are possible in the medium of the expression. The medium in which this differentiation is made becomes an apriority of intentional states, which can only be individuated with its help. It thus holds for higher-level intentions that they are dependent on social media, because they are dependent on the possibilities that such media offer for ascribing intentions. If one accepts this analysis, then the development of a world of higher-level intentions fully accords with Davidson's assumption that having or ascribing (certain) intentional states is dependent on the potential for differentiation of the medium on which the complex behavior that the interpreter interprets is based.

The solution that is proposed here, which sets out from Searlean starting points, finds its way to Davidsonian consequences, and needs to be further worked out, shifts the problem regarding the priority of language or intentionality to the problem of showing the plausibility of the transition between these two forms of intentionality. However, this problem might be solved if we introduce a social practice of interpretation, which I, for the time being, assume here.[31] It remains open—and that is a desired consequence of my deliberations—whether a higher-level intentional state can only be identified by linguistic means, as the example of language acquisition seems to suggest, or whether other, nonlinguistic means could also assume this function. Before exploring this, however, it should be determined whether Searle's naturalist theory of intentionality—which I have thus far drawn on only as a theoretical background in the reconstruction of the fundamental level of intentionality—might not also be suited to allow a reconstruction of higher-level intentionality of which we understand art to be an expression.

4. DOES SEARLE'S THEORY ALLOW US TO UNDERSTAND ART?

In the previous reflections I have attempted to show that it is plausible to use Searle's naturalist interpretation of intentionality as a *starting point* for the development of a form of intentionality, which, in accord with Davidson's postulates, is dependent on the fact that beings that develop this form of intentionality appropriate a repertoire of refined articulation possibilities in a social context. Here, however, it remains an open question whether Searle's theory might not even provide the means with the help of which we could come to an understanding of art that harmonizes with our intuitions. After all, Searle's theory promises to decouple language and intentionality, since language is not a condition or a prerequisite for intentionality. Nonlinguistic forms of expression like art, one might surmise, must then exist in a relationship to the underlying intentionality, which is analogous to linguistic utterances, and it must be possible to reconstruct them independently of language, i.e., as genuine intentional phenomena at the level of conditions of satisfaction.

In order to check this, I would like to turn back to the problem described above, namely, the problem of understanding works of art as products of ordinary action. If "understanding an activity as an action" simply means "describing an activity as intentional," then, if one wants to retain this schema for artistic action, it is necessary to identify intentional states that are supposed to be the reasons for the action that is to be explained. In applying a rationalization of action to artistic actions, it would then be necessary to assume something like the following form, as a modification of (H1):

(H1.1)

    a. *P intends* to express Y.
    b. *P believes* that K is a means to express Y.
    c. Therefore, P produces K.[32]

If we attempt to link (H1.1) to the above reconstruction of the Searlean analysis of meaning intentions,[33] (H1.1) has to be annotated as follows. First, Y must be characterized by certain conditions of satisfaction; second, P must believe that K has the same conditions of satisfaction as Y. These conditions must be fulfilled if we are to be able to maintain the core idea of the Searlean theory of meaning—namely, that mind, in completing an act of expression, "intentionally imposes the same conditions of satisfaction on the physical expression [K] of the expressed mental state, as the mental state [Y] has itself."[34] However, as clear as this analysis appears to be at the outset, on closer examination it is quite confusing. It is clear that artistic actions seldom have the character of expressive, directive, commissive, or declarative acts. In any case, such acts are not *typical* of artistic action. (H1.1) must thus be interpreted in terms of *expressive* acts. Here it is initially questionable how P can come to believe that K is a means to express Y. In contrast to the four mentioned types of speech acts, this belief cannot take recourse in intentionality having a word-to-world or a world-to-word direction of fit, and thus in conditions of satisfaction that are intersubjectively observable. An expression differs from an utterance about an observable state of affairs, whose meaning intention can be related to observable conditions of satisfaction, that is, to the claim that it is true, which is satisfied if the belief that is expressed is fulfilled. For an expression, however, this possibility does not exist. In expressive acts, the belief that K is a means to express Y refers solely to the intention that K *ought to be* a means to express Y. Only the intention to express Y is necessary to determine what is considered an expression of Y. It follows that in the expressive speech act "to believe that K is a means to express Y" is the same as "to intend that K is a means to express Y."[35] However, if intending that K is an expression of the Y-state is sufficient for K to be an expression of the Y-state, then the conditions of satisfaction of the expressive intention are *self-fulfilling*. However, as a consequence of that, such self-fulfilling intentions—which, in interaction with desires, are supposed to ensure that links can be made between the rationalization of action and the standards of rationality of the interpreters—can no longer play an informative or explanative role. For a reconstruction, this structure would revert to an intentional analysis in the following form:

(H1.2)

    a. P desires to express Y.
    b. P desires that K expresses Y.
    c. Therefore, P produces K.

Schema (H1.2), however, now states nothing but that P produced K because P has desires that lead P to produce K. "Explanations" of action of this sort are so free from restrictions that, with their help, *any* behavior can be interpreted as being steered by desires: the cat is on the mat because it wants to sit on the mat or because it wants its sitting on the mat to express a protest about the absence of the person with whom it shares an apartment. In (H1.2) the constitutive function of the conditions of satisfaction can no longer be regarded as a screen against which the individuating of expressive intentional states occurs because, from the perspective of the interpreter, these conditions can be arbitrarily fulfilled. Because there are no restrictions on what can be inserted into (b), (H1.2) can provide arbitrary explanations, which above all share the following characteristics: they are neither informative nor do they clarify an action with a view to intersubjectively comprehensible standards of rationality. Even if Searle's analysis of expressive action may be correct, which, in view of the above-noted consequences, is not easy to believe, his analysis does not provide the theoretical means needed in order to understand *artistic* action. If artistic activities beyond the parameters of (H1.2) are to be explained as actions, it can be assumed either that, with a view to the reception by third parties, beyond the bare meaning intention, the envisioned success of an expression can provide reasons for the choice of a certain means of articulation, or other relations, which limit choices between the content of the meaning intention and the means of the expression, can be found.

In the face of this shattering result, let us initially once again call to mind the problem: (H1.2) places an artistic activity in the context of a meaning intention (Y), which P connects with K, a work of art. Premise (a) indeed fulfills a basic prerequisite for securing artistic action the status of action—the activity is described as intentional. However, it remains questionable how premise (b) is more precisely to be analyzed; this premise is to ensure that an action is able to be related to reasons; further, the explicative character of the rationalization of the action is dependent on it. (H1.1)(b) confronts us with the difficulty of developing a precise view of the belief that artwork is a means for expressing content; for if (H1.1) is supposed to take on the function of rationalizing action, it must be assumed that a robust connection can be made between the products (X) and the assumed goals of the articulation (Y). But what type of relation could that be?

If we assume a strong relation, we must demonstrate the validity of relations between the goals of an expression and the means of the expression, such as the paraphrase or the translation. First of all, however, such strong relations are problematic because it is maintained, for good reasons, that music—as a product of the action of composition—is "essentially *untranslatable*,"[36] and thus it is impossible that there could be a propositional equivalent of what the music intended.[37] If the thesis of the untranslatability of music is to be correct, then, on the basis of the symmetry of the translation relation, there cannot be music-extrinsic intentions that might be able to provide details sufficient to explain the structure of musical works. However, if the assumption that music is essentially untranslatable should turn out to be false, then there is a second question about the rationality of the action of the person who is expressing herself, namely, why P does not simply articulate Y (linguistically). The fact that P articulates K in the face of the possibility of linguistic equivalents could only be explained—absent motives such as that one simply has fun articulating K—if Y cannot be articulated by P except with the help of K. However, if that were the case, then in the rationalization of the action, Y could not be individuated independently of K and would have to be replaced by K. Doing this, however, the explanation of the action would become tautological.

If, in the face of the problem with strong relations, one suggests instead that the relationship between the goal of the expression and the means of the expression be determined with the help of soft relations (such as similarity or "kinship"), then, as a result of the ambiguity about what we might put in the place of Y, the explanatory character of such a rationalization of action disappears; for as a consequence of the ascription of soft relations, the definition of the possible goals of the expression would be subject to so few restrictions that a large number of possible applications of (H1.1) would be placed next to one another, lacking any criteria. In contrast to this, the plausibility of the rationalizations of action according to (H1) is not due to soft relations, but to the fact that for X, in (H1), only truth-conditional sentences, i.e., sentences that are open to intersubjective evaluation, can be employed; consequently, the link to the interpreter's standards of rationality can be secured. However, if we now neither possess strong relations for the connection between K and Y nor are able to secure the link to the interpreter's rationality standards with the aid of soft relations, then we must no longer rely on (H1.1) as the schema for understanding artistic actions or—and this appears to me to be a much higher price—we must no longer ascribe to artistic activity the status of action. For if characterizing an activity as an action requires that the beliefs that we ascribe to actors in potential rationalizations of action are truth conditional, or at least that they can be tested for appropriateness, then it is not clear how a modification of (H1) can lead to a rationalization of artistic action that can fulfill this condition.

In my view these deliberations bring us to the point that it is necessary to replace the action schema (H1) with a schema that allows artistic actions to be explained in a manner that *need not* assume (truth-conditional) propositional attitudes. Such a schema thus must systematically anticipate *that an artistic intention can only be individuated in the medium in which it is articulated.*

In principle, once again it is possible to conceive of two strategies that allow an artistic activity to be described intentionally. While Habermas, with all the well-known problems,[38] has gone the route of introducing a truth-*analogous* validity claim and characterized sincerity as a validity claim that is characteristic for artistic actions, I would like to try to show that artistic action—more fundamentally than in the perspective of a truth derivative—can be understood as a form of action that, by means of a medium, individuates constellations that can be understood as offering a possibility for individuating higher-level intentional states of the recipients. Thus, the view that I would like to bring into play is that by specifying the idea of an intrinsic connection between media and the goals of action that are achieved with its help—which Dewey had quite vaguely formulated[39]—media can be interpreted as "instruments" for individuating higher-level intentional states; with the help of such instruments, these intentional states can also be articulated. However, that is initially a very abstract and provisional formulation, and it must be further developed. Here it is helpful, first, once again to affirm the presuppositions that are involved in rationalizing action with the help of propositional attitudes. Among these presuppositions are the interpreter's knowledge of a language and the assumption that those being interpreted possess a language, possibly a different one, but one that can be translated into the language of the interpreter; with the help of this language, those being interpreted might individuate intentional states and order them into a network of beliefs and desires. In connection with Davidson, it must be assumed that principles of basal rationality span and organize this network.

As a consequence of the assumption that the identity of intentional states arises in a network that is fixed with the help of principles of basal rationality and that an elementary logic is a part of these principles, the entities that are organized in this network must be truth-apt; it is precisely this characteristic that cannot be transferred to artistic intention. It is also the lack of this characteristic that hinders the transfer of a theory of meaning based on conditions of satisfaction; for there is no analogue in artistic acts of articulation to the truth aptness of propositional attitudes, along with the individuation of the propositional attitudes, that secures the connection to a logic of duties which those that are being interpreted have to follow, at least in the perspective of the interpreter. Composing a bar of music—even in highly regimented music—does not render the composer a responsibility similar to that rendered to the speaker who expresses an assertion.

In short, the theoretical situation in which we find ourselves after this look at the conceptual tools that the established theory of mind and theory of meaning provide us for reconstructing the understanding of nonlinguistic intentional expressions is as follows:

1. Within the framework of the standard analysis of action, the interpretation of nonlinguistic works of art as products of common action faces the following difficulty: in accord with this interpretation, one has to understand works of art and the intentional states that they express and that are the cause for their production to be linguistically individuated states. Doing this, however, makes analysis irreconcilable with intuitions that we rightfully have about the understanding of works of art, namely:
   a. Works of art are intentional products of their producers.
   b. Works of art are not completely understood if one identifies the intentions that an artist intended to achieve in producing them.
   c. Works of art articulate thoughts that cannot be grasped by a different means than the one in which the work of art articulates the thoughts—works of art are not translatable.

   There is thus a need for a theory of intentional states that are not individuated (in a [self-]interpretation) by linguistic means.
2. In connection with Searle (and in connection with the functionalist conceptions of intentionality), a concept of nonlinguistic intentionality can be developed using concepts of a basal intrinsic intentionality. With the help of this concept it is indeed possible to overcome deficits in the developmental history of interpre-

tationist theories of intentionality, but the concept of intrinsic intentionality is not suited to allow an intentional description of artistic actions and to open dimensions needed to understand it.

3. Thus: the type of intentionality that it is necessary to apprehend theoretically is a higher-level form of intentionality, which is at the same time not a linguistically individuated form of intentionality. Thus, in conformity with the intuition that artistic media are *means of artistic thought,* one should, in accord with those interpretationistic assumptions that remain fundamental for the reconstruction of higher-level forms of intentionality, attempt to develop a *theory of nonlinguistic thoughts.*

The following section is devoted to the attempt to meet these theoretical demands. In the first step, which is here to be made with a view to a theory of nonlinguistic thoughts, I start from a familiar scenario: two persons with common linguistic competencies discuss a nonlinguistic work of art.

3.2.1.3. After the Concert—An Alternative Analysis

Let us assume the following: after having spent an evening at a concert with someone we hardly know, in the bar after a long period in which the topic strangely did not come up, the topic then turns to the music that we heard just under two hours previously. My question is now the following: Under what conditions would we be ready to say that our companion (P_2) has understood the music that we heard together?

Now among the *minimal* conditions for confidence that P_2 has an understanding of this sort is surely that, during our conversation, P_2 can refer to the various works that we have heard. For example, if we are speaking about the second piece of the evening, then we must expect that P_2 can refer to the characteristics that make the second piece the specific work of art that it is. In short: the person must be able to refer to the work of art as a specific unity or, more precisely, *she must be able to refer to the characteristics that are constitutive for the identity of the work of art,* because no one can understand something that they cannot identify. This prerequisite need by no means be fulfilled using the language of music studies; perhaps it need not even rely on a language at all. If, for example, with the use of singing, gestures, or sketches, P_2 can refer to the characteristics of a piece of music that make that piece of music a piece of music (in the context of the history of music), then the person has fulfilled a central prerequisite for us to be confident that she has understood the piece of music.[40] In any case, we will have considerable doubt that P_2 understands a work of art if P_2's identifying references to the work of art are so unspecific that P_2's "descriptions" of the characteristics do not identify an individual work of art but a set of such works, and in our case, for example, she interprets the last movement of the first piece and the first one of the second as a two-movement work.

To guard against a misunderstanding: what we expect from a person who fulfills the minimal conditions for understanding a work of art is not only the ability to refer to a work of art as an object, as is possible with the help of proper names or identifying descriptions ("Intégrales" or "that music piece for small orchestra and drums that Edgard Varèse completed in 1924"). Rather, it is a matter of the ability to identify the work of art in relation to its *qualities that can be experienced*. But even the reference to the characteristics that can be experienced is not sufficient. For it is not about some identification method with the help of which the work of art can, without a doubt, be filtered from the mass of other works of art on the basis of its empirical characteristics—the way the criminal suspect, with the help of a fingerprint, a DNA sample, or a graphological analysis, can be separated from a set of all potential perpetrators. It is rather about identifying the work of art with reference to those characteristics that are relevant for it *as* this work of art. But which characteristics are those? They are the characteristics that we pay attention to if we, for example, compare the following identifying references to acoustic events:

a. "The piece that I mean is the only one that brings about a feeling in me of cold abandonment."
b. "The piece that I mean consists of two-dimensional crescendo background noises, which sound like a distant, threatening razor, and of light recurring beats as if one were pounding on tin."
c. "The piece that I mean begins "Da-da-daa-di da du di da."
d. The piece that I mean begins

While in (a) reference is made to a subjective association that is not accessible to intersubjective verification and thus hardly offers a suitable indication of the search for the piece, (b) makes reference to the sound structure of the piece, which is described with the aid of comprehensible music-extrinsic sound experiences. Reference (c) presents structural characteristics of the piece that place the listener of the sample in a position to identify the piece whose characteristics are exemplified, as long as the sample does not apply to numerous pieces, and (d) identifies Beethoven's Piano Sonata, Op. 2, Nr. 1 in the form of the index of a volume of sheet music.

The thought that I would like to bring into play in order to more precisely describe the abilities that a person must have before we have confidence that she understands a work of art consists, in short, in connecting this ability to the fact that, in the act of identification, a set of characteristics must be referred to that were relevant for the production of the work of art and are relevant for most of its characteristics that can be experienced. The work of art should not be identified on the basis of contingent characteristics that are external to it, but on the basis of characteristics that it displays because it was made in a particular manner. If the identification is successful in this way, then a recipient refers to the identity of the work of art, which it has by virtue of the fact that it is a *composed unity*.[41] For its part, this identity, which I would like to call the *compositional identity*, has its own presuppositions, which I would like to more precisely explain by once more turning to the continued discussion after the concert.

After a heated debate about the interpretation of one of the pieces performed, our concert companion notices with some indignation that we have spent the past few minutes discussing two different pieces of the evening: she in any case meant the piece "that confronted two themes with each other, where the first one in kernel consisted of three motifs and began with a terse prelude. The motifs of the first theme in the course of the piece hardly varied, quite in contrast to the one motif from which almost all the material of the second theme was developed." If, on the basis of this description, the misunderstanding can be overcome, then it is because our discussion partner can identify the piece of music that we are talking about with the help of attributes that it has before the background of possible musical attributes; further, she supposes that we are all familiar with these.

Implicitly, according to the following pattern, our discussion partner presents us with the characteristics of the piece of music against this shared background: the motif *could* consist of 32nds, 16ths, 8ths, etc.; it *could* be intended that these are played legato, nonlegato, staccato, etc.; the notes *could* progress diatonically or chromatically, etc.; and the motif that I am speaking about consists of diatonically progressing eighths that are intended to be played staccato, etc. The *compositional* identity of a work of art consists insofar in the sum of the attributes that a work of art has against the background of an ordered set of attributes that it also could have had. Those characteristics that are relevant for the compositional identity of the piece, however, are not arbitrary characteristics but *musical* ones. Initially that sounds trivial. However, on closer examination, it is clear that recipients that are able to refer to such attributes cannot be relating to *intrinsic* attributes of objects or events that physically actualize a work of art (for example, sound experiences); rather, they refer to attributes that such events have when "described" in some way. As a listener that has been socialized in a musical practice of listening and/or of making music, a recipient identifies a piece on the basis of a presupposition that is so obvious and for which there is subjectively no alternative; consequently, it easily escapes theoretical attention. She works with the presupposition that the acoustic experiences that were the cause of her perception during the concert were musical events. If such a listener identifies a piece of music, she does not speak of *acoustic* events (as acoustic events), but of (acoustic events as) *musical* events. In doing so, among other things, a listener like this makes use of the vocabulary on the right side of table 3.1.

Competent listeners of course use concepts, beyond the musical vocabulary mentioned, that refer to the organization of the musical material in a piece: they identify a piece by virtue of the fact that it organizes material that they regard as musical material in a certain way. In Davies's

TABLE 3.1

Physical properties	Musical properties
Frequency of the acoustic events	Pitch of sounds
Amplitude of the acoustic events	Volume, dynamics of sound gradients
Temporal sequence of the acoustic events	Tempo, meter, rhythm, agogics
Duration of the acoustic events	Relative duration
Frequency spectrum of the acoustic events	Sound, harmonics

words, "if music is organized sound, to hear music as music is to hear music as displaying organization. To hear music as such is to hear it in terms of the principles of order that give it its identity as the music it is."[42] In a rather technical formulation, we could say: The *compositional conditions of identity* for a work of art K are conditions that are fulfilled in an ordered set M by possible observer-relative attributes. We identify K by characterizing K *as* something that is generated by bringing about some of the possibilities mentioned in M in a specific way. K thus has its identity relative to the possibilities for differentiation that exist in M. In the face of the mentioned reflections on how works of art are identifiable with the help of attributes that are able to be experienced, we are approaching an answer to the question about which attributes assist us in identifying works of art as works of art. For we could say that these attributes are not intrinsic attributes of the events or the objects that works of art bring about, but are observer-relative attributes; here, though, they are not observer-relative attributes in general, but those observer-relative attributes that are amenable to intersubjective assessment. In the face of this clarification, my thesis is now:

(M2) If M is an ordered set of attributes, E_i, and it is the case

 a. that there is a limited set of those action types for which every instance of the action type under consideration brings about intersubjectively observable elements of a class of events or states of affairs in the world, and
 b. every one of these states of affairs in the world actualizes one of the attributes E_i, then M is a medium.

If the compositional identity of a piece of music thus can be provided by characterizing a medium and providing "principles" according to which it is organized, what should motivate us to take the ability to identify a piece of music as an occasion to develop a specific theory of nonlinguistic understanding or even of thinking? Initially, there is no reason not to presume that it is clearly possible to refer to the identity of a work of art by linguistic means, and there is perhaps also no reason not to presume that composers produce the identity of a piece of music by treating musical material in accord with certain principles. Doesn't the discussion of nonintrinsic attributes that characterize the material, but even more, the discussion of the "principles," suggest that composers carry out their work on the basis of a musical practice that is structured by linguistically articulated norms, that is, by rules? In short, isn't the musical practice in which musical pieces are composed and received a thoroughgoing linguistically structured practice in which things or events are what they are because there are constitutive rules that declare them to be what they are within the framework of this practice?

We could say a musical practice functions like a game. Things or events with certain attributes serve as pieces that can be moved according to certain rules; observers of the activities that actualize (or carry out) the game understand a match if they are able to describe the progression of activities as an actualization (or realization) of a sequence of moves that aims to achieve a certain goal of the game. So what reasons are there not to say that composing a minuet is in principle nothing other than achieving a goal in the game of music? What reason is there not to say that Mozart, who composed the piece that our discussion partner described so indignantly, followed the goal of composing a piece in the sonata form in which a multiform, but essentially static, theme is contrasted with a mono-motif, highly malleable theme?[43] The portrayal thus far suggests that artists make plans that they individuate linguistically; here, they view artistic, including nonlinguistic, media as means to achieve these plans. But accepting this analysis brings us into conflict not only with the aforementioned intuition (I_2), but also with the facts of music history.

With a view to the Mozart piece under question, in alignment with the analysis just provided, it would seem obvious that we should identify the piece, inter alia, through its attribute of exemplifying the sonata form. And, given the knowledge of the person who composed it, it would seem obvious that we should ascribe him with the intention of composing a piece that complied with the sonata form. But, first, Mozart *could not have had this intention*; second, knowledge of the concept of the sonata form cannot be a condition for understanding a piece of music that complies with it if we want to avoid the consequence that Mozart did not understand his music, for Mozart was simply not capable of analyzing his music with concepts of the sonata form.

> Moreover, it might be said, Mozart *could not* have analysed much of his music, because the theoretical description of sonata form, the structural

type given life in his music, was offered by musicologists only after his death. If anyone understood music, surely it was Mozart? Yet his understanding was rather applied [than] bookish.[44]

Mozart's music looks like music that is generated by molding a certain material according to given rules or prescripts, but Mozart did not know these rules, so it seems nonsensical to ascribe him with the intention of complying with these rules. On the other hand, it is also clear that composing music, which implements complex organizational patterns, can hardly be explained in reference to dispositional concepts, and it requires a reconstruction in concepts of high-level intentionality and in concepts of orderly thinking. And because it does concern orderly thinking, this suggests that we bring the concept of the rule or the prescript into play as that element on which creative thinking can orient itself.

Precisely in the face of these reflections, one does not want, with no further ado, to accept the demand to set aside the concept of a rule as a theoretical instrument for analyzing aesthetic thinking; indeed, it is perhaps not fully explained exactly how the concept of a rule is to be analyzed in this context. For one could maintain that Mozart could not follow any linguistically formulated rules, but that he followed an *implicit rule* or prescript, a rule he could not have explained offhand but that he could act on. But then, what should an analysis of implicit rule following look like with the help of which it is possible to understand the relationship? If we first take up the reconstruction of the more clearly laid out case of explicitly following rules, then in essence, we encounter the following criteria:[45]

(RF) It holds that a person P follows a Rule R in an action A if and only if

  a. R is a normative sentence that says which attributes A should have;[46]
  b. P is acquainted with R, i.e., R was expressed to P, or P herself expressed R;
  c. P understands R and can explain R, i.e.,

    i. P understands the normative character of R (the *world-to-word direction of fit* of R), and
    ii. P understands the content of R, i.e., P knows how A must be so that it fulfills R.

d. The content of R provides a reason (and a cause) for P to carry out A in the way demanded, i.e., P accepts R as a premise of his practical reflection.
e. It is possible for P not to comply with R; i.e., the fact that P complies with R results from the fact that P accepts and wants to comply with R.
f. P acts in compliance with R.

If one is not able to analyze Mozart's composition of music in the sonata form as specified in (RF) and thus hopes that it is possible to show it to be comprehensible as a case of implicit rule following, then the following question arises: Which of the conditions mentioned in (RF) ought to be given up on or modified in sketching out the concept of implicit rule following?

Conditions (a) and (f) are, of course, indispensable, for the fact that a person acts in such a manner that his action complies with rule R is indeed the initial condition for assuming that a rule-governed behavior exists. Admittedly, condition (f) should be reformulated so as to express that the rule R is a sentence that is formulated by the observer of P's behavior, since it is of course out of the question that the acting individual is a person who explicitly knows R. In a definition of implicit rule following, (f) must mean that P behaves such that an observer who knows rule R can interpret the behavior of P as complying with R. The real problem for sketching out implicit rule following consists in accommodating conditions (b)–(e).

If one accepts the common conceptions of implicit rule following, whose development is motivated, in particular, by the attempt to solve what is known as the rule-regress argument—which arises when an attempt is made to explain the difference between correctly and incorrectly following rules in reference to compliance with rule following—then the general idea used to characterize implicit rule following consists in bringing into play a *cognitive implementation* of those capabilities that make rule-conforming behavior possible.[47] On the one hand, the basic strategy here usually consists in drawing attention to the fact that we do many rule-conforming things without calling the rule to mind or explicitly drawing on the rule; in these cases we have to count *routines* as causes of rule-conforming behavior. On the other hand, it consists in pointing out that rule-conforming linguistic behavior, for example, cannot even be acquired by understanding and learning to follow rules, because this already presupposes that we speak a language; so that one has to expect a nonlinguistic, that is, a nonexplicating, mechanism (*training*) for generating rule-conforming behavior.

However, if we grant that there are sanctioning and nonexplicating mechanisms of training that lead individuals to develop the disposition to display rule-conforming behavior for an observer (under certain conditions), then the question naturally arises concerning how rule-*conforming* behavior that is so conditioned by regularities can be differentiated from rule-*observant* behavior. If one—in contrast to Wittgenstein—does not want to give up on this differentiation, then criteria must be presented that can be shown to be plausible with a view to the *behavior* of a person who is potentially implicitly following rules. To do this, it would be necessary to show that P's rule-conforming behavior B is a rule-observant behavior and that P does not know the rule R that would make the observance of B rule conforming.

Of course there are numerous activities that we regularly engage in without having learned a rule for carrying out the behavior. But not all of these things are at all suited to serve as examples for the implicit rule following that is sought. For example, under certain conditions, to chew one's nails in a certain way is nothing more than a habit, the expression of a psychic disposition; the activity that we are looking for, however, must be immune to a complete, mere dispositional, reconstruction. The "intelligent capacities" that Ryle, in his break with the "intellectualist legend," calls on to demonstrate implicit rule following provide perhaps a more suitable example—capabilities that we acquire through formation; here Ryle assumes that we acquire the ability for rule-conforming action through practices. It is "schooled indeed by criticism and example, but often quite unaided by any lessons in the theory";[48] at the same time, he emphasizes that these abilities can be differentiated from habits that we acquire by training.[49] But how can this distinction be secured? How can the regularist reduction of implicit rule following be prevented? And how can it be precluded that a person only has a chance disposition for rule-conforming behavior? Ryle brings the following criteria into play, which are also of interest for our problem:[50]

1. P is provided with a corrective training.
2. P is able to criticize and correct the rule-deviating behavior of another, P_j, i.e., P is able to instruct P_j.
3. P is able to modify her learned behavior in innovative ways.

Naturally Ryle would like to say that P does not only behave in conformity with a rule, but also that her behavior offers strong evidence that she is rule *guided*, without having access to a formulation of the rule. However, if this case is examined in detail, then we are left only with vague evidence. The first criterion ensures that we, as observers of P, can draw on a history of her behavior so that when we know P's training history, we can assume that P's ability to behave in conformity with rules is owed precisely to this training. If we in this way assume that P's capability for rule-conforming behavior is *acquired*, then everything is dependent on what Ryle means by "corrective." For if the corrections come about like regular occurrences of nature, why should we speak of the training as procuring the ability to (implicitly) follow a rule? From the perspective of the observer of the training history, in any case, the question arises regarding which rule the trainer is following in his sanctions. In this way, however, we just displace the question of rule following from the student to the teacher.

Of course, much depends on how complex the capabilities are that we are assessing. Greeting others with a handshake is perhaps a habit that can be successfully taught with a sanctioning training, without the rule of the greeting ever becoming explicit. But how plausible is the talk of a habit or of nonlinguistic cognitive implementation in the case of complex competencies such as multiplication, which Ryle himself provides as an example? With a view to such capabilities, one rather wants to say that the fact that we perhaps also learn complex abilities from observing practices is no argument at all against the explicitness of rules, since we are, with a view to such abilities, almost forced to assume that P explains the rules that structure the more complex activities within the framework of her lessons in the form of hypotheses that explain the sanctioning behavior of the teacher. How else can we explain that P is able to develop a sanctioning practice herself that is suited to serve as a teaching practice for P_2 if the concern is lessons in multiplication? P could indeed have acquired the disposition to sanction under certain conditions (namely, those of the deficient behavior of his student), but only for those cases in which P herself was positively or negatively sanctioned. However, because the lessons in multiplication that P enjoyed could only have a limited number of multiplication exercises, as a teacher or critic of P_2's multiplication exercises, P must be able to draw on a prescript that enables P to correctly sanction in cases that did not arise within the framework of her education. Even if this prescript was not pointed out to P, P can only work as a competent teacher of multiplication or critic if P has developed the prescript in the course of forming hypotheses that can be applied in a potentially unlimited number of cases. Of course, such a prescript need not take the form of a mathematical formulation, but it should describe a method that, if followed, will allow P to reliably avoid the sanction of her teacher.

Ryle's last criterion is not much better, for with a view to the creativity that is supposed to equip P to creatively accommodate learned behavior, from the interpreter's perspective, the problem arises of how *cases of creativity* can be differentiated from *cases of rule-breaking behavior*. Relative to a cognitively implemented rule assumed by the interpreter, creative behavior can only be identified as such if the presumed rule is not fully followed. If it is completely followed, then the behavior is not creative. It would only be possible to identify with certainty that behavior is creative if P could name a modified rule. This, however, would, in turn, be explicit, and Ryle's criterion of creativity would remain dependent on the "intellectual legend" that he is struggling against.

Above all, in the face of the often-confirmed fact that we do not recite rules when following them and that we do much by routine, it may appear counterintuitive to link rule following to explicit rules. However, it remains questionable how the difference between rule-following action and regular behavior can be secured without relating in one way or another to explicit rules. In my view, there is only one way of speaking of implicit rule following that allows us to accommodate this differentiation; this can be done, namely, if we introduce a division of labor between those individuals who know rules explicitly and can teach rule-conforming action and those individuals whose forms of action are rule conforming as a result of a sanctioning "teaching" practice. The following reflections form the background for this assessment: If we assume that individuals who are said to implicitly follow rules perform rule-conforming action that *contingently* conforms to rules, for example, because of peculiarities of the brain physiology of these individuals, then it is questionable why we should here speak of *rule*-conforming behavior at all. The only thing that might motivate us to do so is the fact that *we* can explicate a rule that the behavior conforms with. Yet, in this case we could just as well provide a natural law to explain the behavior, for if we cannot observe behavior that can be interpreted as the expression of a rule, what evidence would we have for justifiably ascribing an implicit rule? If speaking of rules is supposed to make any sense at all in such cases, then it is only under the condition that *we* know that the fact that people behave in conformity with rules is connected *causally* with explicit rules, for example, in the following way. We know or we justifiably assume that there was a generation of teachers who knew rule R and were able to explain it. This generation of teachers organized a sanctioning practice and placed little value on the explicit transmission of rule R. Then we have the fact that the children of the first generation of students behave in conformity with the rule without any longer having heard the rule from their poorly taught parents at all, a fact that stands in a causal relationship with the explicit knowledge of rules of the first generation of teachers. If we follow this depiction, then, as it were, we shift the explicit formulation of a rule that we, as observers of a behavior that is not caused by the explicit knowledge of the rule, accomplish—whereby this behavior is made a rule-following behavior in the first place—to individuals whose explicit knowledge is the historical cause for the behavior that we view as rule conforming. Of course, the historical framework that I have introduced here can be reduced in scale so that we can also speak of implicit rule following in the sense here in cases in which a person who behaves in conformity with a rule can no longer remember which rule was conveyed in the lesson in which the ability to behave in conformity with rules was acquired.

If, in the face of regular behavior, we want to avoid the arbitrariness of questionable assumptions of implicit rule following, then we must turn to a situation in which an explicit rule was the cause of regular behavior that we can thus describe as rule conforming. If we would like to avoid collapsing the concept of implicit rule following into the concept of regular behavior, we need recourse to a (historical) situation in which the rule was explicit. However, then the concept of implicit rule following is a historical concept that remains dependent on the concept of explicit rule following. With a view to our problem of analyzing rule-conforming composition as rule following, the following is also clear:

1. Because there was no explicit formulation of the standards for sonata at the time *of* Mozart, Mozart could not have conformed to these prescripts in the sense meant by *explicit* rule following.
2. Because there was not a generation of teachers *before* Mozart's time whose explicit knowledge was lost but which caused the transmit-

ted sanctioning practice, Mozart could not have transcribed the prescripts in the sense meant by *implicit* rule following.
3. The alternative between implicit and explicit rule following is exhaustive.
4. Thus, because Mozart's rule-conforming composing cannot be explained either as explicit or implicit rule following, it can*not* be described as rule following *at all*.

In view of the previous analysis, the problem that we confront is that the established methods for describing activities as intentional fail: common rationalizations of behavior confront us with the problem of the translatability of artistic thoughts and the escape promised by descriptions of implicit rule following—which were supposed to undermine the linguistic character of intentional states—has proven itself to be erroneous. However, in the face of the manifest difficulties of providing a suitable intentional description of Mozart's composing, how could we sensibly say that it is possible to *understand* the product of this composition? Of the resources that it is possible to draw on to salvage an intentional description of composing, only two have been partially drawn on thus far: the history of the acquisition of the capability that made it possible for Mozart to write music in the sonata form (to be taken up in more detail in section 1 below); and a systematic investigation of what it means to understand musical *thoughts* (to be taken up in section 3.2.2). In what follows it will become clear that these two perspectives are related.

1. DO IT LIKE THIS: . . . !

In Ryle's reflections, he outlined a training that he thought could transmit the ability to follow a nonexplicit rule, but if we view the training with respect to the conveyance of nonexplicit, yet explic*able* prescripts, then an element that is fundamental for the conveyance of artistic abilities eludes our attention. In the context of reflections on transmitting competencies for performing musical works, Joseph Kerman has pointed out that the transmission of this knowledge takes on a specific form:

> A music tradition [of performance] does not maintain its "life" of continuity by means of books and book-learning. It is transmitted at private

lessons not so much by words as by body language, and not so much by precepts as by *example*. . . . The arcane sign-gesture-and-grunt system by which professionals communicate about interpretation at rehearsals is even less reducible to words or writing. It is not that there is any lack of thought about performance in the central tradition then. There is a great deal, but it is not the kind of thought that is readily articulated in words.[51]

Teaching with the help of examples is not an anomaly in philosophy seminars, but in music instruction it has a different status. For the example in this case does not serve to illustrate an abstract relationship or to depict an exemplary application, but to illustrate the correct articulation of a musical thought. Before Kerman, Kant had already emphasized that the specific function of examples in music lessons is a *necessary particularity* of artistic instruction; interestingly, Kant also thematized this characteristic in contrast to explicit prescripts or rules that, according to his analysis, are unsuited to define the particularities of artistic action. However, because in Kant's view the artifact character of art is also dependent on rules, he had to postulate that these rules cannot have a conceptual character of the sort that allows them to function as premises of an aesthetic judgment. The rules of beautiful art can thus not be invented rules; rather, "Nature in the subject must . . . give the rule to Art, i.e. beautiful Art is only possible as a product of Genius."[52] Geniuses, however, are people whose talent is suited to produce "that for which no definite rule can be given,"[53] that is, individuals who are inventive; it is the work of inventive people that is suited to assume the role of paradigmatic examples in art lessons. However, if we accept the difficult thought that it is nature that provides beautiful art with the rule, then what type of rule are we speaking of?

> It cannot be reduced to a formula and serve as a precept, for then the judgment upon the beautiful would be determinable according to concepts; but the rule must be abstracted from the fact, i.e. from the product on which others may try their own talent by using it as a model, not to be *copied* but to be *imitated*. How this is possible is hard to explain. The Ideas of the artist excite like Ideas in his pupils if nature has endowed them with a like proportion of their mental powers. Hence models of beautiful art are the only means of handing down these Ideas to posterity. This cannot be done by mere descriptions.[54]

Kant's difficulties in reconstructing art lessons are instructive: since even in cases where the students are able to abstract the rule from the product, they are not allowed to orient themselves on an explicit rule in their act of producing, so in the final analysis, Kant can only describe the lessons with psychological concepts; for all that remains for him are *effects* of the paradigmatic work of art. Under the presupposition of the similar proportion of mental powers, these effects should generate similar ideas in the students. In other words, Kant's explanatory problem arises because Kant does not have a concept of understanding that is suited to describe art lessons as a process of understanding and that allows him to reconstruct this, without fissure, in an intentionalist vocabulary.

Kant's discussion of nature as a power that provides art with the rules has broad-reaching consequences for the reconstruction of the inner experience of the artist from an intentionalist perspective. For a (brilliant) artist need *not*

1. be able to describe how she generated a work of art;
2. know the way that ideas are related to a work of art;
3. be capable of artistic productivity according to a plan;
4. be able to convey to others, in the form of precepts, how one creates a work of art.[55]

If, however, all of this knowledge cannot be expected from an artist, then it is clear that an artist has no other means of teaching than her own works (or those of others), and it is also clear that, according to Kant, there are limits to the ability to teach artistic competencies. Indeed, it is possible to learn everything that Newton presented in his principles of the philosophy of nature, "but we cannot learn to write spirited poetry."[56] Regardless of whether one accepts Kant's characterization of an artist as "him whom nature has gifted,"[57] it is very true that "no master has fallen from the skies"; we do assume, for example, that even Mozart could not have composed his pieces without having learned something. Yet, what did Mozart learn from his applied lessons? If one views music lessons with a temporal standard that we also have in mind with a view to language acquisition, then we can certainly say that Mozart—like most schoolchildren today—learned to sing scales, to keep time, to beat simple rhythms, etc.; indeed, he learned this on the basis of the examples of someone who performed these acts. If it turns out that a student has difficulties with the transmission of one of these basic musical competencies, then, by exaggerated singing or performance, the teacher can normally indicate the attributes that were lacking in the student's rendition. In doing this, the teacher hopes—by the exaggeration—to draw the student's attention to precisely those attributes, for she normally could not point to a rule or a precise prescript that can help the student ("Sing the third tone 80 percent higher!") nor could she count on achieving success with such a prescript.

If the student manages to internalize the elementary ability to produce tones at a relatively constant pitch and at relatively constant intervals, the teacher indeed goes on to focus on conveying more complex abilities, but the principle of the lessons remains the same. This principle is: "Do it like this . . . !" And to define "this," the teacher has at her disposal the technique of exaggerated singing or performance and a repertoire of mimics, gestures, and nearly dancelike movements, and now and then also the suggestive power of linguistic comparisons ("Do it like you were an old tired horse that is pulling a heavy cart!").[58] The objective of these techniques is to structure the *playing* of the student *and* to affect or anchor her *listening*, and indeed to do so by means of a *demonstrative* structuring by example or through the appeal to structuring abilities that the student, on the basis of her own experiences, has already acquired.

An elementary music lesson is thus largely free of the transmission of explicit rules and essentially consists in the conveyance of abilities to generate musical events in accord with exemplary patterns and to hear acoustic events as musical events. The latter consists, above all, in the ability to organize the flow of acoustic events according to *types* of activity that one learned oneself in music lessons. It means that one can sing along with a musical performance. If, for the sake of clarity, we accept that the teacher has limited herself merely to familiarizing the student with an extremely reduced form of music—4/4 time, two octaves of the C major scale, and two tone durations (the half and the quarter notes), as well as two dynamic levels (loud and soft)—then a student of such elementary lessons has had successful lessons if she is able to perform within the framework of the possibilities that emerge from these combinations. In the case of this paltry music, with the help of twenty elementary types of activity, such a student would be able to perform a total of sixty types of activities that generate musical events.[59] A student who has completed this paltry class has not learned any rules, but has acquired *know-how* that enables her to perform a set of standardized actions; she has acquired a disposition to hear music as a performance of those types of action, a disposition that can rightly be understood as a part of one's *second nature*—from now on it will be nearly impossible for the student to hear music as a mere acoustic event.

Now let us suppose that this analysis (irrespective of the paltry nature of the lessons) is somewhat instructive. What have we achieved that surpasses Ryle's examples? In contrast to Ryle's examples of a game of chess or of multiplication, we can well imagine that not only the teaching but also the musical practice can manage without rules, even if rules play a large role in our musical tradition. While chess games and multiplication, even if they are taught without reference to rules, are activities that could not arise without linguistic rules, and in the best case, these can be analyzed according to the model of implicit rule following (described above), there is no reason not to imagine that people transmit a music culture without rules guiding it.

Doing this, however, only indicates the first aspect of the difference between chess matches or multiplication and making music. Let us compare the following two cases. Even if we doubt for good reason that there are chess players who would be "instructed" according to a Rylean lesson plan, and in this process would develop a disposition that makes them capable of playing chess, we could imagine, for the sake of argument, a chess player of this sort and assume that this dispositional chess player makes a mistake in the course of a match. In the second case we ought to imagine a dispositional singer, that is, someone who has completed our elementary lessons, making a mistake in the course of a melody by singing a note that isn't in the scale of her music tradition. If we compare these cases with respect to the possibilities that witnesses to the events have available to criticize these mistakes, then we find an interesting difference.

The witness of the chess game might say: "The knight can only be moved so and so, but not the way you have moved it. Your move isn't allowed!" And the player who initially took back his move might again make a false move and look to his critic with a nod. The critic then could insist on his criticism and finally tell the player what he doesn't know: "The knight can only be moved from the field in which it is placed to another field that it can reach if the following rule is followed: 'Move one field straight and one diagonally and increase at every step the distance from the position you started in.'" And he might add this: "The color of the field occupied by the knight changes after every move." What the critic does if the mere reference to the false move is insufficient is nothing other than explicitly state the rule that applies to the figure in question. A critic of someone who multiplied falsely would hardly proceed differently; for if a dispositional multiplier makes a mistake, then the remark "No, three times five is not sixteen, but fifteen!" will hardly achieve anything. Her statement would counter the statement of the one doing the multiplication. But how does the critic know that she is right, and how can she clearly demonstrate to the person doing the multiplication that she is correct? She will name a prescript that the person doing the multiplication does not know, but that leads to results that conform with those of the person doing the multiplication fairly often. She will say, "If you want to multiply two numbers, then note in a row the number of lines corresponding to the first number. The second number then indicates how many rows you have to fill with this number of lines. . . . When you are finished doing that, count all the lines. The number of lines of all the rows is the correct result of the multiplication problem."[60] Knowledge of such a prescript ensures the critic that her criticism was justified, and it forms the basis of her criticism, for with its help the critic can ensure that her own result is correct.

But what rule or prescript does the critic of the false singer draw on? In most cases, on none at all! Let us assume that the tone that the singer is supposed to sing in order to remain within the parameters of the key that has been transmitted is a fifth higher than the directly preceding note: what prescript could the critic state to ensure herself, but also to provide a basis for her criticism? She could sing the tone correctly, but as a rule she would not be able to state a prescript that she has followed in doing so. In musical cultures like ours, which are accompanied by a long history of the scientific study of its physical foundations, the critic could repeat the Pythagorean view of the tetrachord and point to the pitch relationships of strings. She could say that a key stands in the relationship of a fifth to another one if the lengths of the strings that produce the tones are related to each other like two to three. But the ability to use this procedure is a particularity of our music culture. In cultures that make music without recourse, or the possibility of recourse, to a music *theory*, the critic has no choice but to say: "The way that I am doing this is right!" Why? "Because that's how we sing!" However, this means that the critic cannot legitimate or base her criticism on a prescript; rather, just like the teacher, she can only draw on an act of *deixis*. The final authority for her criticism consists in the actions of those in her culture who are thought to know how to do it. She can only point to how they do it. Beyond the existence of correct performances, which form the elements of a system of deictic references, in music cultures there is no authority for rightness.

What makes the case of the elementary music lesson theoretically interesting is thus the particularity that making music can be a practice in which there is right and wrong, but the right (and wrong) can only be demonstrated in deictic actions. However, this also means that the articulation of what is right remains dependent on its performance; and for this type of rightness, a description of rightness with the help of prescripts is not constitutive. We thus should distinguish between two forms of rightness:

(R1) If you (in the context of practice X) want to do it right, then do it like this . . . [an instantiation of the type of activity follows]!

(R2) If you (in the context of practice X) want to do it right, then do it in such a way that you conform to prescript P!

For my reflections, what is most important here is that the articulation of what is right itself need not assume a linguistic form. (R1) of course makes use of linguistic means of reference and the mention of what is right, but what makes what is right right is not characterized linguistically, but is itself demonstrated by means of a nonlinguistic medium. Here it is important to see that formulations of the type (R1) are not common rules. For, by virtue of their deictic components, sentences in the form of (R1) are always connected to contexts in which a right action is performed; although they apply for certain contexts of *application*, they lack the independence from contexts for *expression* that are characteristic of rules. Nevertheless, the deictic illustration of what is right can be understood as a form for making rightness explicit, albeit with the peculiarity that language here only has the function of ensuring the deictic relationship and not of describing what is right or of explaining it.[61] If we assume a deictic form of explicitness in which the performances of the actions demonstrate rightness, we can adhere to the view—from the idea represented above—that rules are of necessity explicit (or in cases of historically implicit rules, must have been explicit); now, however, the analysis of practices in which there is indeed a "right" and a "wrong," but there are no explicit prescripts, no longer presents a theoretical challenge that makes the opaque concept of implicit rule-following attractive. Before I, in what follows, examine the consequences of these insights for the understanding of nonlinguistic works of art, I would like to draw on the returns of the previous reflections for the further development of our still quite rudimentary media-theoretic vocabulary.

First, the vague criterion (M1)[62] can be made more precise. For one, in the course of the reflections it has become clear that the behavioral possibilities are *types* of activities; further, it has become clear that they are activities that *can be learned*. (M1) thus should be replaced by (M3).

> (M3) Every medium includes a limited number of elementary types of activity, understood as in (M2), which can be learned.

In the case of our elementary musical medium, there would be precisely sixty such types of activity; as long as there is, for example, no possibility to bring about a musical event that has a certain length and a certain dynamic value but that lacks pitch (as in the case of many percussive tones), only combinations of dynamic, duration, and pitch—attributes that can be isolated from the interpreter's perspective—will bring about elementary musical events. In order to make an independent term available for such events, I would like to propose the following definition:

> (M3.1) States of affairs in the world or events, understood in the sense of (M2), which arise or are generated by the performance of types of elementary medial activity, are called *media elements*.

In the reduced form of music of the fictive elementary music lessons, every musical event is an implementation of a media element, and each of these media elements can be identified by three attributes, which are attributes from three discontinuous attributive sets (fifteen pitches, two dynamic levels, and two tone durations). In any halfway developed music—especially, however, in other forms of art like painting or sculpture—there are events or states whose attributes cannot be chosen from discontinuous attributive sets, but must come from a continuum of possible attributes. In contrast to the medial elements that can be chosen from discontinuous attributive sets, the difference between two medial elements in regard to such an attribute can be arbitrarily small so that, between two arbitrary elements, a third can always be found. So, for example, between two tones whose dynamic attributes might be selected from a continuum, it would be possible to bring about a third, which is louder than the quieter one and quieter than the louder one. In other words: if x and z are arbitrary tones, in a musical medium in which the dynamic (D) is a continuous attribute: $\wedge x \wedge z([D(x) > D(z)] \supset \vee y[D(x) > D(y) > D(z)])$.[63] In contrast to our elementary musical medium, media in which medial elements can have attributes that are instantiations of possibilities in an attributive continuum allow the formation of an unlimited number of types of medial elements.

The definition (M3.1) primarily has an economic value, for it allows a somewhat less cumbersome manner of speaking; this facilitates the use of it in reference to the products that implement the types of activity, which in many cases interest us, especially as recipients, more than the productive activities. However, (M3.1) also underlines the dependency of the states or events on the implementation of types of activity; this serves to prevent one from mistakenly thinking that these states or events can be identified as such medial events or states independently of their genetic relationship to the practice in which they are generated. In this way, the medial elements stand in a dual relationship to social practices, for, from the perspective of an interpreter or recipient, they are identified with a view to certain nonnatural, nonintrinsic, or observer-relative attributes (see above, pitch versus frequency) and with a view to a certain production history, which expresses the artifact character of the media elements. This precludes a "C" note produced in the desert by the wind blowing over an empty bottle from being a medial element.

With definitions (M3) and (M3.1), however, we still do not have the conceptual means that would allow us to describe music making as medial action, for it is of course clear that bringing about an occurrence of a type of musical activity (singing a quiet G with a half note duration) or bringing about a medial element is not yet making music. However, that someone articulates herself in a medium can be expressed under the presupposition of (M3) as follows:

> (M4) To articulate oneself (or something) in a medium means that one brings about performance sequences of the type of activity that is specific to this medium.

Someone who has learned to move within the parameters of the inventory of the activity types thereby acquires the possibility of combining these types of activity; although this person may not possess a linguistic individuation mechanism for these types of activity, it is clear that the person's disposition to sing the tone at a certain (right) pitch is the prerequisite for the tone being among the materials that the person has to choose from. Further, it would be useful to have a *non*-media-specific concept for the product that is brought about by a sequence that instantiates medial possibilities.

(M5) The product of the performance of a sequence of instantiations of media activity types is called a *medial constellation*.

(M5) ought to accommodate the fact that while all medial products are brought about by sequences of actions, these products themselves do not necessarily have a sequential character. For while in the context of music (or dance), an arrangement of medial elements always has a temporal and thus sequential character, in painting and sculpture this is not the case. With recourse to (M3.1), we can also say:

(M5.1) Every arrangement of medial elements forms a medial constellation.

In a provisional last step in the development of a media-theoretic vocabulary, we can now introduce an expression that allows reference to the possibilities that are provided by a medium for bringing about a medial constellation.

(M6) The set of all possible constellations in a medium M is called the *scope of possibilities* for M.

The size of this set is, of course, only different from infinite if there are, for example, in our case of elementary music, constraints on the length of the songs that can be sung in the framework. The function of the concept of the scope of possibilities, however, is not to organize comparisons of the size of the media; rather, it is to provide a concept for *what is allowed* in a medium, which, as the previous reflections have shown, does not require explicitly formulated criteria.

What have we now gained from the analysis of the elementary music lessons and the specifications of the terminology? Are we nearer to the goal of explaining what it means to have, or to understand, a musical thought? And above all, does this analysis provide us the theoretical means to explain which thoughts Mozart articulated when writing a sonata phrase? Let us thus turn back to the problems that arose in the talk after the concert. In the framework of this discussion, we came up against the problem of explaining the presuppositions that a recipient must fulfill so that we are assured she understands a piece of music.

With the help of the terminology that has been introduced, the criterion—namely, that the recipient must be capable of relating to the identity of the piece of music—can now be specified since we can now say that a recipient must be able to relate to the piece of music that was listened to so that she heard it as a medial constellation, in other words, that she heard the performance as an arrangement of medial elements. Beyond this, the recipient has to hear the performance not only as just any medial constellation whatsoever, but as a specific one: that is, she must not only have a more or less well-articulated hypothesis about the scope of possibilities against which the piece was carried out, but she must also have a hypothesis about the specifics of the sequence of choices that the medial constellation can be depicted as being the product of. If a recipient manages to relate more or less to the position that a work assumes as a medial constellation in a medial scope of possibilities, then she succeeds in referring to the compositional identity of the work. The idea of explaining the conditions necessary in order to understand works of art with the help of a concept of compositional identity can then provisionally be specified by means of media theory as follows:

(CI_0) It is possible to relate to the compositional identity of a medial expression by linguistic means by describing a work as a specific medial constellation within the scope of possibilities of a medium.

But to what degree do the preceding reflections contribute to reconstructing artistic activity as actions and to understanding nonlinguistic expressions? In short: to what degree do our reflections do more than merely redescribe the problems in media-theoretic terms?

1. If media provide sets of basic activity types, then the sequential performance of such activities has a different *status* than the performance of mere dispositional activities. This status allows these activities to be closely related to actions; however, in the

process of providing explanations, we need not appeal to reasons in order for these to count as actions. That these activities have the character of actions is not dependent on the common intentional vocabulary. This is for the following reasons:

a. One can succeed or fail to bring about a type of activity. Consequently, rightly bringing about some type of activity is subject to specific *normative* ideas (*Vorstellungen*), which need not be linguistically articulated, but which can be made explicit through acts of deixis. Although the normativity that is in play here does not manifest itself in explicit linguistic prescripts, it is not reducible to the functional level. For we do not explain what correctly carrying out a type of activity is—as in the case of types of behavior that have arisen in the course of evolution—with a view to a function that this type of activity commonly has. A factual but contingent practice constitutes the basis of the normativity of the practice, not its function. (Do this the way that we do!)

b. Bringing about a sequence of types of activities that we have learned is different from performing dispositional activities under certain environmental conditions, because each time such an activity is carried out, it can be described as a *choice* against the background of alternative activities. The act of carrying out this activity, however, does not appear to be a choice for just the media-theoretic interpreters of the action, but also for the persons who carry it out; they themselves perform the activity with knowledge of alternatives, with knowledge of its arbitrariness, even if, under certain circumstances, they cannot provide a reason for their choice. With the help of this attribute, the performance of medial activities can be interpreted as action if we understand action, in a basic sense, as *chosen activity*. This, however, provides a fundamental concept of action that can form the foundation for an action-theoretic reconstruction of artistic activity insofar as it does not bring any mandatory propositional implications into play.

2. With the still vague concept of compositional identity, means emerge for an identifying reference to nonlinguistic expressions; with the help of this, it is at least possible to articulate necessary conditions for understanding.

Hereby, of course, only the first steps are taken in reconstructing artistic action and in reconstructing what it means to understand nonlinguistic expressions. However, the central question still remains open: namely, what might it mean to think or understand a nonlinguistic thought? It is indeed clear that in the case of understanding linguistic expressions, too, we must pay attention to the structuring and the analysis of expressions. However, our concern is not the grammar of the speaker's language; our concern is to understand her thoughts. Herewith I come again to the above-posed question (see p. 155): What might it mean to understand a piece of music? In the following section I will first attempt to create a place in the philosophy of mind for the idea that there are thoughts whose content and identity are *not* dependent on their position in an inferentially organized network of propositions.

3.2.2. Revisions in the Philosophy of Mind

3.2.2.1. Can Mind Think Without Language?

Davidson has claimed that we should only ascribe thoughts to beings that we can ascribe beliefs to; beyond that, he has attempted to show it to be plausible that the only beings that can have beliefs are those beings that can refer to states of being convinced of something. This was understood to mean that they are able to view the propositions that indicate their respective beliefs as true or false. Only if a being is able, with the help of such second-order beliefs, to draw a distinction between (subjective) beliefs and objective truths does it makes sense to ascribe to this being the ability to have beliefs. However, within the framework of an interpretationist theory of mind, this ability should only be ascribed to beings if they possess a sufficiently complex language, which they use to contrast their subjective beliefs with objective facts within an intersubjective linguistic practice, and in this way refer to an intersubjective truth. It is clear that, in these reflections, Davidson interprets the criteria for thoughts very narrowly—too narrowly in the view of most naturalists, who do not want the discussion of contentful states to be reserved for thoughts as Davidson understands them. However, even in the face of this well-motivated reservation, which my concept of A-intentional states in part attempts to accommodate, I do not want to maintain that

Davidson underestimates the importance of such states for the philosophy of mind; rather, I want to argue that more types of mental states are contentful *for* the beings that have them than his theory allows.

With the help of the previous discussion of higher-level intentional states (thoughts), I have attempted to show that even if Davidson's analysis about those intentional states that are beliefs is correct, this by no means precludes other intentional states from having the status of thoughts, which while not being propositional attitudes are still correlated, like propositional attitudes, to an expressive activity that is sufficiently complex (for thoughts). As already noted, thoughts are individuated by beings who have them; they are not simply discovered or produced by a representational machinery. However, if we expect that beings refer to their thoughts by individuating them, then we obviously require a second-order relation, since a being's reference to its thoughts can only be explained by indicating that the being draws on intentional states with the help of other intentional states. Put differently, a being can only have (nonlinguistic) thoughts if it has thoughts about thoughts. If this is correct, then how is it possible to explain the second-order relation—which Davidson, in reference to beliefs, explains with the help of the truth predicate—with a view to nonlinguistic thoughts?

If we once again call to mind the chief attraction of Davidson's analysis, then it becomes clear that Davidson can manage both the problem of the individuation of thoughts and the problem of second-order reference in *one* theoretical vocabulary. For, with the help of the truth predicate, he can explain both the identity of a proposition as well as the ability of a being to behave with regard to this proposition. Because Davidson does not reckon with nonlinguistic thoughts and thus is able to deal with thoughts analogously to propositions, he entrusts the individuation of thoughts—parallel to the individuation of propositions—to their position in a net that stretches through logical (i.e., truth-functional) relationships:

> Thoughts, like propositions, have logical relations. Since the identity of a thought cannot be divorced from its place in the logical network of other thoughts, it cannot be relocated in the network without becoming a different thought.[64]

Beyond this, however, Davidson can also make a being's ability to have a thought dependent on whether this being can distinguish between two scenarios: the scenario of possessing a logically individuated propositional attitude and the scenario of knowing whether this attitude is true or false. If higher-level, nonlinguistic intentional states cannot be introduced as truth-apt states, the thought of *relational identity*, which integrates Davidson's conception, has to be modified so that the individuating power of the relations are made independent of the concept of truth. With the concept of *compositional identity* I have thus far only introduced a working title for an identity principle with the help of which it should be possible to explain the individuation of nonlinguistic thoughts; however, insofar as the debate about the problem of second-order relations is dependent, from the view of theory formation, on a solution to the problem of individuation, then, first of all, a robust view of the individuation of nonlinguistic thoughts must be developed.

3.2.2.2. An Identity Principle for Nonlinguistic Thoughts

If one attempts, with the help of the principle of relational identity, to check whether two linguistic thoughts, T_1 and T_2, are identical, then the principle of relational identity can be formulated as follows:

> (RIT_1) A propositional state or a propositional thought T_1 is identical with a state T_2 if and only if T_1 and T_2 have the same position in the network of propositional thoughts of a person P_1.

Among other things, that means that T_1 and T_2 have the same truth conditions, but generally that T_1 and T_2 can be substituted for one another without the identity of the thoughts T_n and T_m changing, with a view to which T_1 and T_2 have been individuated. Here what is interesting about (RIT_1) is that the identity of a thought obviously cannot be determined without there being other thoughts whose identities, for their part, refer to the identity of other thoughts.[65]

Because, from the interpretationist perspective, the identification of a position in the network of propositional states is the result of an interpretation—and self-interpretation has no primacy in this schema, but in contrast, self-interpretation is explained according to the model of interpreting others—it must be possible to reformulate (RIT_1) so that (RIT_1) provides the conditions for identifying two different persons' thoughts, the person being interpreted and the person who is interpreting. For the interpretation of others, the relational identity criterion assumes the following form:

> (RIT_2) A propositional state or a propositional thought T_1 of a person P_1 is relationally identical with a state T_2 of P_2, which interprets an expression E_1 from P_1 if and only if T_2 has approximately the same role in the network of propositional thoughts from P_2 as T_1 has in the network for propositional states from P_1 if P_2 thinks that T_2 is true.[66]

With a view to interpreting others, above all, it is clear that the access to a thought is only possible by means of *expressions*; however, because of the primacy of the interpretation of others, this also applies to self-interpretation. An interpreter correlates an expression of the one being interpreted with a metalinguistic specification of its truth conditions; hereby she integrates it into the network of her beliefs, which, however, the interpreter in essence must at the same time read into the one being interpreted. What both of the provided versions of the relational identity criterion formulate for thoughts must thus have an equivalent at the level of the expression.

> (RIE_1) A propositional expression E_1 from P_1 is relationally identical with an expression E_2 from P_2 if and only if E_1 and E_2 can be substituted for one another when expressed under sufficiently similar circumstances, thus that E_1 and E_2 can play the same role in processes of understanding (in similar situations).

Two persons who think relationally identical propositional thoughts have the disposition, when making utterances under sufficiently similar circumstances, to articulate relationally identical expressions. Here the identification of type-identical expressions can initially be ceded to an ability to understand types that, for its part, introduces no further burdensome presuppositions into the concept of relational identity.[67]

In the face of these criteria, what view now emerges about medial expressions and the mental states that are correlated with them? What must an analogous criteria catalogue for nonlinguistic thoughts look like that provides content to the provisional discussion of compositional identity? In order to answer these questions, it makes sense to develop the criteria, beginning with the expressions, because at the level of the expressions no ideas about the constitutive attributes of nonlinguistic thoughts need yet be brought into play; rather, restrictions for the characterization of these attributes can be obtained. An obvious reformulation of (RIE$_1$) for nonlinguistic expressions is:

> (CIE$_1$) A (nonlinguistic) expression E_1 from P_1 is compositionally identical with a (nonlinguistic) expression E_2 from P_2 if and only if E_1 and E_2 can be substituted for one another when the conditions under which the expressions are made are sufficiently similar.

The substitution criterion that can, with a view to linguistic expressions, take recourse in a set of criteria, including truth invariance, requires different proof criteria for nonlinguistic expressions that, however, must transcend the presupposed type identification by perception that is active in both cases. In order to develop an independent concept of compositional identity and to specify the type of identity that might exist between the expressions on this side of the relational identity, it makes sense, first of all, to compare linguistic expressions that have identical attributes in certain respects, but that do not fulfill the established criterion of relational identity.

1. Someone from England says, "You owe me a billion pesetas."
2. Someone from America says, "You owe me a billion pesetas."

The expression "billion" is produced in both cases in the same way, but with a view to the relational position of the sentence in the context of British English or American English, there is a difference of at least 999 thousand million—or billion—pesetas. Thus, the two expressions have quite different truth conditions. Both sentences sound the same, but the identification by means of sense perception is not sufficient for compositional identity, as a look at the expression of the philosophically indispensable parrot shows:

3. The parrot Alex says: "Alexcanspeak!"
4. Tim, Alex's caretaker, says: "Alex can speak!"

The fact that we perceive Alex's expression and the expression of Tim as type identical does not imply their compositional identity, for we cannot presume that Alex synthesizes his expression from syllables that, as linguistic unities, are at the basis of Tim's expressions. Perhaps the difference comes out more dramatically in the following example:

5. The English Garden in Munich.
6. An extraction from nature that by chance looks exactly like the English Garden in Munich.

A comparison of the three pairs of examples shows that only the first case has compositional identity; only in the first case can we presume that the type identity of the expressions is a result of the type-identical production of the expressions. The speakers draw from an established inventory of sounds, from which they form their expressions.[68] From the perspective of the recipient, the compositional identity is not based solely on identification by perception; it is based on identification of something as something. The conditions for the possibility of such a something-as-something identification can now be theoretically used to specify the conditions under which nonlinguistic expressions can be substituted for one another. However, here we must dispense with inferential relations because, given the lack of the truth aptness of the products of nonlinguistic articulation, truth-functional relations are not available to determine identity. However, if we return to the media concept that has been introduced, we find the theoretical resources with the help of which it is possible to provide conditions for substitution. For with the aid of the media concept, a scope for the possible types of action can be fixed, formed by varying and combining elementary types of action. In this scope of action a nonlinguistic expression has an identity:

(CIE$_2$) A (nonlinguistic) expression E_1 is compositionally identical with a (nonlinguistic) expression E_2 if and only if E_1 and E_2 can be described such that two persons P_1 and P_2 have generated the expressions by following the same sequence of choices (from a hypothetical inventory of possible choices).

If the compositional identity of two nonlinguistic expressions legitimizes their reciprocal substitution insofar as it formulates necessary and sufficient conditions for an acceptable substitution, then, with the concept of compositional identity, a concept is also available with the help of which it is possible to determine the identity of those mental states that are *causes* for the articulation of nonlinguistic expressions, and indeed in the following way: In compliance with an interpretationist perspective, the explanation of the criteria of relational identity leads, first of all, from the level of *thoughts* to the explanatory more fundamental level of *articulation*. If (CIE_2) is an acceptable criterion for the compositional identity of an *expression*, then in reversing this in a second step, it is possible to move on from the level of nonlinguistic articulation to the formulation of a criterion for nonlinguistic *thoughts*. Such a criterion comes into purview if we assume that nonlinguistic thoughts indicate dispositions to bring about nonlinguistic expressions.

(CIT_1) A (nonlinguistic) thought T_1 is compositionally identical with a (nonlinguistic) thought T_2 if and only if T_1 and T_2 dispose a person P_1 (or a number of persons) to effectuate compositionally identical expressions.

If the compositional identity of the expressions can be explained in reference to the idea of choice from among a scope of possibilities, then the identity of the thoughts can be explained by employing the idea of options; from an interpretationist perspective, the compositional identity of the observable results of action is the only possible basis for the compositional identity of the dispositional causes and expressions that are being ascribed. If we assume that the alternative forms of articulation are kept in existence by social practices, a criterion for the identity of nonlinguistic thoughts can be formulated as follows:

(CIT_2) A (nonlinguistic) thought T_1 is compositionally identical with a (nonlinguistic) thought T_2 if and only if T_1 and T_2 occupy the same position within the scope of possibilities of the medium.

On the basis of this quite abstract discussion of the identity of nonlinguistic thoughts, how does one now explain what it means to think a nonlinguistic thought? Or, with a view to the example above: what does it mean to think a musical thought? An answer to this question, for its part, can be given in an analogy to linguistic thoughts. If we ask ourselves what characterizes that state of thinking a linguistic thought, we can say that thinking a thought disposes a thinking person to act in a certain way, which is connected to the content of the thought. Someone, for example, who is convinced that the water in his glass is poisoned will not drink it if he does not want to die, and so on. However, besides such consequentalist implications of the belief, which can be expressed in numerous ways, the person certainly has a disposition to express a sentence that provides the content of his belief. Someone who has a thought has this thought by virtue of expressing it internally. In short, linguistic thinking is inhibited speaking. To think a musical thought means, in strict analogy to these reflections, to be disposed toward a musical expression, which means to imagine or to inhibit a musical expression. In contrast to a linguistic expression, which can be translated into a language different from the speaker's, a work of art, which articulates a musical or more generally a nonlinguistic thought, can only be reformulated with the help of compositionally identical expressions. Nothing beyond the compositional identity of such a thought is translatable. We only have access to its content by thinking it ourselves by "quietly (i.e., silently) singing" it.

If we call to mind how conductors or members of small musical ensembles attempt to familiarize other musicians with a musical thought, then we see that competing interpretations of a work lead to different musical thoughts, and their best expression is, in each individual case, apparently of the following sort: "Play daa-dad-daaa-da-ratatataaaa-dam."

Before I attempt to develop a clear, more graphic view of the content of nonlinguistic thoughts, I would like to generally characterize the type of intentional state that we are dealing with if my analysis of nonlinguistic thoughts is correct, and I would like to suggest a more complete integrative depiction of the mental.

In the examination of Searle and Davidson, I earlier[69] suggested characterizing a sort of intentional state (A-intentional states). While these indeed have content, their individuation remains dependent on current or represented conditions of satisfaction; in addition, they have no content *for* the beings that find themselves in such states (as long as these beings only have A-intentional states). I contrasted these intentional states with higher-level intentional states (thoughts), the most prominent representatives of which are, without a doubt, linguistic thoughts, thus propositional attitudes. Under the presupposition of the reflections on the identity of nonlinguistic thought, however, the theoretical means are also now available that allow us to show that there is a reason to include nonlinguistic thoughts in the class of higher-level intentional states. Here, the class of higher-level intentional states must be internally so differentiated that its internal structure can sufficiently accommodate the differences between nonlinguistic and linguistic thoughts *and* their commonalities.

In order to guard against the suspicion that might arise—that classifying nonlinguistic intentional states as thoughts is primarily due to terminological sophistication—there is, however, a need to systematically characterize higher-level intentional states. In drawing this out, it is useful, first of all, to more precisely consider than I yet have what A-intentional states are. Above in (A1)[70] I noted that mental states are those states that dispose beings to differentially respond to their environment and to adjust in a way that precludes being steered by the being. In addition, these states have an identity (that can be articulated by the interpreter of *B*'s behavior), which can be explained in reference to ideas of conditions of satisfaction. As a model for A-intentional states, which I hope is intuitively illuminating, I have introduced a state that, from the perspective of the interpreter of the behavior of a small child that has not yet come to speak a language, might be called a "nonlinguistic desire."[71]

If we characterize the systematic particularities of such states in Searle's terminology, then we can say that such a state is *intrinsically intentional*, which ought to mean that it has an implicit relationship to its *conditions of satisfaction*. A being that finds itself in such a state thus eo ipso has a "consciousness"—avouched for by representational mechanisms—of the conditions of satisfaction specific to this state. This "consciousness" of the conditions of satisfaction is of course not such that a being with A-intentional states could not make these conditions of satisfaction explicit. But beyond the act toward which a state disposes the being, such an A-intentional state must be displayed by a fulfilling or frustrating or surprising behavior on the part of the being that is specific to the state. And this behavior must be a result of the being's ability to differentiate whether the conditions of satisfaction that are specific to its A-intentional state are fulfilled or not. However, it can have the ability to make this distinction only on the basis of *internal* representational competencies; for, because of their world-to-mind direction of fit, in the case of desires, the only possible criterion for this competence for making this distinction lies in the being in question itself.[72] In the context of the reflections here, the form this representation of conditions of satisfaction assumes in the experience of this being can remain open; that is, it can remain open whether it assumes sensory-motor, pictorial, or another form of representation. However, we must then say, regarding the conditions for the individuation of A-intentional states, that these conditions are fulfilled by a sufficiently complex neuronal machinery that human beings contingently happen to have. The interpreter is indeed needed to describe them, but not to establish them; for a (self-)interpretation is not constitutive for the existence of A-intentional states.

To find oneself in an A-intentional state thus means to find oneself in a state that represents conditions of satisfaction. As Searle rightly noted, we can thus not sensibly speak of the meaning of such states because we cannot sensibly distinguish between the state and its content. Searle, however, assumes that this is not a particularity of a certain class of intentional states, but that it applies to intentional states in general. In Searle's words, "Meaning exists only where there is a distinction between Intentional content and the form of its externalization, and to ask for the meaning is to ask for an Intentional content that goes with the form of externalization . . . but it makes no sense to ask for the meaning of the belief."[73]

If we now ask how the content of an intentional state can become the content *for* a being that has this state—thus how a being can reach the level of higher intentional states—then something must come into play that, for its part, is not a representation of conditions of satisfaction, that is, something that is *not* intrinsically intentional; for every further A-intentional state would be no more than a further representation of conditions of satisfaction and would thus not be available for an arbitrary and potentially interpretive relation to another A-intentional state. The problem consists, namely, in the fact that it is impossible to imagine that there is an A-intentional state $I_{(a1)}$ that typifies the conditions of satisfaction of an A-intentional state $I_{(a2)}$. There would simply be no criterion by which to distinguish these two A-intentional states. In other words, A-intentional states that have the same conditions of satisfaction *are* the same states.[74]

Here we have reached a theoretical point, however, from which it is no longer possible to follow *Searle's* theory of intentionality because it does not offer the theoretical resources with the help of which we can reconstruct the level of higher intentional states, and this is for the following reason: If intentional states are introduced by the concept of the conditions of satisfaction, and their identity is dependent solely on, or typified by, this concept,[75] then we cannot see how a being that only has intentional states at its disposal that are characterized in reference to their conditions of satisfaction is able to have intentional states that refer to *other* intentional states; every state that potentially refers to another intentional state would be a state that could manage this solely by means of its conditions of satisfaction. Every successful reference to a state $I_{(a1)}$, however, would have to be able to identify its conditions of satisfaction, and how would that be possible unless the reference-taking state $I_{(a2)}$ had the same conditions of satisfaction? Then, however (see above), $I_{(a2)}$ would be identical with the state $I_{(a1)}$. This relation can also be clarified as follows: because an A-intentional state is a representation of conditions of satisfaction $R(E_i, \ldots, E_j)$, for a representation of this state, $R^*(R(E_i, \ldots, E_j))$, it must be accepted that R^* has conditions of satisfaction $E_i, \ldots, E_j$; for the (A-intentional) identification of an A-intentional state represents its conditions of satisfaction. To counter this analysis, one might object that a suitable reconstruction of the intentional references to $R(E_i, \ldots, E_j)$ does not have the form provided above, but the following form: $R^*(E(R(E_i, \ldots, E_j)))$. The conditions of satisfaction for R^* would be those conditions that are fulfilled by the *existence* of the intentional state $R(E_i, \ldots, E_j)$, but these too are the conditions that R represents. In short, if one takes Searle's fundamental analysis of intentionality as a basis, the attempt to reconstruct higher-level forms of intentionality leads either to an infinite regress, or a duplication of mind, or it collapses because of the concurrence of the referring intentional state and the one being addressed.[76]

If this analysis is correct, then it is not at all clear how Searle, with the help of the representational vocabulary, is to reconstruct those relations between intentional states that are presupposed for higher-order intentional states and thus the basis for any holistic network that is also the foundation for his view of mind.[77] In other words, a mind whose intentional states consist solely in representations of conditions of satisfaction cannot cite itself. If that is true, however, then it is also questionable how the point of Searle's semantics can be salvaged; for how is mind supposed to be able to consciously link the conditions of satisfaction of an intentional state with those of an expression[78] if this mind is not able to refer to the conditions of satisfaction of the intentional state? With an expression an entity does indeed come into play that, for its part, is not intrinsically intentional; however, the intentionally produced relation between an expression and an intentional state presumes a second mind, which can observe the states of the first one, as the conditions of satisfaction for these states would coincide in one mind. If one would like to avoid a mind in the mind of this sort and thus an infinite regress, then it is necessary to accept the idea of a linguistic division of labor, which externalizes the second mind in the form of an interpreter. In short, in order to reconstruct higher-level intentionality, it is necessary to accept an interpretationist strategy; if we want to get a theoretical grasp of higher-level intentional states (thoughts), we must leave the biological theory of intentionality behind[79] and bring something into play that enables a being to behave toward its own intentional states in such a way that it is able to become a self-interpreter, and this can only be something that is itself not intrinsically intentional, that is perceptible, and that thus can be correlated with intentional states by external interpreters.

This, however, is initially only an outline of a theoretical strategic perspective, and it is by no means clear how one can in detail convey an understanding of the transition from a level of intentionality that can be reconstructed in biological terms to higher-level intentional states. In order to ensure that the task confronting us remains manageable—namely, the task of reconstructing this transition—we can first of all limit ourselves to an explanation that is tailored to the case of a being B with A-intentional states that finds other beings in its environment that are potential interpreters of B's behavior that, for their part, have higher-level intentional states. What we are looking for in such an explanation is an *interactionist theory of the emergence of higher intentionality and of consciousness*; on the basis of the genetic character of this theory, we can simultaneously formulate a suitability condition for this to the effect that this theory must be *compatible* with empirical findings about the mental development of children.[80] When I, in the following, reconstruct the process of the development of higher intentionality in four phases, I am not doing so in order to offer an empirically appropriate psychological explanation of this development; rather, I am attempting to show the plausibility of a theoretical *model* of this development that does not start from empirical findings but from the conceptual problems related to designing a process of development of higher intentionality. Within the framework of this model, it is sufficient to allow psychological processes to be identified that *could* serve as the empirical implementations of developmental steps that are postulated conceptually. So, even though the following reflections integrate more empirical material than other parts of the book, they remain committed to the attempt to solve conceptual problems. Here, besides the question of how the development of higher intentionality can be explained, a further question is brought into play: Beyond the admittedly quite formal definition of the identity of nonlinguistic intentional states, how can we explain that such states have content?

3.2.2.3. Back to the Roots

If we aim at an explanation of the transition from basic to higher intentionality for a being B—for example, a small child—under the premise that it interacts with interpreters who already have fully developed intentionality at their disposal, and under these presuppositions, a form of the social "division of labor" is made the basis of higher-level forms of intentionality, then we can initially assume that there is a B-extrinsic mind that can draw on the basic intentional states of B. We then are confronted with the task of explaining how B is able to internalize these references and to achieve them herself independently of the interpreter I.

However, because an interpreter only has reference to the A-intentional states of B via the behavior of B, the center of gravity of such an explanation must be behaviors or (proto-)actions.[81] For an interpreter, only such *observable* activities can constitute an interface for interpretations that employ the vocabulary of folk psychology that the interpreter, because of her higher-level intentionality, has at her disposal. If we start with this intuition, then the following (not particularly dramatic) assumptions are at the basis of our explanation of the development of higher-level intentionality:

(A)

    a. A being B, which in the framework of a social interaction process is supposed to be able to establish a higher-level form of intentionality, must be able to perceive its environment with differentiation, to remember, and to learn.
    b. At the beginning of this process, B must have (in the last analysis biologically explainable) A-intentional states at its disposal.
    c. A-intentional states dispose a being that has them to activities that can be observed by others (proto-action).

d. If the interpreting observers of the proto-action already have higher-level intentionality at their disposal, they can provide intentionalistic explanations of the proto-action of B. (To speak with Dennett, they assume an *intentional stance* with a view to B.)

Having presumed this, three different theoretical options are available for the construction of the first phase of development, depending on which sort of mental states we take as the starting point for the interpretation process and depending on which sort of mental states we allow to have a paradigmatic character within the framework of the explanation.

The *first* option, which perhaps I have appeared to favor thus far because of my insistence on the existence of A-intentional states, consists in making, primarily, the ascription of *voluntary states* the starting point of the analysis; these indeed have paradigmatic status for the characterization of this basic level of intentionality. According to this perspective, in the view of the interpreter, the being B is primarily a being that has *(proto-)desires and (proto-)intentions*, whereby the interpreter views the proto-actions of B (for example, her pointing action) as a means that serves to bring about voluntary A-intentional states. If we accept this option, the basis of our explanation becomes those interactions in which the interpreter interprets the behavior of B primarily according to the following pattern: B wants$_i$ X.[82] Or B wishes$_i$ that X were the case.

A *second* option arises if the activities caused by A-intentional states are not understood primarily as instruments of desire fulfillment, but as means for representing matters of fact. The interpreter understands A-intentional states in this case as *epistemic states*, as *protobeliefs*. If we accept this option, then we make those interactions the basis of our explanation in which the interpreter primarily interprets B's behavior that is interpreted as demonstrative in accord with the following pattern: B believes$_i$ that X is there. Or: B knows$_i$ that this is X.

The *third* and final option provides the possibility of assuming, at or beside the level of A-intentional states, that B primarily expresses itself *expressively*, and its activities are to be understood as an expression of basic *emotional states*, that is, as based on affects. In this case, the interpreter of B's behavior would primarily interpret it in accord with the following pattern: B feels X. Or: B feels X-like.

One could, of course, object to this division, noting that there is no reason at all not to presume that for the real interpretation of B's behavior all of these options are employed. From a theoretical perspective, however, the concern is to distinguish which option is suited to serve as an adequate starting point for a theory of the development of higher intentionality; with a view to this question, it appears clear to me that most of the established theories here in fact make a decision that is closely related to their respective conceptions of the intentional. With a view to the earlier discussed models of Searle and Davidson, it is clear that Searle's model suggests an orientation on voluntary states, and the orientation of Davidson's theory is based on epistemic states. In Searle, the *intention* of mind-to-place intrinsic, nonintentional states or activities under the conditions of satisfaction of intrinsic-intentional states serves as the basic model for the development of inferred (and thus higher) intentionality. For Davidson, in contrast, the development of higher intentionality ultimately aims at *truth*.[83]

In light of these options, let us once again call to mind the task that we are faced with: in the explanation of concern here, it is first of all important to show how mental states can acquire content; second, however, we are concerned with how the content can become content *for* those beings that have these states. Searle's reflections provided for an explanation of theoretical means with the help of which the first part of the task can be handled insofar as A-intentional states can be analyzed in reference to their conditions of satisfaction, but his view lacks the theoretical resources to handle the second part of the task.

If we attempt to identify the theoretical means with the help of which Davidson attempts to manage the second part of the task, then we must assume that Davidson views the model of *triangulation* as the model situation that should be able to yield an explanation of higher-level intentionality. For with a view to the issue of how a being can behave toward the content of its mental states, Davidson claims this is only explainable if it is possible for a being, in communication with an interpreter and in the presence of objective perceptible states of affairs in the world, to generate correlations between (linguistic) reactions and externally caused stimuli. Because "a creature cannot have thoughts unless it is an interpreter of the speech of another,"[84] a situation is needed in which this being can correlate three classes of states: if a thought is a mental state "with a specifiable content,"[85] then in order to identify the content, a second being is needed that has the faculty of perception and that, by innate similarity responses to a class of stimulus patterns, contributes to the identification of the cause of a thought by reacting to this cause in the same way as the being that is to be interpreted. Triangulation is supposed to secure the fulfillment of those conditions that enable the identification of the normal cause of a (truth-apt) thought. However, a problem with triangulation then appears to be that the ability to think is linked to the ability to understand oneself as the apex of a triangle that includes the classes of similarity responses of two beings and an observable stimulus pattern. This, however, raises the question of whether, with a view to the second part of our task, anything was gained at all; for it is questionable whether the ability to be an interpreter of another being does not presume precisely the higher intentionality that we want to explain.

If the triangular situation is to be an explanatory model for how a being can become an interpreter of the behavior of another being, then it is not clear how a being can understand *itself* as the apex of a triangle without already having a complex self-description at its disposal. And even if this consequence is too strong, the problem remains that the child in the triangulation must assume that the (linguistic) reaction of the parents to that event in which the two private perspectives converge articulates *thoughts*. Then, however, the intentionalist vocabulary is already in play; far beyond the assumption that human beings, as members of a species, share perceptual and basic classification patterns, we must assume that children are equipped with competencies of mind reading.[86] However, on the other hand, without these assumptions, which are hardly able to be reconciled with Davidson's philosophy of mind, I do not see how the theory of triangulation can explain how children acquire those competencies that allow them to become interpreters of the behavior of adults since the first concept that the children would have to have at their disposal would be that of a thought.

In contrast to Davidson's externalism, I thus would now like to suggest an externalism that does not emphasize the objectivity of the cause of the stimulus that is perceived by the child and the teacher, and, thus accompanying this, the *epistemic* character of those intentional states that play a paradigmatic role for the development of higher intentionality; this externalism instead argues that the situation of triangulation has assumptions that can be analyzed in a *dyadic* relation in which, first of all, *emotional* and then *voluntative* states acquire paradigmatic character.[87] I would like to develop a multitiered externalism of this sort in the form of a four-phase reconstruction; it sets out in agreement with some results of modern infant research—that emotional states are the starting points of affect-centered communication—and it only introduces voluntative and epistemological states in connection with the structures developed in this first phase. They can, in a manner of speaking, only become the material for the development of higher intentionality if these structures are presumed.[88] Although the theory suggested here is inspired by the results of empirical research, it is important to me to explicitly emphasize that the following reflections are indebted to the development of a reconstructive model and do not claim to be empirically adequate in detail. As a whole, the phase model is a strongly schematized suggestion, which does not claim to do justice to the complexity of the development of thought. An important goal would be reached if, with the help of the sequence of phases, it might be comprehensible how it is *possible*, under certain social conditions, that beings that only have a basic form of intentionality at their disposal develop into beings that can think.

PHASE 1: AFFECT-CENTERED COMMUNICATION

In the first phase I assume that small children have the fixed genetic disposition to express their basic and inborn[89] affects with a mimetic behavior that is solidly connected to these affects. With a view to the assumptions mentioned under (A), this means that (A) assumes the following broadened form:

(A′) (a)–(d) hold; and

    e. B possesses inborn mechanisms that dispose B to react to situations that exhibit certain characteristics with basic emotional reactions, i.e., with *affects* and specific forms of behavior.[90]

The fact that a child finds itself in an emotional state does not mean—not even under the assumption that it is disposed to an expressive behavior—that it has access to this state in some way that exceeds its mere phenomenological experience. Under this assumption, the child has at its disposal neither the ability to draw on the emotional state with the help of mental states nor the ability to change its states by internal means. Starting from this stage, my thesis now is that a child only gains access to its emotional states by means of interpreters, mostly initially women, who react to its emotional expressive behavior with *mimetic responses*. These responses first enable the child to correlate its experience of the affect with something *externally perceivable*; what the child perceives is not just any social reaction, but a reaction that expresses precisely what the child emotionally senses. In short, by means of her mimetic response, the mother *mirrors*[91] the child's emotional state.

Admittedly, it must be presumed that these mirroring mimetic responses are not mimetic articulations that the child misunderstands, as expressions of the emotional situation of its counterpart. This is especially necessary since the "regulation of the childish homeostasis and brain processes [is] extremely environmentally and object dependent, and indeed already at a pre-representational 'pure' physiological niveau,"[92] and children, because of this openness, would be brought into the emotional states that they are confronted with in the mimetic expression. If the mirroring expression of emotions was concerned with reproducing the mimetic expression of the child as precisely as possible, then the affects articulated by the child would be reinforced anyway, also in the case of negative effects. It is thus important that the expression "mirroring" is not to be understood all too literally, and that the process it refers to differs from a copying function in the following respects:

1. The mimetic responsive behavior of the reference person does not occur in every case in which an emotional expression is articulated, but only (sufficiently) *often*.
2. The mimetic responsive behavior of the reference person does not copy the expressive behavior of the child exactly; rather, it is characterized by an *exaggerated* gesture, which *marks* the responsive behavior of the reference person and allows it to be differentiated from her own emotional situation.

According to Watson and Gergely, the two characteristics—that the occurrences are frequent but not lawlike, and that the responsive behavior is marked by exaggeration—now play a central role for the differentiation of the internal states of the child; the regular occurrence of the external indicators makes it possible to identify, with some differentiation, internal states that accompany the occurrence of the affect. Drawing an analogy to the technique of biofeedback—a procedure by which people learn to influence bodily states that usually evade the influence of steering (e.g., blood pressure and the resistance of the skin) by making these states perceptible to them through a sensory apparatus such as help tones—Watson has suggested a fundamental learning mechanism that enables children, on the basis of the above-described *social* feedback mechanism, to perceive their inner states. At the center of this learning model is a mechanism for detecting conditionality, which is triggered especially by frequently, but not always, occurring event–event relations—thus, for example, relations like those we can expect from relations between a child and its reference person. Watson postulates now that this mechanism is oriented to search for those states or activities of the child that, given an external event, maximize the likelihood of that external event.[93]

Under this presupposition, in the phase of affect-centered communication, a first fundamental step of this internal differentiation occurs; this happens as sufficiently frequent incidents of externally marked, mimetic events enable the mechanism for analyzing conditionality to identify, with sufficient reliability, precisely those internal states that allow the external mimetic incidents to occur. Here, with a view to the inner states, this identification is carried out completely at the level of perceptions; for the occurrences of the marked facial expressions of the parents that correlate to the mimetic expression of the child are just as perceptible by the senses as the inner states and processes that precede the parental facial expressions and can be proprioceptively perceived. In short, sufficiently reliably occurring social responses to the inborn expression of emotional states enable the child to identify those proprioceptive perceptible internal states and processes that are specific to the emotional state. At the same time, however, due to the marking, the "mirroring" acquires an affect-regulating function insofar as—after the analysis of the conditionality—it provides the child, inter alia, with the possibility of gaining a certain control over the facial expression of the reference person, a control that is judged positively and that all too happily leads to a reciprocating smile.[94]

The starting point of this first phase is, first of all, a sufficiently stable correlation between (predominantly mimetic) *forms of behavior* that both the child and the adult are able and (partially) disposed to engage in.[95] However, in connection with the sensory identification of inner states, this correlation is expanded for the child so that it learns, with the occurrence of inner states of the affective states, *to expect* the corresponding parental facial expression. For if we can assume that the child has a basic capacity to learn, we can also assume that, when the correlations between its experience and the marked parental responsive behaviors stabilize, the child comes to expect the responsive behavior when it experiences the affects. The way in which these expectations are cognitively achieved—i.e., whether the child forms motoric or visual representations of the responsive behavior—can remain an open question; for the competence to form expectations, we do not presuppose a capability beyond what we expect for higher animals and that we could also describe with the concepts of operant conditioning or within the framework of connectionist models. However, the two elements introduced—i.e., of expectations and representations of the inner causes of the external responsive behavior—are of central importance for further developments. For, on the one hand, these elements can be understood as models for states that can be analyzed in terms of conditions of satisfaction, that is, as models for A-intentional states (see phase 2). On the other hand, under the assumptions that the responsive behavior is engaged in by *both* communication partners and that the communication can be analyzed in terms of effects, it may be possible to expand the means of communication in line with these effects.

In contrast to most externalist theories of mind, the view that is portrayed in the first phase of the four-phase model does not presume that the original material with the help of which the reference of mind to its states is to be organized is made available to the child by linguistically competent adults or by training; rather, I assume that the child itself brings the initial material to the interaction situation, that is, the types of behavior that serve as means of communication. Here, the connection between the expressive behavior of the child and what the behavior expresses is generated not by an interpretation, but by a genetically anchored disposition. However, with the help of external social responses, the child first learns to perceive what its expressive behavior articulates, which the child is disposed to effectuate; in the course of forming expectations, the internalization of this makes a rudimentary form of self-reference possible, which would be much more fragile if the noted constraints did not underlie the expressive means. As limited as these means are, they form the basis for an increasingly plastic and increasingly rich inventory of means of communication.

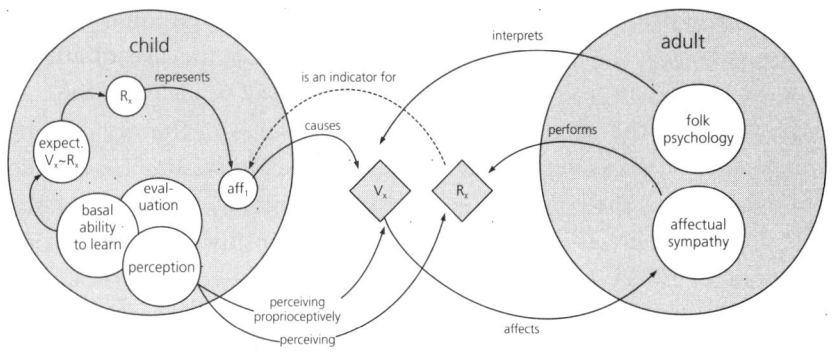

FIGURE 3.1 The development of intentionality: Phase 1

Before I go into these reflections further in the next phase, the scheme of the relations of phase 1 in figure 3.1 should make them more vivid.

PHASE 2: INSTRUMENTAL COMMUNICATION

In the second phase we can broaden the relations that were established in phase 1 such that A-intentional states are integrated into communication. Here we have, in turn, two options. We can assume (like Searle, Dretske, and Millikan) that A-intentional states are biological phenomena, which can be assumed to exist among higher forms of life and can be explained. If we do this, we must then only concern ourselves with integrating them into the already established communicative structures. The second option, in contrast, would consist in placing the existence of A-intentional states in a genetic relationship with the affect-centered communication of phase 1. However, the model that I would like to introduce here is tolerant toward both of these options, and it thus need not make decisions in advance about whether the basis communication of phase 1 is a prerequisite for A-intentionality or not. For there is no reason not to give A-intentional states within the model the same position that the basis affects have in phase 1, as causes of certain forms of behavior of the child. Within the framework of the phase model, we can assume here that the pattern of generating expectations that is established in phase 1 makes it significantly easier to integrate A-intentional states into communication.

If we take the above-provided characteristics of A-intentional states as a basis,[96] then it is clear that we must assume, as in the case of affects, that these states dispose the child to certain forms of behavior. In the case of protodesires, that would be toward forms of behavior that try to bring about states of affairs in the word that satisfy the protodesire. Here we do not assume that the child has access to the content of this protodesire that goes beyond a specific evaluation pattern positively characterizing that state of affairs in the world that constitutes the conditions of satisfaction of the protodesire and negatively assessing a state of affairs in the world that deviates from it. Because, by nature, the means available to small children to fulfill their protodesires are pretty straightforward—the desired things are out of their reach, etc.—there will be numerous activities that fail to fulfill the desires and that will be emotionally assessed correspondingly. If adult reference persons interpret complexes of instrumental activities and emotional evaluations not as resulting solely from their own emotional sympathy, but—because of their folk-psychological competencies—view them as attempts of the child to fulfill a (proto-)desire and to articulate when it has failed to do so, then they can try to bring about the state of affairs that they think is the condition of satisfaction for the nonlinguistic desire of the child. If adults do this correctly often enough, then the activity of the child that is steered by A-intentionality becomes, in the view of the adults, a reliable indicator of the A-intentional state. However, if, in connection with a child's behavior, an adult frequently enough establishes the conditions of satisfaction for the supposed desire, then the reaction pattern of the adult provides empirical material for the child's analysis of conditionality, which is related to the material produced by the parents' mirroring behavior insofar as it allows the child to isolate sufficient quasi-symbolic forms of behavior. Let us assume, for example, that a child wants to be held, that is, it has a protodesire that cannot be fulfilled without the active help of the adult. Then an early form of behavior that is caused by this nonlinguistic desire might consist in an attempt to climb onto the adult, and the articulation of not having achieved this goal might consist in whining. If the adult interprets this behavior to be the result of the aforementioned desire, then with sufficient frequency (though naturally not always), she will do precisely what the child, according to her interpretation, wants. Assuming this, the child's analysis of the conditionality will be able to identify a leaner form of behavior that is sufficient for the fulfillment of the desire, for example, making noise and stretching out its arms toward the adult. If now this behavior leads the reference person to do what the child wants with sufficient frequency, then *the mental representation of this observable implementing action (a mental representation that is anticipated in the course of expectation) indicates precisely the content of the A-intentional state* that the child finds itself in. In other words, *the mental anticipation of the implementing action represents the conditions of satisfaction of the A-intentional state.*[97]

This, however, does not at all completely describe the specifics of phase 2; for, besides the integration of A-intentional states, a further productive problem arises in our model. In contrast to phase 1—in which essentially only the five basic affects serve as causes of the childlike forms of behavior and, via sympathy, the parental reactions—with A-intentional states diverse causes for childlike behavior are added. For the A-intentional states are at least as multifaceted as the things that the child would like to have and the states or events that it would like to bring about. However, this diversity is what makes it necessary that the expressive behavior of a child should be correspondingly sophisticated if the chances for satisfying the A-intentional states are to keep step with the differentiations. However, in the example above, the strategy with the help of which it becomes possible to articulate more differentiated A-intentional states is succinctly sketched out. If we assume that there are numerous situations in which the child remains dependent on the implementing action of adults, then the child's analysis in cases like wanting to have x, wanting to have y, etc., leads to a reduction of the variety of forms of behavior. There ends up being only one, which has the same outcome in all of these cases: it consists, namely, in arousing the attention of the adult and *pointing* to x or y.

With pointing behavior, the child has found a form of articulation that stands at the threshold of medial forms of articulation; the practice of pointing can be described as the use of a medium whose medial configurations are composed of a type of arm/hand movement and directions; here, what a token of such a protomedial form of behavior refers to covaries depending on the direction in which the child points. In this way, the articulation is differentiated at the same time that the application context is universalized.

If the mechanisms of phase 2 are established, interpreters can understand the behavior of children relative to their A-intentional states as *choices of expressive means*, which if performed under the given social

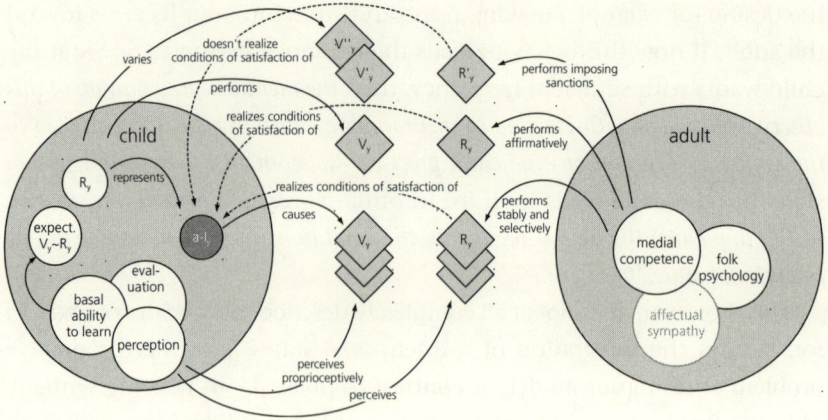

FIGURE 3.2 The development of intentionality: Phase 2

conditions, makes it more probable that these states will be fulfilled. But the children do not yet choose these means on the basis of reflection about adequacy, which would imply a second-order relation to the A-intentional states: they have rather a disposition to use an expressive resource, which they have learned to partially control. Now, how can the decisive transition to a higher level be reconstructed? Thus far we have only prepared *one* element of this higher level, namely, that of socially conveyed representational access to one's own intentional states. A further attribute of the higher level—namely, the ability to autonomously individuate intentional states—marks the attainment of higher intentionality; this will be introduced in the next phase. Figure 3.2 makes the essential structures of the (earlier) phase 2 somewhat more vivid.

PHASE 3: MEDIAL COMMUNICATION OR THE DEVELOPMENT OF
B-INTENTIONALITY

In the phase of instrumental communication in essence the expressive behavior of children is oriented toward achieving states of affairs in the world that, from the perspective of A-intentional states, have the status of conditions of satisfaction; in contrast, a basic characteristic of phase 3 consists, among other things, in the fact that the communicative acts have conditions of satisfaction that, for their part, are communicative acts. Merely in order to have a name, I initially call this type of intentional state "B-intentional." What is specific for these states ought to become clear as we pass through phase 3. From the perspective of communication acts that are oriented toward communicative responses, those addressed by such medial acts are not those who implement the states of affairs in the world that A-intentional states are oriented to bringing about; rather, they are beings *whose expressive (medial) reactions constitute the conditions of satisfaction for B-intentional states.* In a certain respect, phase 3 is concerned with a communication for communication's sake; here elements of phase 1 will be further developed and elements of phase 4 will be prepared, which, for their part, can be understood as further developments of pointing. However, before this will be comprehensible, an analysis, carried out in several small steps, needs to show how this is possible.

In the first phase, with the help of affect "mirroring," an initially external representation, and later an internal representation (via expectations), of internal states is developed with the help of which a first step beyond a mere phenomenal experience is possible. In contrast, in the reconstruction of phase 2, we have laid open a *self-controlled* form of articulation, even if the states that are articulated are not under the control of the child. Under these assumptions, the characteristic of phase 3 can initially be described as a new combination of these elements; here the ability to control expressive resources is not in the service of A-intentional states, but in the service of articulating emotional states, an articulation that is successful if the expression is shared by the addressee. While the basis of phase 2 is constituted by the correlation between childlike expressions and parental reactions that are actions for implementing A-intentional states, the B-intentional states of phase 3 are oriented to those reactions of the parents that, in phase 2, appear as epiphenomena of the interaction. On the one hand, of course, these reactions are linguistic (see phase 4); on the other hand, however, they are also mimetic, gestural, prosodic, onomatopoeic, etc., and they accompany many of the occurring or absent implementing actions. Unlike the reactions that are linguistic in a narrower sense, these articulations primarily aim to produce effects in the children. They are not supposed to be understood like linguistic expressions, but should structure and modify the experiences of children by accompanying aspects of certain situations with medial expressions—for example, by accompanying the lifting of the child with the expression "uha!" or "uupsa!" or by noting when the baby is tired, "ve-e-e-ry ti-i-i-red." What is interesting about these expressions is not that they—like the last one—can have a linguistic meaning; it is rather the effect of the expression on the child.[98] With such expressions the parents in a certain respect interpret the experiences of their children by producing medial expressions whose effects on themselves fit the experience imputed to the children. If we assume that parents perform these expressions—which are formed with the help of (ad hoc) media—with sufficient frequency in the appropriate situations, then we can assume that the children associate types of experiences with types of expressions, that is, they connect the medial expressions with those experiences that have occurred in the contexts in which the medial expressions have been introduced.

A further decisive step for the development of B-intentional states can be made plausible if we assume that children have the natural disposition to imitate the behavior of adults and thereby especially attempt to imitate their medial expressions. If this is the case, then children and their parents exchange the roles of producers and recipients, and the children can expect their performative acts to illicit the symptoms of those effects from their recipients that they normally experience if they perceive the corresponding expressions.

If one takes into consideration the structures of the communication situation that are possible under the mentioned assumptions, then it is striking that the proposed reconstruction exhibits a series of basic parallels to Dewey's reconstruction of aesthetic communication.[99] As noted, Dewey characterized the specificities of aesthetic communication situations by, on the one hand, labeling the aesthetic production a form of articulation whereby producers try to *anticipate* its effects on the recipients; on the other hand, he described the reception of a (nonlinguistic) articulation against the background of communicative intentions attributed to the producer. Above all, Dewey's analysis of the producer's perspective can be of use to us in reference to a nonlinguistic communication situation between adults and children who do not yet have thoughts; for our scenario indeed allows that the adults play the role of producers with fully developed intentionality. In conformity with the above assumptions, let us suppose the following situation. In the eyes of the adults, the child is making an uneasy, frightened impression. In the face of this, the adult sings the child something calming. Here the adult anticipates the effects that singing in one way or another (quiet, soft articulation, slow tempo, repetitive structure, somewhat ritardando) will (hopefully) have on the child, and she anticipates this reaction by viewing her own standard reaction to singing in these forms as the model. The adult thus uses means that she has available because of her socialization in a musical culture in the attempt to produce the effects in her recipient that these means normally produce in herself.

In a further, but not necessarily temporally later, step, from the perspective of aesthetic production, we can now view the child as the producer: here we of course are not allowed to assume the higher-level intentionality that is to be developed. Under this constraint, there is no problem, however, in assuming that children observe the effects their imitating or spontaneous nonlinguistic articulations have on the adults and correlate those effects—in the case of imitation—with the effects that the parental articulations commonly have on themselves or—in the case of spontaneous articulations—with the effects that articulations have on them.

Even if such interactions may initially be fragile, mechanisms for stabilizing communication in this phase, in which communication is centered on expected effects, can be introduced in the form of two interaction patterns that suggest themselves and that only slightly add to the assumptions required; here, however, they are neutral with a view to the mental competencies that we assume the child has. For, first, we can assume that the adults maintain relatively *stable* reactions to the children's articulations. Here we can either assume that the reactions of the adults *are* relatively stable because of their own socialization history or we can assume that the adults artificially stabilize their reactions in order to improve the chances that the child will be able to form expectations about the reactions.[100] Irrespective of how the relative constancy of the reaction comes about, it forms the basis on which the children can establish stable expectations—connected with internal perceptions—regarding the effects of performances on others. Second, however, we can also expect that over time the adults increasingly link their reactions[101] to conditions for conformity such that their reactions are reinforced if the children make use of means of articulation that the adults (with a lot of goodwill) are able to identify as instantiations of sequences of medial elements of those media that they also make use of in their articulating behavior. If one assumes that children have an interest$_i$ in these reactions (insofar as they confirm their expectations), then we can expect that they optimize their articulations with a view to the benefits of the reactions and in doing so increasingly fulfill the standards that regulate the articulation practices of the adults.[102]

The basic idea of the third phase—with the help of which it is to be explained how children develop the ability to consciously individuate intentional states and in doing so reach a first level of higher intentionality—is to enable them, within a responsive social framework, to become producers of the kind of medial expressions that are directed toward them. Of course, to explain the development of those competencies that children must have available to them as medial producers, we cannot take recourse in the explicit forms by which such knowledge is conveyed; this would assume that the children would already have to have competencies of mature interpreters at their disposal. If we want to avoid this assumption, then we have to assume that children, on the one hand, imitate the medial expressions of their parents, but that, on the other hand, they bring about spontaneous variations in the process of doing so. If, for example, the repetition of the childlike performance by the adult, or other observable "interpretive" reactions such as gestures, is connected with such expressions under the described social conditions, but as regular reactions, then the children can link the performance of types of articulating acts with the expectation that the types of articulating acts with which the parents react will occur.

Following the A-intentional states, B-intentional states are oriented toward external reactions, but they do not aim at those reactions that lead to changes in the world. Rather—following affect-centered communication—they are aimed at changes related to the expressive behavior of the parents. The conditions of satisfaction of B-intentional states are not states of affairs in the world in general; rather, they consist initially in the expressive behavior of the recipient, caused by the expression. With this unspectacular step a new level of development is reached insofar as, above all, expressions now relate to expressions. In this type of a communication situation, a relation is thereby achieved at the level of expressions that, at the level of mental states, constitutes a necessary characteristic of our concept of a higher-order mental state: namely, the relationship of one mental state to another mental state. With a view to the existence of thoughts, it is of decisive importance that this relationship exists within *one* mind. But in any case, herewith and with a division of labor, we have achieved by means of the proposed reconstruction a form of the relation of expressions to expressions and indeed of expressions that are caused by mental states.

In two concluding steps, I would now like to investigate how these constraints can be sublated in phase 3 so that it is possible for the child to relate a mental state that is the cause of an expression to another mental state, which anticipates—as an expectation—the effect of the expression. To do this, on the one hand, the competence of the child to produce medial expressions, not only spontaneously or in imitation, but also "systematically," must be developed (this will be discussed in [a] below); on the other hand, so must the ability to inhibit the performance of the expressions (see [b]).

a. In regard to an increasingly orderly production of medial expressions, we can assume that, at the beginning, the parents secure a correlation between spontaneous childlike expressions and their own expressions by imitating the expressions of the child. Little by little, by imitation, the child takes elements of the parental expressions into its repertoire so that at a certain point it approximates the medial expressions. If the parents now make their own responsive practices increasingly dependent on the child expressing itself in a way that conforms to the internal structures of the parental media, and here increasingly also make use of responses that conform to their own media standards, then we can expect the mechanism of conditionality analysis to isolate elements of the childlike articulation practice that more frequently lead to a responsive behavior.

We can thus assume that the ability of the child to construct expressions by combining elements that result in rewarding reactions from the parents is conveyed in the course of analyzing the practical consequences of communicative action until the competencies of reproducing the internal structure have been passed over to the child. With these reflections we have gained a further element for the reconstruction of (nonlinguistic) higher intentionality, namely, stabilized relations between standardized types of articulation and reactions, which form the basis for expectations that connect with inner states and acts of articulation. These expectations are, first of all, primarily related to the behavior of communication partners and not to third parties outside of this dyadic relation. Relations of this sort form the basis for the development of higher intentionality insofar as, in the process of forming expectations, the expressive tokens obtain satisfying conditions, which *they acquire solely through and in a communicative process*. Unlike Searle, we thus do not need to assume that mind "intentionally" assigns nonintentional phenomena, such as expressions, conditions of satisfaction of intrinsic-intentional states; rather, we can assume that expressions obtain conditions of satisfaction in the form of expected reactions.

If a child can, with variation, actualize combinations of elements of a medium and can form expectations about the reactions that occur among the recipients, it is able to individuate simple B-intentional states. These states have an identity insofar as there are alternatives to them that can be generated by varying medial elements or parameters; they therefore have a *compositional identity*. From here, it is only a further step to inhibiting the performance, and in doing so, to having an imaginative anticipation of the effects at one's disposal so as to think a *nonlinguistic* thought.

b. How it is possible that children learn to inhibit expressions and to perform them *in foro interno* is a question that cannot even begin to be adequately addressed here; it is in the last analysis an empirical question. In the context of this model, I thus will limit myself to showing that it is plausible that an explanation of this ability need not bring intentional states into play that go beyond the level of B-intentional states. In the end, I thus only attempt to show the plausibility that thoughts, which solely exhibit compositional identity, are not dependent on propositional states to be actualized, and consequently that already at the level of B-intentional states all of the general characteristics of thoughts can be satisfied. The explanation that we are seeking must provide the transition, for example, from the ability to sing something to the ability to merely imagine singing it. If we observe how children learn to read silently, we can assume that this ability is simply acquired as the steering of an activity that was initially only able to be carried out publicly becomes more encompassing in the sense that control over the execution of the activity includes, little by little, the repression of the motoric expression. However, the increasing independence of the child from external addressees is more important than this increase in motoric control: while at the beginning of phase 3 we assumed that, by means of the reactions of the recipients of its expression, the child develops the ability to relate to the effects that the expression has on it, we can now assume that, in the process of forming expectations, step by step the child internalizes the views of external recipients and in this way can correlate medial expressions with the effects they have on it, effects it learned to isolate with the help of the recipients' reactions.

To what degree does the ability to think nonlinguistic thoughts indicate a form of *higher-level* intentionality? An initial indication that nonlinguistically individuated thoughts possess a new status is the fact that we cannot characterize these mental states as intrinsically intentional; they do not have their content as intrinsic conditions of satisfaction, but because they create a disposition to behavior that, under certain social conditions, can structure the perception and the experience of the recipients. They do not acquire intentionality because mind transfers the conditions of satisfaction of an A-intentional state to them; instead, they have content that is dependent on a social context because specific medial configurations trigger certain partially observable effects in the recipients (including the producers), effects that, in the process of forming expectations, are linked to the performance of the configurations. To the degree that the child, with the help of reactions to its spontaneous or imitating articulations, manages—with conditionality analysis—to isolate those internal states that are sufficient or necessary conditions for the occurrence of these reactions, its articulations acquire content that is initially determined largely in dependence on the reaction of the recipients. And to the degree to which the child can anticipate this reaction, and thereby can internalize the external observer, the content of the B-intentional state is determined by the experience of the performance of that expression toward which the state is disposed. This content, however, is content *for* the child; it is accessible to the child insofar as it is able to arbitrarily bring about medial expressions. It can bring about actions that can be generated on the basis of clear, easy-to-remember alternatives and that can be described as productive selective actions insofar as the expressive actions synthesize something whose content cannot be individuated by other means than the identification of a medial configuration. As a medial expression, this provides an offer for structuring the perception of the recipients and replicating it (internally); the recipient is in a position to do these things because of her own medial competence. Herewith it is possible to communicate medial individuated configurations: one and the same B-intentional thought can be thought by different persons just as two persons can have one and the same belief. Unlike the content of a belief, however, its content is as individual as the experience of the medial expression.

The fundamental pattern that is exposed in phase 3 also remains basic for advanced forms of medial communication, which exist in their most

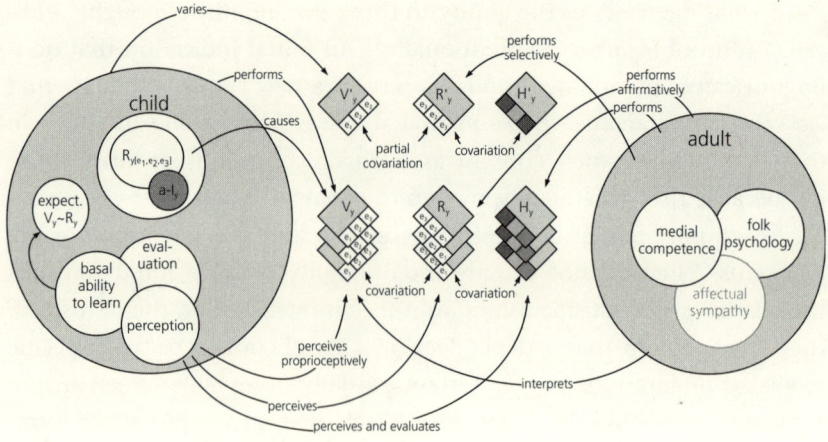

FIGURE 3.3 The development of intentionality: Phase 3

developed form as art, even if a part of the sophistication of media and of medial strategies is not conceivable without the occurrence of language. For even the developed medial communication remains related to a level of the differentiation and the structuring of perception and experience, which is developed in phase 3 for the first time. As states with a compositional identity within the scope of possibilities of a medium, B-intentional states are states that could not be individuated by the beings that have them without the appropriate media, nor could those beings understand them within the framework of the reception of medial expressions—that is, replicate them internally—without the appropriate media (see figure 3.3).[103]

PHASE 4: LINGUISTIC COMMUNICATION OR THE DEVELOPMENT
OF C-INTENTIONALITY

With phase 4 we finally reach the level of intentional states whose content has a propositional form; that is, we reach the level of those states whose identity and content can be provided by means of the standard interpretationist theory with recourse to their position in an inferentially structured network. Here it is clear that inferential networks are constituted by certain normative relations, which, in the final analysis, are based on the truth-aptness of many elements of such networks. In the context of these reflections I will not go further into whether the specifics of these C-intentional states ought rather to be described with a Davidsonian or a Brandomian vocabulary. Within the framework of the four-phase model, I can limit myself to explaining how the level of C-intentionality behaves in a genetic respect to the preceding forms of intentionality.

If we explain the specifics of B-intentional states at a fundamental level by maintaining that they are states that have a compositional identity, then C-intentional states can be understood as a level at which medial expressions (or B-intentional states) are linked in a network of normative relations, and indeed the type of normative relations that a radical interpreter assumes if she correlates expressions of a being with states of affairs and other expressions of this being. However, herewith something comes into play at the level of propositional attitudes that opens the primarily dyadic communication of level 3 to the world and thus to objectivity. Relations among medial expressions and experiences of the producers and recipients of the expressions are no longer in the foreground; instead, relations between medial expressions and states of affairs in the world are. While I could take recourse in the communicative structures of affect-centered communication in order to introduce the B-intentional states, the development of propositional states can be explained, on the one hand, with recourse to structures of instrumental communication, on the other hand, however, also with recourse to the mechanisms of medial communication. For basic forms of linguistic communication can be described against the background of the preceding phases as forms of communication in which the reference to the world—which comes to expression at the level of instrumental communication through pointing—is differentiated and explicitly articulated with the medial means developed in phase 3.

The basic idea for the characterization of *linguistic* communication thus ought to be that some of the introduced medial expressions acquire *new roles* that are increasingly subject to normative restrictions in the course of the development. Hereby the normatively determined roles acquire a dominant status; this is expressed in the fact that the compositional identity is subordinated to the interpretability of linguistic expressions. Insofar, namely, as an interpreter of linguistic expressions must assume that the speaker fulfills the demands of minimal rationality, she places the expressions in a normative context in which they can play the role of declarations, desires, commands, etc. While the compositional identity of nonlinguistic expressions remains related to experience, in linguistic utterances it comes to the service of the content-avouching power of normative relations that must therefore also come to the fore in the explanation.

If we first of all begin by viewing language as a medium in the sense of phase 3 and, accordingly, viewing linguistic communication as a form of medial communication, then the difference between B- and C-intentional states can be made clear—or each of them, with their related type of expression, can be made clear—if we call to mind a communicative use of language that is caused by B-intentional states. Hereby we would, so to say, assume that, in this linguistic communication, people speak in the same way that they make music in musical communication. A use of language of this sort (which to our ears sounds "inauthentic") can be clarified in an exemplary way in reference to onomatopoeic linguistic usages, which appear to be enclaves of medial communication from phase 3. For these usages are oriented on experience that is generated by the pronunciation or hearing of onomatopoeic statements by a speaker or hearer, an experience that exhibits structural perceptual similarities with the experience to which the expression is a reaction.[104] However, as a rule precisely these relations between attributes of linguistic expressions that are amenable to sense experience and those of expression situations (*Äußerungssituationen*) are of subordinate importance for the specific possibilities of language; they serve—as in the example of prosody—rather to lessen the ambiguity of meanings that are already in play independently of these relations.[105]

Unlike the contents of B-intentional states and of the expressions caused by them, linguistic utterances have content that is prototypically not determined in the relation between the expression and the sense experience of the expression (or the sense experience of the social consequences of the expression), but in other relations. The central characteristic of linguistic utterances, the fact that they can play a role in the game of giving and asking for reasons, is based rather on a relation that is accessible to all participants of linguistic communication, namely a relation between expressive *actions* (*Äußerungshandlungen*) and intersubjectively accessible expressive *circumstances* (*Äußerungsumständen*). To the degree that the expressive actions are assumed to meet conditions of appropriateness, whose fulfillment can be intersubjectively examined, expressions are subject to normative demands; this is fundamental for their ability to articulate reasons.

If we place these reflections in the context of a genetic perspective, then we can proceed by linking the reference to states of affairs in the world, which already exists at the level of A-intentional states, with medial expressions so that following up the pointing actions of phase 2, the medial expressions are linked with *social fulfillment circumstances* (*soziale Erfüllungsumstände*). If we thus assume a child that can perform the pointing actions of phase 2 and the medial expressions of phase 3, and further assume that among its A-intentional states there are certainly some, perhaps many, the conditions of satisfaction of which the child itself cannot actualize, then we obtain an interface for expanding the inventory of pointing actions if we assume that the social environment of the child treats some of its medial expressions as substitutes for pointing actions, for example, according to the following pattern: on the one hand, the parental interpreters establish stable relations between types of expressive actions and actions that *achieve* the putative conditions of satisfaction of the child's A-intentional states; on the other hand, they establish relations between types of expressive actions and actions that *do not achieve* the putative conditions of satisfaction of the child's A-intentional states. Here the types of expressive action employed by the parents are constituted such that the child can instantiate these types of action by itself. If these prerequisites are fulfilled, the child will develop the disposition to perform an expressive action that instantiates the type of expression that correlates with the implementing action if the child finds itself in an A-intentional state with conditions of satisfaction that it cannot fulfill by itself, but that it can imagine in the form of the expected implementing action.[106] With the parental expressive actions, however, at the same time the pool of expectable reactive actions (*Reaktionshandlungen*) is broadened so that types of parental expressive action can come to indicate types of parental implementing action. To the degree that children manage to perform tokens of parental expressive actions, they manage to *articulate* the content of the A-intentional states for which the expressive actions indicate conditions of satisfaction. Admittedly—and this is the contribution of the development in phase 3—the types of expressions do not enter into a relation with the implementing actions as monolithic unities, but as medially structured so that modifications of the internal structure can covary with the modifications of the connecting actions (*Anschlusshandlungen*).

If, in the face of this analysis of Searle's discussion—that an expression obtains meaning when mind arbitrarily confers to it those conditions of satisfaction that a mental state has—we can then modify this manner of speaking in order to avoid the above exposed difficulties so that we say an expression has content by virtue of the fact that the recipient of the expression confers content to it by reliably reacting to this expression in a certain manner. Here the reliable reactions, for their part, are the basis on which the one expressing herself forms expectations. In contrast to the process of establishing reaction expectations in the context of phase 3, in cases of linguistic utterances, we assume that the expectations are related to reactions that bring about observable states of affairs in the world, or that assume the existence of such states, that is, states that A-intentional states are typically oriented toward. In contrast to the nonlinguistic medial expressions, the fulfillment of the conditions of satisfaction for linguistic expressions is accessible to intersubjective examination. For unlike the medial responsive behavior of the adults in phase 3, which of course also brings about events in the world, the states of affairs in the world that are the conditions of satisfaction for linguistic utterances are prototypically states that can be observed from both communication partners *in the same way*. Because, on the basis of A-intentionality and the means of medial communication, something comes about that we could call a triangulation, and it is thus possible to connect the use of linguistic expressions that intrinsically lack content to the existence of conditions of satisfaction that can be intersubjectively examined, it is possible to individuate content with normative relations.

The four-phase model that is suggested here assumes that inhibited or implemented medial articulations must have a compositional identity *before* they can obtain an inferential content. It thus appears that this analysis competes with the Fregean (and Davidsonian) conception of the compositionality of language. For while Frege deduces the structure of language from the contribution of sentence components to the truth functionality of the sentence, here the thesis is that the compositional identity of expressions is more basic than the contribution of the sentence components for the truth functionality of an utterance. It is, however, important to see that, on the one hand, this is concerned with a genetic primacy that is still reconcilable with the theoretical primacy of the sentence, and that, on the other, as a theoretical primacy, remains limited to the context of nonlinguistic communication.[107] For the framework of the four-phase model, one specificity of linguistic utterances is that normative relations steer the medial possibilities by subjecting the scope of possibilities of a medium to inferential relations.

The result of phase 4 is a form of communication in which the medial expressions take on roles that are lent to them because they obtain the status of claims, promises, and orders in the context of social interactions. Those medial expressions that have truth conditions or conditions of satisfaction are linguistic utterances, and those states that can be described as inhibiting medial expressions with conditions of satisfaction are linguistic thoughts.

Of course, the model that is proposed here does not claim to be able to explain a linear history of the development of higher intentionality. It is especially important that the impression not arise that every higher level presupposes the *completion* of the one preceding it; for a realistic view of the development would certainly have to expect that the development of phase-specific competencies are also interlocked with one another. This model would fulfill its goal if it could provide an answer to the question of how it is possible that (biologically sufficiently complex) beings develop a mind under certain social conditions without thereby having to presuppose capabilities at the beginning of the development whose development is precisely what is to be explained and without thereby reducing mind to a phenomenon that is completely able to be causally or functionally described. The model attempts to balance two strategies that Brandom respectively calls "assimilationist" and "exceptionalist."[108] For while, from the bottom up, a continuity with the representationalist vocabulary is sought (the level A-intentionality), for the two stages of higher intentionality the exceptionalist motif that emphasizes the specific difference between thoughts and intrinsic-intentional states is fundamental. Here the content of nonlinguistic and linguistic thoughts is owed to social practices that are erected on natural foundations, but that become unfixed from these to the degree that communicative acts are structured by typified performances that are intrinsically free of content.

3.2.2.4. A More Comprehensive View of Intentionality

One goal of these overflowing reflections has been to develop a view of intentionality and thinking that provides a place for the possibility of understanding thinking as something that is not thoroughly linguistically constituted, without getting entangled in the shallowness of phenomenological introspectionism and without losing sight of the specificities of mind by following a radical naturalization strategy. I have suggested dividing the set of intentional phenomena into the class of functionalistically determinable intrinsic-intentional states and the class of higher intentional states that I also call thoughts. I have related the existence of thoughts, regardless of whether these are linguistic or nonlinguistic, to three conditions that the beings that have thoughts can only acquire socially. The ability of a being to think thoughts is presented, in this perspective, as a capability to internalize processes that are initially actualized as social processes. Here two developmental lines run parallel in which performative competencies and interpretive competencies are developed by internalizing relations between the performances and (interpretive) forms of reaction. In the course of this process, beings that are socialized in a medial practice acquire

1. the ability to *individuate performances* consisting of medial elements by synthesis;
2. the ability to *anticipate the reaction* of a recipient to their medial performances; and
3. the ability to inhibit a performance.

While the first condition guarantees that the performance of a medial constellation has the status of an action insofar as, in each performance within a medium, the being also has had socially conveyed alternatives available that could have been chosen from, the second condition ensures that the content-lending correlations of the medial constellation are connected to sufficiently stable social reactions that are, however, in principle malleable and covary with the compositional identity of the constellation. The specificities of the correlations cannot be comprehended in the concepts of natural law or functionalism. Finally, the third condition can only be fulfilled if a being is practiced in medial performance practices so that routines emerge for performing medial elements (and constellations). The following conditions that come about in the process of socialization form the background of this reconstruction: the standardization of expressive behaviors, the standardization of reactions to norm-conforming expressive behaviors, as well as the varying and consequently individualizing of the expressive behaviors within a norm-conforming framework.[109] If we assume the existence of these capabilities, then the following basic definition of thinking can be provided, which is not limited to linguistic thoughts:

> (ND) Thinking is the individuating of an inhibited, medial performance within the scope of possibilities of a medium, whose effects on potential recipients of the performance are anticipated.

Every mental state that is individuated in a manner sufficient to (ND) is—unlike A-intentional states—a higher mental state that has content and an identity for the being that individuates such a state. Such a state has an *identity* for this being insofar as it must be able to bring about this state using a mental operation that can be described as an inhibited medial performance. For that being, each of these states is thus a state for which there are alternatives relative to which the existing state has an identity. Such a state has *content* insofar as the being that individuates it assumes an interpretive relation toward it which prototypically is an anticipation of the (medial) reaction(s) of recipients of the medial constellation, but it can later also assume the form of the reception by the producer.[110] If this analysis is plausible, then we can say that besides linguistic thoughts, nonlinguistic medial mental states are also one kind of higher-level intentional state. For both types of states can only be individuated with the help of means that, for their part, are not already intrinsic-intentional and that must be kept in existence[111] in a social interpretation practice.

Before I finally go into the question of whether nonlinguistic thought can be understood in this sense as second-order intentional states, and thus fulfill Davidson's second-order criterion, I will provide a summary of the types of intentional states that I have established in the preceding reflections as theoretical entities of an expanded interpretationism. I propose differentiating between three types of mental states with content:

(AI) A-intentional (intrinsic-intentional) states

   a. The ascription of A-intentional states is legitimate from the perspective of the interpreter if the interpreter's explanation of a particular behavior must assume that the being that is to be interpreted (*B*) has at its disposal nonlinguistic representations not only of existing states of affairs of the world, but also of *nonexisting* states of affairs, and these representations are the causes for *B*'s behavior. A-intentional states dispose the beings that have them to differentially respond to their environment. Here the differentiating behavior must be such that it orients itself in reference to internal criteria$_i$ so that these criteria$_i$ provide an explanation of the behavior in the sense that they identify a state of affairs in the world and the behavior can be understood as bringing about exactly that state.
   b. The A-intentional states befall the beings that have them. A being whose most developed mental states are A-intentional states does not have the possibility to refer to these states. In other words, the content of A-intentional states is never another intentional state. If a being finds itself in an A-intentional state I_{a1}, there is no reason for a change to a state I_{a2}; there are only causes.
   c. A-intentional states are *intrinsic-intentional*, that is, they are not intentional by virtue of a (self-)interpretation. They have content that an interpreter can rightly ascribe to them on the basis of the behavior of *B*, but they have no content *for* the being that has the ascribed A-intentional states.
   d. A-intentional states occupy a position between those mental states that we call perceptions and those mental states that we call thoughts. They share with perceptions the intrinsic relationship to a content that we can imagine is conveyed through functional mechanisms; they share with thoughts (B- and C-intentional states) the individuation in relations that are characterized by rightness or appropriateness, but that in the case of A-intentional states can be completely naturalized.[112]

(BI) B-intentional ("medial intentional") states, in contrast, are states that beings impute content to when, in performing the acts that these states dispose them toward, they assume an interpretive relation toward them.

a. B-intentional states assume that behavioral alternatives are available; here, these behavioral alternatives *are not thought to be intrinsic-intentional*.
b. A B-intentional state I_b is individuated in such a way that this individuation can be steered by B insofar as B is able to implement constellations of intrinsically empty behavioral alternatives (and to inhibit the performance of these).
c. I_b has a compositional *identity* that provides its position in the scope of possibilities of a medium.
d. I_b has *content* for B because B correlates I_b with another mental state, prototypically of a cognitively implemented expectation with regard to the behavior of a recipient (which can be B itself) or an experience.

(CI) C-intentional (propositional-intentional) states are those B-intentional states whose contents are truth-apt for the being who has these states.

A map that I would recommend for orientation in the zoo of mental states would thus look schematically something like figure 3.4.

With the preceding "revisions" in the philosophy of mind, it should be shown to be plausible that we can expect intentional states that are thoughts insofar as they have content and an identity for the being that individuates these states. In a concluding reflection I would now like to examine whether these nonlinguistically individuated B-intentional states fulfill the second-order criterion that Davidson views as foundational for the existence of thoughts. Let us recall: Davidson claimed that only those beings can have thoughts that have the *concept* of thought at their disposal. In doing this, Davidson fixed on a concept of thought that implies a second-order relation such that the being that has a mental state has a thought if and only if it has thoughts about this state—if it, for example, believes that this mental state is true or false.

Davidson's reconstruction of thought as a second-order intentional phenomena has a double function within his theory. On the one hand, the second-order relation guarantees that the contents of thoughts are the products of (self-)*interpretation* of mental states. On the other hand, this move vouches for the possibility of assuming an antirealistic position about the existence of thoughts insofar as the second-order relation ensures that thoughts can be apprehended as theoretical entities of

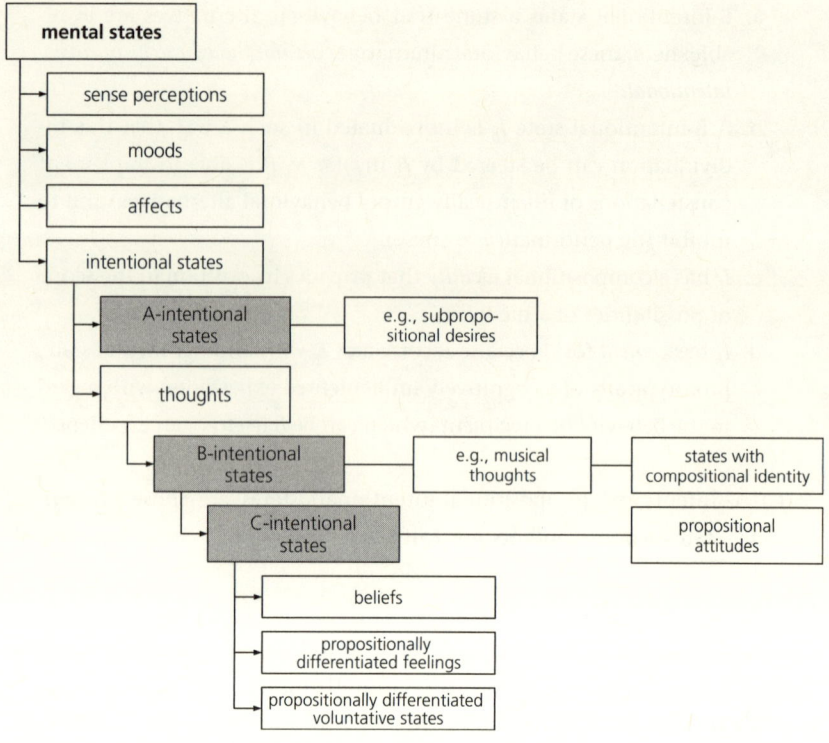

FIGURE 3.4 Types of mental states

(self-)interpretation. Even if one can take a relaxed stance about the ontological question,[113] a position that understands itself as expanding interpretationism must clarify whether there is a higher-order relation that can articulate the content of B-intentional states without thereby having to take recourse in the interpretive resources of a (meta-)*language*.

In principle, two perspectives are available to us to investigate this question. For one, we can question whether it is possible, by means of a nonlinguistic medium M_1, to refer to a B-intentional state that has been individuated in M_1, and indeed in the way that we can refer to a linguistically individuated mental state by means of language. For another, however, we can also examine whether it is possible to articulate the content of an M_1-individuated B-intentional thought by means of a nonlinguistic medium M_2. In both cases we would be able to examine whether nonlinguistic media provide resources with the help of which it is possible to refer to B-intentional states in such a way that their content is articulated.

Because the only medium needed to specify the meaning of a linguistic utterance is the language in which the utterance was generated, and we can thus use any natural language as a metalanguage, the possibility, by means of language, of providing the content of expressions in this language appears precisely to be the formal attribute that makes language a model case of a medium that allows second-order relations to be implemented. If we accept that metalinguistic ability is the standard for the possibility to develop second-order mental phenomena—thus thoughts—then we can only justify the view that nonlinguistic mental states are coequal to these if we can show that nonlinguistic media can also be applied *meta-medially*. Put concretely, can we, for example, refer to music by musical means or refer to painting by the means of painting and in doing this interpret the constellations to which we are referring?

Initially there appears to be no special difficulty connected with the idea that it is possible, for example, to refer to music by musical means; for imitation, citation, and satirizing are established aspects of musical practice. If, for example, we accept Goodman's analysis, we can see that we by no means need exaggerated analogies in order to explain the possibility of citing with the help of nonlinguistic media. From the analysis of linguistic citations, Goodman gains, first of all, two necessary presuppositions for the possibility of citation. Citing must primarily solve two problems: it must include what is cited (in the form of a paraphrase), and it must ensure the reference to what is cited either by naming it or by denoting it through predication.[114] Criteria for direct and indirect citations can now be provided by modifying these necessary conditions: while the direct citation must denominate and incorporate the cited material, indirect citations can also secure the denotation not by explicit denomination, but by predication and guaranteeing the incorporation of what is cited by (nonidentical) paraphrasing.[115] For music and painting, which Goodman discusses as examples of nonlinguistic media, it is indeed necessary that constraints for the possibility of citation are accepted, but the principal possibility of citing is not called into question by these constraints. So in both cases, analogues to the quotation marks of language can be found or thought of.[116] Here, in the case of painting, one must account for the fact that there can be no replications in the sense in which different inscriptions of a word are replications of the word, because works of painting are always unique.[117] As a result of the lack of an analogue to the alphabet and the lack of criteria for the determining that the citation and what is cited are the same, in painting there is no exact analogue to the direct linguistic citation. A theory of musical citation, in contrast, must account for the fact that music usually denotes nothing at all. For this reason, in the framework of music the problem is not with direct citation, but with indirect citation insofar as it is difficult to provide criteria for a musical paraphrase. But the problems of musical citation are restricted to difficulties that can be limited to a certain way of incorporating what is cited into a citation, and these problems do not obviate the possibility of direct citing. Considering these constraints, there is no reason not to assume that in nonlinguistic media it is also possible to refer, by means of a medium, to entities and to those thoughts that are generated by their help.

With a view to the problem of nonlinguistic second-order relations, Goodman's reflections throw light on the fact that it is possible, with the help of nonlinguistic media, to refer to nonlinguistic thoughts insofar as a reference can be organized by means of these media that can be reconstructed as an exemplification of the attributes of a medial constellation. It remains questionable, however, whether this reference plays a constitutive role for the existence of a B-intentional state. For the fact that this reference is possible does not mean that it is necessary for the existence of a B-intentional thought in the same way as having a belief about a propositional state is necessary for the existence of a thought. Davidson apparently links the existence of thought to the following criterion:[118]

(T) P has a thought T if and only if

1. P believes (desires, etc.) S [formal: $(T(P, S)]$ and
2. P believes that P believes (desires, etc.) S [formal: $T(P, G(P, S))$].

Because P, however, can only fulfill the condition (T)(2) if P has the *concept* of belief at her disposal, only those beings can have thoughts that have a language that provides the conceptual means for reference to mental states. If one now confronts B-intentional states with the criterion (T), then the following options are available:

1. We reject criterion (T) or a reformulated variation of (T) for nonlinguistic thoughts.
2. We admit that B-intentional states are only thoughts if a person who thinks them has *linguistic* beliefs about these states.

3. We attempt to develop an *equivalent* to criterion (T) that can be actualized with the help of nonlinguistic media:

   a. by making *medial forms of reference* to B-intentional states the presupposition for the existence of nonlinguistic thoughts; or
   b. by identifying a *general attribute* of B-intentional states that *implies* a certain (perhaps weaker) form of a second-order relation.

What is clear at the outset is that the *first option* has very high costs, for in opposition to the claim that B-intentional states are mental states *for* the being that has them, we must clearly show how this is possible without criterion (T) or a variation of it being fulfilled in her mind. In a certain way, (T) includes the nucleus of an interpretationist theory of mind, that is, a theory that explains the being-*for*-a-being of a mental state using concepts of self-interpretation or self-ascription. The first option is thus simply incompatible with the interpretationist foundation of the theory of conscious medial thoughts proposed here. The *second option* appears to be too defensive insofar as it falls back behind the level of the reflection on the content of nonlinguistic thoughts; after all, these reflections have shown that the content of a medial constellation in the form of an experience that is connected to carrying it out is a content for the being that carries it out. However, we can view the second option as a fallback option for the case in which it can be shown that every form of self-interpretation of mental states is connected with the availability of concepts. We must then accept the idea that B-intentional states are indeed intentional states that a being itself can practically individuate, but whose identity (and content) can only become conscious if identity and content become the object of a propositional attitude. However, a fallback option should only be taken up if it is clear that the attempt to develop an equivalent for the linguistic form of reference to mental states entails insurmountable problems. Let us then first of all consider the *third option* in its two variants.

In the context of its genetic reconstruction, I said that medial expressions (and their B-intentional causes) have content insofar as they are connected with experiences that accompany the performance of medial constellations. If we compare this constitution of content—which is a content *for* the performing being *insofar* as it is this being that has the performance-dependent experiences with the relation that forms the basis of (T)—then the following difference stands out: while, according to Davidson's criterion, consciousness is connected with the fact that a being refers to a propositional state by means of concepts, the content in the context of introducing B-intentional states is ensured by something that indeed is *caused* by a medial performance (namely, the experience), but not by the fact that a medial performance is *interpreted*. Thus the question of concern here is not really whether to cast doubt on whether B-intentional states have content, but whether beings can articulate this content by nonlinguistic means so that the content *in the perspective of the self-interpretation is content for the being that finds itself in a B-intentional state*. According to interpretationist premises, nonlinguistic thoughts would have *content* in a formidable sense for the being that has them only as interpreted intentional states, and it is clear that linguistic interpretations are model cases of such self-interpretations. If then there is to be an interpretation of (T) that is befitting to nonlinguistic thoughts, this criterion (NT) must connect the existence of a nonlinguistic thought to the existence of a nonlinguistic interpretation, and in fact, more precisely, to the existence of a nonlinguistic interpretation of a B-intentional state.

What reasons are there not to view the correlation of two nonlinguistic thoughts as an interpretive relation? What reason is there, for example, not to say that a red-chalk drawing interprets a watercolor or that a dance interprets the content of the piece of music to which it is performed? But it remains questionable—even if this is admitted—whether the possibility of the existence of an interpretive relation between two nonlinguistic thoughts can provide a sufficient basis for the reformulation of (T). This would, namely, take something like the following, unsatisfying form.

(NT_1) P has a nonlinguistic thought M_1 if and only if

1. P thinks M_1; and
2. P thinks M_2; and
3. P thinks that M_2 articulates the content of M_1.

Apart from the fact that a propositional state appears in (NT_1)(3), and (NT_1) could thus not be fulfilled by beings who do not have a language at their disposal, the criterion does not accomplish what (T) does. For (T) not only prescribes that a being must be able to articulate the content of a mental state if a thought is to exist; rather, it prescribes that it also must be able to ascribe this mental state to itself. However, if B-intentional states have no predicative structure, this means that, with the help of a nonlinguistic state, no predication can be carried out in which a being ascribes to itself a mental state. If the interpretive relation is not fundamental in (T), but a *self-ascribing relation*, then it is clear that this relation cannot be produced by nonlinguistic means. And then it is also clear that Davidson's criterion (T) in essence is a much stronger reformulation of the Kantian view that "the *I think* must be *capable* of accompanying all my presentations."[119] In contrast to Kant, Davidson would claim that a mental state *M* is a thought if and only if *M is* accompanied by the "I think."[120] If we assume this interpretation, then the consequence is obvious: it must be accepted that there is no direct nonlinguistic equivalent for the "I think"; insofar as this is the case, B-intentional states are only thoughts if a being ascribes to itself a B-intentional state with the help of the idea "I think," which can only occur with language. In contrast to this, Kant's formulation of a more liberal way of speaking of this would make it possible for B-intentional states to be thoughts, because they can become objects of self-ascription with the help of the "I think," regardless of whether they are this for contingent reasons or not.[121] There is no reason not to say that thoughts like the following are possible:

Regardless of whether one assumes the liberal interpretation (with which I sympathize) or the stricter one, the preceding reflections appear to show that B-intentional states are thoughts, understood as self-ascribed—and thus conscious—thoughts, if the being that has B-intentional states refers to these—or can refer to these—with the help of a self-ascription that can only take place with the help of language. Here, however, it should not be forgotten that the "I think" only *articulates* a difference that this being can make, also without language, namely, the difference between its own states and the states of other beings.

In conclusion, let us examine the option of formulating (3b) as an equivalent for the criterion (T) with the help of general attributes of medially individuated intentional states. An attribute that all B-intentional states share is that—in contrast to A-intentional states—they are states that a being can actively individuate. However, such a being must have a *consciousness* of the optionality of every B-intentional state. A being that does not *know* that there are alternatives to every medial performance *M* does not have a B-intentional thought that is, at the same time, the cause for the performance of M. What reason is there not to view this consciousness of the optionality of B-intentional states as the general attribute, which fulfills the second-order relations in the required manner and then correspondingly to advance the following criterion:

(NT_2) P has a nonlinguistic thought M if and only if

1. P thinks M; and
2. P knows that there are alternatives to M that P could think.

As an objection to (NT_2) one might point to the fact that demand (2) brings a form of knowledge into play that is propositionally differentiated so that (NT_2) increases the dependency of having a thought on having a linguistic thought. Because it is difficult to see how consciousness of the optionality might be implemented in P independently of linguistically articulated knowledge, to retain the idea of (NT_2), only an external ascribing perspective remains available to us:

(NT_3) P has a nonlinguistic thought M if and only if

1. P performs a medial constellation K.
2. Interpreters of the medial performance of P can only understandably explain the performative practices of P by assuming that P individuates her B-intentional states by actualizing constellations within the scope of possibilities of a medium (and in doing so partially exploits these possibilities).
3. The performance of K by P is caused by a B-intentional state to which P had alternatives, as her performance shows.[122]

The following results from our reflections regarding the ability to satisfy the second-order criterion, understood as a self-ascription: self-ascriptions are connected to media in which one can say "I" and thus can articulate a self-reference that is indeed possible at the level of prelinguistic and nonlinguistic thought, but at that level it cannot be the object of a belief or of a thought. We can indeed describe the identity and the content of a nonlinguistic thought as an identity and a content[123] *for* the being that has this thought, but we can only articulate the belief that it has this thought by employing linguistic means. Anyway, this at least is the preliminary conclusion: nonlinguistic thoughts can become the object of a self-ascription so that—if one follows Kant—the status of thoughts cannot be denied to them as long as we do not identify consciousness with self-ascriptions that are *carried out*.

3.2.2.5. Back to the Concert

Based on the difficulties of developing an adequate understanding of artistic action by means of the established theory of action, I have taken to developing a more comprehensive view of mind, employing the means of media theory; this is a view in which nonlinguistic thoughts also have a place. Now it is time to examine whether, by expanding the theory of mind with the help of media theory, a conception for understanding artistic action can be developed that is reconcilable with two basic intuitions, namely, that works of art are not translatable and that they are understandable. To do this, it is necessary to address the question of the adequate form for rationalizing artistic actions as well as the question of the content of nonlinguistic artistic thoughts: for, on the one hand, the gap that was left by the rejection of the common rationalization schemata (H1) must be closed (this is to be taken up in [b] below); on the other hand, it is necessary to examine whether the analysis of nonlinguistic thought employing the concepts of compositional identity does more than provide a technically bogged-down theory ([a] below).

   a. The fact that the identity of a B-intentional state can be explained by media-theoretic means can indeed be viewed as an explicative advance; for in any case we have an identity criterion for nonlinguistic thoughts available. On the other hand, the comparison with propositional attitudes immediately shows that an identity criterion alone is hardly able to account for our expectation that a thought—be it linguistic or not—has content; for even if the identity of a propositional attitude can only be explained in reference to ideas of its inferential position, the entire network of inferential relationships cannot be created without the existence of mental states that have a noninferential content.[124] If the concept of nonlinguistic thought is not to remain pallid, the analysis cannot merely consist in providing identity criteria. Rather, precisely in the context of understanding artistic action, it must be made clear that these thoughts are about something. If the explanation of the structural attributes of works of art did nothing more than analyze their medial identity, it could hardly be plausibly explained why works of art can move us in such specific ways. So, what are B-intentional states concerned with?

If we call to mind the position that B-intentional states assume within the framework of the genetic reconstruction of the four-phase schema, we begin to see the contours that an answer to this question will be able to take. For in a certain respect, medial expressions, which are caused by B-intentional states, take on the position of those communicative, expressive behaviors that articulate affects at the level of affectual communication. However, while the communicative role of the emotional expressive action is ensured by a genetically fixed relation between affects and expressive behavior, the possibility for medial articulation opens up a space for expressing something that surpasses the experience of basic affects, but that is nonetheless an experiencing or perceiving. To determine this experience two perspectives are available: for, on the one hand, it is possible that a person finds herself in a state that disposes her to an (inhibited) performance of certain medial configurations; on the other hand, however, the (inhibited) performance itself can occur as an object of an experience that can be communicated with the help of a medial configuration.

The basic idea for determining the content of a medial constellation, or for determining the corresponding B-intentional state, claims—in agreement with the hypothetical history of its origins—that the function of medial communication consists in the fact that the producer of a medial constellation makes an object of her own experience accessible to the addressee; in this way, it becomes an object of the experience of the recipient. Here, two situations can be distinguished. The producer has an arbitrary experience E_1 and tries to generate a medial constellation that causes an experience E_2 in the receiver, namely, an experience that is sufficiently similar to E_1. If this is successful, then the producer can view the medial constellation as a means of sharing the experience E_1. Another possibility is for the artist to use the medial possibilities of a medium, while in the course of experientially varying and recombining them, to create an object of experience that is of interest, independently of its specific preceding experiences. In both cases, it holds that

(M7) Media are means with the help of which experiences can be communicated.

Unlike the linguistic *descriptions* of experiences, in the course of individuating the *objects* of experience, media allow experiences to be communicated. If this reflection is used to determine the content of a medial constellation, two preliminary definitions result: one is connected to the experience that produces it, and one is more general, giving up the connection to the producer.

> (M8) The content of a medial constellation is the experience that the producer connects to its realization.

> (M9) The content of a medial constellation K is the experience that the reception of K brings about in its recipient.

If we, in turn, use these determinations in order to define the content of a medial-intentional state, we can establish it as follows:

> (CB) The content of a B-intentional state is the experiences that cause the inhibited performance of the medial constellation that the B-intentional states dispose us to perform.

Against the background of these definitions, the portrait of medial communication that we are sketching out describes media as means of communication that open the possibility to overcome the exclusive privacy of experience by structuring these objects on the basis of intersubjectively established alternatives so that the experience can obtain the function of a nonlinguistic interpretation on the basis of those competencies that allow the interpreter to structure the experiences that she has by perceiving medial constellations in line with those intersubjectively shared medial competencies; this is done by reproducing its medial structure. Here it is of decisive importance that this object of experience exhibits a medial structure—i.e., it has a synthetic character—that shows that this structure can covary with the experience and is not an opaque monolithic object. In short, medial communication is the attempt to avert the impossibility of conveying phenomenal experience; this is done by generating constellations—with the help of media—that, as objects of the addressees' experience, should enable the addressees to have an experience that is similar to that of the producer in relative ways if the recipient structures the object in the same way as the producer.[125]

b. Applying this to the problem of the rationalization of artificial actions, the preceding reflections allow a schema to be formulated that, on the one hand, makes it possible to describe artistic activities with the help of a practical syllogism as activities caused by reasons; on the other hand, however, it does not prescribe that each of these reasons be interpreted as an intentional state that is, eo ipso, a propositional attitude. If we can expect that B-intentional states are able to occur as parts of the rationalizations of action, then rationalizations of artistic actions can assume the following form:

(H2)

a. With the help of the possibilities of a medium M_1, P_1 individuates a B-intentional state $I_b(K)$;
b. With the help of the possibilities of a medium M_n, P_1 generates a product whose identity in M_n is subject to the same—or sufficiently similar—conditions of identity as $I_b(K)$ in M_1 ($n \geq 1$);
c. P_1 wants to express $I_b(K)$;
d. Thus: P_1 makes K accessible for another P_n.

Before I evaluate (H2) with a view to the problem of understanding artistic action, I would like to quickly comment on the premises of the syllogism.[126] Premise (a) states essentially that "P_1 thinks a nonlinguistic thought by anticipating and inhibiting the performance of a medial action." At the same time, premise (a) ensures that (H2) is connected to the intuition that works of art are not translatable; for although in (a) only the individuation of a nonlinguistic thought is discussed, the genetic context for introducing B-intentional states places the inhibited individuated medial constellation in the context of those effects that a perceptible actualization of this constellation could have on recipients. However, for the implemented medial configuration that is externally perceptible, it holds, then, that it can have effects that are in an elementary sense connected to the implementation of the configuration in a specific medium, and indeed because these effects do not occur in the recipients' perception in another media. Insofar as the effects on the recipients are intractably connected with the means by which they are generated, all "translations" of the work of art that do not bring about these effects fail. Premise (b) should clearly show that P_1 does not stop with the thinking of a nonlinguistic thought, but precisely implements the action that would be inhibited in (a). In this, premise (b) anticipates two possible cases: P_1 could implement those medial actions whose inhibited execution identifies the nonlinguistic thoughts in (a) so that the individuating medium and the implementation medium are identical, or another (nonlinguistic) medium could be used whose scope of possibilities allows the implementation of a compositionally sufficiently similar medial configuration. Premise (c) functions to connect the nonlinguistic thoughts with a desire or an intention that is necessary for the practical syllogism. Thus (c) contains a reference to the nonlinguistic thought $I_b(K)$. However, this reference does not imply the linguistic reconstruction of the identity conditions of the thought $I_b(K)$; rather, it can be analyzed as a deictic form of reference or as a sufficient characterization.

According to (H2), the action character of an artistic activity now no longer depends on ascribing persons with intentional states, which can in principle be stated linguistically; rather, we can now expect that it is possible for people to have intentional states individuated by means of nonlinguistic media. On the basis of their identity *in their medium*, we can refer to them by means of another medium (often only with constraints). The process of individuating works of art can now be described as a production process. Within this process, the product emerges through steps in which choices are made from an inventory of intersubjectively accessible possibilities. Because the intention is able to be individuated—even for the producer—only in dialogue with the specific possibilities of the medium being used, language does not necessarily come into play in the individuation of the intention of the work of art, as long as the work of art in question is not itself linguistic. In contrast to (H1.1), (H2) only contains the formulations of propositional attitudes in premises (b, c). In premise (H2)(c), reference is indeed made to $I_b(K)$, but this reference can only be guaranteed after $I_b(K)$ is already individuated in an artistic medium. Besides this reference to the B-intentional state, which is determined in the process of producing a work of art, the premise, however, also ensures the ability to connect to the folk-psychological understanding of action explanations, which remain obtuse if they fail to refer to desires or intentions.

In an important respect, (H2) can be read as emphasizing the communicative dimension of artistic action without thereby conflicting with the intuition that works of art are untranslatable. Beyond that, however, (H2) also allows us to specify Dewey's reconstruction of artistic communication. Dewey interpreted the specifics of aesthetic communication as follows: P_1 produces a perceptible phenomenon K with a view to the reception of K by other persons P_n ($n \geq 1$), and a person P_2 receives K with a view to its having been intentionally produced by P_1.[127] Now it is clear why Dewey came to his view that there is a double determination of the *intrinsic* relationship[128] between the means and the ends of expressive actions. For media are *of necessity means* for individuating B-intentional states insofar as their compositional identity is connected with the respective media; on the other hand, media are means that stand in an intrinsic relationship to goals insofar as the product *consists of* these means, because, as a product, it *is* the implementation of a medial constellation. Under the premise that the medial communication serves the communication of experience, it is now, however, also clear that we are not dealing with two forms of intrinsic relationships here, but only with one: for as a means for individuating a nonlinguistic thought, which is the inhibited form of a medial performance, media are, at the same time, the means that structure the performance that can be experienced.

In addition, however, with the help of these reflections—extending beyond Dewey's accomplishments—we can plausibly demonstrate why a form of aesthetic communication that is implemented by medial means shows any promise of success whatsoever and why (H2) is a *rationalization* of action insofar as an artist can expect to be able to achieve her communicative goal by publishing or performing the work of art. For if we can assume that the recipients share the medial competencies of the artists to the degree that they are able to medially structure the produced object and thus are able to replicate it in accord with medial differentiations, then the probability increases that the replicating structuring of this produces an inner experience that is similar to that of the artist. I will return to these problems in chapter 4.

3.2.3. Problems of Field Research

In the previous section I have attempted to clearly show how the media theory proposed here can be applied to reconstruct processes of understanding nonlinguistic expressions (in reference to the example of artistic expressions). Here I have assumed that both the interpreter and the producer have a completely developed interpretation language and socially developed medial competencies at their disposal. In the second step, which now follows, I would like to investigate what media theory might add in the situation of radical interpretation, thus in the "prototypical situation of contemporary analytic philosophy."[129] The situation of radical interpretation here provides us particularly with the chance to examine whether the concept of compositional identity is an independent concept, which can be explained without reference to the Fregean perspective of truth functionality; for Frege, and following him, Davidson, have claimed that the syntactic structuring of the object language is precisely a product of the analysis of the input that linguistic elements provide in determining the truth function of the sentence that is to be interpreted.

By entering into a situation of (sufficiently) radical interpretation, we, however, enlist in a situation in which it is not clear whether those being interpreted speak a language; we, however, hold firmly that the interpreter is in full possession of an interpretation language. Let us, for example, observe the situation of an ethnolinguist who, within the framework of a prestigious research project, has to investigate an ethnicity that was, until recently, undiscovered. According to the working hypothesis of the ethnolinguist, the members of the Mulang speak a language in which, apparently, numerous important differentiations are made by articulating the few syllables of the language at various pitches. This fact does not irritate the researcher much initially, for he also knows such techniques from Chinese. However, because the number of syllables is quite small, quite a lot is dependent on the reception of pitch. In the hope of better establishing his hypothesis, for which he initially has formulated a few empirical indices in the form of T-theorems, the field researcher requires musicological help from his home university. The ethnomusicologist who was hurriedly flown in, however, realizes after only a few days of intensive observation of the Mulang that her colleague has been mistaken. In truth, what the ethnolinguist understood to be a language is nothing other than *singing*. Shocked by this diagnosis, and mindful of the potential damage to his reputation as a researcher, the linguist first assumes that his colleague is inexperienced and mistaken. The musicologist, however, confronts him with the following finding. If one analyzes the pitch sequences *exactly*, the following somewhat surprising view emerges: the sequences are organized in quasi-eight-tact phrases, which are organized cyclically; here a correspondence between the first and the fifth "tact" are quite frequent. Beyond this, over a long period of time, systems of ordering such sequences can be found. With their help, the sequences are often organized into complex rondo-like schemata. All of this escaped the colleague's notice, above all, because the Mulang use a quite small-step tone system—with intervals that are considerably smaller than our half-tone steps—which easily escapes our notice.

However, the ethnolinguist, who thinks he can see what this is all boiling down to, now waves it aside. What the colleague is presenting in this analysis does indeed exhibit a certain similarity with the structuring of an expression in the object language through a metalanguage, but beyond identifying syntactic relations, this structuring also semantically identifies the elements of the object-language expression that are integrated by the syntactic relations. And, according to the ethnolinguist, there simply is no equivalent to this semantic identification in the ethnomusicologist's analysis, which by the way is completely arbitrary because it imposes the concepts of the European music tradition on the alleged singing of the Mulang.

The musicologist admits that the attributes of the Mulang's singing, which she has mentioned in her analysis, make this objection obvious, but she thinks the irritation can be cleared up in the following way: the elements from which the singing of the Mulang is comprised can be impeccably identified in our staves, which must take on the function of a meta-"linguistic" translation medium; thus far she has found no token that could not be noted—at least with sufficiently good ears—with the help of our staves system. These comments do not really improve the atmosphere; the remark about imposing the concepts of the European music tradition has particularly agitated the musicologist. After all, in her view there is in principle no difference between her procedure and the procedure of the ethnolinguist; for just as the linguist reads his rationality standards and beliefs into the expressions of the Mulang, she hears the familiar musical structures there.

For an outsider it is perhaps easier to see that the musicologist is right about this; for there really is an interesting correspondence between the procedures of the researchers. Both researchers use a medium for their interpretations with the help of which they structure the articulation sequences of the Mulang.

Fully indebted to his Davidsonian education, the linguist attempts

1. to identify linguistic unities, which he holds to be truth-apt, as well as their components;

2. to correlate expressions that can be formed from these elements with metalinguistically expressed truth conditions, i.e., to formulate T-theorems for the types of expressions;
3. to collect evidence for the T-theorems by searching for expression situations in which the hypothetical truth conditions are fulfilled;
4. to discover covariations between the compositional structure of the linguistic unities and their truth conditions.

The musicologist, in contrast, attempts

1. to identify medial constellations and their elements;
2. to correlate the expression of those constellations with expression situations that she views from the perspective of her own experience of these situations;
3. to find evidence for her correlation hypotheses that indicates that certain songs are only performed under certain hypothetical, individual psychic, social, or natural conditions.

But the parallels of the researchers are more far-reaching, for they employ a medium in their interpretations of the Mulang, with the help of which they ascribe intentional states to them. In complete conformity to the above analysis, to do this they use the possibilities for differentiation, which make available to them an already known medium that, in the framework of their interpretations, plays the role of a "meta-"language. For there is no dissent among the two colleagues about the basic status of the behavior that is to be interpreted insofar as they both describe the behavior in question as *action*, which is intimately related (e.g., instrumentally) to the intentional states that each of them ascribes to the Mulang.

The principal divergences exist in these procedures primarily with a view to their starting hypotheses. As a charitable interpreter, the ethnologist must assume that the ascribed intentional states, more precisely the propositional attitudes ($A \rightarrow S$), can only be individuated in a network of further propositional attitudes, which comply with certain demands for coherence and correspondence, which, for their part, can only be fulfilled under the premises of the *truth aptness* of the propositional contents and a truth-functional integration of the contents. Against this background, he assumes that a set of expressions can be identified that are made by their speakers in agreement with the interpreter's assumption that they are held to be true, and he explains successful coordination processes among the Mulang on the basis of the (causally embedded) shared view that certain things hold true.

It is these truth-related assumptions that the musicologist neither needs nor is directly suited to accept as starting premises. For the musicologist need not assume that the Mulang make music for the purpose of truth-conditional representation in order to be able to ascribe to them shared intentional states. However, she does want to maintain the intentional ascriptions. She categorically rejects a description of the behavior of the Mulang that views the singing as an epiphenomenal sound, comparable to the humming of bees. She rather claims that the Mulang could also not sing; that their extraordinarily differentiated musical practice is based on a sensibly ordered system; and that a conscious, subtle varying practice can be detected in the songs of the individual singers. The set of the differentiations that the musicologist needs in order to interpret the musical practice of the Mulang as a practice that consists of musical *actions* must describe the scope that the Mulang draw on when singing. In the interpretation of the musicologist, this set of differentiations forms a *hypothetical medium*, and indeed one that would lose its hypothetical status particularly if, on the basis of this assumption, she could herself carry out actions that the Mulang accept as singing and be integrated into their practice of singing.

The researcher underlines this last mentioned thought—that her thesis has a "pragmatic verification"—with an excursus about rules, since for her analysis she is by no means, as her colleague believes, dependent on the assumption that the Mulang orient themselves in their musical practice on explicitly, linguistically agreed-on rules. The singing is indeed an action, which assumes that the singers are familiar with the musical entities, but this could be explained by the participation in a social practice that includes correcting nonlinguistic sanctions without the systems of differentiations that it is based on ever becoming explicit. On the whole, the comparison with a game is more suggestive; here the participants learn to play by practically being integrated into the practice. An important aspect of such games, without agreed-on rules, is the nonverbal action of competent players, which novices would find to be sanctioning behavior; although the introduction of such a game is not dissimilar from training, the model of conditioning misses the main point. For in contrast to a conditioning, which anchors a causally describable routine in a being that limits its scope of behavior under certain basic conditions, for the young Mulang who are introduced to the practice of singing, it opens up a scope of action that provides numerous alternatives. It is thus by no means impossible that those playing music would have intentional states and that their activities in the framework of games are activities, even without linguistic rules. In short, one can assume that the Mulang *first* intentionally sing and, in doing so, draw on a set of possible actions that are generated with the help of a nonlinguistic practice of drawing distinctions; to do this, however, it is not necessary to assume, *second*, that the mental states that the Mulang articulate with the help of singing are linguistically structured. In contrast, precisely with the concept of nonlinguistic mental states, one could accommodate the intuition that artistic intentions cannot be translated into linguistic intentions.

The ethnologist admits that the musicologist's thesis offers an interesting theory about the phoneme practice of the Mulang, but he is critical of the fact that the musicologist effectively provides no theory about the reason that the Mulang make music, and especially of the fact that she cannot explain why individual Mulang in certain situations sing one rather than another sequence. What the musicologist lacks is an explanation of the behavior of the Mulang that makes use of *reasons or even of thoughts* in an essential sense. In order to deal with this objection—which has a certain weight since it questions in a certain sense whether the analysis of the musicologist is in fact concerned with a form of understanding—the musicologist sketches out two strategies:

1. Within the framework of the first strategy, she accepts that the ascription of reasons always presupposes a language, but she questions that ascribing reasons or having reasons is constitutive for action. It is sufficient for actions that an activity is *chosen* from among possible forms of behavior.[130] If one accepts this strategy, then it is necessary—in conformity with the musicologist—simply to insist that a behavior that is carried out against the background of similarly alternative choices has another status than a behavior for which there are no such alternatives *for the actor*.

The first objection of the ethnologist to this strategy is obvious. With smug undertones, he asks: "For which form of animal behavior, for example, is there no alternative for those animals? Can't we always describe the behavior of reasonably complex animals as the realization of behavioral options that these animals have? Doesn't a bee have the option of flying onto one or another flower? And doesn't a bird have the option to sing this or that melody?"

The musicologist, who has been shaking her head while listening, does not even think about dropping these ideas. First of all, it is questionable what it is supposed to mean that a bee chooses among different flowers, for the flight of the bee over a meadow can be reconstructed completely in a causal—if necessary, however, in a functionalist—vocabulary. There is no problem imagining that a causal mechanism is implemented in a bee that leads it to fly onto all flowers that would be classified in a certain way, according to its perception, as long as its body exists in certain states. In any case, to our knowledge, the order in which bees fly onto flowers does not demonstrate a certain pattern; nor, in any case, she believes—should such a pattern exist—can intelligible variations of such patterns be made out.

At the same time, she specifies her criteria by pointing out that the concept of intelligible variation does not presuppose a mere change in activities, but a variation that is based on discrete, identifiable elements, thus a type of variation that assumes the type-token differentiation.

The musicologist characterizes the case of the bird as admittedly interesting and challenging, for the singing of the bird satisfies a number of criteria that her *theory of actions, as a chosen activity*, is based on. So it can be said that birds in a certain sense learn to sing, that birds vary their singing, that a refined varying practice is "honored" in social (i.e., sexual) relations, and that the influence of external causal factors is hardly suited to explain the "creative" aspect of singing. On the other hand, however, it is questionable whether the singing of the bird cannot be completely explained with a functionalist vocabulary. For the new work on birdsongs shows that the singing serves both to court and to acoustically mark a territory for a specific singer. If one would like to ascribe mental states to birds on the basis of this analysis, one is hardly required to assume more than the disposition to signal something like, "This territory is taken by me, singer X," and "I am an attractive male." Beyond that, however, for the case of bird singing, one simply cannot make out a social practice that can be sensibly interpreted as a *teaching* practice.[131]

Of course, it is difficult to prove this difference in individual cases; it is, however, possible to draw on further criteria. For example, the following addendum: behavioral alternatives can be prognotized in line with certain parameters; they result from an arbitrary pattern of alternatives that exhibits an intelligible order and whose differentiating attributes cannot be reduced physicalistically. Above all, this last point—the criterion of immunity to physicalist reduction—is important and must be better worked out in a developed version of the theory. However, it would be possible to maintain the following.

The attributes of the (alleged) musical actions of the Mulang that the musicologist has used for support in her analysis of the behavior of the Mulang are not physicalist attributes, but "medial" attributes, so she claims. Here, this means the following: her description of the music of the Mulang does not refer to the physicalist parameters such as frequency, amplitude, duration, or the frequency spectrum, but to parameters such as the key, volume, dynamic, tempo, rhythm, and agogics, such as tone and harmony. One could indeed imagine an agreement between the vocabularies such that every musical parameter X, with the value a, can be ordered to a physical parameter Y, with the value b, but *these relations are not reversible*. As an example, the colleague calls to mind the history of standard pitch a, which has remained constant as a musical entity since it was introduced into European music but viewed physically moved from 415.5 hertz in Bach's time to 457 hertz in 1880, after all a difference—musically spoken—of more than a half tone. Accordingly, described physically, the action of playing a C note at Bach's time was a different choice than it was at Mahler's time, while musically they have remained the same. The theory of action that views it as chosen activity is thus by no means unrefined; for in any case, the following criteria must be fulfilled so that an activity (X_1) can be described as an action.

1. X_1 is an activity that can be carried out at least by some members of a group of beings.
2. There are alternatives (X_n ($n \neq 1$)) to X_1 for which it holds that
   a. X_n share a series of attributes with X_1; and
   b. X_n distinguish among themselves with respect to at least one attribute;
   c. some of the attributes with the help of which X_n can be distinguished are socially conferred attributes (so that there is a history of these attributes).

3. The alternatives can be allocated to various forms of social reactions insofar as they often lead the observers of the action, which implements one of the alternatives, to different connecting actions.

2. The second strategy of the musicologist accepts the argument that reasons are essential for actions, but attempts to defend an alternative analysis of reasons, which does without the concept of truth. From her research journal, it can be seen that, in the conflict with the colleague, she pursued this strategy with the following arguments. First she claimed, certainly to the surprise of her colleague, that the procedure of ascribing reasons for the behavior—which by virtue of having reason ascribed to it is action—of persons who express themselves linguistically would not differ in principle from the procedure that she would follow to explain the singing, which is based on reasons: so, as the linguist counts the expression situation as one of the causal effects on the speaker, it would certainly still be possible for her to take internal factors—for example, inner *perceptions*—to be causes for the behavior of musical articulation. The disadvantage of such a construction is indeed obvious insofar as it is necessary to forgo the (alleged) public character of external, causal-effecting occurrences, understood as causes,[132] but that by no means implies a principal lack of intersubjectivity.

The singers could initially assume that softer relationships exist between the choice (or structure) of the singing and external situations, that are also externally perceptible or sensible by others, which could be comprehended by potential interpreters. These relations are softer than causal relationships above all because the perceptions cannot simply be interpreted as effects brought about by expression situations; rather, one must assume the singers' experience of the situation, which is itself evaluative. There is, however, no problem imagining that expression situations, which, for example, are influenced by the weather, trigger sufficiently similar perceptions in the singers and the listeners, so that the song can exist in an articulatory (and in a certain sense interpretive) relation to these perceptions. If, however, the singers can assume that the relation by which their singing is related to their inner states (perceptions, feelings, etc.) could be understood by others insofar as others could interpret the perceptions that they link with the singing to be *precepts for identification or an expression of an inner state* in which they could find themselves, then what reason is there not to say that the singers had reasons for their action? These are indeed not reasons that we can only individuate if we attribute truth-apt beliefs to the singers, but they are nevertheless reasons.

The response of the linguist to the first strategy is not known. Above all, he was demonstrably irritated by the second strategy. He objected that if we ascribe a singer P a rationalization for her singing action S, this in essence assumes the following form (which complies with [H1]):

1. P thinks S expresses feeling F.
2. P would like to express F.
3. P does S.

And it is clear that P holds the sentence "S expresses F" to be true. To what degree then is the discussion here of reasons in a sense that is not dependent on the concept of truth? The musicologist responds with a counterquestion: What does it mean to speak of "truth" in connection with a subjective belief that is not amenable to examination? However, the following is more important than an answer to that question.

If the Mulang hear a song, then they have an experience that, among other things, leads to the emergence of feelings. We expect that the Mulang have a disposition to react to various events with feelings, and it is, first of all, this disposition that is responsible for the emergence of feelings. Then we could assume, under the assumption that there is a practice that introduces variances into the singing, that the Mulang could make discoveries of the sort *that certain songs bring about certain feelings*. They perceive the song and they perceive effects of the song. (There could also be other nonlinguistic reactions to these feelings, for example, gestures or grimacing, so that social repercussions of a song could be correlated to activities to which the Mulang emotionally react.) What reason is there not to assume that the Mulang vary their singing with a view to the feelings it produces and to maintain that the song comes to symbolize the feeling that it generates? And why shouldn't we be allowed to assume that, with a differentiation of the song, there is a differentiation of the feelings, and thus of the mental states of the Mulang? In contrast, there is no reason not to maintain that the musical forms of expression make available the *only suitable means* for identifying the feelings that are expressed or generated with their help. Herewith, however, we would come to the heart of a thesis that is stronger than the thesis that the activities that can be depicted as resulting from choices are actions. We would arrive at the thesis that, besides language, there are other means for individuating mental states or thoughts, and these nonlinguistic means for individuation make it possible for beings to refer to these states.

But what have we gained with a view to the problem of the structuring of the expressions that are to be interpreted by the interpreters? More precisely, on the basis of the reflections, can it be plausibly shown that it is possible to structure the expressions in a way that is not dependent on the interpreter taking the "syntax" of the expressions from the perspective of the truth functionality of the hypothetical components of the expression? Can it thus be shown that the structuring of a medial expression in fact is independent of a concept of compositional identity, which in the late Fregean manner is explained employing the concepts of truth functionality?

The look at the problems of field research should have made it clear that it is possible to structure a medial expression using media-theoretic means, which is independent of the concept of truth. Admittedly, to do this, the design of the situation of radical interpretation must be broadened. In contrast to Davidson's construction of the situation in which it is initially sufficient that the interpreter correlates utterances of an individual speaker with utterance conditions, the situation in a media-theoretic perspective must be designed so that the interpreters can *simultaneously* observe expressions of a being that articulates itself and the effects of these expressions in a social context. The media-theoretic interpreter is dependent on the observation and analysis of the social practices of producing and receiving medial expressions. If this presupposition is fulfilled—a presupposition that remains compatible with the idea of radical interpretation—then the empirical data that must be analyzed in order to make it possible to identify elements of the medial expressions is available to the interpreter; such an identification is possible insofar as the interpreter can simultaneously observe that the reactions of the respective recipients covary with the *structure* of the medial expression and not with accidental attributes that appear when an expression is made.

3.2.3.1. Summary

If we put ourselves in the position of an interpreter of odd beings *B*, who are physically rather like us, but do not engage in activities that are sufficiently similar to our speaking, we must accept an especially prejudice-free type of observation in order to determine whether these beings have something that we should call media. Under these conditions, when would it be justified to say that these beings have media at their disposal? Now, this interpreter must (of course with the help of his language)

1. identify types of performances
    a. that can be performed by more than one individual;
    b. that, on the basis of bodily and the ascribed mental capabilities, *could* be performed by most B_j;
    c. that will lead to regularly observable changes in behavior for those B_i who witness a performance P_x; here some of these behavioral changes are implementations of P_x-similar expressions; and
2. classify some of these types of performances into sets (because of 1[b]) so that the performances can be described within each such set as performances that share certain perceivable attributes and that differ with respect to other perceivable attributes. (These types of performances are sufficiently similar to one another and are distinguished on the basis of changes in the attributes that are responsible for their similarity.)

At an elementary level, from the perspective of the interpreter, media are thus initially sets of transindividual types of activity, which the interpreter views as belonging together in varying ways. In order to have an example, let us suppose some B_i perform quite a number of bodily movements, without any of them making a sound. The interpreter proceeds as follows:

1. On the one hand, the interpreter classifies the movements that she identifies as "walking," "breaking something off," etc.; on the other hand, she classifies types of movements that are displayed by some B_i and that lead, with a reasonable regularity, to changes in the behavior of those who perceive these latter movements.
2. The interpreter sorts out those behavior-changing types of movement

    a. that are only visually perceptible, only pertain to the hands, and can be described as consisting in a variation of the position of the fingers (crossing the index and the middle finger, spreading out all the fingers, etc.), and those

b. that are only visually perceptible and that lead to an optical change in the cliffs (color one place on the cliff with red color, another with white color, one covered with moist lime, etc.).

In the case of the alleged finger-positioning medium, technically this means something like the following: the angle of the fingers and their distance from one another form the *elementary parameters* of the medium, and every type of finger positioning is a *medial element* or a *medial constellation*. With a view to the last distinction, the interpreter can only be sure if she has good reasons to think that individual finger-positioning performances do not lead to behavioral changes in the recipients, but that sequences of such performances do. If the sequences bring about behavioral changes, then the types of position constitute medial elements, and the sequences constitute medial constellations. If the performance of types of finger positioning is already sufficient for behavioral changes, then the medium is so simply structured that media elements and media constellations are coextensive. A medium whose elements at the same time also depict all the medial configurations that are possible for it has a scope of possibilities that is described completely by the list of all the performance types that are possible by applying its elements. The scope of possibilities of a medium that, for example, allows more complex medial configurations to form by sequencing finger positioning has, accordingly, a theoretical scope of possibilities whose power corresponds to the number of all the medial configurations that can be created by the sequencing types of finger positioning (a number of possibilities that of course only differs from infinite if additional restrictions on the length of the sequences come into play).

It is clear that our interpreter brings her entire language to bear in theoretically organizing her observations of *B*. But the interpreter is more than a theoretically distanced observer of *B*'s practices: she herself classifies the types of performances relative to her reactions, and in producing this classification (for example, of certain finger positionings), objectively measurable attributes of the act of finger positioning are not relevant; what is relevant are rather those attributes that the interpreter, on the basis of contingent mechanisms (for example, of pattern recognition), classifies as belonging together. The interpreter classifies on the basis of observer-relative attributes that the events or the states have for her, and she can assume that the reactions of *B* occur on the basis of the same attributes. The example of the cliffs should illustrate that the interpreter also can find support in the *consequences* of activities, which, in the form of relatively stable states of affairs in the world can be detached from the performances that bring them about. Admittedly, these states of affairs are only relevant as long as they are interpreted as consequences of the activity of *B*.

3.2.4. Interpretation Without Linguistically Apt Interpreters

In the last step of the introduction to a media theory from a broadened interpretationist perspective, I will attempt to show that, employing media-theoretic means, an assumption can be put to rest that is a premise of all the preceding reflections aimed at explaining the possibility of thoughts, the assumption, namely, that the transition from A-intentional states to thoughts is carried out with the help of external interpreters who already have thought available to them. In the following I would like to clarify, on the basis of a myth about the origins of media, that we can do without this assumption, that the interpretationist perspective can be reconciled to a genealogical perspective, and that consequently its phylogenetic problems can be overcome. Here it is important to avoid presuppositions of the established interpretationism, which, with a view to the question of how the primacy of the interpretation for the emergence of language, meaning, and mind can be reconciled with assumptions of evolutionary theory, is pacified with the answer that all speaking beings have parents who already possess an interpretation language. On the one hand, this information, however, opens a question of interest to evolutionary history—namely, whether we should assume that people who indeed must have undergone a transition from a nonspeaking species to a speaking humanity had parents, who, in opposition to interpretationist assumptions, *on the basis of their genetic endowments*, were interpreters of their children. On the other hand, one cannot see offhand how this transition can be construed to have been gradual, since the ability to ascribe rationality that is attributed to the interpreters has the character of a constitutive all-or-nothing criterion, which eludes a gradualist reconstruction. A myth of the origin of media must consequently be able to tell a story of the *development of competencies for interpretation*. Here it is decisive that these competencies can be understood to be gradually developed, but at the same time that the qualitative niveau characteristic for beings with thought can be designated.

Against the background of the previously developed four-phase model,[133] the task that we are confronted with regarding the construction of this myth can also be described as follows: we must tell the story of the social development of medial and interpretive competencies in which, at least at the beginning, all of the interpretive abilities of the adults that we can assume within the four-phase model initially have to be replaced by arrangements of dispositions in the beings that interact with one another. For unlike the interactions in the four-phase model, in the list of characters of the myth, no interpreters can be listed who already have a fully developed mind at their disposal. Of course—and the expression "myth" should emphasize this—this is not an empirically adequate development story; the goal of the myth would be reached if it were shown *how* such a story *could* be told in the interpretationist framework broadened by media theory, without the inadmissible assumptions.

At the center of the myth there is a group of primates that perhaps includes about eighteen individuals of various ages and of various physical statures. Outside observers are left with the impression that a hierarchy has been established in accord with these differences, which, for example, is seen in the fact that the weaker animals draw aside from the stronger ones if they cross paths. An idea of the myth is to assume that precisely this asymmetry in power between individuals is a basic aspect of those dispositional reconstructable social constellations that allow the individual interpretive competences of mental beings to be substituted in explanations.

3.2.4.1. A First Version

Let us now go to the edge of a clearing: one of the strong individuals (Alpha) suffers now and then from an itch on a place on his back that he cannot reach. After a failed attempt to ease the itch by scratching his own back, Alpha blurts out a noise that is obviously perceptible by the others; some of them look to the source of the sound. Alpha responds to the fact that he cannot manage to ease the itch with a nervous aggressive behavior, expressing frustration, and with threatening gestures and minor encroachments; in doing so, he agitates the weaker animals. Delta, one of the weaker animals, is obviously bothered by these bouts and devises a behavior that makes it possible for Alpha to stop the tedious interruption to the napping: he scratches Alpha. In reaction to this, Alpha calms down and the agitation of the group abates. However, it is not long before Alpha is once again afflicted, and once again a sufficiently similar noise is blurted out. Then Delta does what earlier had already restored the peace and quiet. If this interaction pattern becomes somewhat established, for Delta, Alpha's noise acquires the status of a sign, an indication. Its meaning$_i$ is parallel to the meaning$_i$ of seeing stinging nettle, which the animals avoid touching after sufficiently frequent experiences that touching it leads to an unpleasant skin irritation. And Delta's scratching intervention is parallel to the avoiding of stinging nettle.

If we look more precisely at our burdening assumption, it is clear that so far, in any case, we have not assumed that Alpha was following an intention when he produced the noise or that bothering the group was related to intentions. Alpha merely has the disposition to react to a disturbance to his well-being that he could not redress with a noise and with aggressive behavior. And Delta has the disposition to avoid experiences that he assesses as negative; so Delta reacted to the noise as if it were a sign for the occurrence of an ill feeling. As far as I can see, there is no reason not to say that Delta interprets$_i$ Alpha's noise *by behaving in a certain way*; here this interpretation is nothing other than a "perceiving as," which leads to a form of behavior.

For the further development we must now assume that Delta's acquired disposition to react to Alpha's noise is not a form of behavior that admits no exceptions. We must thus assume that Delta can also hear the sound without the soothing behavior ensuing as an effect. In other words, it must be possible to understand the acquired disposition as making it probable that the corresponding behavior is performed, but not as making this inevitable. Just as animals that are fleeing accept the contact with stinging nettle at a cost, it must be possible for Delta to accept the aggression at a cost, if other dominant impulses determine Delta's behavior. If this is possible on the basis of Delta's biological endowment, then the following scenario is possible. If Delta does not react to the noise in the tested way, this then has consequences for the other members of the group; for Alpha's aggression is directed at lower-ranking animals with a relative lack of specificity. If the animals of this group can *observe* a sufficiently stable connection between Alpha's noise and Delta's pacifying action—and we can assume that the animals, as primates, intensively observe one another—then it is not temerarious to assume, for example, that, for the sake of his own quiet, Gamma, an animal that occupies a similar position in the hierarchy to Delta, reacts to Alpha's noise, should Delta at some point not intervene for some time, with a behavior that is equivalent to Delta's, thus appeasing Alpha. What this step yields is that an interpretive correlation between the noise and the appeasing behavior becomes detached from Delta's instantiations of this relation, and it can now be instantiated by other animals. However, even if this correlation is, as it were, integrated into the cultural stock of the group in this way, in any case, we are here dealing with interpretations via action, and indeed via action that is directly *preference relevant*.[134]

In order to move beyond the outlined pattern, a further step is now necessary: for one, the (aggressive) behavior that functioned as a negative reinforcement for the performance of the preference-relative behavior must also be performed by other individuals than merely Alpha so that not only the interpretation of the behavior but also the reinforcement behavior are able to be disconnected from the original protagonists. For another, interactions must be established in which the interpretive behavior is not directly preference relevant, but in which it, for its part, has a demonstrative character. The first step could be achieved simply if the stronger members within the group of the lower-ranking animals, through preference-relevant behavior, urge the relatively weaker animals to react to the noise in the established way. In this way, they would ensure the extension of a reliable structure of reinforcement, which ought to lead to the establishment of a correlation between the sound and the designated form of behavior in the group. However, although this step looks easy, it appears to entail too many assumptions. For the animals that urge the weaker ones to engage in the appeasing behavior are interpreters in an overly demanding sense; we would have to explain their behavior by assuming that they understand the observable connection between the noise and the appeasing actions of other animals as a "semantic" relation, which they use to achieve their preferences. This, however, would be irreconcilable with the conception of intrinsic-intentional states, for intrinsic-intentional states systematically preclude the reference to other intentional states, because they, as a result of their individuation through conditions of satisfaction, would be identical with these states, or a duplication of mind would be implied.[135]

On the other hand, however, the step is too small insofar as only a deficient interpretation could be reconstructed in which the meaning$_i$ of an expression could not be provided by another expression, but in the form of a preference-relevant connecting behavior. However, this is irreconcilable with the interpretationist framework, because an interpretationist theory of content is based on a correlation between expressions whereby the interpreting expression is itself interpreted, thus is interpretable.

If I see things correctly, then the relations in this version of the myth can be analyzed on the basis of the ascription of intrinsic-intentional states. We at no place assume that the interacting primates ascribe intentions to one another so that a second-order mental relation would be brought in play. In order to proceed beyond this level, it would have to be possible to take recourse in a model that we were able to draw on with no problem in the four-phase reconstruction: what we would need is a model for the *internalization of an interpreter* or for the internalization of an interpretation. However, in solving the phylogenetic problem of the development of mind, we do not have interpreters—in any case those with the common semantic and folk-psychological competencies—at our disposal. If, in the face of this problem, the myth is to have any chance whatsoever of fulfilling its explicative function, then we must introduce interpreters whose interpretive competencies are adapted to these assumptions. These interpreters would not have to be steered by beliefs in their interpretations, but could be moved by dispositions. And it would have to be shown to be plausible that these dispositions themselves are malleable so that the interpretive$_i$ behavior that they cause can be modified and differentiated in reactions to this behavior. Unlike instrumental communication, which I have attempted to develop in the first version of the myth, the second version might rather play out in a framework that is related to the phase of affective communication.

3.2.4.2. The Phylogenesis of the Mind, the Second Take

From the perspective of affective communication, we now observe animals that have dispositions to react to certain social events with expressive$_i$ forms of behavior. This is not uncommon among higher primates: if playing pups surpass what is tolerated by the adults, they are responded to with threatening gestures; if they are fondled by other animals, they put on a "playful face"; if they are separated from important reference animals, they exhibit signs of sadness$_i$. Let us then presume that all animals in the group are disposed to express their emotions$_i$,[136] with facial expressions, bodily posture, noises, etc. Nothing prevents us from describing these expressive acts and the attentive observation in a functionalist vocabulary that places these forms of behavior in a close relationship with the survival of the group. With a view to the construction of an interpretive relation, whose internalization would simultaneously be the birth hour of mind, expressive acts assume an interesting position insofar as we can expect, on the one hand, that all members of a species of primates have a genetic disposition to react to types of expressive acts (by performing expressive acts) so that stable reactions are ensured. On the other hand, however, we can also assume that such reactions can be learned, so that types of reactions can have a history, which is connected to traditions$_i$ within the group and, for example, do not occur in other groups of the same species. Besides a set of inborn forms of behavior, we also find in the group forms of behavior that are passed on through associative learning.

If we next assume that animals are endowed with brains that allow them to carry out analyses of conditions in Watsons's sense[137]—and this is not an assumption about the existence of intentional states—then, on the basis of the observation of interactions that are appropriate for such analyses, we can justifiably assume that the animals learn to identify types of bodily states proprioceptively that sufficiently frequently lead to certain expressive social responses, regardless of whether the relative stability of the reaction has genetic or historical causes. Let us further assume that playing$_i$ is a widespread practice, especially of the pups in the group, and indeed a practice that—in contrast to the practices of nonhuman primates that we know about—entails *varying* the performance of expressive behavior. Then we can imagine that, in the framework of such playing, expressive types of behavior become established because, on the basis of the shared genetic dispositions, we can expect that some of the expressions that are developed when playing might activate the attentiveness patterns of their recipients and lead to an expressive connecting behavior, which is tied to the previous performance of certain expressions. Within the framework of such playing we thus should be able to see interactions in which individuals react to gestures with other gestures and to noises with other noises, and not with immediate preference-relevant activities. If we assume a playful practice of this sort, then, with the help of conditionality analysis and the processes of forming expectations that can be explained with the concepts of associative learning, we must be able to show the plausibility of the further steps. Let us assume that, in the framework of playing, Delta performs a gesture G, which captures Gamma's attention in a special way, and Gamma reacts with sufficient frequency to the performance of G, for example, by imitating the gesture. Then Delta's conditionality analysis leads him to identify the necessary and sufficient conditions for the form of behavior that Delta must carry out in order to get Gamma to imitate the behavior. If this interrelation becomes stabilized, then Delta will come to expect that Gamma will react to the performance of G with the performance of G; one can imagine that when that reaction does not occur, Delta's reaction will aim at generating conditions that satisfy the expectation. Here, if expressive reactions occur often enough, Delta will identify the proprioceptive perception of the state that leads to the performance of a behavior with a state that normally brings about a certain reaction.

Again, in contrast to the implementation of this construct in the four-phase model, here we cannot assume that recipients are endowed with folk-psychological competencies. Thus a theoretical framework is needed in which a complex balance is possible between a sufficient constancy in the reactions and a sufficient performative "freedom." In the model here, the causal effect of a protomedial expression on the recipient of the expression ensures the constancy of reactions; this can be explained, for example, by species-specific attentiveness patterns, specificities of perception, and dispositions to imitative learning, as well as a positive evaluation of the imitating performances.

Once this level of interaction is reached, the behavior is interpreted$_i$, not by preference-relative activities, but by intrinsically empty forms of behavior that become connected with the activities by being embedded in a network of expectations. At this fundamental level, behavior that reacts to the failure of what is expected to occur must and may thus not be understood as a sanction. It has no normative significance. In contrast to Brandom's view, here sanctions are thus not placed in a fundamental theoretical position, establishing correctness or rightness by positively or negatively reinforcing forms of behavior.[138]

The possibility of further developing these rudimentary media is now primarily dependent on two factors: first, the possibilities of a species to differentiate the scope of possibilities of media and to use them articulatively; second, the possibilities of a species to place types of performances under conditions of appropriateness, which in the case of nonlinguistic performances are experiential contexts and in the case of linguistic performances are prominently truth conditions or conditions of satisfaction.

If I am correct, in the construction of a myth that attempts to make the social origin of mind intelligible, media-theoretic means can allow an intermediate step, which—because we expect a form of communication without reasons—permits the process of establishing communications media to be decoupled from a process of applying communicative media with reasons.[139] If one accepts the view sketched out here, then the origin of mind is not based on sanctions, but on play.

3.3. FURTHER THEORETICAL FOUNDATIONS OF MEDIA THEORY

The preceding sections of this chapter should clearly indicate how the interpretationist theory of mind, of meaning, and of action can be broadened by means of media theory so that those cases of communicative action that do not play a paradigmatic role for the established interpretationism can be adequately understood. For this, I have introduced a media concept that apprehends media as means for individuating thoughts. In the following I would like to further hone this concept, for one, by pursuing the question of what it means to say that there are media: in short, in which way do media exist?

In a second step, on the basis of the earlier developments, I will suggest an ordering framework that makes it possible to subjugate the ubiquitous talk of media to criteria. To this end, I suggest a typology for media with the help of which it should be possible to examine which of the types mentioned at the beginning of chapter 2 can rightfully be characterized as media and how these media behave toward one another.

3.3.1. Comments on the Ontology of Media

As we have seen, among the striking deficits of the system-theoretic media conceptions is the remarkable evasion of the following questions.

Which epistemological access do we have to media? Which forms of existence do they have? In the preceding chapter I attempted to show that this deficit is no coincidence; for both Parsons as well as Habermas must assume—because of the double function that they burden the media with as intersystematic entities and as action-coordinating social entities—that media have both objective effects and intrinsic attributes accorded to them independently of us, as well as observer-dependent attributes that are dependent on us for their existence and that only have effects because actors ascribe these attributes. On account of the dependency of social systems on the emergence of improbable communications, Luhmann's expression "There are systems!"[140] can be extrapolated as "There are media!" But rather than squarely addressing the question of the ontology of media, as a result of his trust in a naturalized epistemology, he assumes that such questions are purposeless.

A media theory that attempts to cast off its provisional status should, however, be able to answer the question of whether media exist like stones or shovels, like paper or banknotes, like balls or games, like noises or languages. If, in the face of these alternatives, we attempt to specify the ontological status of media, we will initially tend toward the choice of the second disjunctive; from the series of the second disjunctives, we will tend to maintain that the form of existence of media is more comparable to the form of existence of banknotes, games, and languages than to the form of existence of a tool. The background for this classification is the thesis that:

(M10) Media are social entities.

An ontology of media would thus have to clarify what social entities are and what form of existence they have. In order to approach a robust answer to this question, I would like, first of all, to attempt to use the theoretical apparatus that Searle developed in his third larger work, *The Construction of Social Reality*, from 1995. In connection with a critical presentation of Searle's basic reflections, I will take up those parts of his program that are independent of the specific presuppositions that indeed are characteristic for Searle's purposes but that are incompatible with the basic assumptions of my reflections. Among these is, for example, the assumption that intentionality is *completely* a biological phenomenon and does not first come into play in a social practice of interpretation.

Beyond that, however, all of those assumptions in which language plays a fundamental *and* exclusive role for the origin of social entities must lead to a modification of his analysis.

Searle's reflections, which, in the first step, aim to examine the presuppositions of our social reality, assume first of all that these presuppositions

> neither are made accessible by *sense experience*;
> nor are accessible from an *internal phenomenological* perspective insofar as the objects with whose help we act socially do not reveal anything specific to the phenomenological view;
> nor can be apprehended from an *external behaviorist* perspective, because the mere description of social behavior does not bring the structures into view that make this behavior possible;
> nor become transparent in reference to the assumption of cognitive science or linguistics that the behavior of social actors can be understood to be the result of *unconscious rule following* (particularly if it is assumed that these rules are, in principle, not accessible to consciousness), because the rule following itself is a part of the explanandum.[141]

In order to gain a more precise view of the social reality and its presuppositions, Searle attempts, first of all, to position the forms of existence of social facts within the framework of a three-level rough ontology, which he portrays in broad strokes on the basis of the atomic structure of the material and the evolutionary theory of life:[142]

(1) Materially, the world consists entirely of particles that are subject to force fields and organized into systems, whose borders are drawn by causal relationships so that the relation between entities of the first level of ontology can be described in a causal vocabulary. (2) Some of these systems are living systems; these types of systems develop by mutation and natural selection. One fraction of these systems has developed subsystems that we call nervous systems, which, for their part, are able to generate consciousness; here consciousness is understood as a biological and to that extent as a physical attribute of higher-developed nervous systems. (3) Along with consciousness, intentionality is developed, i.e., the ability of mind to represent other objects and states of affairs in the world; here intentionality is an attribute of the mental representations through which they refer to something or are oriented toward something.

It is obvious that this rough ontology is quite problematic and is incompatible with the interpretationist assumptions of my view insofar as it views consciousness and intentionality as biological phenomena. Nevertheless, the problems initially do not pose a serious obstacle to the usefulness of the Searlean apparatus insofar as they are not dependent on a certain interpretation of the rough ontology and the steps of the rough ontology can also be reconstructed to be reconcilable with the assumptions of interpretationism.[143] For Searle, the rough ontology initially only has the function of providing the background for an epistemological question, namely, the question of how we have access to social facts within this ontology. The distinction between intrinsic and observer-relative features of the world is foundational for the access to social facts.[144] Here, *intrinsic features* are those that exist independently of the observer, that is, all of those features of the entities of rough ontology that exist independently of mental states, including the existence of mental states. Searle distinguishes *observer-relative features* from intrinsic features, that is, from those features whose existence is dependent on the existence of observers that ascribe a feature to an object or process in reference to their perceptions, beliefs, and expectations; an example is the feature of being a tool. Unlike intrinsic features, observer-relative features are not ontologically objective but ontologically subjective. The status of ontological subjectivity, however, by no means precludes entities that possess such features from being objects of epistemically objective judgments. In contrast to aesthetic assessments, judgments about whether something is a tool or a word are not merely of an epistemically subjective nature; rather, despite the ontologically subjective status of the feature of being a tool or a word, they are epistemically objective. Figure 3.5 provides the course, within the apparatus of the Searlean distinction, that we must follow in order to encounter the type of judgment that is specific to the features of social entities.

Against the background of this distinction, the following is decisive for every arbitrary observer-relative feature F_b: namely, logically precedent to F_b inhering in an object O is that *it appears to us that F_b* inheres in that object; for "seeming to be F_b is a necessary condition of being F_b."[145] Searle connects his hope that he has found an adequate starting point for the investigation of social facts to this particular consequence—namely, the primacy of *ascribing a nonintrinsic feature* over the inherence of the feature. Besides the analysis of the ascription of nonintrinsic features,

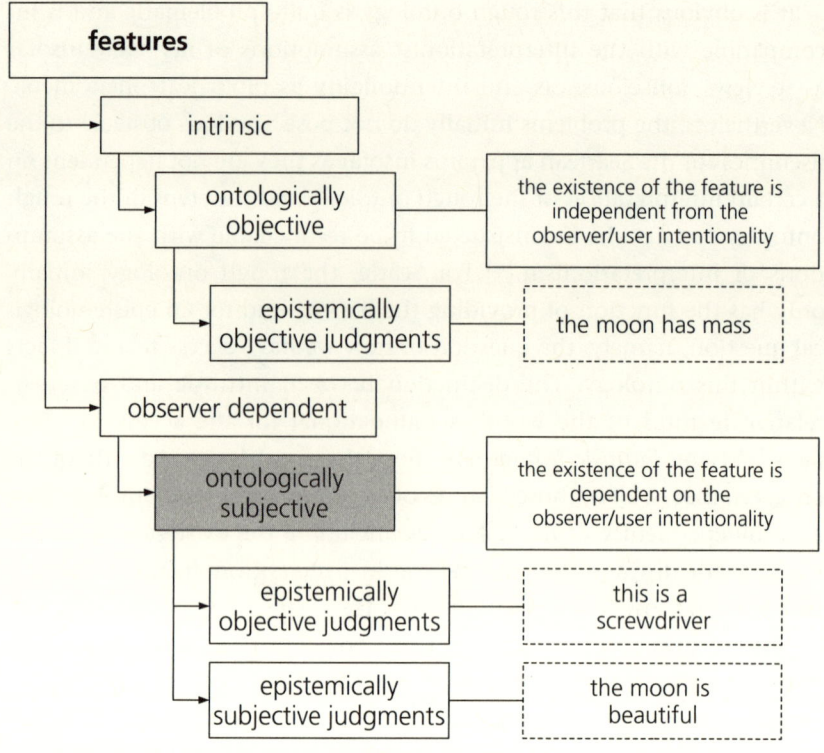

FIGURE 3.5 Searlean types of features

which Searle investigates in reference to the example of the *assignment of a function* (1 below), the concepts of *collective intentionality* (2 below) and the generation of institutional facts by *constitutive rules* (3 below) are the theoretical instruments with the help of which Searle attempts to illuminate the structure of social facts.

1. Against the background of the apparatus in figure 3.5 for drawing distinctions, *functional assignments*, in which an object G is ascribed a function Y, can be qualified as follows:

   a. For all functions Y, it holds that they are observer-relative features.
   b. From this it follows: functional assignments *do not* introduce *any new intrinsic facts*.

c. Functional assignments operate with observer-dependent *values*.
   d. Under the presuppositions (a)–(c), the schema "G has function Y" can be analyzed as follows:

   i. G and Y are parts of a system that is in part defined in reference to purposes, ends, and values.
   ii. It is *expected* that G performs Y (even if G occasionally, or even often, fails to do so).

This specific type of functional assignment can be action related ("This is a screwdriver"), or it can play an epistemic-theoretical role, whereby the functional assignment acquires the status of a heuristic hypothesis ("The lungs provide the body with oxygen"). Among the action-related functional assignments Searle counts those that assign a representational or presentational function to an object. So, stamps on paper could take on a function analogous to tools relative to presentational intentions.

2. If we now accept that functional assignments are a necessary criterion of social facts, then the question arises regarding how functional assignments—beyond mere individual acts of assignment—can acquire a social character so that they can become an object of an epistemically objective judgment at all. Searle entrusts the solution to the problem to a theory of *collective intentionality* (*we-intentionality*). His simple claim is: collective intentionality is a primitive biological phenomenon that cannot be reduced to forms of individual intentionality.[146] To provide an example of a behavior that might be explained with the help of the phenomenon of collective intentionality, Searle introduces pack-hunting animals, which is supposed to prove that beings without language can pursue common, i.e., coordinated, goals, and sometimes even with a division of labor. Here, Searle places a lot of value on the view that collective intentionality, as is also shown, for example, in a soccer match ("We are playing soccer"), cannot be reconstructed from the first-person intentionality of the individual players ("I play soccer, Y plays soccer, and . . ."). In an adequate reconstruction of the relationships between we- and I-intentionality, it should rather be shown that "wanting X collectively," in the sense that "we want X," is the presupposition required so that individuals can pursue intentions that refer to X, under the assumption of this common desire. Here Searle emphasizes that the assumption

of we-intentionality is compatible with methodological individualism because we-intentionality is not dependent on its implementation in higher-order subjects and is thus not damaging for his rough ontology. With a view to the explanation of social facts, it follows then that:

> (WI) We-intentionality is a necessary condition for the emergence of social facts. Individuals who contribute to fulfilling these conditions share an intentional state with others of the form "We intend X."

Regardless of how one judges the analysis of we-intentionality in detail, it is in any case clear that a mechanism is needed that ensures functional assignments the status of epistemological objectivity. However, that appears to me initially only to assume that, for example, all of those participating in a game can draw on criteria that can be intersubjectively examined in order to be able to move in a field of shared functional assignments.[147]

Although the microanalysis of collective intentionality is not of enormous significance for my reference to Searle's theory of social entities, I do not want to fail to mention that Searle's analysis of we-intentionality is problematic in two respects.

From a quasi-epistemic perspective, it is *first* questionable whether the view that "We intend to do X" can be analyzed differently than "I intend to do X, and Franz intends to do X, and Paul . . . ," because the ascription of an intention can only take recourse in individuals as objects of predication. For if we analyze the deictic expression "we," we do not point to a higher-level entity with the expression, but to a bunch of individuals who are the bearers of intentionality and who integrate the bunch into a group; the subject pointed to, as the subject of the intention, is not a collective, but an individual. It is instructive to test this analysis on cases in which someone is deceived about what the object of the intention of the participants is. If, for example, it is found out that the opposing soccer team has been bribed (as occurred with Schalke 04 in the 1970s), and a basic condition for the soccer game—namely, the desire to win—is not fulfilled, then the proposition that is supposed to express the intention of the participants as "We intend to play soccer" is not applicable for half of the players, and it is questionable how the intention of the honest players should have been indicated under these conditions after it was found out that this was a case of deception. In this situation—if one wants to retain an intentional description—one must indicate the intention by saying, "*I* intended to play soccer, but the others did not." From this, it follows that "not: we intended to play soccer."

As a result of the reservation just expressed, it is, *second*, admittedly difficult to see how it can be precluded that the mere synchronized pursuit of I-intentionality is counted among the cases in which the coordination of those actions that are commensurate with the intentions are among the things intended. However, this particular distinction does not appear to me to be a problem if we shift the commonality of the intending from the collective subject to the content of the intention: "*I* intend, *together with* P_x, to do F, and the other persons P_x intend to do F with me." (Often, however, it is not even necessary to explicitly indicate the term "together with," because it is implicit in formulations like "I want to play tennis," "I want to play in a quartet," etc.)

Searle's affinity to an analysis of shared intentions in the form of we-intentionality can surely be explained by the fact that he views intentionality as a biological phenomenon, and he wants to treat the collective hunting of animals as an example of we-intentionality. With a view to the above-introduced distinction between simple and higher-level intentionality, however, I believe I can account for the advantage of this analysis, which primarily lies in the fact that it can be favorably linked to behavioral research; indeed, I can do so while gaining greater precision. It is plausible that pack hunters or that demonstrators who are fleeing from mounted police can evaluate situations with a view to whether they correspond to the conditions of satisfaction of their A-intentional states or not, and a collective behavior occurs that can be well described under the assumption of collective ends. But it is very questionable whether the individuals that form the groups can behave toward their A-intentional states by weighing alternatives. This kind of collective behavior, which needs to be explained, can be elucidated by noting that it is precisely causal mechanisms that condition the A-intentional states and thus the coordinated behavior. To emphasize the difference from Searle, I have characterized the analysis of the phenomenon that I prefer as *shared* intentionality. It is:

> (SI) Shared intentionality is a necessary condition for the emergence of social facts. Individuals who contribute to fulfilling these conditions share

intentional states with others in the form, "I intend to do X together with others, and I believe that the others intend to do X together with me and believe that I intend to do X together with them."[148]

3. With the concept of *constitutive rules*, Searle attempts to introduce a criterion for further internal differentiation of social facts that ought to make it possible to distinguish between mere social and institutional facts. The concept of constitutive rules, which Searle had already introduced[149] in the 1960s in connection with a distinction from Rawls, postulates a type of rule that, in contrast to regulative rules, does not have the function of influencing behavior that exists independently of these rules; rather, such rules function first to make possible the actions that they simultaneously regulate. Unlike regulative rules, constitutive rules do not have the form of a hypothetical imperative ([If Y, then] do X!) but the form of defining sentences:

(CR) X counts as Y (in context K)!

With the help of constitutive rules, we can, for example, determine what a legal move of the pawn is (in chess) or what a banknote is. Constitutive rules establish possible actions; certain social practices are constituted by carrying out those actions. In contrast to arbitrary conventions, sets of constitutive rules produce institutional facts.

With the three elements—namely, of action-related function, we-intentionality (or better, shared intentionality), and constitutive rules—Searle now has the building blocks from which a differentiated ontological view of social reality can be constructed in which institutional facts are a subset of the social facts that are ascribed their institutional status by constitutive rules. In detail:

(SF) A fact is a *social fact* if and only if its existence implies *collective intentionality* and allows the assignment of an action-related function.[150]
More precisely:

   a. Collective intentionality exists in a *minimal sense* if beings behave in such a way that their behavior can best be described under the

assumption of shared goals (the case of collective intentionality [as A-intentionality] among animals).
b. Collective (shared) intentionality exists in a *developed sense* if there are beings that share at least one goal, one belief, or one preference X, whereby for X it holds that

   i. the beings believe reciprocally of each other that they find themselves in intentional state X (besides other intentional states);
   ii. the beings carry out actions that are caused by having X and that are understood by these beings as the realization of the conditions of satisfaction for X.

The definition of *institutional* facts now fits precisely the conception of social facts:

(IF) A social fact is an *institutional fact* if and only if its existence implies collective (shared) intentionality in the sense that the content of collective (shared) intentionality aims at the validity of constitutive rules or it implies the validity of constitutive rules;[151] more precisely,

   a. There are beings that create social facts as understood in (SF).
   b. These beings assign attributes to objects or states Y through collective intentionality, which cannot be described in a physicalist vocabulary (status functions).
   c. These beings permanently accept the assigned status function.
   d. The status assignment takes the form of constitutive rules (CR).

With recourse to Searle's analysis of social reality, the question about which ontological status media have can be more precisely answered, for we can now ask whether, beyond thesis (M10), it should also be accepted that media are *institutional* entities. Against the background of the Searlean analysis, it is clear that media can only be considered institutional entities if their existence is fundamentally dependent on language; Searle assumes very clearly that constitutive rules are linguistic rules. This means that if we cannot make sense of a concept of nonlinguistic constitutive (somehow implicit) rules, we would have to draw the conclusion that media are social but not institutional entities. Formulated differently, where media have institutional attributes, they are dependent on language.

An interesting question is now whether the demonstrative rules[152] reconstructed in the first section of this chapter might be able to take on the status-assigning function that is carried out by constitutive rules. As far as I can tell, this would mean that the content of a rule like "Do it like this...!" would have to entail something like "View or treat X (in context K) as Y!" Even if following a demonstrative rule could be described as if the rule follower treated something as something in context K, the ability to follow a demonstrative rule does not imply that there is knowledge of following a constitutive rule. Because Searle, however, makes the content of a constitutive rule into an object of the intentional states with which beings assign status functions, it must be assumed that they are conscious of the content of the rules. Although demonstrative rules can be understood as a form of explicit rules, it makes no sense to understand them as constitutive rules.[153] This analysis does not preclude some media from being institutional entities. In these cases, however, it is clear that such media (among them possibly money) are dependent on language insofar as the constitutive rules that apply to them must be explicitly stated in language. I thus accept the thesis:

> (M11) All media are social entities, and some media are at the same time also institutional entities.

Thesis (M11), which answers the question of the ontological status of media, allows at the same time a dynamization of the schematic discussion of linguistic and nonlinguistic media; in this a development in the history of the media can be accounted for that applies linguistic precepts to media that were originally nonlinguistic in a radical sense and that subjects these media to linguistically formulated regimentations. This historical process, which can be illustrated, for example, in reference to tempered tuning or twelve-tone music, can be interpreted ontologically as a process of transforming media into institutional entities.

3.3.2. A Media Typology

At the beginning of chapter 2 I presented a heterogeneous list of objects that are said to be media. The question that I finally want to pursue in what follows—and answering this in some respects challenges my reflections—is whether, with the help of the above-developed criteria, media can be limited, and thus whether it is possible to decide if something is a medium, and whether media that are obtained in accordance with this criteria can be sensibly classified. In the course of the attempt to develop a typology of media with the help of the criteria that have been worked out, it will be necessary to explain how the consequences of the theory that are developed here are related to common manners of speaking. Are the manners of speaking in general simply too undifferentiated and in need of reform, or can at least some of these everyday manners of speaking be reconstructed within the parameters of the terminology developed here?

However, before we take up the discussion of this question, it is necessary to call to mind that because of false substantiation, a typology of media runs the danger of taking a false course. Dewey already pointed out that it is impossible to indicate "where one [medium] begins and the other ends."[154] And he clearly indicated that this is not the result of a defect in the set of criteria that is available to us, but that it is systematically based on the fact that it is completely dependent on *how something has been used*. With a consciousness of the primacy of the pragmatic perspective, proposing a media typology thus necessarily entails the relativizing of the systematic demands of this typology; it means that it is based in a certain, historically contingent social process in which certain practices of application are established and others are not. A media typology is thus a typology that is specified for a certain historical situation. It reflects what we do with certain types of actions, but not intrinsic attributes of things.

And a further remark about the status of the typology is necessary: If we are interested in classifying some range of phenomena, then we can in principle attach any criteria to the range of phenomena that are selective with a view to the phenomena. However, if the classification is supposed to do more than echo the criteria used, then it is sensible to work with criteria that articulate specific attributes of phenomena in some range of phenomena. A media typology could secure such criteria by drawing not only on the fundamental criteria that characterize the range of phenomena in general, but also on those that arise from the possible relations between the phenomena. To this end, one can outline prototypical operations that are possible among the medial constellations. (I will only do this here in a very provisional and schematic way.)

3.3.2.1. Elementary Media Operations

If we have two medial constellations, we then can ask what relationship they can have to one another, and we can refer to the types of activities that actualize instantiations of this relationship as medial operations. The reach of the possible relations is here stretched by two extreme cases: the case that allows the two medial constellations to be substituted for one another boundlessly and the case in which two medial constellations stand in a relationship of boundless difference to one another. Let us begin with cases in which a higher degree of reciprocal substitution between two medial constellations is possible: if two medial constellations relate to one another such that the reception of K_1 and K_2 makes possible the same medial structuring by competent recipients, then K_1 and K_2 can represent each other in the sense that the two constellations in the most demanding cases cannot be distinguished from each other by the senses. In order to generate a constellation K_2 for a given constellation K_1 that can represent K_1 in every respect, something like a perfect copy would have to be produced. So, something would have to be generated that we could, in connection with one of Danto's thought experiments, call a materially identical double,[155] something that, after being produced, could only be distinguished from the original with the help of knowledge of the production history. If the two products were stored by a grumpy curator in unmarked boxes, the identity of the original would be lost with the passing away of the curator because there would be no procedure left by which they could be distinguished.

If one gives up on the condition that the difference between K_1 and K_2 cannot be determined by any means whatsoever, another form of the substitutability of K_1 and K_2 can be exposed. For example, K_2 could represent K_1 not with respect to all attributes but only with respect to relevant ones, and precisely those attributes that are fundamental for the compositional identity of K_1 might be among those. In order to guarantee this interchangeability, it is not necessary, for example, that the color of a picture K_2 has the same chemical structure as that of K_1. It is enough that the light reflects in a way that is not distinguishable to the human observer.

At the level of this limited form of substitutability, different conditions for substitution come to light, depending on how the medium in which K_1 was individuated is characterized. If we ask someone to read Davidson's "The Conditions of Thought," we will not be indignant if the person reads a photocopy of the article; for the photocopy, we at least expect, should in any case have all of the sensibly perceptible characteristics that are sufficient so that, when reading the copy, one reads the same text that is found in the book in which it is originally published (*The Mind of Donald Davidson*). Whether the text is blue or black plays no role, and even some poorly legible letters may be able to be deciphered in reference to the context. However, what we expect from such a surrogate K_2 is that a recipient of K_2 ascribes it the same compositional identity as K_1. Similarly, two performances of a musical work substitute for one another in this way if both of them enable competent listeners to identify the same score as the basis of the performances,[156] or, as in the case of oral stories, they enable listeners to generate the performances themselves, which will be accepted by competent listeners as articulations of the corresponding musical thought.

The relations that exist between the original and the copies or between performances can be understood as relations that can be brought about by actions that instantiate a generally operative pattern that I would like to call reproduction. The following preliminary criterion attempts to define reproductions with recourse to the concept of compositional identity and to widespread intuitions:

(R_1) Given a constellation a in a medium M_a, a *reproduction* of a exists if and only if a constellation a^* is generated in a medium M_a^* ($[M_a^* \neq M_a] \vee [M_a^* = M_a]$), whose compositional identity in M_a^* is sensibly and functionally equivalent to that of a in M_a.

Reproductions are operations that can be distinguished at two levels. At the level of physical processes perceptible objects must be produced that lead (under similar circumstances) to sufficiently similar perceptions. And the objects are sufficiently similar if competent recipients can identify the same medial constellation with their help. Because not all perceptible attributes of an object are necessarily of those attributes that are varied in a medial practice, the second condition provides the mentioned success criterion for successful reproductions. With respect to the participating media, this means that the medium in which the reproduction is carried out at least provides the differentiation possibilities that are necessary to determine the compositional identity of the constellation from which one sets out.

Setting out from this ideal type for determining reproduction, we can now set about to successively modify the substitutability relation (*Vertretbarkeitsverhältnis*) between medial expressions. The following, in part hopefully fictive, examples present cases in which people assume that such substitution relations are satisfied.

a. A person whom we have asked to read Davidson's "The Conditions of Thought" read a text that was published under Davidson's name with the title "Voraussetzungen für Gedanken."
b. A person whom we asked to read Baudelaire's *Les Fleurs du Mal* read a book with the title *Flowers of Evil*.
c. It turns out that the author of an essay that, according to the title, ought to contain an analysis of Kandinsky's *Bleu de Ciel* (1940) composed this on the basis of a black-and-white photograph of the picture.
d. An important literary scholar publishes an article on Dante's *La Divina Commedia* solely on the basis of his knowledge of Liszt's *Dante Symphonie*, which was composed in 1856.

Of course, none of these cases establishes a merely arbitrary relation between the two medial constellations mentioned in each example, but these relations differ considerably with respect to whether the second-named constellation can substitute for the first. If the German translation of "The Conditions of Thought" is successful, then we do not assume that the German text resembles the English one in a way that can be experienced by the senses, but we expect that the medial constellation that constitutes the translation is true under the same conditions as the original. Or, put differently, we expect that the two texts contain the same determinations, so that the same entitlements and responsibilities accrue for someone, regardless of which of the two versions he adopts. As is well known, literary texts that do not merely make use of characteristics that are able to be articulated in terms of validity conditions, but that also make systematic use of sensible attributes pose more broad-reaching translation problems. In any case, the reader of an English translation of *Les Fleurs du Mal* might miss effects that the text typically has on French readers, because expressions in the context of the French-speaking community are part of a certain connotative environment that cannot be reproduced in English, or because the text possesses certain sensible aspects that are not able to be reconstructed in English (alliteration, onomatopoeia, rhythmic structures, rhyme, etc.). With a view to these characteristics, which can be of fundamental importance for the compositional identity of a work of art, it may be impossible to reproduce sensible equivalents in the medium in which the substituting medial constellation is supposed to be produced. What we expect from translations in these cases is that at least functionally equivalent forms are found.

(T_1) Given a constellation a in a medium M_a, a *translation* of a exists if a constellation a^* is produced in a medium M_a^* ($M_a^* \neq M_a$) whose compositional identity in M_a^* is functionally equivalent with that of a in M_a.

In the case of the painting by Kandinsky, we at first glance have a similar situation, which is aggravated by the fact that the target medium is systematically poorer than the source medium insofar as black-and-white photography can reproduce brightness attributes but not color attributes. And although we can recognize some of the relevant structures of the work of art in the photograph, all of those differentiations that are connected to the color or that can only be obtained by assuming different perspectives toward the picture (the surface structure) are lost. Because the colors of the original are not able to be distinguished in black-and-white photography if they have the same brightness, the photograph cannot substitute for the original in regard to these attributes. Because these differences and the effects of the color escape the author of the essay, here we should no longer speak of a translation; the attribution of brightness values to color cannot guarantee the functional equivalence.[157]

Finally, in writing his article, the literary scholar relies on a substitutability relation that simply does not exist. Indeed, in a certain respect Liszt's symphonic poetry mirrors the tripartite structure of Dante's work, and the internal structuring of the parts displays a relationship to the sections in Dante's work insofar as the parts convey experiences with musical means that are described in *The Divine Comedy*. But these relationships are limited, on the one hand, by the fact that the musical structures articulate those subjective experiences that the composer had while reading the literary work; on the other hand, the musical constellations cannot reproduce those literary aspects that depend on the predicative structure of language. Even if the compositional identity of the symphony were obtained by following prescripts that relate medial attributes of the literary work to medial attributes of the musical work without ambiguity, the symphony alone could not represent the literary work. On the one hand, such prescripts could not guarantee the substitutability relation with respect to the sensible attributes; on the other hand, the substitutability relation would, for a recipient, remain dependent on the knowledge of the prescripts so that the target constellation would lose its medial independence since, under the aegis of linguistic prescripts, it would mutate into a literature that contingently uses musical medial elements.

These last two cases are ideal type instantiations of a relation that is implemented by the operation of transposition. Transpositions create medial constellations that cannot be substituted for the initial constellation; as transpositions, they are only of interest to those who know the initial constellation. If this prerequisite is fulfilled, then transpositions can provide interpretations in a broader sense, interpretations that articulate the proposals for structuring the perception of the initial constellation by means of another medium.

(TP_1) Given the constellation a in a medium M_a, a *transposition* exists if and only if an a^* is generated in a medium M_a^* ($M_a^* \neq M_a$) whose compositional identity exists in a conceivable relation to the compositional identity of a in M_a.

What might an operationalizable test now look like that could be used to determine which of the mentioned ideal type operations has formed the relationship between two medial constellations? One test like this could orient itself on the following question: Is it possible to find the medial constellation K_1 for a given medial constellation K_2 that forms the basis of the production of K_2 by the implementation of one of the media operations? In light of this question, it is clear that the degree to which we hold reproductions, translations, and transpositions for invertible operations differs. For while we expect of copies and translations that it is possible to identify, among all of the possible constellations that are possible in a medium, those medial constellations that might serve as source constellations for the operations, we do not expect this of transpositions: Let us assume the existence of a medial constellation that is supposed to be a reproduction. We must expect that a medial-competent recipient is able to identify, from all of the possible constellations in a *medium indi-*

viduationis, those that could have served as the model. And in the case of a translation, too, it must be possible for competent recipients to single out the original from all of the possible texts in French. In short, *Flowers of Evil* is then a translation of *Les Fleurs du Mal* if one can, with its help, identify *Les Fleurs du Mal* from all the French texts.

If both successful reproductions and successful translations enable competent recipients to identify the initial constellation, then, with a view to the test, what is the difference between a reproduction and a translation? Although the reproduction initially looks like the more demanding medial operation, a reproduction does not necessarily imply a reference to the compositional identity of the initial constellation; even a person who cannot write could reproduce a text by sketching a copy, and, in the end, photocopiers manage this without a pattern-recognition program. However, for translations this reference to the compositional identity of the initial constellation is necessary. For even the translation of the text "The Conditions of Thought" into codes of signals can only be carried out if the medial elements of the initial text are correctly identified.

Of course, we do not expect this from transpositions; we do not expect to be able to identify *La Divina Commedia* with the help of the *Dante Symphony*. But neither do we expect that there is no intelligible relation between the two works whatsoever. What a transposition might do can be called an interpretation in a broad sense, an interpretation that provides a specific accentuation of the compositional identity of the constellation that it refers to by means of another medium.

From the perspective of the question regarding whether and how we can identify medial constellations, the criteria (R_1), (T_1), and (TP_1) can now be reformulated as follows:

(R_2) A medial constellation b in a medium M_b is a *reproduction* of a medial constellation a in M_a ($[M_b \neq M_a] \vee [M_b = M_a]$) if and only if a, in the scope of possibilities of M_a, can be identified on the basis of the sensible perceptible attributes of b.

(T_2) A medial constellation b, in a medium M_b, is a *translation* of a medial constellation a in M_a ($M_b \neq M_a$) if and only if a, in the scope of possibilities of M_a, can be identified on the basis of the compositional identity of b in M_b.

(TP$_2$) A medial constellation b, in a medium M_b, is a *transposition* of a medial constellation a in M_a ($M_b \neq M_a$) if and only if the compositional identity of a in M_a is interpreted by the compositional identity of b in M_b.

One can complain that these reflections have a rather schematic character and ought to be refined in many respects,[158] but it is important to see that the elementary medial operations—if they are to be able to take over a function for the study of the possible relations between media—must be characterized in a way that is not merely relying on the specifics of particular media. If the characterization of the elementary medial operations is able to help provide orientation through the jungle of the media without thereby interfering with the possibility of further differentiations, then it will have fulfilled its objective here.

Let us thus return to the problem set out at the beginning. In a first run-through, on the basis of what has been worked out in this chapter, I will attempt to show the plausibility of a media typology. Here, I will, at the same time, investigate how the everyday ways of speaking about the term *medium* and its theoretical ideas are related to the distinctions under discussion.

As we set out to offer a typology, the first selective criterion that is available to us for this classification work consists in examining whether something is used to individuate thoughts (i.e., A- or B-intentional states). As I have shown, this question cannot be answered independently of the question of whether something is used in a social interpretation practice as a means for individuating thoughts. As a result of the interpretationist perspective of the theory of higher-level intentional states, fulfilling this individuation criterion entails a step toward desubjectivization. If we want to answer the question whether something *is* a medium, then we must ask the following question: besides a being that avails itself of states of affairs of the world in a systematic way for expressive purposes, is there at least one further being that ascribes thoughts to the first one as a result of her interpretation of the expressive behavior? We do indeed expect that producing and interpreting beings are identical; however, both from a genetic and a systematic perspective, self-interpretation is derivative from the interpretation of others, and from a criteriological perspective, we must demand ascription conditions that can be observed from a third-person perspective. An answer to this question must clearly be distinguished from an answer to the question of whether something *could be* a medium.

I would like to characterize the following means of communication as *first-order media*: these are means of a social interpretation practice that help make possible articulation acts that have a compositional identity within the scope of possibilities of a medium and that are provided with content due to interpretive connecting behavior. Means of communication that play the role of first-order media in the social community are the fundamental basis for individuating and ascribing higher-level intentional states.

If one accepts the reflections with the help of which I have attempted to show that both linguistic and nonlinguistic intentional states have a right to be classified as thoughts, then a quite heterogeneous set of different media meet this first criterion, which we should be able to further sort out in a second step; for the means for individuating thoughts that have now been characterized can be further differentiated, and indeed relative to the *kind* of thought that can be individuated with their help. The distinction between truth-apt and non-truth-apt thoughts provides one fundamental possible way to distinguish thoughts, and it is clear that media that individuate truth-apt thoughts, that is, propositional attitudes, are *languages*. Hereby the set of those languages is characterized as a genuine subset of first-order media that encompasses particularly those media with the help of which truth-apt thoughts can be individuated and ascribed. Within the set of languages, for example, vocal and sign languages can be distinguished, depending on which physical parameters are varied in the expression behavior. Here, however, to be granted the status of a first-order medium, it is important that, for example, a sign language does not, for its part, fall back on routines for individuating thoughts employed by a vocal language.[159] If we take into purview the possible relations between linguistic articulations, then the set of (natural) languages can also be characterized by the fact that it is possible to translate among all languages. Tokens of linguistic expressions cannot only be reproduced but also translated insofar as it is possible that a linguistic utterance in context C can be represented (or substituted) by another linguistic utterance that has the same truth conditions in context C.[160]

In clear contrast to languages, as one class of first-order media, is a class of media that—like languages—can assist in individuating and ascribing thoughts; however, the difference here is that these thoughts are not truth-apt. Besides languages, with which C-intentional states can be individuated, *non*linguistic media, with which it is possible to individuate

B-intentional states, comprise a further subset of first-order media; for by virtue of the criterion of compositional identity, B-intentional states possess a media-dependent identification criterion on their own. Thus, these media are potentially independent of language; their potential for individuating thoughts assumes neither linguistic agreement (for example, in the form of explicit rules) nor a necessary linguistic transfer of medial competencies.

If the full theoretical potential of elementary medial operations is exploited for determining the relationship between first-order media, then it is possible to maintain the following: in contrast to the case of linguistic utterances in different languages, it is *not* possible to translate between two medial constellations that are generated using nonlinguistic (artistic) media. In contrast to linguistic utterances, for nonlinguistic medial constellations the *transposition* is the only intermedial operation that is available. Further, however, also with a view to the relation between linguistic and nonlinguistic expressions, because of the lack of truth aptness of nonpropositional thoughts, neither can nonlinguistic expressions be translated into linguistic expressions, nor, conversely—in accord with the symmetry of the translation relation—can linguistic expression behavior be translated into linguistically independent first-order media. If we accept the idea that the characteristic of first-order media is that, with their help, it is possible to think thoughts, then the distinction between natural languages and nonlinguistic media can be explained in terms of media theory by the fact that nonlinguistic media can only be involved in intermedial relations as instantiations of transposition. In contrast, it is possible to translate between different linguistic utterances. Examples of these nonlinguistic media are, of course, artistic media such as music, dance, painting, graphics, sculpture, etc.[161]

Two types of first-order media that are clearly distinguishable are thus, first, languages and nonlinguistic (artistic) media. However, in the face of the differentiation we have made, greater problems are posed by the question of whether this provides an exhaustive catalogue of the class of first-order media or whether views, like those brought into play by sociological media theory—for example, money, power, or law—are further first-order media. In order to have a right to the status of first-order media, it must be possible to show that thoughts whose identity is linked to the position in the scope of possibilities of a medium can be individuated with their help.

It appears to me to be clear that a person in a negotiating situation who, for example, lays $954 on the table expresses in this act that she is ready to pay exactly this sum for the goods offered by the seller. Yet it is questionable whether we can ascribe to this person the intentional state that is expressed in this offer without assuming that this person has individuated this state with language. One could now claim that, independently of the established "medium" of money, this person could not find herself in the intentional state that is characterized by holding the goods to be properly valued at $954. More specifically, however, we are faced with two questions: on the one hand, it is an open question whether an intentional state is conceivable that is not able to be sufficiently determined independently of the individuation possibilities of the potential medium of money; on the other hand, it must be explained whether there could be a medium of money without the medium of language. As far as I can see, however, both questions must be clearly answered with "no." For the intentional state of "being ready to spend $954 for W" can only be individuated by a person who has this state in the context of common beliefs, and the fact that the formulation that provides the content of the intention names a monetary amount is only understandable to the person herself if she has background beliefs of the following sort: "For $954 I have to work forty hours. In this time, I cannot produce W myself." But also "Dollars are a lawful currency that can be exchanged for goods." And "I would also be prepared to exchange W for 140 pounds of coffee." All of the attributes of money relevant for the person can be linguistically expressed. Beyond this, it is also clear that money is not a medium that exists independently of language; for money—all the more so as intrinsically worthless money—must be brought into social existence in an act of explicit institutional agreement with the help of constitutive rules. Even if we need not assume that all users of money are conscious of the principal fact that it has an institutional character, well-rehearsed routines of monetary exchange can only be explained if we assume that the users, for example, know that it is against the law to produce money oneself, that an old used bill is worth as much as a new one, that a nickel has the same value as five pennies, etc. However, even the thoughts that a money user has in a specific situation in which she uses it are largely of a propositional nature; for the specific ameliorations that the use of money provide for the formation of beliefs and intentions, as well as for actions, are part of a network of linguistically individuated intentional states and can be understood as a refinement of intentional states that exist independently of money. If we assume that a natural language contains numerals, that the person in question can count, and that the person knows what an exchange is, then the thoughts of the person that are related to money can be described as the mere refinement of the thoughts that the person could also think independently of the money-specific competencies. All differentiations are the result of the fact that the person expands the evaluating vocabulary by expressions that use money as the standard of evaluation, an evaluation that is also possible independently of this standard, even if it can be articulated especially efficiently with the help of this standard. In short, intentional states that can be articulated with the help of money are not independent of language; in the best-case scenario, the domain of the intentional states that can be individuated with its help provides for an amelioration of the intentional states that need to be individuated by language. This classification of money in the context of language is also confirmed by the fact that sentences, whose relational identity is partially dependent on the fact that they contain expressions for monetary amounts, can be *translated* both into other languages and into those sentences that contain no such expressions, but that have the same truth conditions; for example, the sentence "*P* is prepared to pay $954 for this book" can be translated into the sentence "*P* is prepared to exchange 140 pounds of coffee for this book."[162] Because all of the other phenomena—that in the context of sociological theory formation should be understood in accord with the example of money—are integrated into a holistic context of explicit institutional agreements to the same degree as money, a detailed discussion of phenomena such as power, influence, or law is unnecessary here, especially since the generalization procedure, to which they owe their classification as media, is extremely dubious.[163]

Higher-order media can be differentiated from first-order media, which are the irreducible means for individuating thoughts. Particular to such higher-order media is that their medial *elements*—or a set of medial elementary constellations—exist in a sufficiently unambiguous classificatory relation to the medial *elements* of a medium M_1, which is already used in an interpretive communicative practice to individuate thoughts. Let us assume a community in which a vocal language is spoken that consists of twenty-six types of phonemes; then a higher-order medium (M_2) could classify every type of phoneme into another event type or state type, for example, per character or per elementary constellation of characters. Here the event types or state types that form the medial elements of M_2 have different physical attributes than the medial elements of M_1.

Higher-order media, like phonetic transcripts or notation and medial codes (codes of signals, ASCII), assume that there are already medial constellations that have been individuated in first-order media; with a view to the compositional identity of these medial constellations, they can prove their value as target media for translation operations. Insofar as the successful use of higher-order media is dependent on equivalence relations or reproduction relations between sets of medial elements (or elementary constellations), and thus on compliance with explicit prescripts, I view higher-order media as linguistically dependent media that can only arise historically if there is a medium in which the reference to the first-order elements of the medium is possible as well as the individuation of explicit prescripts.

With higher-order media, the possibilities for communication that are available in a social community can be considerably broadened; in particular, the physical attributes of elements of second-order media can allow medial constellations whose performance within the framework of first-order media is elusive to be translated into forms that endure longer than the physical implementations in a first-order medium. But even in writing, where this is managed, and where articulations of greater dimension and greater complexity are made possible, articulations in second-order media remain connected to the potential to individuate thoughts in first-order media. In other words, it is not possible to write something that one could not (internally) say or sing.

If, against the background of the previous reflections, we ask how that which is called media in the McLuhan tradition is related to the differentiations made here, then, in the face of the basic classification criterion—which draws its classifying power from its connection with the conditions for individuating thoughts—two answers must be provided. Some of what the McLuhan tradition refers to as media belongs to *higher-order* media; other things are not media at all, because they do not have anything to do with individuating thoughts—they are things that we simply use as *tools*, which are based on the implementation of physical and not medial relations. However, it is worthwhile to differentiate the class of tools so that it is at least understandable how McLuhan could come up with the idea of presenting such heterogeneous phenomena as language, the alphabet, print, and radio, but also electric light, electric energy, paper, and the wheel as examples of media. While the alphabet and script can be classified as second-order media, we must view the wheel and electric light simply as tools that exist without a direct, significant connection to media. For radio, television, paper, and print, things may look different. In these cases we are dealing with tools or technologies that, at least, play a role in medial practices.

On the one hand, we can observe that tools and technologies for generating physical realizations of medial constellations can play an important role. If, for example, we take second-order medial constellations such as written texts into purview, a surface is needed on which a text can be written or printed. Here writing instruments and writing surfaces play the role of *medial tools*; diverse physical objects and materials can fulfill this role.[164] Even if different tools for implementing medial constellations might have different advantages and disadvantages with a view to the durability, the power expended, the readability, etc., these differences are hardly of conceptual significance, even if innovations in these areas can have broad-reaching social consequences and can be directly relevant for aesthetic reception.

On the other hand, however, this assessment raises the question of whether we should analyze phenomena like photography, film, radio, telephone, television, video, etc., in the same way or whether qualifying them as sets of medial tools is to do too little. Because an answer to this question raises numerous specific problems, I will here only suggest a criterion with the help of which the question can be addressed in principle.

First, with a view to the phenomena mentioned, we should clarify what we are talking about and avoid the idiosyncratic ambivalence that is implicit in the expressions mentioned. To do this, we should distinguish between the medial tools that, in the most demanding case, are *nècessary* means for physically implementing medial constellations and the medial constellations themselves, which we, for example, call radio dramas, photographs, films, or videos. Medial tools in this sense can be microphones, cameras, developers, cathode ray tubes, speakers, that is, any of those technical means that lead to the implementation of a perceptible product and in this respect stand in the tradition of paintbrushes and violins. The use of technical instruments that serve the reproduction and distribution of physical implementations of medial constellations should be distinguished from the necessary role that technical instruments can play as medial tools. These tools are the arsenal of technical devices that

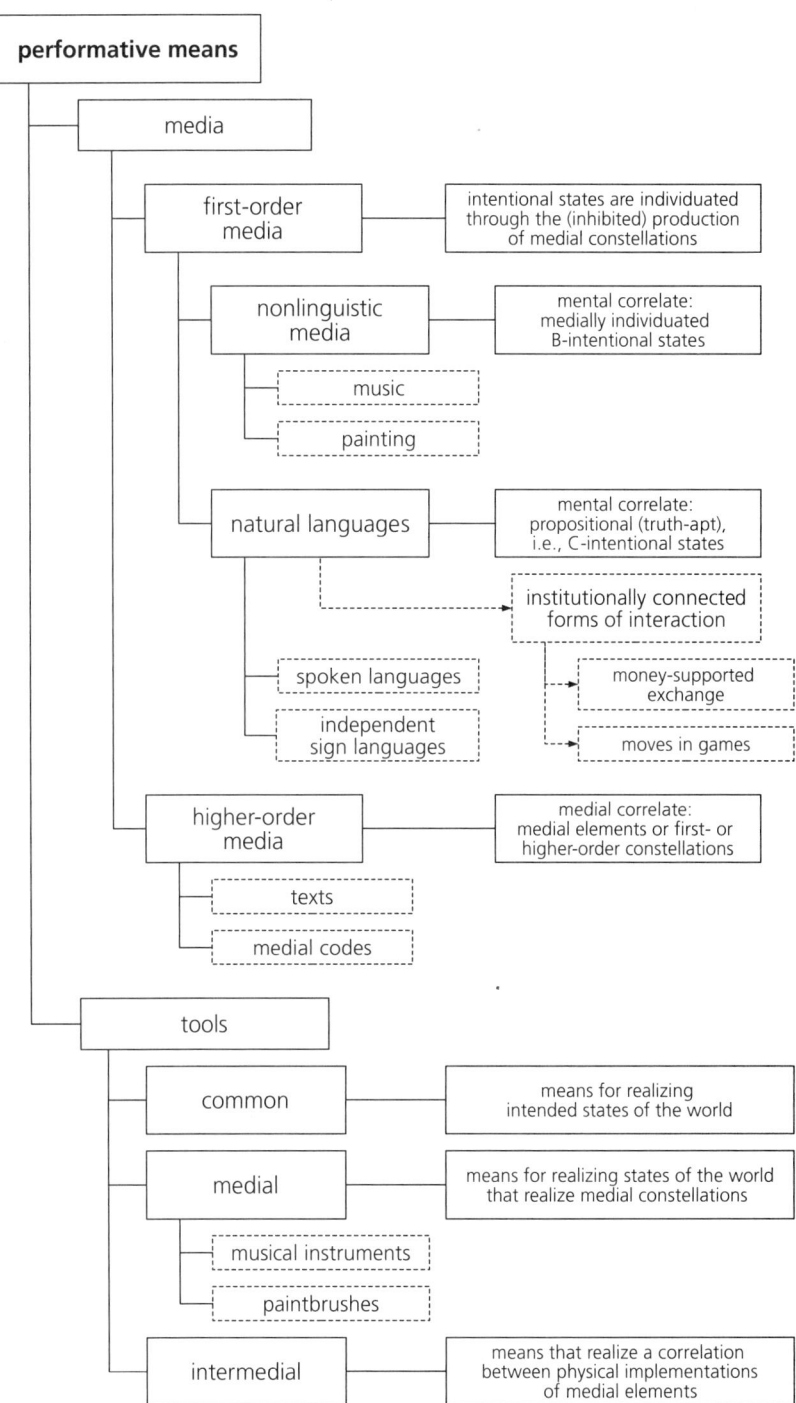

FIGURE 3.6 A typology of media

motivate one of the popular everyday ways of applying the media concept and that in common use do not serve the initial production of a medial constellation, but, like photocopiers, serve reproduction, or, like radio systems, serve the distribution of physically implemented medial constellations. In the framework of the perspective suggested here, we can call these tools *intermedial tools*.

The suggestion here is not characterized by a particular sensitivity to the details that play a role in the context of relations between medial constellations and the processes of physically implementing them; nevertheless, with its help, a perspective can be distinguished in which stable distinctions can be established between media and medial constellations, on the one hand, and medial tools, on the other hand. For in contrast both to the medial tools and to the intermedial tools, only perceptible products that are able to be experienced are medial constellations, which have identities within the scope of possibilities of their medium. Whether the concern is with medial constellations in nonlinguistic or linguistic media depends on whether such products are caused by B- or C-intentional states. Because media are understood as limited sets of learnable alternatives for action that bring about intersubjectively perceptible states of affairs in the world or events that implement medial attributes, media-specific action alternatives can include the use of tools or instruments. But the tools are not media.

If I am correct, on the basis of the fundamental description of media as a means for individuating thoughts, we obtain a perspective that allows us a reasonably organic classification of media and tools. For an overview, see figure 3.6.

4 / THE CONSEQUENCES FOR A CONCEPT OF RATIONALITY

At the end of chapter 1 I argued that an adequate theory of rationality can only be developed on the basis of a comprehensive analysis of processes of understanding. Such an analysis is only comprehensive if it includes the understanding of nonlinguistic communicative actions that can account for the untranslatability of nonlinguistic articulations. In conformity with one use of the concept of a "medium" in everyday language, I then assumed that some processes of nonlinguistic understanding are implemented with the help of means that are analogous to the medium of language, which makes verbal communication possible. Because no stable concept of medium can be found in the contemporary theory landscape—despite the fact that the media concept plays a central role in the most influential social theories of our day—in chapter 2 I set out to develop the main features of a general media theory. This should in particular show itself to be up to the task of making nonlinguistic processes of understanding, as they paradigmatically appear in aesthetic communication, accessible to theoretical analysis within the framework of an interpretationist theory. If the intuition is correct that an adequate concept of rationality must be developed on the basis of an adequate concept of understanding, then it is now time to examine what benefits the media-theoretic amelioration of the concept of understanding has brought to the theory of rationality. In other words, the issue is to examine whether this book rightly bears the title *Media of* Reason. This chapter is thus devoted to addressing the question of the degree to which our view of rationality can be refined by the proposed media-theoretic means and the consequences that this might have for the further development of the project of the Enlightenment.

With a view to the mentioned issue, two possible benefits of the media-theoretic amelioration of the concept of understanding are to be distinguished, which I will attempt to balance in succession. For one, *explicative* benefits may result from the fact that a concept of understanding that is broadened in this way allows us to apply our view of rationality more comprehensively and with greater differentiation and greater homogeneity, so that we can, for example, clearly show, with such a concept, the degree to which aesthetic communication instantiates rational competencies and what the differences from the established forms for instantiating reason consist in. From the perspective of the study of the explicative benefits, I hope to be able to show that the common critique of rationality is attractive because it is based on a view of rationality that centered on—historically plausible but contingent—philosophical explications of rationality that only take account of linguistic competencies. For another, however, one can also expect a *normative* benefit from a theory of rationality ameliorated by media theory. From the perspective of the study of the normative benefit, I would especially like to examine whether we ought to understand reason in the Humean tradition rather as a bundle of such competencies with the help of which we can best achieve our respective contingent preferences, or whether, following a Habermasian impulse, general norms can be obtained from the analysis of understanding—now with a complete variety of processes of understanding at our disposal—whose normative power is not dependent on specific interests, that is, on particular norms that would be relevant for the conception of Enlightenment processes.

4.1. THE EXPLICATIVE BENEFITS

If we inquire into the explicative benefits of the reflections on media theory for a theory of rationality, then it is obvious that we must address the question of what reason is. As we saw in the introduction, there are a series of well-established answers to this question. Admittedly, particularly using these theories in the attempt to understand what artistic action is, we encountered numerous problems, precisely the problems that motivated us to develop the media theory. However, from the fact that the established rationality theories do not provide any particularly favorable instruments for analyzing artistic actions, it by no means automatically follows that these conceptions of rationality are to be fundamentally modified. In order to determine the explicative benefit of media-theoretic reflections we should thus examine whether medial action *can be subsumed* under the existing concepts of rationality. We must thus examine whether, starting with a well-contoured understanding of rationality, we can also understand artistic action and nonlinguistic thinking as instantiations of already sufficiently specified rational abilities. Only if we show that this is not possible can we justifiably assume that our view of rationality *itself* must be differentiated in order to provide a place for abilities, the analysis of which has not yet been able to contribute to a characterization of rational competencies, although the same set of entities can be characterized with the help of these abilities as can be characterized with the classical definition of reasonableness. In the framework of these reflections, the concern is thus not to grant one ability or another a place among the range of exemplary rational competencies; rather, we must show that they have a rightful claim to this status.

4.1.1. Media as Mere Instruments of Reason?

However, if, to begin with, one pursues the first path, then a charitable reader of the media-theoretic reflections might come to the conclusion that they may well yield something interesting about media, art, and nonlinguistic communication, but that media in principle are nothing more than instruments that can be used by actors with artistic, expressive, or general communicative intentions. If that is the case, however, then the connection between media and reason appears to be purely external. Then, in this perspective, media come into purview, under the assumption of existing intentions, only as possible instruments for implementing such intentions. They contribute nothing to defining reason, which reflects on the adequacy of these means. Even if this objection is based on a specific understanding of reason, one could maintain the thesis that each of the concepts of reason that was explained in chapter 1 in principle would be able to integrate the media-theoretic reflections so that the respective definition of reason of each of them would remain untouched. In the face of the list of paradigmatic rational competencies schematically summarized in the findings of the reconstruction of the established concepts of rationality,[1] we must be able to say the following: *If* rationality essentially

1. is a culturally conveyed competence of actors to orient themselves with the help of transindividual but context-varying standards in action situations (Kambartel), *then* even in the context of aesthetic phenomena, or more generally in contexts of nonlinguistic communication, this competence may *arise* and *develop*;
2. is to be understood as a set of normative demands, which, if followed, ought to promote the production of forms of life that find general agreement, that are generally perceived to be acceptable, and that present a suitable basis for justified developments (Mittelstraß), *then* we can assume that (some, perhaps even many) people will tend to view the expressive and communicative possibilities that depend on the social existence of media as a characteristic of generally acceptable conditions of life;
3. is the competence of communicative actors to subject their communicative actions to universal validity claims and thus to fulfill conditions required to criticize and, hence, understand them (Habermas), *then*, under the assumption that communicative actors pursue communicative objectives, it is certainly possible that they make use of nonlinguistic means in doing so; here, however, the adequacy of these means in the case of expressive action is only subject to limited intersubjective examination;
4. is the competence of actors to optimize their actions and beliefs relative to their well-understood individual interests (Gosepath), *then* media can be means to implementing such optimizations;
5. is understood as a set of normative demands that are directed to interpreters who want to describe and understand the behavior of beings as action by imputing desires and intentions to them (Davidson), *then* such interpreters might feel compelled to impute to these beings expressive intentions that they implement by means of media;
6. is understood as a competence of systems to reduce the complexity of their environments under conditions of self-maintenance and to assume a perspective that relates the selectivity of the systems to the improbability of their existence (Luhmann), *then* we

can easily imagine that they accomplish this by the use of medial means—whatever that means.

If we go through the individual points, it quickly becomes clear that all the concepts are able to integrate the media-theoretic reflections insofar as they can view (nonlinguistic) media as means for implementing communicative intentions as well as other desires. From this perspective—which completely concurs with the intuition of the charitable reader—media appear to be instruments, and indeed instruments like dough hooks or toothbrushes. They are a part of what Heidegger called equipment (*Zeug*). If one wants to evade this kind of assimilation (*Vereinnahmung*), then it must be shown that the main point of media theory has escaped the allegedly charitable reader, and, as a result, he deals with a sterilized media concept that virtually guarantees the subsumption of media under an antecedent rationality concept. If I am correct, this subsumption is possible because the established concepts of reason assume a specific relationship between reason and language, which, for its part, has consequences for the relationship between reason and media. For what would happen if, in the face of the above finding, we were to say: now media behave exactly like language. Media *and* language are means for fulfilling (communicative) ends. I think that the proponents of conceptions of reason would attempt to show the validity of the view that the relationship between language and reason is fundamentally different from the relationship between media and reason insofar as reason is something that simply cannot exist independently of linguistic competencies. The connection between reason and language is accordingly constitutive rather than instrumental.

However, precisely because, according to this view, reason exists independently from nonlinguistic media, the concepts can place media under the umbrella of reason in the way sketched out above; here media do not play a part in constituting reason. However, as I attempt to show in what follows, this is only plausible if one falls back behind the media concept that I have developed. Because the established theories believe that they can solely entrust language with constituting reason, they are able to apprehend the relationship between reason and media as merely instrumental. If we would like to oppose the view that media have a mere instrumental status, then we must first of all understand what makes the constitutive relationship between language and reason so plausible and why it also appears to be clear that nonlinguistic media cannot play a role in constituting reason.

With a view to the relationship between language and reason, in essence the four following theoretical motifs can be offered as arguments for the constitutive relationship. *First*, language is thought to make possible the individuation of (higher) intentional states, i.e., of *contentful* mental states; this comes to expression, inter alia, in the fact that having a thought is identified with the inner articulation of a sentence. However, because only beings with thoughts can be rational, it is at the same time clear that only linguistic beings can be rational. *Second*, language is apprehended as making the development of a *self-relationship* possible, so that only one who masters a language can develop the ability for self-reflection and with it the ability for self-criticism. However, because self-criticism is a condition for the process of weighing alternatives, which is specific to rational beings, rational beings have to be linguistic beings. *Third*, because only language is considered to allow the formulation of *rules*, and the ability to orient one's actions on principles, i.e., on rules, is a basic dimension of rational behavior, one would have to deny nonlinguistic beings a fundamental aspect of rationality. Finally, *fourth*, only language is entrusted with the ability to make something *explicit* that our behavior is implicitly based on. By making something explicit, however, one places it in the realm of *reasons*; here it is subject to the light of critique. And, of course, only beings that operate within the realm of reasons are considered rational beings.

Even if these four motifs are connected with each other in diverse ways and are weighted differently in the different conceptions of rationality, they nevertheless depict the core of those beliefs that form the background for the view that only linguistic beings can be rational beings. Because it is unclear what it might mean for a thought to have content if this content cannot be linguistically articulated, and because, beyond this, it is unclear how nonlinguistic media might make a self-relationship possible, how they could explain the formulation of rules or the elucidation of implicit norms, it appears at the same time to be evident that the relationship between nonlinguistic media and reason is external, in a word, instrumental. If one would like to show that this assessment is wrong, then one must show that and how nonlinguistic media can assume roles that are comparable with the role of language with a view to the competencies mentioned above. In short, one must answer the question of whether it is also sensible to say that nonlinguistic media have the ability to be constitutive conditions for reason.

4.1.2. Media as Conditions of Reason

In what follows I would like to proceed by discussing the four mentioned motifs relatively concisely. I will look into whether it is possible to imagine that their basic relations can also be realized by means of nonlinguistic media. While the reflections of chapter 3 were marked by the attempt to buttress an intuition, now I will not mince words in treating the ideas developed there, but will attempt to examine them as forthrightly as possible.

4.1.2.1. Content

From an interpretationist framework, to speak of the content of thoughts is to speak of theoretical entities of interpretation. Content is what we assume if we *understand* beings by rationalizing their behavior. Here we impute to them states that have an identity within a holistic network of propositional attitudes, which, for its part, is structured inferentially. According to this basically Fregean perspective, however, content then has the form of a sentence of necessity, because sentences are the smallest unities that can play inferential roles, i.e., the role of reasons.[2] However, with Brandom, we must then say that musical *expressions* or works possess no content, because they cannot be put into the form of sentences, and thus they cannot be understood within the framework of the inferentialist theory of content. For "understanding in this favored sense is a grasp of reasons, mastery of properties of theoretical and practical *inference*."[3] If one accepts this view, then it follows (according to interpretationist premises) that those mental *states* that are causes of musical action cannot have content. If, in contrast, on the basis of the reflections of the previous chapter, one wants to claim that the B-intentional states that I postulated there certainly have content, then this content can certainly not be due to the fact that these states can play the role of premises or of conclusions. If B-intentional states are supposed to measure up to linguistically individuated thoughts in the sense of having content, then an interpretive relation is required that ascribes them content without thereby imputing to them the status of reasons.

In the previous chapter I proposed[4] that nonlinguistic expressions, in the context of the social interactions that they are developed in, acquire content by virtue of the fact that, in a first step, through the formation of expectations, they are correlated with the regular reactions of the recipients of such expressions, and, in a second step, they are joined to those reactions that the producers of such expressions experience for themselves or anticipate as reactions of potential recipients. With a view to the process in the course of which expressions and reactions are joined to one another, we need not assume that the constancy of the reactions to types of expressions, for its part, is supported by the recipients' reason-guided behavior. We can thus assume that the content of nonlinguistic expressions is ascribed by a form of social interpretation that is itself not a linguistic interpretation. However, if interpretation is the only way in which a mental state or an expression can acquire content, and there are nonlinguistic interpretations, then there are beings that fulfill *one* prerequisite for being rational beings—namely, of having thoughts with content—without necessarily thereby being linguistic beings. With B-intentional states we have not yet entered the realm of reasons, yet we have left the realm of nature insofar as we are concerned with *socially conferred* content.

A fundamental pragmatic prerequisite for the ability to socially confer content is that media—regardless of whether these are nonlinguistic or linguistic media—are not instantiated by types of expressions that themselves already have content, independently of social interpretations. In other words, it requires types of expressions that are *semantically intrinsically empty*, i.e., that have no intrinsic content. Here it should hold:

> (IC) A form of behavior B has intrinsic content if and only if recipients of B react to B as they would react to a *natural sign*.[5]

Given a certain biological endowment in a recipient R, R cannot receive a form of behavior that has intrinsic content B without reacting to B as if that which B stands for is present; in the case of natural signs, this consists in a cause C that brings about B. Here B is caused by C and only

C. In contrast, only those expressions are suited to be types of medial expressions that bring about states or events that do not play the role of natural signs, because these would indicate—in a way that authenticates natural law—the states of a being that brought them about.[6]

The media-theoretic analysis thus draws our attention to the fact that the social dealings with types of activities that are semantically intrinsically empty create the foundation for our ability to develop something that is called mind; for the operation of mind consists in dealing with (inhibited) types of expressions that obtain content in the context of social interaction. Here, with nonlinguistic media—as with languages—the differentiation of content is dependent on the differentiation of the medial constellations.[7] In the development of this foundation of mind, nonlinguistic media thus mark an important step, which is further specified by language. In this way, from a media-theoretic perspective, we at the same time gain a clearer view of the role of language; here, an advantage of this perspective is that it allows language to be described in a theoretically homogeneous vocabulary as a specific medium—a medium, namely, that is subordinate to normative restrictions that allow it to become a medium for giving and asking for reasons. If the creation of content justifies the intimate relationship between language and reason, then we must account for the fact that nonlinguistic means also make the individuation of content possible if we replace the mere instrumental relationship between reason and media with a constitutive one. If, beyond that, it can be shown to be plausible that the content that can be individuated with the help of nonlinguistic media cannot necessarily be articulated with the help of language—if then this content is connected to certain forms of nonlinguistic articulation, which, for their part, cannot be translated—then we can claim that this content cannot be reduced to what is able to be linguistically articulated. For nonlinguistic medial expressions this is fulfilled in particular by the fact that the experiencing of the medial expression remains linked to those physical attributes that the implementation of a medial expression exhibits. At the same time, the ability to substitute, paraphrase, and translate linguistic expressions shows that the medium of language has, to a significant extent, been emancipated from the sensory elements that constitute one of the causes of the untranslatability of nonlinguistic medial expressions.

4.1.2.2. Self-Relationship

An answer to the question of whether a sphere that is rightfully denoted a sphere of linguistically independent self-interpretation can be characterized by media-theoretic means will have to be positioned in reference to two views: on the one hand, to the interpretation that quite self-assuredly tends, for example, to understand the painting of children as a form of expression by which children develop a relationship to themselves; on the other hand, to the interpretation that becoming well versed in a medial practice means only that one possesses a disposition to react to experiences by producing certain pictures. While the first position interprets the children's pictures as a nonlinguistic form of self-interpretation, the second one views those pictures as mere symptoms; and while the first position has to postulate something like a self-relationship, which at any rate is not necessarily generated with a linguistically realized self-interpretation, the second position assumes that the symptomatically understood pictures can only be observed as material of an interpretation from the perspective of an interpreter that possesses language.

Within the framework of the four-phase model, I have attempted to show that it is plausible that medial constellations obtain content in the phase of medial communication by virtue of the fact that individuals who are familiar with a medial practice react to the medial performances of children in an exemplary way. These reactions succeed reactions to affect-steered expressive behavior in which reference persons mirror the states of children in a process of marked mimetic communication. If medial behavior is joined to the expectation of a nonlinguistic response behavior, and the response behavior covaries with the compositional identity of the medial expressions, then a child that is socialized in a medial practice learns to order medial expressions in line with the proprioceptive perception of the act of carrying out the expression and in line with the effects of the social response behavior on itself. In this process, types of medial expressions become the means for referring to types of experiences.

Already at an elementary level, nonlinguistic medial constellations can thus assume a form in which, by virtue of the effect of the medial means on themselves, producers of medial constellations can envision experiences. Because these means do not have any intrinsic meaning, like the mimetic expressions of affects, constellations can obtain meaning in line with their receptive effects. Because the medial production of medial constellations is a self-controlled form of articulation, and the production can be controlled by the producer in line with its effect on the producer, for their producers medial constellations are instantiations of a self-relationship. Here, with medial means, they refer to an experience that is adequate or inadequate relative to the state in which they find themselves. Then, however, one can say that the medial constellations structure the access to those states, relative to which, on the basis of their effects, they are adequate or inadequate.

4.1.2.3. Rules

With a view to the problem of whether the aspect of rational action that makes it possible to follow maxims or principles, that is, to follow rules, can be reconstructed by media-theoretic means, we must, first of all, distinguish between two levels. On the one hand, it is clear that in order for an action to be defined as a rational action, it is not required that the action have a rule-following character. For rational actions, we do not necessarily expect the content of rules to establish the reason for the action. In order to understand an activity as a rational action, what we need are reasons (in the framework of assuming minimal rationality) that we can ascribe coherently. On the other hand, the ability to follow rules or to act on the basis of principles is a specific characteristic and prominent aspect of rational action.[8] If language is the only medium for formulating principles, then we must admit that nonlinguistic media cannot contribute to constituting this aspect of rationality. However, I have attempted to show that we can plausibly postulate a special form of explicit rules with the help of the concept of demonstrative rules that is characterized by the fact that it articulates rightness nonlinguistically and medially.[9] However, because the normative component is articulated within the parameters of this concept, with the help of an imperativist linguistic form, the possibility that explicit rules can exist in a language-independent form appears to be dependent on our ability to demonstrate how the imperativist component can also be nonlinguistically implemented. In attempting to show this, we are confronted with the following task: if we want to reconstruct the concept of rule following solely using nonlinguistic instruments, then we must ensure that both the part of a rule that characterizes the right or wrong behavior as well as the part that articulates the imperative character that is expressed by rules can be implemented nonlinguistically.

In connection with the conception of demonstrative rules, we, after all, find ourselves in an interesting theoretical position, namely, that we can implement these two components by different mechanisms, and it is not necessary to burden one concept alone—for example, the concept of a sanctioning practice—with the task of specifying the content and conveying the imperative.[10] The strategy sketched out here is thus a strategy of decoupling the individuation of the content of rules and the implementation of the imperative modus. And because the concept of demonstrative rules allows us to entrust the individuation of the content of nonlinguistic rules to a deictic practice, a sanctioning practice could limit itself to conveying the imperative. For this, we must only assume that, for example, a teacher, who can deictically refer to and bring about what is right, negatively sanctions a student if and only if the student, for example, makes a mistake in the production of medial elements.

Admittedly, it can be objected that the deictic practice is overtaxed as a content-individuating mechanism insofar as, in deictic situations, it is not at all clear *what* is being pointed *to* or *what* is demonstrated as right. In opposition to a deictic individuation mechanism, one could thus formulate an objection along the line of arguments on which Føllesdal[11] bases his objections to Davidson's causal reference theory: just as, in the triangulation situation, there is a lack of clarity about the cause of the similar reactions among students and teachers, so with the deictic individuation mechanism, there is a lack of clarity about what the sanctioner is really pointing at. Is the nonlinguistic vocal instructor concerned about the positioning of the lips, the effects that the singing has on animals in the surroundings, or the pitch? Arguments of this type can perhaps not be dispelled in principle, but they can be largely rebutted if sufficiently strong restrictions are introduced for deictically implemented teaching practices that are carried out without the help of language. Acceptable deictic practices—that is, practices that can be accepted as mechanisms for individuating the content of nonlinguistic rules—must then exhibit the following characteristics:

1. The right performance must be *repeated* frequently.
2. The repetition of the right performance, which is held stable, *occurs in different contexts* in which the deixis does not refer to attributes that are varied.

3. The right performance is *marked* by nonlinguistic means, normally by exaggeration.

While this last criterion admits a potential attribute of deictic action that is deeply rooted in the prelinguistic communication between infants and their reference persons,[12] the first and second criteria prescribe characteristics for deictic actions whose meaning can be made plausible in the conditionality analysis or other neuronal models of learning: the repetition functions to establish a type, and varying the environmental conditions functions to validate the type *ex negativo*.

In light of the consequences—which are difficult to take into purview—I do not want to commit myself;[13] yet a strategy may begin to show itself that makes rule-following behavior possible, even independently of language. If this analysis allows medial competences to be described as competencies of rule following that are not joined to a linguistic form of explicit rules, then, as a character of rational action, the competence to act according to rules or principles is not linked to language either.

4.1.2.4. Explicitness and Reasons

If we explain a particularity of rationality in a Brandomian perspective so that reason consists of the ability to make explicit the inherent norms of rightness in social practices and thus to make them potential objects of critique, then it is not possible to see how elucidative rationality could have an analogue in nonlinguistic thinking. For from the perspective of elucidative rationality, medial practices may indeed be based on standards of rightness, but these practices do not make things explicit, and, when they do, they require language. In short, I do not see how we can understand nonlinguistic communicative practices to be practices that make their *normative* basis explicit. Nonlinguistic medial practices instantiate rightness; however, without language they are not able to form rightness into rules or principles, and thus to explain it. If we view the rightness that is specific to a specific medial practice, then we can say that what is considered right in this practice, what is accepted as right, can be made explicit in a *deictic* practice. What is right can be demonstrated at any time, and the function of the demonstrative rules consists precisely in providing what is demonstrated with an exemplary character. Here the concept of demonstrative rules[14] allows us to accommodate the fact that it is possible that what is right (in a given social context) cannot be made explicit linguistically at all. But it is important to see that, with this form of explicitness, it is only possible to affirm that which is considered right. In the context of the mere deictic reference to what is right, critique is not carried out by critiquing explicit norms, but by bringing about other paradigmatic forms that are endowed with the status of rightness by becoming media of communication and thus being passed down. In these contexts, "critique" is carried out more by replacing what is valid than by disputing the justification of what is valid.

On the other hand, one could maintain that, with the help of nonlinguistic media, it is possible particularly to make explicit what the content of a medial constellation is. We could then say that medial constellations, for example, make the structures of experiences explicit. This, however, would imply that something would be made explicit by medial means that exists independently of its being articulated. And this does not appear to me to be the case. For van Gogh's *Peasant Shoes* does not make anything explicit that someone with a practiced eye could discover about peasant's shoes or—after having seen the picture—that can be perceived *about such shoes* with hindsight. The picture shares rather a B-intentional state or an experience that is reliant for its individuation on the individuation of the picture.

What about the possibility of understanding *reasons* as something that can be implemented by nonlinguistic medial means? If we view B-intentional states as medial thoughts, that is, as states that have content and an identity for the being that thinks these thoughts, then there is no reason that B-intentional states cannot assume the role of reasons. This assessment can also be supported by the fact that B-intentional states are among those mental states that, by virtue of their content, can also play the role of causes of action. On the other hand, this attribute of the mental cause of an action depends on the existence of a rationalizing interpretation of the activity that actualizes the action, in which the cause is regarded as a reason. I have proposed (H2)[15] as a schema for rationalizing artistic action; and in the first premise of (H2)—fully analogous to the common rationalizations of action in which beliefs or desires are ascribed—a medial intentional state is ascribed. In addition, the medial intentional state would also fulfill the counterfactual criterion for identifying the right causes of an action: if *P* had not found herself in state $I_{b'}$, P would not have produced the work of art. Notwithstanding, the medial intentional state has a different status than, for example, the desire to express I_b. Such desires or beliefs are irreducible components of explanations of action, and I_b only plays the role of a reason in contexts that incorporate desires and beliefs. The fact that I_b plays the role of a reason in (H2) is dependent on the fact that I_b is embedded in the context of desires and beliefs. Because I_b is neither a belief nor a desire, I_b requires this context in order to be a reason. In short, medial intentional states can function as reasons, but we can only ascribe them this function in the context of the classical intentional vocabulary.

4.1.2.5. Summary

The attempt to describe competencies characteristic of rational action as competencies that can be carried out by medial means has yielded the following view:

1. Mental (B-intentional) states that are individuated by media have *content*, and they have this content *for* the beings that have these states. But, unlike propositional states, here it frequently is not possible to express this content in any but one—and only one—medial constellation.
2. Media can be understood as the conditions for the development of a self-relation, because, with the help of medial-affecting experiences, beings can draw on inner states.
3. Media are products of social practices that can be understood as practices that are guided by rules without needing to assume that what is right is characterized linguistically. But medial practices only instantiate this rightness; in a narrower sense, they are not means with which rules—as with the help of language—can be formulated. Admittedly, the correctness of this evaluation is posited on the implausibility of a form for articulating rules that is completely supported by deictic means.
4. Strictly speaking, media do not make anything explicit. But they allow an access to structures of perceptions and experiences that we must assume are partially structured independently of media and language insofar as the acquisition of media and language

competencies already presuppose the ability to identify medial expression types.

5. Medial intentional states can take on the role of reasons insofar as their content can be causes for medial action. But it is only from the perspective of an interpreter capable of speech that they claim to take on the role of reasons.

4.1.3. Another Perspective

The questions of the preceding sections are concerned with appropriating the diagnosis that rational competencies are based on linguistic capabilities. With this perspective, I have tried to clarify the degree to which these competencies can be understood as being based on medial competencies. However, it is specific to such questioning that the reason-*constitutive* aspects of media are described according to standards of paradigmatic linguistic capabilities. One can, however, also question whether media generate a *specific* reason-constitutive achievement that is not brought adequately into view from the perspective of linguistically authored competencies or that is not brought into view from that perspective at all. In order to make this plausible, it must be demonstrated that the concept of reason, which media are supposed to make an independent contribution to constituting, within the parameters of this procedure, is not just broadened precisely to include those aspects that guarantee that the media make a constitutive contribution. In other words, one must ensure that the concept of reason has an inner homogeneity such that it is not so malleable that it merely embodies all those capabilities that one places in a constitutive relationship to it. If this threat is not precluded, then arbitrary constituting relations can be designed so that the concept of reason would only reflect what one is presently characterizing as its constituting basis. If one thus wants to show that media make an independent contribution to defining reason, then this contribution must be included in a conception of reason in such a way that it can be defined independently from these specific contributions. In the introduction to this book I provided a diagnosis—namely, that the theory of rationality is converging toward a theory of understanding as the fundamental level of explication—and I stated that the core rational competencies are those that allow us to understand something. If media are thus supposed to be able to contribute to defining reason, then it must be possible to illustrate this contribution with the concepts of understanding.

Before I attempt to show the specific contribution that nonlinguistic media make to the competence of understanding, in a short excursus I would like to show that some of Kant's thoughts can be read as a suspenseful attempt to characterize a broadened concept of understanding (*Verstehen*) that moves beyond the view that the process of understanding is carried out solely by conceptual-linguistic means. In doing this, I would like to show, within the framework of what is possible here, that theoretical motifs of the Kantian aesthetic can be reformulated by media-theoretic means within the framework of the interactionist paradigm, while avoiding some conceptual ambivalences and counterintuitive presuppositions.

4.1.3.1. Kant's Theory of Aesthetic Experience as a Theory of Nonconceptual Understanding

> Very little is there to reveal things to us . . .
> —I. Bachmann[16]

In his *Critique of Judgment*, Kant, among other things, sought to show that aesthetic experience is based on specific competencies that cannot be reduced to theoretical or practical competencies for dealing with objects of aesthetic experience. In contrast, as Höffe vividly describes, "in the aesthetic relationship to the world . . . [there is] a *distinct form of rationality*," which "can neither be traced back to objective cognition nor to morality, nor to both."[17] In the context of the reflections here, it is, of course, of particular interest that Kant sees a particularity of this form of rationality to lie in the fact that we develop interpretive thought in aesthetic experiences, which have content that systematically evades conceptual articulation. In what follows I would like to suggest an interpretation of Kant that aims to uncover theoretical motifs that are suited to serve as links for the theoretical formulation of nonconceptual *rational* competencies.

As is well known, Kant conceives of the particularity of aesthetic experience such that in aesthetic experience sensibility and spontaneity interact with one another in such a way that the representations (*Vorstellungen*) that we form of a sensory-perceived phenomenon are brought together, under the direction of the reflective judgment, with conceptual productivity such that an integrated representation emerges without the perceived phenomenon thereby being subsumed under a concept. In contrast to the *determinant* judgment, which subsumes the particular that is provided by the senses under the general, a rule or principle, that is provided by the understanding (*Verstand*), the *reflective* judgment searches for the general under which the particular that is provided through intuition could fall. As reflective judgment, in this it proceeds—according to the subjective transcendental principle—to view the particular, in accord with its form, as purposive for our cognitive faculty.[18] If we now examine the representation of a particular from the perspective of the subject that has the representation, then we come up against its aesthetic constitution insofar as it is subject to a specific evaluation by taste—an evaluation in which the purposiveness of the object for our cognitive faculty is judged. If objects of sensory experience manage to bring imagination and understanding into a harmonious relationship—without this having been intended—then this relationship generates a feeling of pleasure that Kant traces back to the purposiveness of the object of the representation for the reflective judgment, which is not dependent on its conceptual determination.[19]

In this perspective, an aesthetic experience does not emerge as an exotic special kind of experience, but as a fundamental kind of experience; on the basis of it, the conditions of the elementary individuation of experience can be analyzed without the need for a concept of the object of experience. The analysis of aesthetic judgment thus also aims at an explication of experience, which does not allow the conceptual structuring of intuitions. For even if, in contrast to the common experience, we do not end up, within the framework of aesthetic experiences, with a conclusive conceptual structuring of intuitions, the process in which the sensibility and spontaneity interact with one another is not in vain. From the perspective characteristic of judgment toward subjective purposiveness of the form of the object for our cognitive faculty, the object provided in the experience is indeed, on the one hand, apprehended independently of concepts; on the other hand, however, this is carried out precisely by virtue of the fact that the intuition and the concepts come together in *cognition generally* (*einer Erkenntnis überhaupt*).[20]

1. The concept of cognition generally, which Brigitte Scheer places at the center of her interpretation of Kant,[21] here has the function of characterizing a synthesizing activity of mind, which emerges from the free

play of imagination and understanding in the face of an aesthetically experienced phenomena and "need not yet be cut short by the stipulation of a concept."[22] Representations of objects of aesthetic experience do not have an identity due to the fact that they are (identifying and) identified by means of the classifying power of concepts, but due to the fact that they exist in a (challenging) relation to our cumulative possibilities to make phenomena intelligible. I suggest that we interpret the expression "cognition generally"[23] as a characterization of a kind of intentional state that indeed stands in an interpretive relation to an object of experience, but neither in order to identify the object nor to subsume it under concepts. If we would like to more precisely understand how such states are theoretically designed, then we must above all more precisely understand the unique place of the conceptual in aesthetic experiences. If we call to mind Kant's thoughts about the role of concepts in the context of aesthetic experience, then, however, the following ambivalent view emerges:

a. Concepts are necessary conditions for referring to objects of experience at all; they are, as Kant showed in his *Critique of Pure Reason*, necessary conditions for the knowledge-constitutive synthesis.
b. Insofar as the aesthetic experience is oriented toward the sensory appearance of things, their conceptual determination plays no role: aesthetic judgments are not knowledge judgments.[24]
c. Because aesthetic experience puts into motion the free play of the cognitive faculties, which understanding, with its concepts, necessarily participates in, concepts are a necessary condition for aesthetic experiences, even if having an aesthetic experience does not entail the conceptual determination of an object.
d. In principle, the structure of what emerges with the free play of the cognitive faculties, namely, cognition generally and aesthetic ideas, evades conceptual articulation.
e. The ability to judge an object of experience aesthetically is not a conceptual power, but a power of feeling (*Gefühlsvermögen*).[25]

If I am correct, the ambivalences of these motifs can be resolved if we limit the role of concepts so that concepts, on the one hand, play a necessary, though not a sufficient, role for the possibility of aesthetic experiences; on the other hand, however, especially for determining the content of an aesthetic experience, they are insufficient. Because Kant does not want to understand aesthetic experiences as experiences that simply have not *yet* led to a synthesis that identifies the object of the experiences—which would thus merely be an early stage of a process that, for contingent reasons, is incomplete—a solution must be found in which conceptual aspects are among the necessary framework conditions of aesthetic experience, but wherein they are not part of what defines those experiences. To do this, I will attempt to understand Kant's reflections such that his concern in identifying "cognition generally" is with a nonconceptual form of intelligibility, a form of comprehensibility (*Einsichtigkeit*) that sensory objects can have for us because they confront us as if they were made *for us* and our cognitive apparatus. However, while Kant joins this relation to the point that, from the perspective of understanding, we must view this "fitting" in the case of natural objects as coincidental, and we thus cannot expect it,[26] and our pleasure comes to indicate that we fit into nature, I would like to orient myself on a less perplexing view of the comprehensibility of sensory objects. I would like to claim that it is necessary to reformulate Kant's view, namely, that the fit of nature to our cognitive faculty can be made plausible not with causal concepts, but with teleological ones, in such a way that human artifacts are the exemplar for teleological structure, and we only derivatively describe nature with teleological concepts. To speak with Dennett, when faced with nature, we assume the *design stance*, which we initially rehearse with reference to human products. However, if, in inversion to Kant's weighting, we place the primacy of the artistically beautiful before the naturally beautiful, and analyze aesthetic phenomena at a fundamental level as communicative phenomena, then the nonconceptual form of intelligibility can be shown to be more plausible. While the first view certainly stands in contrast to Kant's ideas, a series of links can be found in Kant's text that supports an emphasis on the basic communicative structure of aesthetic experiences.

2. In the analytic of the beautiful, in which Kant is concerned with the analysis of aesthetic judgment, the communicative function that such judgments can take on plays an important role with a view to determining the validity claim (quantity) of the judgment of taste. Kant analyzes aesthetic judgments not as merely subjective evaluative-expressive acts that have no claim to general validity, but as evaluations that allow those who are making the judgments to lay a claim to a transindividual dimension of aesthetic experience. The basis for this potential "general validity" (*Gemeingültigkeit*) of aesthetic judgments is that the different recipients have the same mental apparatus, the game states (*Spielzustände*)

of which are supraindividual. Kant can thus expect a "universal capability of communication of the mental state in the given representation,"[27] which is not brought into being by concepts. In comparison to Kant's general strategy, namely, to show that nothing can stake a claim to being a principle of reason that cannot be followed by all—thus that is not in a basic sense transindividually intelligible—the reference to the ability to communicate pleasure, which begins from a representation in reflection, seems rather weak. For there appears to be no particular reason—that can be explained and thus transindividually accepted—why an aesthetic judgment can be demanded of everyone; there appears rather to be an empirical cause, namely, that we share a certain mental endowment. Further, however, beyond the fact that a representation has led to a pleasure originating from reflection, the content that is communicated with the help of judgments of taste is not further determined.[28]

In contrast, if we do not view the communicative function of aesthetic judgments but of works of art, another element is introduced that Kant calls *Geist* and that could also be called *Esprit*. We expect that works of art originate from the "faculty of presenting aesthetical Ideas." And an "aesthetic Idea"[29] is a "representation of the imagination which occasions much thought, without, however, any definite thought, i.e., any concept capable of being adequate to it; it consequently cannot be completely encompassed and made intelligible by language."[30]

However, the *intersubjective* principle from which the presentation of aesthetic ideas can take on a communicative function remains unclear. Kant does not even view the faculty of expressing aesthetic ideas as a competence that is intersubjectively acquired in order to portray something with the help of aesthetic (and not "logical") attributes, but as a *talent*, which he understands as a natural gift.[31] That the talent is apprehended as a natural gift, for its part, has the function of reconciling the artifact character—which is connected to precedent rules—that every work of art possesses with the view that a work of art should not merely be viewed as resulting from the arbitrary following of rules that can be conceptually explained: "But since at the same time a product can never be called Art without some precedent rule, Nature . . . must give the rule to art, i.e., beautiful Art is only possible as a product of Genius."[32] Herewith, however, the freedom from which the genius creates, in contrast to the systemization otherwise found in Kant, is precisely not a freedom that results from mind's connection to comprehensible principles, but from the "innate mental disposition (*ingenium*) through which Nature gives the rule to Art."[33] In order to avoid these difficulties, a procedure is required with the help of which the particularities of the aesthetic experiences and articulations can, in harmony with the Kantian intuitions,[34] be connected with recourse to transindividual structures, which nonetheless do not simply have the form of explainable rules. In short, we must identify structures that make possible an intersubjective practice that is open to all. If, as I believe, nonlinguistic media can play this role without what is articulated with their help being subsumed under the conceptual, then it should be possible, in a clearer way, to maintain Kant's intuition that the aesthetic attitude is based on a separate form of rationality. A necessary condition for this, however, is precisely that aesthetic practices are described as communicative practices.

3. If we attempt to accommodate this last-mentioned condition, then we must free Kant's aesthetic—entirely in the sense of Hegel—from the primacy of natural beauty and maintain without qualification that natural beauty is derivative from the beauty of artifacts.[35] For Kant, the concept of nature especially plays a foundational role because, with its help, Kant can grant aesthetic phenomena an ambivalent position between a separate purposive *freedom*, which protects the phenomena from being subsumed under purposes, and a formal *purposiveness* for our cognitive faculty. Using the concept of purposiveness, Kant articulates the possibility of structuring nature, which he views as a subjective prerequisite for the possibility of experience. The faculty of placing sensory appearances under the perspective of formal purposes is the faculty of structuring sensory appearances in accord with an assumption that makes it plausible that the sensory appearance is made for us. The fact that we experience this as "beautiful" positions us in a specific way toward nature. But this assumption would, of course, lose all quasi-religious connotations if the phenomena were made *for us because* they were made by other people. If, along with Hegel, we view art as a form by which we develop a relationship to ourselves and link the possibility of such a relationship to the requirement that others stand in an interpretive relationship to our articulations, then a concept of beauty that leans on Kant's views can be explained with recourse to the success of communication that does not owe this to explicit rules, which are, because of this, potentially generally valid rules. In this sense we might be able to call an artifact

"beautiful" if we manage, with its help, to communicate experience. According to this view, beauty is an attribute that an experience of the intelligibility of a perception possesses; here the medial structuring of an object succeeds such that, in this, we generate an integrated episode of experience. If we assume that cognition generally, in the sense I have explained above, is made possible by the fact that the sensory object of experience is nonconceptually structured, and we further assume, in line with interactionist requirements, that the means for this structuring are not inborn but are socially acquired, then the "general validity" of judgments of taste can be made understandable in a simple way.

Of course, one could claim, against this reconstruction, that this is irreconcilable with Kant's definition of beauty as "the form of the *purposiveness* of an object, so far as this is perceived in it *without any representation of a purpose*,"[36] because beauty in the proposed reconstruction would be viewed from the perspective of communicative ends. But because of the formal purposiveness relative to our cognitive structure, the reconstruction of the formal purposiveness using concepts of communicative intelligibility remains sufficiently connected to the Kantian definition. It can thus still serve as a reconstruction insofar as the intelligibility of nonconceptual communicative artifacts is projected onto artifacts similarly to the way the subjective principle of formal purposiveness is projected onto nature. An assumption serves as a subjective condition for the possibility of judging such objects aesthetically; namely, it is necessary to view those experienceable things that other people generate as having a form that is lent dimensions by the structure of our capacity for having experiences. If one now understands formal purposiveness as resulting from the fact that the objects of experience display a medial structure with which we are familiar, at least in principle, then those tensions can be avoided that characterize Kant's description of the role of rules in the context of aesthetic experiences. For, on the one hand, aesthetic judgment is "a special faculty for judging of things according to a rule, but not according to concepts."[37] On the other hand, "every art presupposes rules by means of which in the first instance a product, if it is to be called artistic, is represented as possible."[38] Here, however, the work of art should not leave a trace "of the rule having been before the eyes of the artist and having fettered his mental powers."[39] Kant appears to want to bring these different motifs together in the following argument:

a. There are rules that artists must follow if they want to create works of art at all, because the character of works of art as artifacts depends on it.
b. Nothing is a work of art that merely applies rules.
c. Because conceptual rules are general, and by following them only applications like (b) can be produced, the rules named in (a) cannot be rules that are able to be fully conceptually determined.
d. "Therefore beautiful art cannot itself devise the rule according to which it can bring about its product," and "Nature in the subject must ... give the rule to Art."[40]

If I am correct, (a)–(c) can also be integrated into conclusion (d').

d'. Thus: the *necessary* rules that artists follow are demonstrative rules as laid out in (R1).[41] They only prescribe how the material from which the work of art is formed is produced, but not how it is to be used in order to produce a work of art.

In my view, conclusion (d') would have the great advantage of being able to situate artistic production in an intersubjective social context, and thus it would be connected better than (d) with Kant's basic intuition that links the possibility of rationality with the condition for the existence of practices that are in principle open to all. If these practices are analyzed as communicative, then we can say that aesthetic communication is centered around the communication of experiences, and indeed in the sense that experiences are communicated in the form of medial-structured objects of perception. And Kant himself points out that the structuring competencies, that is, those capabilities that allow us to position a perception in the light of the products of imagination, are socially transmitted. Kant writes:

> The skill that men have in communicating their thoughts requires also a relation between the Imagination and the Understanding in order to associate intuitions with concepts, and *concepts again* with those concepts, which then combine in a cognition. But in that case the agreement of the two mental powers is *according to law*, under the constraint of definite concepts. Only where the Imagination in its freedom awakens the Understanding, and is *put* by it *into* regular play without the aid of concepts, does the representation communicate itself not as a thought but as an internal feeling of a purposive state of the mind.

Taste is then the faculty of judging *a priori* of the communicability of feelings that are bound up with a given representation (without the mediation of a concept).[42]

In the *Critique of Judgment*, with the concept of "cognition generally" and the concept of the "aesthetic idea," Kant introduced two concepts that can be interpreted as products or objects of a nonconceptual understanding. I think Kant's observation that successful works of art present specific challenges for our structuring capabilities is correct and would like to suggest that a particularity of aesthetic experience consists precisely in the fact that what the subject of an aesthetic experience provides for structuring the object is not merely conceptual (in the narrower sense), but precisely is an attempt to *reconstruct* the phenomenon *medially*. From the perspective of these considerations, we would try to explain the preestablished harmony that is assumed by aesthetic judgment to exist between the forms of artifacts and the structure of our cognitive faculties to result from the fact that we share medial competencies with the producers of aesthetic phenomena. The core of aesthetic experience would thus lie in the correlation of an experienced phenomenon with those structuring medial-interpretive correlates that—because of our familiarity with the medium in which the work of art has a compositional identity—have a history of *generating experiences*. As a consequence of these reflections, aesthetic experience is thus described as a kind of experience that integrates experienced phenomena at a fundamental level into the realm of things toward which we can behave interpretively.

In the *Critique of Judgment* Kant centered attention on a dimension of aesthetic experience that must evade every merely experience-centered aesthetic, and he attempted to show that aesthetic experience possesses its own rationality. However, because Kant must define all the particularities of this rationality in relation to conceptual competencies, and the analysis of the communicative functions of aesthetic experiences is not available to him in a systematic way for determining the specifics of rationality, his determinations turn out, on the one hand, to be strangely formal, and, on the other hand, to be oddly negative. From a media-theoretic perspective, one can concur with Kant that aesthetic experiences are *not* exclusively conceptually structured; that the production and interpretation of works of art do *not* or can*not* follow conceptually explicit rules; that the content of works of art can*not* be conceptually identified;

292 / THE CONSEQUENCES FOR A CONCEPT OF RATIONALITY

and, finally, that aesthetic experiences are *not* limited to an appreciation of sensory impulses, but are characterized by a certain form of reflection. However, insofar as one can say with media-theoretic means that this reflection results from a medial structuring of experiences, and the competencies for such acts of structuring that are acquired in communicative processes form the core of nonconceptual reason, a perspective emerges that allows the difficulties of the Kantian track to be avoided. This would at least indicate how a philosophy of media based on interactionist basic beliefs could reconstruct those competencies that have thus far largely found no place in the philosophy of the *linguistic turn*.

4.1.3.2. The Rationality of Medial Understanding

The examination of Kant has at least shown that my attempt to uncover a special form of mental activity in aesthetic forms of experience, which is subject to distinct principles, is a project that is not without its historical precursors. In the following I will attempt to establish that this kind of mental activity is a form of understanding, and that the analysis of this can contribute to the explication of rational competencies. Here, those correlations in which medial constellations (K) either appear as interpreting structures or that are themselves the object of an interpretation by medial structures must form the basis of such an analysis. Systematically then, the following correlations can appear:

(C1) P interprets X with the help of K.

(C2) P interprets K with the help of K'.

In order to be able to analyze both cases separately, apart from the fact that X is not a medial constellation, there should be no restrictions about what X can represent.

1. In examining the correlation (C1), we are examining the relations that form the basis for the fact that a medial constellation (K), from the perspective of a person (P), can assume a form in which P develops an interpretation of something (X); and the one standard case (to which I will limit myself here) may be that P taps a sensory experience. In this

perspective K is a means for articulating the attributes of X in a form that is determined in some way by X.

Let us assume a very simple example: In the sky we can see very deep-hanging, dark clouds. It is humid. The body of P feels heavy, etc. If we assume that there is some form in which P has a sensory awareness of this, then a medial constellation could be a form in which P structures and identifies aspects of the experience of the situation by using relations between medial elements to articulate the attributes of the experience of the situation.[43] In contrast to the case of a linguistic description of the experience, however, the generated constellation K would itself constitute something that P initially taps in a sensory reception. However, P is at the same time connected to K in another way, for as the producer of K, the medial structure of K is transparent to P. In this case, understanding would constitute a correlation between two experiences; here the medially generated experience would be connected with the capability to generate this by medial means.

Admittedly, in this analysis we have assumed that P already understands K, for only under this assumption can K become a means to understanding X for P. Of course, this assumption is met, in particular, if P is the producer of K. However, if this assumption is not met, then we must analyze the case (C2). For if K is not transparent to P from the perspective of the producer, then K must be understood medially, even by an interpreter. In other words, K must be interpreted with the help of K'.

2. So, if we must analyze what it means to understand a medial constellation (K) by the medial means (K'), then two levels are to be differentiated; for one level of understanding is related to the reconstruction of the *identity* of a medial constellation, and another is related to the *content*. Here the level of understanding, as a specific form of reference to the identity of a medial constellation, can be analyzed in the context of two different cases:

   a. The simpler case is one in which the interpreter P perceives a medial constellation K, which consists of media elements that P is practiced in bringing about. This is the case, for example, if P hears a song that she herself could sing. An interpreter like this will structure the perception of the song such that she organizes the flow of acoustic perceptions, breaking them up into a sequence of activities that actualize those media elements whose constellation is specific to K. P does not simply perceive K; rather, she comprehends the structure of K by an inhibited performance of K'. Insofar as P in this way manages a performative reconstruction of the perception of K, the perception does not simply befall P; rather, P refers to the compositional identity of K by performing something internally that has the same compositional identity as K. At this level, to interpret K simply means to identify K against the background of medial alternatives by producing K', and K' is compositionally identical to K.

b. A more complex case exists if an interpreter is confronted with a sensory-structured artifact K^*, which has a structure that—in part or fully—evades a medially structured replication (*Mitvollzug*) by P. Let us assume that P knows or assumes that K^* is a communicative artifact and that it was created with an expressive intention. Then how could the medial aspects of the understanding be explained with respect to the apprehension of the identity of K^*? I would like to suggest that we analyze this more complex case as follows: P attempts to structure K^* so that K^* is apprehended like a constellation whose compositional identity exists in a *hypothetical medium*. P thus attempts to organize the sensory-perceptible attributes so that they can be described as medial attributes. Here, P, so to say, integrates K^* into a network of distinctions that consists of systematic alternatives to the attributes that K^* depicts. In this way, P places K^* within the scope of possibilities of a hypothetical medium and determines the compositional identity of K^* relative to this scope of possibilities. Here P at the same time drafts patterns for the comprehension (*Nachvollzug*) that can be described as sequences for realizing medial elements.

Of course, it seems questionable that an interpreter of K^* could design a hypothetical medium without the help of language. However, while this possibility should not be precluded, the construction of the hypothetical medium can be described as the attempt to test forms of practical comprehension. This, however, raises the question of whether every practical comprehension ought to be considered a form for understanding the identity of K^*. Obviously this cannot be the case; understanding is a concept that implies success, so it should be possible to provide criteria for *successful* medial understanding. While quantifying the normative benefits, I will attempt to show what such criteria might look like.

Having now gained an idea of understanding by employing concepts that refer to the compositional identity of a medial constellation, what it means to understand its content is still to be explained. As I have shown in chapter 3,[44] the content of a medial constellation is initially dependent on the exemplary reactions of (parental) recipients that covary with their medial structure. This dependency of the content on compositional identity continues in developed medial practices. The content, however, becomes independent from the exemplary reactions of others to the degree that the initially external reception is internalized. However, then, by specifying (M8) and (M9)[45] more precisely, it can be said:

> (M12) The content of a medial constellation is the experience that accompanies the comprehension of its compositional identity.[46]

If the content for both producers and recipients is formed by reference to the compositional identity of a medial constellation, then one can say that, with the help of medial practices, processes of understanding can be organized. However, this means that the medial competencies that these processes are based on must be counted among the competencies of understanding; as such, they form the core of the rational competencies. Beyond that, through these reflections, the portrayal of the communicative function of medial expressions takes on clearer contours. For in the context of interpersonal communication, media obviously allow contents to be transmitted in more independent forms; it is through their dependency on transindividual individuating patterns that these are able to be communicated.

In the last section in which the explicative benefits of a media-theoretic amelioration of our understanding of rationality is quantified, I would like to clearly show that existing medial practices always at least partially realize the rationality potential of medial understanding.

4.1.3.3. The Inherent Rationality of Media Practices

In the preceding chapter I have defended the thesis that nonlinguistic media play a foundational role in the process of the development of higher intentional states. In doing so, in an explicative perspective I have clearly shown that media make a necessary contribution to the realization of those structures that exemplify a minimal rationality and, thus, are constitutive for our mind. In the following, I would like to clearly show that medial practices can be described *as if* they are oriented on certain principles. I will thus attempt to show that our dealing with media, particularly with artistic media, exhibits an inner systematization that can be described as resulting from the social implemented fulfillment of conditions for constituting media.

If we consider a community in which certain medial practices have been established, then we can say that, in this community, certain (demonstrative) rules hold that subject the behavioral scope of medial-interacting members to certain media-constitutive restrictions; we can at the same time say that it is precisely these restrictions that the actors, first of all, owe to the medially structured possible actions. The freedom to perform this or another medial constellation, to choose this or another action alternative, presupposes that the members of the community can move amidst a scope of alternatives whose existence is owed to the observance of restrictions. To that extent, we can say:

(M13) All successful medial practices realize the principle of productive constraint.

But (M13) is not sufficient precisely insofar as it sets out from an implicit counterfactual assumption, namely, the assumption that beings can subject their behavior to constraints *before* they have acquired medial competencies. If we consider the case of a novice who is socialized in a medial practice, it appears that the "negative freedom" that the novice would have to constrict can only be ascribed from the perspective of an observer that already moves within the scope of alternatives that is due precisely to the adherence to restrictions. For only from the perspective of beings with media competence can forms of behavior be interpreted as behavioral *possibilities* that, for beings that do not yet have these competencies, do not represent possibilities they could choose from. (M13) thus already presupposes that the participants in a successful medial practice move within a scope of alternatives that is dependent on media-constitutive restrictions. However, as long as a being only has A-intentional states at its disposal, it does not have the possibility to constrain *itself*, because it does not have possibilities that are possibilities *for it*. But this comes down to the following:

> (M14) Media are fundamentally social mechanisms for constituting basal rationality, insofar as only those beings can be rational that have action alternatives that are alternatives for them.

Besides these elementary implications of medial practices that are constitutive for action and mind, quasi-economic principles play an interesting role. So, a medium in the sense of (M2)[47] plays the role of mediating between a few medial attributes—often organized in simple grids—and a sphere of complexity that can be built on the basis of the medial elements. Insofar as the possible choices are organized in a grid with relatively few attributes, from the perspective of an actor, the possible choices are more clearly arranged, and they are easier to use in developing arbitrarily complex medial constellations. With a view to the communicative function of the media, this means that because one can learn to bring about simple medial elements, and any medial constellation can be analyzed in media elements, medial constellations can in principle be both reconstructed and reproduced. At the same time, any medial practice characterizes spheres of various degrees of plasticity by devoting stronger resistance to changes in the set of media elements than to changes at the level of the production of medial constellations.

Besides these limitations, which develop in complexity, it can be maintained that every factual implementation of a medial practice looks *as if* the participants in the practice orient themselves on the principles for securing communicative success. I have already mentioned one property that is relevant in this respect:[48] medial elements are semantically intrinsically empty; consequently, the constitution of medial constellations is not bothered by primary forms of semanticity. Other properties of medial practice can be interpreted as culturally developed successors to that *marking* that we got to know as a property of parental response behavior in the phase of affectual communication.[49] Examples of such properties are forms for contextually characterizing medial expressions, as, for example, they are realized with the help of frames and stages. Further quasi principles for securing communicative success aim at something that could be called the economy of attention; for, as a rule, medial constellations are placed in a context that ought to make it clear to the senses what is a part of the medial performance and what is not. In short, as a rule, medial performances take on their contours against a sensorily uninteresting (redundant) background.

These rather cursory remarks should merely show it is plausible that the relations of understanding that were reconstructed in the preceding section were not only carried over from a theoretical perspective to the medial constellations, but that structures can be found in the existing medial practices, whose meaning (*Sinn*) is tapped with a view to the individuation and transference of intelligible objects of experiences.

4.2. THE NORMATIVE RETURNS

By balancing the explicative returns (or benefits) for the view of rationality ameliorated by media-theoretic reflections, the plausibility of the following view should be shown. Nonlinguistic media allow correlative structures to be actualized with which it is possible to individuate contentful mental states, but with which experiences can also be structured and communicated and with which we can develop a self-relationship at a basic level. The reflections in connection with the determinations of the specifics of processes of medial understanding have led us to a point where we could see a particularity of medial processes of understanding to consist in the following: a medial interpreter taps an experience by attempting to reconstruct the compositional identity of the medial constellation by medially structuring the medial constellation that is to be understood, if necessary by means of a hypothetical medium. Admittedly, here it has remained an open question whether *every* comprehension of the structure of a medial expression can also be considered an *apprehending* comprehension. In other words, what the *conditions for the success* of adequate medial interpretations consist in has remained an open question. In a last step I would thus like to propose a principle that can serve as a standard for a good interpretation and that, in the best-case scenario, ought to result in a nonlinguistic analogue to Davidson's principle of charity. Here, however, from the outset we must be aware of a difficulty: a principle like this will not be able to have recourse to the type of normative relations (e.g., inferential ones) that exist between ascribed propositional contents in linguistic interpretations.

4.2.1. A Principle of Medial Understanding

In order to construe a situation of radical medial interpretation, let us assume the case of an interpreter of a sensory-perceptible artifact K, who does not have the capability to routinely identify the medial structure of K. In this situation, should *every* correlation between K and the scope of possibilities of a hypothetical medium be considered a case of understanding? Or can criteria be provided with the help of which a boundary can be drawn between *correlations based on understanding* that exist between the sensory attributes of K and hypothetical scopes of possibilities and some other correlations?

If we assume that K had a set of perceptible attributes $E_1, E_2, \ldots, E_n$, then we could judge the correlation that K has to a hypothetical medium according to how many of the E_i can be viewed as attributes of medial elements. Here it is, of course, not clear from the outset which of the E_i are *relevant* attributes of the object of experience. An interpreter can indeed prescind from any attributes that cannot be perceived in the context of the presentation of the object of experience—attributes like the weight of a drawing, the crystal structure of an applied pigment, etc.—but among the *contextually accessible* attributes, all perceptible attributes are *potentially* relevant. However, because it is not clear which of the perceptible attributes are in fact relevant, a medial interpreter could be prompted to consider as many sensory-perceptible attributes in the scope of possibilities of her hypothetical medium as possible. She thus must adopt the following principle:

(1) Maximize the number of those sensory-perceptible attributes that you apprehend as medial attributes in the medial structuring of an object that you want to understand as a communicative artifact.

This *maximization* principle, however, does not integrate the attributes that are taken into account. In the worst case, a hypothetical medium would be put together namely from a number of medial elements identical to the number of attributes taken into account. The interpreter could thus postulate a medial element for the implementation of each medial attribute, which would contradict the idea that the structure of a medial constellation must be able to be tapped on the basis of a manageable number of medial elements. A medial interpreter is thus prompted to replace the simple maximization principle with a more mature principle that combines the maximization demand with a *minimization* demand. This principle would have the following form:

(2) If you structure a sensory-perceptible phenomenon with the help of a hypothetical medium, then keep the number of medial elements whose combination implements the maximum perceptible attributes of the phenomenon as small as possible.

This principle prompts the interpreter of a nonlinguistic expression to apprehend the maximum amount of sensory-perceptible complexity of the expression as a product of a minimum number of different medial action types. I believe that this principle has a counterpart for the producer of medial constellations. If one considers that not a few artists in the process of creating a work (K) produce a number of preliminary studies and sketches, then one can ask why, in a series of sketches, $S_1, S_2, \ldots, K$, one passes over from a sketch S_n to S_{n+1}, and in particular what, in the view of the artist, distinguishes K from all the sketches. Of course, one could reconstruct this process by assuming, within the framework of an instrumentalist understanding, that S_{n+1} is simply preferred to S_n because S_{n+1} better expresses what the artist wants to express. But this reconstruction assumes that the artist has some access to S_i that is independent from what she wants to express.

In my view, one can understand the reflections that lead to K being granted a special status compared to the sketches as an answer to questions like the following: Does the medial constellation depict something that is identified as a unity in perception? Are all of the applied elements necessary in order to give a medial constellation the character of an integrated unity that can be experienced? Does the medial constellation obtain an "independence" such that the integration of the elements prevents their disintegration? If these questions actually play a role in the decision about which medial constellation is preferred in comparison to the sketches, then one can understand the question about the necessity of the applied elements to mean that an artist anticipates the minimization demand directed to the interpreter. In the same sense, the question of the unity in the perception and the question of the "independence" can be understood as anticipating the pressure, which arises from the minimization demand, to reconstruct the work from the smallest possible number of densely integrated elements. Because the maximization demand prompts the recipients to pay attention to any potentially relevant attribute of the work, artists must expect that the recipients will include all sensory-perceptible attributes of a work in the medial structuring.

Simply following the mentioned principle cannot secure a good interpretation. For numerous interpretations are always possible, and the suggested principle is only selective if these interpretations significantly differ in their breadth and their level of integration. In this respect, it is no different than the *principle of charity*, for Davidson also expects indeterminate interpretations. Admittedly, with the help of this principle, correlations of understanding can be distinguished insofar as correlations are subject to restrictions that prescribe that interpretive correlations orient themselves on the conditions for individuating medial constellations insofar as differentiating an object that can be experienced is linked with perceiving it as a unity. In other words, the restrictions articulate conditions for successfully conveying experiences with the help of medially structured objects of experiences, and, with them, the conditions for the transindividual individuation of B-intentional states so that the discussion of medial processes of understanding in any case appears to be justified. Under the assumption that the core rational competencies can be explained in reference to concepts related to competencies of understanding, this in turn means that medial processes of understanding can be drawn on to determine rational competencies. But then it must also be possible, aligned with the model of that catalogue,[50] which explains rational competencies as prerequisites for the ability to understand and for the de facto understanding at different levels—to characterize basal, habitual, and optional rationality in the context of medial competencies:

1. In the context of medial action, *basal* rationality legitimizes a manner of speaking about beings whose activities can in part be described as if they use sensory-perceptible states of affairs in the world or processes for communicative purposes.

This implies especially that basally rational beings

a. have a typified repertoire of semantically intrinsically empty behavioral alternatives that they use to produce medial constellations;
b. teach the production of medial elements;
c. frequently react to the expression of medial constellations by expressing medial constellations; and
d. frequently use types of medial constellations so that these co-vary with the circumstances of the expression.

If these criteria are not fulfilled, then the behavior of these beings loses the status of action. However, this is not because we cannot ascribe reasons for the expression, but because we cannot ascribe a medium that allows the individuation of higher intentional states and legitimizes the assumption that these beings choose their activities against the background of alternatives that are alternatives *for* them.

2. *Habitual* rationality can only be assigned to those beings that fulfill the criteria of basal rationality and participate in a social practice of *interpretation*. In communicative practices, such beings frequently act in compliance with

a. principles of the economy of attention; and
b. principles of the economy of individuation.

3. At the level of medial practices, *optional* rationality is also a second-order rationality. It presumes a medium, language, with which beings can draw on their medial practices. Here, forms for realizing medial practices or medial strategies themselves become the content of intentional states, and indeed in the perspective of the systematic formulation and opening up of forms of articulation. With respect to the ability for medial articulation (on the part of the producers) and the ability for medial interpretation (on the part of the recipients), the maximization of optional rationality underlies *education processes* and the development of an *artistic* or *aesthetic attitude*.

The criteria of optional rationality are normative insofar as the realization of optional medial rationality prescribes the further development of articulatory possibilities and interpretive capabilities. Norms of medial rationality demand that their addressees

a. maximize the articulation possibilities by
   α. making full systematic use of the scope of possibilities of the media; or
   β. developing new medial strategies; or
   γ. developing new media; and
b. maximize the interpretive capabilities by
   α. attempting to maximize the originality of the medial constellation in their interpretations;
   β. developing new strategies of medial comprehension;
   γ. tapping new forms of the medial organization of possibilities of experience,
in order to systematically expand the means that we have at our disposal for the processes of (self-)understanding.

4.2.2. Media of the Enlightenment

In the definition of (A1), I described the Enlightenment as a process in which we develop and learn to understand our abilities to understand.[51] In the preceding reflections I have attempted to plausibly show that an adequate and comprehensive understanding of our capabilities to understand must also include forms in which nonlinguistic media play a key role. For nonlinguistic media are both means for articulating and means for developing articulations; they are means for developing a self-relationship as well as means with which we can individuate contentful intentional states. In short, they are means for nonlinguistic thinking.

In many places, but especially in chapter 3, the development of my reflections is influenced by the impulse to understand the possibilities that nonlinguistic means offer us as *sui generis* possibilities. That means that these determinations often occur independently of language or after setting aside language. However, it is important to see that this impulse is indebted to the theoretical interest in, if possible, bringing everything into view that is possible in media without language, and it does not attempt to play down the significance of language. I hope, to the contrary, that my reflections have contributed to better understanding the prominent role of language. For if language can be understood as a medium that shares part of the phylogenetic and ontogenetic history of origins with nonlinguistic media, then, in a theoretically homogeneous vocabulary, it can be clearly shown which normative relations a nonlinguistic medium must be embedded in so that it can take on the role of a language. If the justification of medial expressions is tied to normative criteria, which, for their part, are connected to intersubjectively accessible truth-conditions, then a nonlinguistic medium is transformed into a language.[52] And because linguistic utterances can themselves be counted among the truth conditions for linguistic utterances, a metalinguistic reference is possible in language for which there are only limited functional equivalents in nonlinguistic media.

However, none of this changes anything about the finding that nonlinguistic media have a specific capacity available especially to make experience intersubjectively communicable.[53] In nonlinguistic medial expressions, the possibility of arousing our sensibility is connected with the possibility of structurally tapping this sensory dimension of the reception of medial articulations and, through this structuring, of making it intersubjectively accessible. Because medial articulations have a compositional structure, in the course of a comprehension they convey their sensory attributes, but also indications regarding their development (*Erschließung*); such a reconstruction can orient itself on the compositional identity of a medial expression against the background of a regularly structured scope of possibilities. This specific combination of an intelligible structure and sensorily "dense" perceptible attributes forms the basis on which medial interaction processes can be viewed as processes of understanding, and it forms the basis for the fact that a principle for judging interpretations can be characterized, but without the following of this principle ensuring interpretive success. Here, however, interpreting medial expressions is related to interpreting linguistic utterances even if interpreters of linguistic utterances, because of the normative relations between sentences, are subject to considerably more restrictions than the interpreters of nonlinguistic medial expressions.

If the discussion of medial interpretations can be shown to be plausible in this way, then we can understand the development of medial articulation competencies and interpretation competencies to be genuine components of the Enlightenment process. We can, in a basic manner, claim that this process is more complex than its critics would have us believe.

For as paradigmatic cases of developed aesthetic communication, in this view, works of art play neither the role of a compensatory or correcting mechanism that relieves us of conceptual work nor the role of enigmatic expressions whose rationality must be unlocked with aesthetic commentary or critique.[54] The proposed concept should rather reveal that one can take seriously the thought that aesthetic communication is a full-fledged dimension of the development of rationality. To the degree that the development of medial and linguistic competencies in the context of educational processes is the development of competencies of understanding, and the articulated self-understanding is a necessary condition for knowing who we are and what we want, to this degree, the development of these competencies is a value that does not stand in need of an external justification. Because justifications of what is required, for their part, presuppose a self-understanding, those practices in which we transmit and develop the preconditions for developing self-understanding constitute unconditional values; for we are what we are *for us* only within the framework of linguistic *and* medial self-interpretations.

Media, understood in the manner developed here, are media of reason in a twofold sense: they are media that lead us to reason, and they are something in which our reason is realized.

NOTES

FOREWORD

1. Jürgen Habermas, *The Theory of Communicative Action: Reason and the Rationalization of Society*, trans. Thomas McCarthy (Boston: Beacon Press, 1984), 2.

1. INTRODUCTION

1. Jürgen Habermas, *The Philosophical Discourse of Modernity*, trans. Frederick G. Lawrence (Cambridge, MA: MIT Press, 1987), 83ff., esp. 94–95. Bernhard Lypp, among others, has pointed out that those interpreters who center their diagnosis of an anti-Enlightenment program around the concept of the will to power do not go far enough and thus do not gain a view of Nietzsche's idea of a "new enlightenment." Bernhard Lypp, "Über die Selbsterzeugung der Aufklärung," in *Der Traum der Vernunft: Vom Elend der Aufklärung*, ed. Akademie der Künste Berlin, 195–308 (Darmstadt: Luchterhand, 1985).

2. Cf. Jean-François Lyotard, *The Differend: Phrases in Dispute*, trans. Georges Van Den Abbeele (Minneapolis: University of Minnesota Press, 1988).

3. Cf. Jean Baudrillard, *Symbolic Exchange and Death*, trans. Mike Gane (London: Sage, 1993).

4. Cf. Theodor W. Adorno, *Negative Dialectics*, trans. E. B. Ashton (London: Routledge, 2000).

5. Cf. Lyotard, *Differend*, 158.

6. Cf. Baudrillard, *Symbolic Exchange and Death*, 5.

7. Cf. Adorno, *Negative Dialectics*, 5–6.

8. Cf. Georges Bataille, *The Accursed Share: An Essay on General Economy*, trans. Robert Hurley (New York: Zone Books, 2007).

9. Jean-François Lyotard, *The Postmodern Condition: A Report on Knowledge*, trans. Geoff Bennington and Brian Massumi (Minneapolis: University of Minnesota Press, 1985), 29.

10. Niklas Luhmann, *Social Systems*, trans. John Bednarz Jr. and Dirk Baecker (Stanford, CA: Stanford University Press, 1996), 473.

11. Here, for example, when the concern is with the epistemological demands of Enlightenment theories, the discussion is still of an orientation toward objective truth, as if there were never a critical, epistemologically sophisticated debate of scientific theories in the philosophy of science, besides Kuhn's. For his part, Kuhn became something of a patron saint of the postmodern. Cf. Jürgen Habermas, "Modernity: An Incomplete Project," in *The Anti-Aesthetic: Essays in Postmodern Culture*, ed. Hal Foster (Seattle: Bay Press, 1991), 12.

12. Cf. Jean-François Lyotard, "Re-Writing Modernity," *SubStance* 16, no. 54 (1987): 3–9.

13. Cf. Lyotard, *Postmodern Condition*, 37.

14. Ibid., 25.

15. Cf. ibid., 28.

16. Cf., e.g., ibid., 27.

17. Even in Luhmann, who, with the book *Social Systems*, provided a "supertheory" with universalist claims (cf. Luhmann, *Social Systems*, xiii) and who to that extent is an opponent of critics of broader theoretical claims par excellence, the case is more complex. More on this later.

18. Here I do not want to go into the diverse inconsistencies of the reception by postmodern critics, which are influential, for example, in the debate with Habermas's theory of the modern. Here I will only mention that Lyotard, for example, assumes that "Jürgen Habermas . . . thinks that . . . modernity has foundered" (Jean-François Lyotard, "Answering the Question: What Is the Postmodern?" in *The Postmodern Explained to Children* [Sydney: Power Publications, 1992], 2).

19. Habermas, *Philosophical Discourse of Modernity*, 409.

20. Ludwig Nagl has pointed this out: "The best-guarded, best-repressed secret of the postmodern philosophers, their philosophically half measured critique of the subject, for which it attempts to compensate with literary exuberance, consists in the fact that, despite the radical pathos of its performance, it suffers from a deficit of radicality. It, however, runs the risk, for reasons of inconsistency, of collaborating because its deconstruction actions—given that these are offered a reading public for comprehension—presuppose that an irrevocable part of the use of reason is able to function, which the material deconstructions attempt to discredit completely" (Ludwig Nagl, "Zeigt die Habermassche Kommunikationstheorie einen 'Ausweg aus der Subjektphilosophie'?" in *Die Frage nach dem Subjekt*, ed. M. Frank, G. Raulet, and W. van Reijen [Frankfurt: Suhrkamp, 1988], 346). Such self-contradictions are especially crassly striking in formulations like the following: "The consensus has become an outmoded and suspected value. But justice as a value is neither outmoded nor suspect. We must thus arrive at an idea and practice of justice that is not linked to that of consensus" (Lyotard, *Postmodern Condition*, 66). Among other things, it is questionable who this sentence could be directed toward and with what goal, if agreement with the diagnosis and approval of the consequence were taken to be a suspect goal.

21. Lyotard, *Postmodern Condition*, xxv.

22. Ibid. It also stays an open question, what the incommensurable should be.

23. Niklas Luhmann, *Observations on Modernity*, trans. William Whobrey (Stanford, CA: Stanford University Press, 1998), x.

24. Ibid., ix.
25. Ibid., 18.
26. Ibid., 23.
27. Lyotard, "Re-Writing Modernity," 8–9 (my emphasis).
28. Odo Marquard, *Die Erziehung des Menschengeschlechts: Eine Bilanz*, in *Der Traum der Vernunft: Vom Elend der Aufklärung*, ed. Akademie der Künste Berlin (Darmstadt: Luchterhand, 1985), 125.
29. Ibid., 129.
30. Luhmann, *Observations on Modernity*, 6.
31. Ibid., 18.
32. Luhmann, "Biographie, Attitüden, Zettelkasten," in *Archimedes und wir*, ed. Dirk Baecker and Georg Stanitzek (Berlin: Merve Verlag, 1987), 126–127.
33. Habermas, *Theory of Communicative Action*, vol. 1, *Reason and the Rationalization of Society*, trans. Thomas McCarthy (Boston: Beacon Press, 1984), 398.
34. Luhmann, "Biographie, Attitüden, Zettelkasten," 127–128.
35. Richard Rorty, "The Priority of Democracy to Philosophy," in *Objectivity, Relativism and Truth* (Cambridge: Cambridge University Press, 1991), 193.
36. Ibid.
37. Richard Rorty, "Solidarity or Objectivity," in *Objectivity, Relativism and Truth* (Cambridge: Cambridge University Press, 1991), 24.
38. Ibid., 26.
39. Rorty, "Priority of Democracy to Philosophy," 196. I believe Rorty is mistaken if he thinks that what irritates us about his texts is the loss of "two sorts of metaphysical comfort [universal species-specific rights and the hope for indissolubility of our culture]" (Rorty, "Solidarity or Objectivity," 31). It is much more irritating that he simply assumes democratic structures of society, that is, structures that have normative implications, as a form of play within which social practices are preserved or not. It is difficult to imagine that, within this liberal framework, we are supposed to depend on any merely imaginable experiment being permitted, and in an evolutionary process in which the "genotype" of various theoretical concepts is made phenotypically visible in the form of social practices, it can only be determined a posteriori which catastrophic, surprising, or pleasant consequences result, and there is no possibility to preclude certain experiments in advance with the help of theoretical critique. Rorty's naïve celebration of experimentation seems strange to me against the background of the catastrophic historical developments, not least of all in the twentieth century, which can hardly be explained without assuming that, at least short term, a sufficient number of members of a society were quite satisfied with the practical value of the typical theories, social practices, and institutions, so that they watched the organization of terror and destruction while doing nothing. But even when the experiment of democratic societies fails, Rorty hopes that "perhaps our descendants will remember that social institutions *can* be viewed as experiments in cooperation rather than as attempts to embody a universal and ahistorical order" (Rorty, "Priority of Democracy to Philosophy," 196).
40. See p. 30.
41. Jürgen Mittelstraß, "Von der Vernunft: Erwiderungen auf Friedrich Kambartel," in *Der Flug der Eule* (Frankfurt: Suhrkamp, 1989), 131.
42. Ibid., 128.
43. Ibid., 122.

44. Ibid., 129.
45. Ibid., 132.
46. Cf. ibid., 136.
47. Ibid., 138.
48. Jürgen Habermas, *The Theory of Communicative Action*, vol. 2, *Lifeworld and System*, trans. Thomas McCarthy (Boston: Beacon, 2000), 77.
49. Cf. Habermas, *Reason and the Rationalization of Society*, 69.
50. Cf. Jürgen Habermas, "Discourse Ethics: Notes on a Program of Philosophical Justification," in *Moral Consciousness and Communicative Action*, trans. Christian Lenhardt and Shierry Weber Nicholsen (Cambridge, MA: MIT Press, 1999), 65.
51. Habermas, *Reason and the Rationalization of Society*, 398.
52. Cf. ibid., 287; and Jürgen Habermas, "The Dialectics of Rationalization," in *Autonomy and Solidarity: Interviews with Jürgen Habermas*, ed. Peter Dews (London: Verso, 1992), 100.
53. Jürgen Habermas, "The Unity of Reason in the Diversity of Its Voices," in *Postmetaphysical Thinking: Philosophical Essays*, trans. William Mark Hohengarten (Cambridge, MA: MIT Press, 1992), 139–140.
54. Jürgen Habermas, *Theory and Practice*, trans. John Viertel (Cambridge: Polity, 1988), 40.
55. Subsequent to Habermas's analysis, *The Dialectic of Enlightenment* by Adorno and Horkheimer has to be understood as a prominent example of such an autodestructive construction. Cf. Habermas, *Reason and the Rationalization of Society*, 283.
56. Cf. Karl Marx and Friedrich Engels, *The German Ideology*, ed. C. J. Arthur (New York: International Publishers, 2004), 45–46; and Karl Marx, *Capital: A Critique of Political Economy*, 3 vols. (New York: Cosimo, 2007), 1:273.
57. Cf. Jürgen Habermas, "What Is Universal Pragmatics?" in *On the Pragmatics of Communication* (Cambridge, MA: MIT Press, 1998), 35: "What begins as an explication of meaning aims at the reconstruction of species competencies."
58. Robert Brandom has also alluded to the connection of articulated self-understandings and specific aggregates of attributes. Cf. Robert B. Brandom, *Making It Explicit* (Cambridge, MA: Harvard University Press, 1994), 3–4.
59. This criterion, which appears trivial, still precludes all forms of strong incommensurability from fracturing the process of the Enlightenment process.
60. Cf. Rorty, "Solidarity or Objectivity," 23. Cf. also Udo Tietz, "Vernunft und Verstehen: Bemerkungen zum Verhältnis von formaler und materialer Rationalität," in *Sich am Denken orientieren*, ed. Simone Dietz, Heiner Hastedt, Geert Keil, and Anke Thyen (Frankfurt: Suhrkamp, 1996), 84–102.
61. Cf., with a reference to different languages, Donald Davidson, "On the Very Idea of a Conceptual Scheme," in *Inquiries Into Truth and Interpretation*, 183–198 (New York: Oxford University Press, 2001).
62. Cf. Hilary Putnam, *Reason, Truth, and History* (Cambridge: Cambridge University Press, 1981), 119ff.
63. Cf. Axel Honneth's contribution in Wolfgang Bonß, Helmut Dubiel, Gerhard Gamm, Heidrun Hesse, Axel Honneth, Christa Karpenstein-Eßbach, Gerd Kimmerle, Discussion leader: Christa Hackenesch, *Die Zukunft der Vernunft: Eine Auseinandersetzung* (Tübingen: Konkursbuchverlag, 1985), 113.
64. I would even like to maintain that one can only do justice to the "others" if one can recognize them as the others, before the screen of one's own standards, in

their concrete particularity, while the glorification of the others leads precisely to their exclusion. Slavoj Žižek, *The Ticklish Subject* (London: Verso, 2000).

65. The model of the constructive vote of no confidence secures at the same time the intuition that criticism can never be allowed to lead us into a situation in which we simply lose our evaluative standards: every critique of evaluative standards that is accepted with reasons can only be accepted against the background of further developed standards.

66. Habermas, *Reason and the Rationalization of Society*, 2.

67. So, in the past few years a few anthologies and even monographs on the theory of rationality have been published. As exemplary works I would like to mention Axel Wüstenhube, ed., *Pragmatische Realitätstheorien: Studies in Pragmatism, Idealism, and Philosophy of Mind* (Würzburg: Königshausen & Neumann, 1995); Karl-Otto Apel and Matthias Kettner, eds., *Die eine Vernunft und die vielen Rationalitäten* (Frankfurt: Suhrkamp, 1996); Wolfgang Welsch, *Die Zeitgenössische Vernunftkritik und das Konzept der transversalen Vernunft* (Frankfurt: Suhrkamp, 1995).

68. In what follows I draw on the following works of Herbert Schnädelbach: "Observations on Rationality and Language," in *Reason and Its Other: Rationality in Modern German Philosophy and Culture*, ed. Dieter Freundlieb and Wayne Hudson, 49–66 (Oxford: Berg, 1993); "Vernunft," in *Philosophie: Ein Grundkurs*, ed. E. Martens and H. Schnädelbach, 77–110 (Reinbek: Rowohlt, 1986); "Rationalität und Begründung," in *Zur Rehabilitierung des* animal rationale*: Vorträge und Abhandlungen* (Frankfurt: Suhrkamp, 1992), 61–78; "Rationalität und Normativität," in *Zur Rehabilitierung des* animal rationale*: Vorträge und Abhandlungen* (Frankfurt: Suhrkamp, 1992), 79–103.

69. Cf. Herbert Schnädelbach, "Philosophie als Theorie der Rationalität," in *Zur Rehabilitierung des* animal rationale*: Vorträge und Abhandlungen* (Frankfurt: Suhrkamp, 1992), 41–60, esp. 44ff. A similar history of reason—albeit with different consequences—is embraced by Wolfgang Welsch, leaning on Gianni Vattimo.

70. Schnädelbach, "Philosophie als Theorie der Rationalität," 43.

71. Cf. introduction, pp. 2ff.

72. Cf. Schnädelbach, "Philosophie als Theorie der Rationalität," 43.

73. Ibid., 47.

74. Cf. Schnädelbach, "Rationalität und Normativität," 82.

75. Ibid.

76. Cf. pp. 33ff.

77. Schnädelbach, "Philosophie als Theorie der Rationalität," 47.

78. Ibid., 48.

79. Schnädelbach, "Rationalität und Normativität," 79–80.

80. Ibid., 82–83.

81. Cf. ibid., 80ff. (with additions).

82. Manfred Frank, "Two Centuries of Philosophical Critique of Reason and Its 'Postmodern' Radicalization," in *Reason and Its Other: Rationality in Modern German Philosophy and Culture*, ed. Dieter Freundlieb and Wayne Hudson (Providence, RI: Berg, 1993), 77.

83. Herbert Schnädelbach, "Über die Vernünftigkeit der Geschichte und die Geschichtlichkeit der Vernunft," in *Vernunft und Geschichte* (Frankfurt: Suhrkamp, 1987), 9.

84. As an example of a rationality concept that drops all normative ambitions, one should at least point to Luhmann's concept of rationality. Setting out from

Parsons's impulse that rationality cannot be explained in reference to particular actions but only in reference to actions systems (cf. Niklas Luhmann, *Zweckbegriff und Systemrationalität* [Frankfurt: Suhrkamp, 1991], 14), within the framework of his program, Luhmann converts action categories into system categories, and he understands reason initially as a function in the process of system differentiation, which for its part is a form for dealing with complexity. Rationality is "above all else a reduction of complexity" (Luhmann, *Zweckbegriff und Systemrationalität*, 14); it is the ability of a system to work off environmental complexity and to maintain itself under a reduction of environmental complexity (cf. Luhmann, *Zweckbegriff und Systemrationalität*, 179). Rationality should no longer be determined against this background of existing or chosen ends, but goals are apprehended as *one* form of the reduction of complexity in that they provide "the basic problem of maintaining existence in a complex and changing world that, as such, is not instructive, not capable of deciding a system-internal, workable version" (Luhmann, *Zweckbegriff und Systemrationalität*, 190).

By transforming his system theory to a theory of self-referential systems, Luhmann radicalizes the reduction of the rationality concept to problems in dealing with complexity, and rationality comes to characterize a perspective of systems toward themselves: "The concept of rationality merely formulates the most demanding perspective on the system's self-reflection. It does not signify a norm, a value, or an idea that confronts real systems. . . . It merely indicates the keystone of the logic of self-referential systems. If one introduces it into the system as a point of reference for self-observation, this makes it truly ambivalent: it then serves as a viewpoint for critiquing all selections and as a measure for its own improbability" (*Social Systems*, 477). However, as a result of the reduction of rationality to a perspective, it remains a mystery how criteria for such a critique can be developed and what the normative basis on which the critique might orient itself would be. If a system achieves rationality to the degree "that it reintroduces the difference of system and environment within the system and is not guided by its (own) identity but by difference" (Niklas Luhmann, *Ecological Communication*, trans. John Bednarz Jr. [Cambridge: Polity, 1989], 131), then it remains incomprehensible how this is supposed to be possible at the level of functional differentiated social systems, for a differentiated system can only know this difference with the help of subsystem-specific means, i.e., partially. Luhmann, who himself sees this, comments laconically: "Modern society's principle of differentiation makes the question of rationality more urgent—and at the same time insoluble" (*Social Systems*, 477). What Luhmann wrote about the rationality concept in later works is not much clearer than his elaborations within the framework of the theory of social systems. What can be observed is that the rationality concept, as a result of the system-theoretic transformation, has forfeited any ability to connect to the perspective of actors. So it remains completely unclear what it means at the level of "psychic systems" to orient oneself in connection with the reintroduction of the difference between system and environment. I do not see that Luhmann gets beyond the attempt to incorporate a concept into system theory for which it lacks the appropriate means needed to provide a stable construction. Where the rationality concept is decoupled from the perspective of acting individuals in a serious way, a plausible explanation of what precisely this concept is supposed to mean can hardly be offered. A concept of system rationality remains derivative of the rationality that system theoreticians themselves assume.

85. Cf. Friedrich Kambartel, "Vernunft: Kriterium oder Kultur? Zur Definierbarkeit des Vernünftigen," in *Philosophie der humanen Welt* (Frankfurt: Suhrkamp, 1989), 34.
86. Ibid., 34–35.
87. Ibid., 43.
88. Ibid., 42.
89. Mittelstraß, "Von der Vernunft," 128.
90. Ibid., 124.
91. Ibid., 129.
92. Ibid., 132.
93. Ibid., 138.
94. Cf. ibid.
95. Habermas, "Dialectics of Rationalization," 100.
96. Habermas, *Reason and the Rationalization of Society*, 8.
97. Cf. ibid., 10.
98. Cf. ibid.
99. Ibid., 8.
100. Ibid., 9.
101. Ibid., 15.
102. Habermas, "What Is Universal Pragmatics?" 37.
103. Ibid., 52.
104. Ibid., 50.
105. Cf. ibid.
106. Ibid., 49.
107. Habermas, *Reason and the Rationalization of Society*, 308.
108. Cf. Habermas, "What Is Universal Pragmatics?" 73.
109. For a discussion of Davidson's meaning-theoretic strategy, which retains the meager premises of a truth-conditional semantic program and his reflections on a theory of rationality that are connected to this, see p. 58.
110. Cf. Habermas, *Reason and the Rationalization of Society*, 276–277.
111. Ibid., 297.
112. Ibid., 298.
113. Herbert Schnädelbach, "The Transformation of Critical Theory," in *Communicative Action: Essays on Jürgen Habermas's Theory of Communicative Action*, ed. Axel Honneth and Hans Joas (Cambridge: Polity, 1991), 15.
114. Habermas, *Reason and the Rationalization of Society*, 305.
115. Ibid., 288.
116. Cf. ibid., 289.
117. Ibid., 290.
118. Ibid., 291.
119. In contrast to this, Habermas has characterized the level of interpersonal relationships, at which illocutionary success can occur, as "extramundane" (ibid., 293).
120. Habermas, "Dialectics of Rationalization," 100.
121. Habermas, *Reason and the Rationalization of Society*, 294.
122. Cf. ibid., 329, 333ff.
123. The cultural sphere of values of Max Weber will be integrated, as it were, into the reconstructive basis of the rationality concept.
124. Habermas, *Reason and the Rationalization of Society*, 119.
125. Cf. p. 86.

126. Cf. Thomas McCarthy, *The Critical Theory of Jürgen Habermas* (London: Hutchinson, 1978).

127. Habermas, *Philosophical Discourse of Modernity*, 409 (my emphasis).

128. Cf. Habermas, "Dialectics of Rationalization," 102; and Habermas, *Reason and the Rationalization of Society*, xlii.

129. Habermas, *Reason and the Rationalization of Society*, 364.

130. Ibid.

131. Habermas, *Lifeworld and System*, 304.

132. Habermas, *Reason and the Rationalization of Society*, 41. It thus appears that to judge truthfulness, we must change precisely to the level that Habermas subjected to the diagnosis of perlocutionary effects, namely, the level of the descriptions of affairs in the world. Here, the "internal" connection presents nothing more than a hypothesis of the observer.

133. Ibid., 42.

134. Cf. ibid., 41.

135. Cf. Jürgen Habermas, "Erläuterungen zum Begriff des kommunikativen Handelns," in *Vorstudien und Ergänzungen zur Theorie des kommunikativen Handelns* (Frankfurt: Suhrkamp, 1986), 605.

136. Habermas, *Reason and the Rationalization of Society*, 23.

137. Cf. Jürgen Habermas, "Discourse Ethics," 95. Habermas claims that, on the one hand, with the help of reference to performative contradiction to the basic rules of argumentation in which critics become embroiled, the *lack of an alternative* to rules of argumentation can indeed be shown, but not the *justification* for these rules. As a reconstructive discipline, universal pragmatics remains limited to reconstructions, which are in principle fallible, presenting the rule competence of those who participate in argumentation at all.

138. Because Habermas also places communicative action and discourse in an evolutionary perspective (cf. *Lifeworld and System*, 313), one must also expect the objection that the form of the examination procedure is historically contingent and, for its part, remains subject to the process of evolutionary development.

139. Cf. p. 34.

140. Jürgen Habermas, "Intentionalistische Semantik," in *Vorstudien und Ergänzungen zur Theorie des kommunikativen Handelns* (Frankfurt: Suhrkamp, 1986), 332.

141. Cf. Noam Chomsky, *Rules and Representations* (Oxford: Blackwell, 1982), 39, 188.

142. Cf. ibid., 47ff.

143. Among the empirical indications for generative linguistics is that the input on the basis of which children would have to learn hypotheses about the rules of the language that is to be learned are so deficient that the factual learning of languages cannot be shown to be plausible without the assumption that children have a generative capacity.

144. In the face of this unattractive analysis, Habermas would perhaps draw our attention to the fact that, with a view to the competencies of competent speakers, he has spoken of an "*intuitive* rule consciousness" (cf. Habermas, "What Is Universal Pragmatics?" 33; my emphasis) and with an allusion to the fact that the knowledge of rules is able to be made explicit, but is not necessarily de facto explicit, the regress can be ended. However, then it is questionable whether the concept of an intuitive consciousness of rules is not a *contradiction in adjecto* and whether one might not bet-

ter speak of action-governing habits—whereby here it would admittedly be unclear what status habits that are to be *causally* reconstructed ought to be able to take on for a theory of meaning. One could object that my concept of rules is too rigorous, but I do not see what it might mean to follow a rule whose content is not cognitively accessible to me such that I could explicitly articulate it. I suggest a particular (demonstrative) form of the explicitness of rules below; see p. 155.

145. Stefan Gosepath, *Aufgeklärtes Eigeninteresse: Eine Theorie theoretischer und praktischer Rationalität* (Frankfurt: Suhrkamp, 1992).
146. Ibid., 15.
147. Ibid., 11, 95.
148. Cf. ibid., 15.
149. Cf. ibid., 50–51.
150. Ibid., 79.
151. Ibid. (Here, S stands for persons, t for the point in time, and p for the propositional content of the belief.)
152. Ibid., 249.
153. Cf. ibid., 108, 110, 112, 119–120.
154. Ibid., 192.
155. Cf. ibid., 198.
156. Ibid.
157. Ibid., 188.
158. Ibid., 98.
159. Ibid., 245.
160. Cf. ibid., 219.
161. Cf. ibid., 220.
162. Cf. ibid., 256.
163. Ibid., 257.
164. Ibid., 258.
165. Ibid., 260.
166. Cf. ibid., 263.
167. Cf. ibid., 272.
168. Cf. ibid., 273.
169. Cf. ibid., 301.
170. Ibid., 304.
171. Ibid., 97.
172. Ibid.
173. Ibid., 376.
174. Cf. ibid., 49–50.
175. Schnädelbach, "Rationalität und Begründung," 62.
176. Ibid.
177. Cf. ibid., 63.
178. Ibid., 67.
179. Ibid., 62.
180. Ibid., 68; cf. Herbert Schnädelbach, "Rationalitätstypen," in *Philosophie in der modernen Kultur* (Frankfurt: Suhrkamp, 2000), 274–275.
181. Schnädelbach, "Rationalität und Begründung," 68.
182. Ibid., 69.
183. Ibid., 70.

184. In connection with reflection on dealing with the hermeneutic circle (cf. Martin Heidegger, *Being and Time*, trans. Blackwell Publishing Ltd. [Oxford: Blackwell, 1962], 153; and Hans-Georg Gadamer, *Truth and Method*, trans. Joel Weinsheimer and Donald G. Marshall [London: Continuum, 2004], 178) two modes of circularity can be distinguished that present a general reformulation of the hermeneutic reflections. Operations—which have as necessary conditions the partial or hypothetical anticipation of the results of the operation—in principle allow the relationship between the anticipation and the results to be dynamized. In connection with such operations *dynamic circles* can be generated that are tolerable as long as the anticipation of the results of the operation are not complete. In contrast, operations whose necessary prerequisites preclude partial anticipations lead, when there are such anticipations, to *vicious circles*. Here it is significant that the fact that justifications of justifications as well as justification standards are imaginable that avoid becoming vicious circles. As long as the condition that we make progress in determining the *preconception* in each round of justification is fulfilled, that is, as long as we manage to dynamize the circle productively, we are by no means in a methodologically unacceptable position. The prescription for productivity that is implicit to this idea is of course related to Lakatos's criterion of progressive problem shifts. Cf. Imre Lakatos, "Falsification and Methodology of Scientific Research Programmes," in *Criticism and the Growth of Knowledge*, ed. Imre Lakatos and Alan Musgrave, 91–196 (Cambridge: Cambridge University Press, 1970), esp. 116ff.

185. This is Gosepath's thesis; see p. 46.

186. X must rather be rational in a broader sense so that X can be false.

187. Cf. Schnädelbach, "Rationalität und Begründung," 70.

188. Ibid., 72–73.

189. Ibid., 62, 73–74.

190. Cf. ibid., 63.

191. Cf. Schnädelbach, "Rationalitätstypen," 277–278. I wonder, however, whether it is auspicious to view this dimension of reason in connection with Cassirer or Langer as competencies of *symbolic* use or as *symbolic* rationality, especially because the view of content or meaning associated with the concept of the symbol is not sufficiently distant from linguistic meaning.

192. Habermas has characterized the concept of communication or reaching an understanding (*Verständigung*) as the "bring[ing] about [of] an agreement (*Einverständnis*) that terminates in the intersubjective mutuality of reciprocal comprehension" ("What Is Universal Pragmatics?" 23).

193. Joachim Schulte, "Nachwort," in *Der Mythos des Subjektiven: Philosophische Essays*, ed. Donald Davidson (Stuttgart: Reclam, 1993), 112.

194. Habermas has used the core thought of truth semantics precisely as the starting point for an enhancing strategy; indeed, he has done this, first, with reference to the type of linguistic entities and, second, with a view to the dimensions of validity of these entities, which are broadened from truth conditions to conditions for acceptability in order to allow not only claims to truth but also claims to sincerity and rightness to be encompassed so that a theory of meaning can be secured for expressive and normative speech acts. Third, he has applied this with a view to the interpretive situation, which is conceived of as a shared intersubjective communication practice.

195. Willard van Orman Quine, *Word and Object* (Cambridge, MA: MIT Press, 1960), 28.

196. Davidson has attempted to show—even when including grave cases of deviant speech in which there is not a set of shared rules—that even in the case of malapropism or radical idiolects the conditions for the possibility of understanding are not fundamentally withdrawn.

197. Cf. Donald Davidson, "Radical Interpretation," in *Inquiries Into Truth and Interpretation* (New York: Oxford University Press, 2001), 125–126.

198. Cf. Donald Davidson, "Truth and Meaning," in *Inquiries Into Truth and Interpretation* (New York: Oxford University Press, 2001), 22.

199. Ibid., 23.

200. For an excellent introduction to Tarski's procedure, see Wolfgang Künne, "Wahrheit," in *Philosophie: Ein Grundkurs*, ed. E. Martens and H. Schnädelbach (Reinbek: Rowohlt, 1991).

201. Cf. Davidson, "Truth and Meaning," 36.

202. However, for some of these problems, studies have been done, not a few by Davidson himself. Cf. Donald Davidson, "Quotation," in *Inquiries Into Truth and Interpretation*, 79–92 (New York: Oxford University Press, 2001). Donald Davidson, "On Saying That," in *Inquiries Into Truth and Interpretation*, 93–108 (New York: Oxford University Press, 2001). Cf. Tyler Burge, "Reference and Proper Names," *Journal of Philosophy* 70 (1973): 425–439. Cf. Gilbert Harman, "Moral Relativism Defended," *Philosophical Review* 84 (1975): 3–22. Cf. John Wallace, "Positive, Comparative, Superlative," *Journal of Philosophy* 69 (1972): 773–782.

203. Davidson discusses this problem himself as anomalous T-theorems ("'snow is white' is true if and only if 'grass is green'"). Cf. Davidson, "Truth and Meaning," 25.

204. It is of fundamental significance that this assumption has *un*specified content; for if an interpreter had to work with assumptions of the type "*P* believes *x*," "*P* wants to say *x*," then we would return to the difficulties of an intentionalist semantics. However, with this assumption an initial correspondence theory motif of the principle of charity (*Nachsichtigkeit*) is at the same time brought into play, which is explained below.

205. Cf. Davidson, "Truth and Meaning," 25. "This is snow" is true if and only if the speaker is pointing to snow.

206. Føllesdal bemoans a principal defect of publicness in the causal reference theory (regardless of whether in the Quinean variant of stimulus meaning or on the basis of the causal effects on speakers in Davidson), among other reasons, because it may not be clear offhand that the causes that are the basis of the actions are in fact the same ones. Føllesdal, "The Status of Rationality Assumptions in Interpretation and in the Explanation of Action," *Dialectica* 36 (1982): 301–316.

207. Donald Davidson, "The Conditions of Thought," in *The Mind of Donald Davidson*, ed. Johannes Brandl and Wolfgang L. Gombocz (Amsterdam: Rodopi, 1989), 198.

208. Ibid., 193.

209. See p. 182.

210. An alternative model of the origin of thoughts is presented below; see pp. 183–203.

211. Donald Davidson, "Rational Animals," *Dialectica* 36 (1982): 321 (my emphasis).

212. Davidson, "Radical Interpretation," 137.

213. Donald Davidson, "How Is Weakness of the Will Possible?" in *Essays on Actions and Events* (New York: Oxford University Press, 2001), 41. Cf. Rudolf Carnap, *Logical Foundations of Probability* (Chicago: University of Chicago Press, 1951), 211.

214. Davidson, "How Is Weakness of the Will Possible?" 41.

215. Cf. Quine, *Word and Object*, 20; and Donald Davidson, "Incoherence and Irrationality," *Dialectica* 39 (1985): 348.

216. Cf., e.g., Gosepath's sixth principle of practical rationality; see p. 49.

217. Cf. Davidson, "Incoherence and Irrationality," 347–348.

218. Cf. Alexander Becker, *Verstehen und Bewusstsein* (Paderborn: Mentis, 2000), 102–107. Cf. also Daniel Dennett, "Intentional Systems," in *Brainstorms: Philosophical Essays on Mind and Psychology* (Cambridge, MA: MIT Press, 1981), 3–22.

219. Compare both pertinent works: Donald Davidson, "Paradoxes of Irrationality," in *Philosophical Essays on Freud*, ed. R. Wohlheim and J. Hopkins, 289–305 (New York: Cambridge University Press, 1982); and Davidson, "Incoherence and Irrationality," 345–354.

220. Davidson, "Incoherence and Irrationality," 347.

221. See p. 69.

222. See (A1), p. 15.

223. Cf. Habermas, "Unity of Reason in the Diversity of Its Voices," 134 (my emphasis).

2. WHAT ARE MEDIA?

1. Cf. the article D. G., "Medium (semiotisch)," in *Enzyklopädie Philosophie und Wissenschaftstheorie*, 4 vols., ed. Jürgen Mittelstraß, 2:829–831 (Stuttgart: Metzeler, 1984). In the *Historischen Wörterbuch der Philosophie* and other pertinent works, the concept is not listed.

2. Jan Künzler, *Medien und Gesellschaft: Die Medienkonzepte von Talcott Parsons, Jürgen Habermas und Niklas Luhmann* (Stuttgart: Enke, 1989), 1.

3. Cf. Knut Hickethier, "Das 'Medium,' die 'Medien' und die Medienwissenschaft," in *Ansichten einer künftigen Medienwissenschaft*, ed. R. Bohn, E. Müller, and R. Ruppert, 51–74 (Berlin: Sigma, 1988).

4. Cf. Friedrich Knilli, "Medium," in *Kritische Stichwörter zur Medienwissenschaft*, ed. W. Faulstich, 230–251 (Munich: Fink, 1989); Werner Faulstich, *Medientheorien: Einführung und Überblick* (Göttingen: Vandenhoeck & Ruprecht, 1991).

5. Cf., e.g., Bertolt Brecht, "Radiotheorie 1927–1932," in *Gesammelte Werke*, vol. 8, *Schriften zur Literatur und Kunst, Politik und Gesellschaft*, 117–137 (Frankfurt: Suhrkamp, 1976). Siegfried Kracauer, *Theory of Film: The Redemption of Physical Reality* (Princeton, NJ: Princeton University Press, 1997); Vilém Flusser, *Die Schrift: Hat Schreiben Zukunft?* (Göttingen: Immatrix, 1989). Faulstich provides an overview of the numerous such works about particular media in *Medientheorien*, 18–86.

6. As far as I can see, Faulstich is an exception. See his *Medientheorien*, where he also introduces media theories (Parsons, Habermas, Luhmann, J. S. Schmidt), even

if very schematically, which are applied beyond mass communication theory or aesthetic means of expression.

7. See pp. 93ff.

8. In a further publication, I soon hope to be able to provide a detailed reconstruction and critique of the media theories that are only sketched out here, but especially also of the attempt to (mis)understand society as an autopoietic system.

9. Cf. Talcott Parsons, *Actor, Situation und normative Muster* (Frankfurt: Suhrkamp, 1994), 32.

10. Here, *A* stands for adaption, *G* for goal attainment, *I* for integration, and *L* for latent pattern maintenance.

11. Talcott Parsons, "Some Problems of General Theory in Sociology," in *Social Systems and the Evolution of Action Theory* (New York: Free Press, 1977), 236.

12. Cf. Talcott Parsons, "On the Concept of Political Power," in *Proceedings of the American Philosophical Society* 107, no. 3 (1963): 259; Talcott Parsons, "On the Concept of Influence," *Public Opinion Quarterly* 27, no. 1 (1963): 37–62, esp. 45; Talcott Parsons, *Societies: Evolutionary and Comparative Perspectives* (Englewood Cliffs, NJ: Prentice Hall, 1966), 29; and Talcott Parsons, *The System of Modern Societies* (Englewood Cliffs, NJ: Prentice Hall, 1971), 4, 9. Because every system that is differentiated in AGIL-conforming subsystems has to solve integration tasks, Parsons is forced to identify four media in every such system. Because the social system is only one of four subsystems in the action system, for the action system and its subsystems alone it is necessary to determine twenty media. Even the eight that are portrayed here raise doubt that robust criteria for all media can be distinguished.

13. Cf. Parsons, "Actor, Situation and Normative Patterns," originating in 1939, but not printed in Parsons's lifetime; German version, *Aktor, Situation und normative Muster: Ein Essay zur Theorie sozialen Handelns* (Frankfurt: Suhrkamp, 1994), 163. See also Talcott Parsons, "On Building Social Systems Theory: A Personal History," *Daedalus* 99, no. 4 (1970): 870.

14. Stefan Jensen has proposed the following standard formulations for the four media of the social system: for *money*: "offering money—looking for goods!" For *power*: "Have power—desire to reach goal X!" For *influence*: "Have solved problem X—offering relief and orientation for allegiance!" For *value commitment*: "Norm X is right or true—X should be accepted!" See Stefan Jensen, "Einleitung," in *Zur Theorie der Interaktionsmedien*, by Talcott Parsons (Opladen: Westdeutscher, 1980), 25, 26, 37, 46–47.

15. Talcott Parsons, "On the Concept of Value Commitments," *Social Inquiry* 38 (1968): 143. Cf. also Talcott Parsons, "The Present Status of 'Structural-Functional' Theory in Sociology," in *Social Systems and the Evolution of Action Theory* (New York: Free Press, 1977), 107–108.

16. Cf. Parsons, "On the Concept of Value Commitments," 143.

17. Talcott Parsons, "Social Systems," in *Social Systems and the Evolution of Action Theory* (New York: Free Press, 1977), 189.

18. Ibid., 198.

19. Ibid., 190.

20. Parsons, "On the Concept of Political Power," 242.

21. Künzler, *Medien und Gesellschaft*, 40; and cf. Parsons, "On the Concept of Political Power," 242, 247.

22. Cf. Jürgen Habermas, *The Theory of Communicative Action*, vol. 2, *Lifeworld and System*, trans. Thomas McCarthy (Boston: Beacon, 2000), 262.

23. Ibid., 266.
24. Cf. ibid.
25. Cf. ibid., 318.
26. Cf. Jürgen Habermas, "A Reply," in *Communicative Action: Essays on Jürgen Habermas's Theory of Communicative Action*, ed. Axel Honneth and Hans Joas (Cambridge: Polity, 1991), 259: "What I do not see ... is how a system rationality, be it the market-mediated rationality of the medium of money or the organization-mediated rationality of the power medium, can be criticized from this action theoretic vantage point and then rejected for being inverted purposive rationality." Cf. also Simone Dietz, *Lebenswelt und System: Widerstreitende Ansätze in der Gesellschaftstheorie von Jürgen Habermas* (Würzburg: Königshausen & Neumann, 1993), 185.
27. Habermas, "A Reply," 257.
28. Cf. Jürgen Habermas, "Handlung und System: Bemerkungen zu Parsons' Medientheorie," in *Verhalten, Handeln und System*, ed. W. Schluchter (Frankfurt: Suhrkamp, 1980), 95–96.
29. Cf. Habermas, "Handlung und System," 80; Habermas, *Lifeworld and System*, 263.
30. Habermas, *Lifeworld and System*, 263 (my emphasis).
31. Ibid., 390.
32. Ibid., 365.
33. Cf. Habermas, "Handlung und System," 95ff.; regarding "law," cf. Habermas, *Lifeworld and System*, 365; regarding "mass media," ibid. 573.
34. The bifurcation is reproduced with a view to law, which as a steering medium substitutes for linguistic understanding, but as an institution it remains connected to lifeworld processes of understanding.
35. Habermas mentions a limited ability of power to circulate, which is shown in the "form of position-bound administrative authority" (Habermas, "Handlung und System," 88); it is worth considering whether it is people here who circulate relative to positions rather than power that circulates relative to persons.
36. Cf. also Künzler, *Medien und Gesellschaft*, 69.
37. See Niklas Luhmann, *Social Systems*, trans. John Bednarz Jr. and Dirk Baecker (Stanford, CA: Stanford University Press, 1996), 442, where he writes: "The concept of system (as we use the term in our investigations) always stands for a real state of affairs"; or ibid., 12: "The ... considerations assume that there are systems."
38. Cf., e.g., Niklas Luhmann, "Veränderungen im System gesellschaftlicher Kommunikation und die Massenmedien," in *Soziologische Aufklärung 3* (Opladen: Westdeutscher, 1981), 309; and Luhmann, *Social Systems*, 138.
39. Cf. Luhmann, *Social Systems*, 139–145.
40. Niklas Luhmann, "Einführende Bemerkungen zu einer Theorie symbolisch generalisierter Kommunikationsmedien," in *Soziologische Aufklärung 2* (Opladen: Westdeutscher, 1975), 171. Luhmann here obviously has abandoned Parsons's understanding of the concept of contingency in the context of social interactions.
41. Luhmann, "Einführende Bemerkungen," 172.
42. Ibid.
43. Luhmann, *Social Systems*, 160.
44. Cf. Umberto Eco, *Einführung in die Semiotik* (Munich: Fink, 1985), 57, 60.
45. Niklas Luhmann, *Trust and Power: Two Works* (Chichester, UK: Wiley, 1979), 128.

46. Luhmann, "Einführende Bemerkungen," 172. It is more than questionable whether the fact that one can maintain the falsity of a sentence *p* with the help of negation should be expressed such that some information is expressed in another version than if one claims *p*.

47. Cf. Niklas Luhmann, "'Distinctions directrices': Über Codierung von Semantiken und Systemen," in *Soziologische Aufklärung 4* (Opladen: Westdeutscher, 1987), 14–15. Cf. also Niklas Luhmann, "Codierung und Programmierung: Bildung und Selektion im Erwachsenensystem," in *Soziologische Aufklärung 4*, 182–201 (Opladen: Westdeutscher, 1987).

48. Cf. Luhmann, "Einführende Bemerkungen," 175; Niklas Luhmann, "Ist Kunst codierbar?" in *Soziologische Aufklärung 3* (Opladen: Westdeutscher, 1981), 246. Cf. also Niklas Luhmann, "Die Unwahrscheinlichkeit der Kommunikation," in *Soziologische Aufklärung 3* (Opladen: Westdeutscher, 1981), 28; and Luhmann, *Social Systems*, 161. Here the concept is no longer used, but the motivational aspect of communications media continues to play a central role.

49. Niklas Luhmann, *Ecological Communication*, trans. John Bednarz Jr. (Cambridge: Polity, 1989), 45. One may ask whether the discussion here is of values and rules or of prescripts, thus of things that one might speak better about using a different type of language.

50. Künzler, *Medien und Gesellschaft*, 89.

51. Cf., e.g., Marshall McLuhan, *The Gutenberg Galaxy* (Toronto: University of Toronto Press, 1992), 8: "The abstracting or opening of closed societies *is the work of the phonetic alphabet*" (my emphasis).

52. Cf. Marshall McLuhan and Eric McLuhan, *Laws of the Media: The New Science* (Toronto: University of Toronto Press, 1988), 68ff.

53. Cf. McLuhan, *Gutenberg Galaxy*, 7–8.

54. Cf. also Paul Goetsch, "Der Übergang von Mündlichkeit zu Schriftlichkeit: De kulturkritischen und ideologischen Implikationen der Theorien von McLuhan, Goody und Ong," in *Symbolische Formen—Medien—Identität*, ed. W. Raible (Tübingen: Narr, 1991), 115–116.

55. Goetsch, "Der Übergang von Mündlichkeit zu Schriftlichkeit," 116.

56. Marshall McLuhan, *Understanding Media: The Extensions of Man* (New York: McGraw-Hill, 1966), 23.

57. Cf. McLuhan, *Understanding Media*, 35. This thought is by no means so original as McLuhan appears to presume. Arnold Gehlen had summarized the "sense" of technology as "the principle of *organ-replacement*, which now from the outset is placed beside *organ-relieving* and *organ-surpassing*." See Arnold Gehlen, *Anthropologische Forschung* (Reinbek: Rowohlt, 1961), 93–94; cf. also Arnold Gehlen, "Man and Technique," in *Man in the Age of Technology*, trans. Patricia Lipscomb (New York: Columbia University Press, 1980), 3.

58. McLuhan, *Understanding Media*, 36.

59. Ibid., 23–24.

60. Ibid., 24.

61. Cf. McLuhan, *Laws of the Media*, 3. Also: "Utterings are outerings, so media are not *as* words, they *are* words" (ibid., ix).

62. Cf. John Dewey, *Art as Experience* (New York: Perigree, 2005), 1, 11.

63. I go more precisely into the communicative elements in Kant's views, which I think are underestimated. Cf. pp. 286–287.

64. Cf., e.g., the following formulation: "When [the form of an object of industrial art] is liberated from limitation to a specialized end and serves also the purposes of an immediate and vital experience, the form is esthetic and not merely useful" (Dewey, *Art as Experience*, 121).

65. Cf. Dewey, *Art as Experience*, 50, 53, 56.

66. Cf. ibid., 110.

67. Ibid., 207.

68. I use this expression differently than Habermas's expression, "giving something to understand" (*Zu-verstehen-geben*), not to characterize a parasitic (strategic) mode of communication, but to express the offering character of works of art and their wide-reaching need for interpretation. See Jürgen Habermas, *The Theory of Communicative Action*, vol. 1, *Reason and the Rationalization of Society*, trans. Thomas McCarthy (Boston: Beacon, 1984), 288.

69. Dewey, *Art as Experience*, 66.

70. Ibid., 205.

71. Ibid.

72. I am focusing on the example of bricks in detail because, given its reappearance in the summary (ibid., 253), it is hardly to be viewed as a slip.

73. Cf. Dewey, *Art as Experience*, 239, where he writes: "The trait that characterized architecture in an emphatic sense is that its media are the (relatively) raw materials of nature and of the fundamental modes of natural energy." He also writes (229) that architecture "expresses also enduring values of collective human life."

74. Ibid., 209.

75. Cf. Georg Wilhelm Friedrich Hegel, *Phenomenology of Spirit*, trans. A. V. Miller (New Delhi: Shri Jainendra Press, 1998), 117.

76. Dewey, *Art as Experience*, 298.

77. Cf. ibid., 110, 298.

78. Ibid., 248.

79. Ibid., 299.

80. Cf. Immanuel Kant, *The Critique of Judgment* (New York: Cosimo, 2007), 112–113.

81. Dewey, *Art as Experience*, 235.

82. Cf. John R. Searle, "What Is a Speech Act?" in *Readings in Language and Mind*, ed. H. Geirsson and Michael Losonsky, 110–120 (London: Blackwell, 1996); and John R. Searle, *The Construction of Social Reality* (New York: Free Press, 1995), 27ff., 43–51.

83. Cf. John Rawls, "Two Concepts of Rules," *Philosophical Review* 64 (1955): 3–32.

84. Dewey, *Art as Experience*, 66.

85. Ibid., 349.

86. Here I would like to correct my views in Matthias Vogel, "Medien im Experiment der Demokratie," in *Demokratischer Experimentalismus*, ed. Hauke Brunkhorst, 104–143 (Frankfurt: Suhrkamp, 1998), in which I set the focus of the establishment mechanism nearly exclusively on constitutive rules. Although Dewey provides indications of corresponding views, the concept of performative proliferation appears to me to harmonize better with numerous other views of Dewey.

87. Dewey, *Art as Experience*, 282.

88. Ibid., 298.

89. Ibid., 349.

90. Ibid.

91. Ibid., 192.
92. Ibid., 281–282.
93. Ibid., 281.
94. Ibid., 253–254.
95. Ibid., 299.
96. Ibid., 109.
97. Cf. Ernst Cassirer, *The Philosophy of Symbolic Forms*, 4 vols., ed. J. M. Krois and D. P. Verene (New Haven, CT: Yale University Press, 1955); and Susanne Langer, *Philosophy in a New Key: A Study in the Symbolism of Reason, Rite, and Art* (New York: New American Library, 1954), chaps. 6–7.
98. Dewey, *Art as Experience*, 204.
99. In light of the uneasy things that could be connected with the motif of unifying art, it is important to emphasize that this motif does not have the character of creating unity in exclusive communities (for example, among folk groups), but is characterized by a universalist tendency, which emphasizes the unity of all human beings. Cf. ibid.
100. Ibid.
101. Martin Seel has taken up these ideas and further developed them. He writes, "Dewey said that the work of art that is experienced as successful *constitutes* the 'experienceability' of the experience, which it, at the same time means solely in *this* work." Cf. Martin Seel, *Die Kunst der Entzweiung: Zum Begriff der ästhetischen Rationalität* (Frankfurt: Suhrkamp, 1985), 174. Admittedly, Seel takes up only the experiential aspect of Dewey's theory, and he is distrustful of an immediate communicative function of works of art, leaning on Adorno's dictum that "No artwork is to be described or explained in terms of the categories of communication" (Theodor W. Adorno, *Aesthetic Theory*, trans. R. Hullot-Kentor [Minneapolis: University of Minnesota Press, 2004], 144). Yet even if works of art should not be understood without much ado as means for realizing communicative intentions, I cannot see that a fundamental perspective of the communicative role of works of art that is oriented on the medial structure of the works threatens their status as works of art. In contrast, the possibility of explaining how works of art can acquire a specific meaning is dependent on this view of understanding; see p. 119.

3. TOWARD A GENERAL THEORY OF MEDIA

1. Jean Baudrillard, "Requiem for the Media," in *For a Critique of the Political Economy of the Sign*, trans. Charles Levin (St. Louis: Telos, 1981), 164.
2. In chapter 4 of *Verstehen und Bewusstsein* (Paderborn: Mentis, 2000), Alexander Becker provides outlines of an alternative approach to an interpretationist theory of art.
3. In the context of my reflections, musical works of art are considered a paradigmatic example of nonlinguistic expression. For economy of presentation, I will first go into nonmusical works of art after I have substantially developed the basic conceptual apparatus of media theory. It is clear that the background for this procedure is the thesis that what is said about music also applies mutatis mutandis to other artistic media. Readers who, in the face of the paradigmatic function of music, might be reminded of the problems that arose in Parsons in connection with the generaliza-

tion of the attributes of the paradigmatic medium of money, can take comfort in the explication of the media concept that is independent of music and art.

4. Anton Webern, *The Path to the New Music*, ed. Willi Reich (Bryn Mawr, PA: Presser, 1963), 42.

5. Theodor W. Adorno, "Music and Language: A Fragment," in *Quasi una fantasia: Essays in Modern Music*, trans. Rodney Livingstone (London: Verso, 2002), 6. In the same text (2–3), we find the following, no less paradoxical formulation: "The language of music is quite different from the music of intentionality. . . . Music aspires to be a language without intention. . . . There is a dialectic at work. Music is permeated through and through with intentionality. This does not just date from the *stile rappresentativo*, which deployed the rationalization of music in an effort to exploit its similarity to language. Music bereft of all intentionality, the merely phenomenal linking of sounds, would be an acoustic parallel to the kaleidoscope. On the other hand, as absolute intentionality it would cease to be music and would effect a false transformation into language. Intentions are central to music, but only intermittently." However, cf. also: "If painting and music do not converge by means of growing similarity, they do meet in a third dimension: both are language" (Theodor W. Adorno, "On Some Relationships Between Music and Painting," *Musical Quarterly* 79 [1995]: 71).

6. Eduard Hanslick, *On the Musically Beautiful*, trans. Geoffrey Payzant (New York: Liberal Arts Press, 1957), 30 (my emphasis). Hanslick's vote has historical predecessors. So, for example, already at the beginning of the eighteenth century, Johann Mattheson wrote: "Instrumental music [is] nothing . . . other than tone language or sound talk" (*Der vollkommene Kapellmeister* [Hamburg: Christian Herold, 1739], 82).

7. Cf. Donald Davidson, "On the Very Idea of a Conceptual Scheme," in *Inquiries Into Truth and Interpretation* (New York: Oxford University Press, 2001), 183–198.

8. As is well known, Kant placed music there side by side with humor: "Music and that which excites laughter are two different kinds of play with aesthetical Ideas or with representations of the Understanding through which *ultimately nothing is thought*. . . . It is not the judging of the harmony in tones or the sallies of wit . . . but the furtherance of the vital bodily processes, the affectation that moves the intestines and the diaphragm, in a word, the feeling of health (which without such inducements one does not feel) that makes up the gratification felt by us; so that we can thus reach the body through the soul and use the latter as the physician of the former" (Immanuel Kant, *The Critique of Judgment* [New York: Cosimo, 2007], 132; my emphasis).

9. Cf. Christoph Rueger, ed., *Die musikalische Hausapotheke: Audio CDs* (Geneva: Ariston, 1999).

10. Of course, this is not to say that the widespread use of music as a (ritual) intoxicant is a deficient use, but only that this does not exhaust what music is.

11. Fred Lerdahl and Ray Jackendoff, *A Generative Theory of Tonal Music* (Cambridge, MA: MIT Press, 1983). Here I just mention the differences in individual ways of listening and the historical dynamic of music, in contrast to the relative constancy of the linguistic grammar.

12. Here and in what follows, I ignore additional presuppositions with which (H1) must be supplemented, e.g., that X has no consequences that clash with important preferences of P (that are not stated in [a], etc.), in order to be considered a suitable rationalization of an action of P, because these differentiations of (H1) are of no importance for the considerations here.

13. By speaking of "existence," I do not mean to suggest any specific realistic position with regard to intentional states. Propositional attitudes "exist" in interpretation theory generally only as ascribed states of those interpreted (they are *theoretical entities* of explanations of action) so that interpretationism does not imply a realistic theory of intentional states. However, it is clear that the difference between *possible* reasons and *effective* reasons suggests a realistic interpretation insofar as the identification of effective reasons is based on the identification of those reasons that *are causes* of the action that is be explained.

14. Cf. Donald Davidson, "Rational Animals," *Dialectica* 36 (1982): 321.

15. Cf. ibid., 322: "My thesis is . . . that a creature cannot have a thought unless it has language."

16. Cf. ibid., 324.

17. Here I am prescinding from the role that Davidson assigns to surprise, as a necessary and sufficient condition for having thoughts (ibid., 326) because surprise, in the face of facts that do not confirm one's own expectations or beliefs, is, in my view, a psychic symptom that contingently occurs, or not.

18. John R. Searle, *Intentionality: An Essay in the Philosophy of Mind* (Cambridge: Cambridge University Press, 1983).

19. Ibid., 5.

20. Ibid., 27.

21. Cf. ibid., 176ff.

22. Ibid., 161.

23. Cf. ibid., 164.

24. Ibid., 177.

25. Ibid., 164.

26. This distinction is not the same as Brandom's distinction between *simple intentional systems* and *interpreting intentional systems*, for besides the parallel that A-intentionality does not enable a being to interpret another being, there is the difference that Brandom's simple intentionality "lies in the eye of the beholder" and thus is derivative from the developed form of intentionality (cf. Robert B. Brandom, *Making It Explicit* [Cambridge, MA: Harvard University Press, 1994], 60–61), while I expect that beings with A-intentional states manage to individuate A-intentional states, and thus become able to differentiate between states of affairs that satisfy their intentional states and states of affairs that do not. Beings with A-intentional states are thus not interpreters of their intentional states, but they evaluate the world *relative to the content* of their A-intentional states, contents that they are not able to articulate themselves.

The estimation that there is prelinguistic intentionality is provided some empirical support by more recent works on infant research. With a view to numerous empirical works, Martin Dornes, *Die frühe Kindheit: Entwicklungspsychologie der ersten Lebensjahre* [Frankfurt: Suhrkamp, 1997], cf. 66–76) suggests a three-level mental theory that describes the development of mind as a development from perception to images to words, a development that starts with a phase of *sensory-motor thinking*, which achieves the recording of sensory-motor affective schemata (dominant in the first year) by coupling perceptions of reality with sensory-motor effects, and proceeds through a phase of *pictorial thinking* (greater than twelve months) in which the ability to evoke fantasies and sequences of images is reached at the age of one and a half, thus to a point of time in which the third phase is reached, the phase of the "linguistic coding of the psychic." Here it is interesting that Dornes already expects *"intentional expressions"* at the first level; children (less than nine months) intentionally employ expressive forms of behavior after observing the effects of pure involuntary expressions on their guardians (instrumental crying), and these forms of behavior are contextually suited to probably nonconscious intentions. Evidence of a genetic coding of prelinguistic competencies, on which the identification of other intentional beings is based, is provided by Baron-Cohen in his functionalist analysis of autism; see Simon Baron-Cohen, *Mindblindness: An Essay on Autism and Theory of Mind* (Cambridge, MA: MIT Press, 1995).

27. Later in the text (see p. 178), there are more refined views on the conception of the transition between both forms of intentionality.

28. Ruth Millikan has submitted a detailed proposal about how, with the help of a reproduction history of basic intentional states, the teleological and observer-relative category of function can be reconstructed as an intrinsic category. Cf. Ruth Garrett Millikan, *Language, Thought and Other Biological Categories: New Foundations for Realism* (Cambridge, MA: MIT Press, 1995). Using Millikan's teleo-semantic vocabulary, one could say that A-intentional states are "intentional icons," whose "proper function" is "to map" to issues or objects, for given the reproduction history of children's pointing actions to an object (under normal social conditions), tokens of such pointing have the function of identifying their "real value" as the desired object (cf. especially chaps. 15–18). Wolfgang Detel provides a more detailed overview of the program and the problems of teleo-semantics in "Haben Frösche und Sumpfmenschen Gedanken? Einige Probleme der Teleosemantik," *Deutsche Zeitschrift für Philosophie* 49, no. 4 (2001): 601–626; and Wolfgang Detel, "Teleosemantik. Ein neuer Blick auf den Geist?" *Deutsche Zeitschrift für Philosophie* 49, no. 3 (2001): 465–491.

29. Searle, of course, does not understand his thesis as one that should remain limited to the basic case of intrinsic intentionality. Below (see p. 137), I go into the difficulties that arise if one entrusts Searle's meaning-theoretic program with the reconstruction of art.

30. A more abstract and technically more precise formulation of the transition can be found on p. 178.

31. Below an attempt is made at least to show this in some rudimentary way (cf. p. 233).

32. Edgar Allan Poe appears to have been convinced that artistic action should be understood according to the pattern of (H1.1). Approximately a year after he wrote "The Raven" in "The Philosophy of Composition" (1846), he provided a portrayal of the composition of the poem. His report does not lack a bit of involuntary humor; large portions read like a quite strained pseudorationalization. Cf. Edgar Allan Poe, "The Philosophy of Composition," *Graham's Magazine* 28 (1846): 163–167.

33. Cf. p. 129.

34. Searle, *Intentionality*, 164.

35. Cf. Searle, *Intentionality*, 174, where, among other things, it succinctly says: "Since there is, in general, no direction of fit in expressives, there are no conditions of satisfaction other than that the utterance should be an expression of the relevant psychological state. If I intend my utterance as an expression of such and such a state then it will be an expression of that state, though I may of course not succeed in communicating that expression."

36. Susanne K. Langer, *Philosophy in a New Key: A Study in the Symbolism of Reason, Rite, and Art* (New York: New American Library, 1954), 234.

37. I will return to the problem of untranslatability; see p. 254. What is initially decisive is that even music that follows the view that music is language (Hans Werner Henze) can never ensure the general character of the semanticizing of the musical material, except perhaps from the indexical elements and techniques of citation; nor does it ever exhaust itself in semantic elements of that kind. Cf. Hans Werner Henze, "Die Folgen der Vereinsamung," *Die Zeit* 34 (1979): 31. For the general use of the language metaphor in connection with music, see Peter Faltin, "Ist Musik eine Sprache?" in *Die Zeichen: Neue Aspekte der musikalischen Ästhetik 2*, ed. H. W. Henze (Frankfurt: Suhrkamp, 1981), 32.

38. Cf. p. 41.

39. Cf. p. 100.

40. The fact that this is hardly controversial among some leading musicologists shows that this by no means is a strained or artificial criterion. Cf. Stephen Davies, *Musical Meaning and Expression* (Ithaca, NY: Cornell University Press, 1994), 325, 330ff. See also Peter Kivy, "It's Only Music: So What's to Understand?" *Journal of Aesthetic Education* 20 (1986): 1–74. A systematic, i.e., general meaning-theoretic use of the identification criterion as a criterion of understanding is presented by Ruth Millikan, *Language, Thought and Other Biological Categories: New Foundations for Realism* (Cambridge, MA: MIT Press, 1984), chap. 15. Within the framework of a functionalist semantic, she conceptualizes the understanding of a concept (or a thought) with the content X as the ability to identify X.

41. Herewith I take up a thought that Dewey, according to my reconstruction, drew on to determine the specifics of aesthetic reception. See p. 98.

42. Davies, *Musical Meaning and Expression*, 325.

43. Cf. Mozart, String Quintet in G Minor, K. 516.

44. Davies, *Musical Meaning and Expression*, 337. The specifications of the sonata form on the basis of the attributes thought characteristic of it today (the contrast of two antithetic themes at various tonal levels in the exposition; the production and the illuminating of references between these themes as it is carried out; and the summarizing, homogenizing presentation of the musical material of the exposition in the reprise [in the key of the phrase]) were first codified by Adolf Bernhard Marx in 1845, fifty-four years after Mozart's death. In 1840 the piano teacher and instructor of Liszt, Carl Czerny, wrote, "In no treatise . . . which has yet appeared, has the manner of constructing a sonata . . . been fundamentally described" (quoted in William S. Newman, Article "Sonate," in *Musik in Geschichte und Gegenwart* [Munich: Deutscher Taschenbuch/Bärenreiter, 1965], vol. 12. Newman cites the English version of the "Schule der Tonsetzkunst").

45. I would like to thank the participants of the Thursday colloquium, but especially Alexander Becker and Wolfgang Detel, for numerous helpful discussions about the concept of a rule.

46. Causal consequences of A can, of course, be among these attributes.

47. It should be clear that the regress problem cannot be solved by bringing implicit rules into play, for in order to correctly follow them, an (infinite number) of implicit rules of compliance also have to be drawn out. Brandom thus pursues a three-level strategy that views rules (i.e., explicit norms) as the explicitly achieved norms of a social practice that is structured by implicit norms (rightness), which for their part draw on factual, individual, and societal regularities.

48. Gilbert Ryle, *The Concept of Mind* (Chicago: University of Chicago Press, 2000), 41.

49. Cf. ibid., 42.

50. Cf. ibid., 42ff.

51. Joseph Kerman, "The State of Academic Music Criticism," in *On Criticizing Music: Five Philosophical Perspectives*, ed. Kingsley Price (Baltimore: Johns Hopkins University Press, 1981), 196, quoted in Davies, *Musical Meaning and Expression*, 337–338 (my emphasis).

52. Kant, *Critique of Judgment*, 112–113, B 182.

53. Ibid., 113, B 182.

54. Ibid., 114, B 185. Spacing (rather than italics) is used for emphasis in the original.

55. Cf. ibid., 112, B 182.

56. Ibid., 113, B 184.

57. Ibid.

58. A good example of this way of establishing correlations between the tone characteristics of instruments and musical motifs, on the one hand, and imaginary music-extrinsic characteristics, on the other, is the lasting contribution to music pedagogy of Prokofiev's "Peter and the Wolf."

59. The elementary types of activities—to sing C, D, E . . . (fifteen possibilities), to sing a loud/soft tone (two possibilities), to sing a half or a full tone (two possibilities)—are types of activity that only reveal themselves from an analytic perspective, for within the musical world of the student there are only types of activities that perform attributes in all three dimensions—pitch, dynamic, and tone duration.

60. This procedure of course applies only for natural numbers. I will not go into the modification to this procedure necessary for other types of numbers.

61. Of course, one can doubt that the concept of a demonstrative *rule* is an auspicious choice. However, insofar as a demonstrative act is a *normative* act and indicates a rightness that displays a certain *generality* and, if necessary, is *explainable as a rule*, the characterization in general appears to me to be pretty appropriate.

62. See p. 116.

63. For the differentiation between continuous and discontinuous attribute sets as a differentiation between types of "information spaces," cf. David J. Chalmers, *The Conscious Mind: In Search of a Fundamental Theory* (New York: Oxford University Press, 1997), 277–282. Chalmers relies on Shannon's distinction between discrete and continuous communications systems in Claude E. Shannon and Warren Weaver, *The Mathematical Theory of Communication* (Urbana: University of Illinois Press, 1963), 34. Cf. also Turing's distinction between discrete and continuous machines in Alan Mathison Turing, *Collected Works of A. M. Turing: Mechanical Intelligence*, ed. D. C. Ince (Amsterdam: Elsevier Science, 1992), 109.

64. Davidson, "Rational Animals," 321.

65. I think that the fact that a holistic net forms the presupposition for the identity of individual thoughts offers a good reason for Davidson to at least defend a *two-level* theory of intentional states insofar as one can hardly imagine that this net unfolds, so to speak, in one act. It is more probable to assume that the structure of the net can find support in an existing structure of A-intentional states that are individuated not by relations of logical inference, but by causal, dispositional, sedimented relations.

66. This formulation, which appears very wide reaching at first glance, results from the fact that the networks of two persons whose behavior is reciprocally intelligible to one another do not allow differences about the whole. Cf. Donald Davidson,

"Verbs of Action," in *Essays on Davidson: Actions and Events*, ed. B. Vermazen and J. Hintikka (Oxford: Clarendon, 1985), 91, where he notes that "propositions are identified by their logical properties, inductive and deductive, their role in determining evaluations and actions, and their relations to the world, the interpreter can do no better in general to interpret an utterance of a speaker than by keying it to a proposition of his own such that if he (the interpreter) believed the propositions true it would play approximately the same role in his reasoning, actions, and feelings as it would play in the economy of the speaker were he to believe his utterance true."

67. Here I rescind from problems that could arise for radical interpreters under unfavorable conditions, namely, to distinguish what is an element of an expression and what is merely an irregularly correlated epiphenomenon.

68. In the case of the parrot, we cannot expect this as long as Alex doesn't enjoy the benefits of syllable-centered instruction (Ma-ma, Au-to, etc.) and we witness that Alex makes use of free variations syllables.

69. See p. 130.

70. See p. 130.

71. The model of A-intentional states can, from the paradigmatic case of prelinguistic desires, for example, be expanded to prelinguistic "expectations," because within the framework of research on object permanence the hypothesis can be corroborated that six- to seven-month-old children—thus certainly prelinguistic—for example, continue to "believe" for approximately one minute in the continued existence of objects that have (covertly) disappeared. Even five-month-old infants are surprised if objects do not have the causal influence on a situation (preventing motion) that they are supposed to if they—as initially perceived—are at a certain place, but have been secretly removed; they perform object-specific motions to reach for an object that cannot be seen by them so that we must assume that they have representations of attributes of these objects available, that is, nonlinguistic representations. Cf. Dornes, *Die frühe Kindheit*, 108ff.

72. It is important to see that this phenomenon is different than in the case of perception, for example, among animals; for the content of an A-intentional state is not explained, as in the case of perception, (solely) by external stimulation and a perceptual machinery, but by a behavior that can be explained relative to an internal state whose generation is opaque. However, on the other hand, this does not imply that a being that has nonlinguistic desires has a second-order thought.

73. Searle, *Intentionality*, 28.

74. This is true as long as they have the same direction of fit. Cf. the following footnote.

75. As is well known, Searle defines intentional states as having or representing conditions of satisfaction (content) *and* as having a *direction of fit* (modus) (cf. Searle, *Intentionality*, 22). In the context of these reflections, however, which are concerned with the reference to a *content*, we can disregard the direction of fit, for the direction of fit only says something about the means by which (through the world or mind) the conditions of satisfaction of an intentional state have to be fulfilled; it contributes nothing to its content.

76. Remarkably, Searle does not make any effort at all to get a theoretical grasp on higher-level forms of intentionality. This seems to be because consciousness, in his view, is not a phenomenon that stands in need of explanation; for even "the consciousness of the conditions of satisfaction is part of the conscious belief or the

desire, since the intentional content is internal to the states in question" (Searle, *Intentionality*, 22).

77. Ibid., 19.

78. Cf. ibid., 167.

79. As far as I can tell, Millikan's refined biological theory of intentionality (Millikan, *Language, Thought and Other Biological Categories*) also offers a plausible explanation for the transition to higher-level forms of intentionality. Millikan's basic idea (in a certain sense Hegelian) is to objectivize the concept of *function* (*proper function*), which is typically viewed as observer relative, by making the reproduction history of entities (including intentional states) on the basis of ascriptions of function. On the basis of a refined theory of proper functions, Millikan constructs a three-level theory of intentionality. At the *first level*, the concern is to analyze that kind of intentionality that an occurrence of an intentional state (*intentional icon*) has as a member of a reproduction family. Such a token has *aboutness* if we can expect from its elements that it identifies that which is to be pointed toward—given the reproduction history of the occurrences of its type—which has real function. At the *second level* the concern is to explain what it means that a being grasps what one of her intentional states is about; this ought to be possible if a being is able to indicate the referent of an intentional icon by correlating it with another intentional icon. This work should be done by an *interpreter* that has the proper function to identify, under "normal conditions," that the tokens of a type of intentional icons have the same real value or that their elements, under normal conditions, point to the same objects or circumstances. At this second level, above all, problems are brought up by the question about the criteria on the basis of which the interpreter can manage this, for she needs not only the ability to determine the type identity of the tokens of intentional icons, but also the ability to *immediately* identify those objects or circumstances that such a token is supposed to be pointing to. The product of this double identification is supposed to be a belief, that is, a second-order intentional state. However, here the suspicion arises that even Millikan's interpreter is a mind-internal mind, for the achievements of the interpreter are the same as the achievements that a theory of mind must be concerned with explaining. At the *third level*, which also entails difficulties that I would just like to mention here, the concern is to indicate the criteria according to which one can check to see whether those things that an intentional state is about exist and whether it is about those objects or circumstances that one supposes it is about ("Epistemology of Identity"). At the third level, it is above all problematic that Millikan links the test regarding whether a belief is about that which it is about, according to the work of an interpreter, to the characterization of attributes that, under the presupposition of their empirical incommensurability with other attributes, identify *one* object or circumstance among all the possible ones. Millikan's theory is far too complex to be done justice within the framework of cursory remarks, but given the enormous terminological complexity of her theory, a sophisticated discussion would also spring from the parameters of this work. However, it is important for me to emphasize that my remarks about the difficulties, which are specific to the present form of Millikan's theory, are by no means meant to imply that it is impossible to solve these problems within the framework of her theory. However, for this, precisely the potential must be tapped that results if intentional icons are systematically linked to expressions.

80. Further, on pp. 233ff., I attempt to show that this premise of the presence of interpreters who have fully developed intentionality can be eliminated. Only at this level can interpretationism be considered a theory that can be reconciled to phylogenetic explanations of the emergence of higher intentionality.

81. *Proto-action* here refers to those activities that are caused by A-intentional states. In my model example, for instance, this is a pointing action, aimed at a desired object. The relation between such an activity and its mental cause is somewhat different from the relation between mere behavior and its mental cause: the A-intentional state can function *in the eyes of an interpreter* of the activity as a cause and a *reason*.

82. I am using the subscript i in order to clarify that the mental expressions that are marked with it are ascribed from the perspective of an interpreter with fully developed intentionality. The expressions are letters of an interpretation language.

83. Davidson's concept of truth is, of course, a semantic concept, but every implementation of this concept in the context of an interpretation has an epistemic dimension insofar as a speaker who is assumed to hold her expressions to be true is placed in an epistemic relation to her environment.

84. Donald Davidson, "Thought and Talk," in *Inquiries Into Truth and Interpretation* (New York: Oxford University Press, 2001), 157.

85. Donald Davidson, "The Conditions of Thought," in *The Mind of Donald Davidson*, ed. Johannes Brandl and Wolfgang L. Gombocz (Amsterdam: Rodopi, 1989), 193.

86. Cf. Baron-Cohen, *Mindblindness*, who, along with an "intentionality detector," postulates an "eye direction detector" and a "shared attention mechanism," as well as an inborn "theory of mind mechanism."

87. I think, in other words, that Davidson's externalism in the end is a scientific reconstruction of the acquisition of language and of the development of thinking that—if it is understood as an empirical model—also has the disadvantage of not being particularly refined; it must live primarily in the hope of gaining empirical support.

88. With regard to the development of communicative competencies of infants and small children, the following rough development scheme can be held to be relatively well established (cf. Dornes, *Die frühe Kindheit*, 73ff., 142ff.):
1. *Pure expression* through nonarbitrary behavior, e.g., behavior expressing pain. This means, for example, that an event E_1 (pain) causes in P_1 a nonarbitrary expression of behavior B_1.
2. *Intentional expression*. A behavior B_1 of the nonarbitrary *type* is intentionally deployed after the effects of pure expressions (on a person) have been observed (e.g., instrumental crying or pointing behavior [before nine months]). Intentional expression is characterized by directionality, contextual suitability relative to the (probably not conscious) intentions. In connection with the experience that P_1 can influence P_2 with V_1, P_1 wants$_i$ to influence P_2 by V_1 in such a way as to improve the emotional situation of P_1.
3. *Intentional communication*. From nine months of age, one can observe, for example, that demonstrative actions are extended with the fixation and observing of those addressed. An interpreter of such activities can hardly but assume that P_1 has the intention$_i$ of communicating X to her, and to show P_2 that P_1 wants$_i$ to communicate X. Intentional communication at this basic level comes in two forms: (a) *protoimperative acts* (instrumentally pointing to X in order to

get P_2 to bring X) and (b) *protodeclarative acts* (pointing to X in order to direct the attention of P_2 to X).

Above all, intentional communication appears to be an impressive indication that children who cannot yet speak can have intentional states. It appears to be an indication that prelinguistic children already have a level of "secondary intersubjectivity" (ibid., 142). This level ought to be reached if P_1 carries out protodeclarative acts, for such acts appear to aim at sharing a mental state with those addressed by the protodeclarative act. However, I would like to point out that there is a competing reconstruction of the protodeclarative acts employing the concept of "zest for competence" (*Kompetenzlust*). Primarily with the intention of retaining thin assumptions, in the following I assume this weaker interpretation. A stronger analysis, however, would also be irreconcilable with my characterization of A-intentional states, because it would already bring aspects of higher intentionality into play, without having a reconstruction of these elements at its disposal.

89. The following basic emotions are thought to be such culturally invariant affects: interest/curiosity, surprise, disgust, happiness, sadness, irritation, and fear. Cf. Dornes, *Die frühe Kindheit*, 40; and Paul Ekman, "Biological and Cultural Contributions to Body and Facial Movement in the Expression of Emotions," in *Explaining Emotions*, ed. A. O. Rorty, 73–102 (Berkeley: University of California Press, 1980).

90. With a view to the relationship of the affects to the A-intentional states it can here remain an open question whether affects can be understood as a subset of A-intentional states. I lean toward the assumption that affects are less specified states than A-intentional states, because basic affects of one type can occur in various situations that differ from each other in numerous respects. By assuming that affects are independent, genetically established mechanisms, one indeed increases the number of "things" that go into the model, but not the scope of the assumptions regarding the goal of reconstruction, for one takes a step back to something more primitive rather than taking a step in the direction of higher intentionality.

91. I here take up the metaphor that György Gergely and James Watson make use of in their brilliant article "The Social Biofeedback Theory of Parental Affect-Mirroring: The Development of Emotional Self-Awareness and Self-Control in Infancy," *International Journal of Psychoanalysis* 77 (1996): 1181–1212.

92. Michael Dornes, *Die emotionale Welt des Kindes* (Frankfurt: Suhrkamp, 2000), 199.

93. The mechanism uses two independent submechanisms that analyze the conditioned structure of probabilities of event–event correlations. One mechanism analyzes which future event is *sufficient* so that a conditioned incident occurs, while the other mechanism analyzes the relative probability that a given event has another (internal) event as a *necessary* antecedent. If a child can always bring about an event by its own activity, then the first mechanism provides a sufficiency-index value of 1.00. However, should this event also occur without the activity of the child, then the necessity-index is smaller than 1.00. A child gains maximal control in this model by diminishing the set of internal events and states so that only events and states remain that provide a high sufficiency- and necessity-index value.

94. I will not go any further into the affect-regulative aspect of social feedback theory, and in the framework of the model, I view it only as a functional support for the approach. For more here, see Gergely and Watson, "Social Biofeedback Theory of Parental Affect-Mirroring," 1194–1196.

95. It is an everyday experience that adults also remain disposed to react to a mimetic expression of the basic affects with these affects and the corresponding mimic; this is supported by the fact that the forms of marked mimetic and prosodic contact with children are largely culturally invariant.

96. See p. 130.

97. As an important condition for adequacy for phase 2, we could formulate the demand that the model of the development of intentionality for phase 2 must make theoretical means available that allow the problem that one is confronted with to be skirted if one can take recourse solely in the attributes provided by Searle's definition of A-intentionality for developing higher-level intentionality. The externalization of the indicator events gives us an important advantage for meeting this demand. For in contrast to Searle's intrinsic and thus monological intentionality, in our model, the interpreters lend a sufficiently stabile reacting power that can take on precisely that *role of observation* that would have to be taken on, in a Searlean mind—in which intentional states solely represent conditions of satisfaction—by a second mind-internal mind. The observer brought into play at this level is, on the other hand, not *primarily* an interpreter who interprets the alleged states of the child verbally (and thus in a way that is incomprehensible for the child), but one who interprets them mimically, prosodically, or with connecting actions, i.e., nonverbally.

98. In many cases, the parents in such circumstances take up expressions that the children have themselves produced in certain situations.

99. Cf. p. 98.

100. In this phase, it must thus be possible to observe interactions over a time that do nothing more than affirm these correlations. In this phase children do not have to be described as passive students, for they "steer" these affirming interactions by "remunerating" the adults with their happiness about the fulfilled expectations.

101. I am thinking here in particular of the following: imitation of childlike articulations, mimic, gestures, and dancing movements.

102. With a view to the internal structure of expressions, we can naturally say, in light of the expression practices of the parents, that perhaps not all but some of the parental expressions are instantiations of medial configurations. This amounts to saying that they can be described as the implementation of medial possibilities. Here we can assume with no difficulties that most adults know the elements and parameters that their expressions can be described as variations and constellations of, be that in the form of an explicit linguistic knowledge or in the form of deictic identification.

103. I will come back to this relation and its meaning for a theory of understanding art. See p. 215.

104. Because one could have the suspicion that already at this level a form of triangulation exists, it is important to see that pure onomatopoeic expressions do not *refer* to *objects*, but *express* aspects of characteristics that can be experienced. That does not mean that such expressions (as, for example, "bow wow") cannot acquire a referential function, then, however, function as linguistic expressions. Only then is it no longer a matter of experience (*Erleben*) but of perception (*Wahrnehmen*).

105. Irrespective of this fact, lyric poetry is a use of language in which sense attributes of linguistic expressions can play a central role.

106. The development of this type of disposition is, of course, especially probable if the interpreter frequently denies the fulfillment of the conditions of satisfaction

when the corresponding expression is not performed, whereas when it is performed (in any case in the framework of the learning phase), it is reliably guaranteed. In other words: here what Wittgenstein rightfully called "training" occurs.

107. I go into this problem more precisely on p. 220.

108. Cf. Robert B. Brandom, *Articulating Reasons: An Introduction to Inferentialism* (Cambridge, MA: Harvard University Press, 2001), 11.

109. There is a technical sense to the discussion of norm conformity here, which remains reconcilable with the view that a norm can be made explicit in a social community only in the form of paradigmatically demonstrative acts. See p. 220.

110. In chapter 4 I will go more precisely into the forms in which we can relate to the content of nonlinguistic thoughts. See pp. 153, 155.

111. On the ontology of media, see p. 240.

112. Following Millikan, *Language, Thought and Other Biological Categories*, one could say that the identity and the content of an A-intentional state I_a is determined by an interpreter device, which comprehends the reference of I_a with a view to the *normal function* from I_a, but does not test the appropriateness of this state.

113. That is possible especially because Davidson's antirealism undoubtedly brings up numerous difficult questions regarding mental causation.

114. Cf. Nelson Goodman, *Ways of Worldmaking* (Indianapolis: Hackett, 1978), 43.

115. Cf. ibid., 42–43.

116. For example, painted frames in painting or quotation marks in scores that could, for example, be performed auditorily by inserting pauses.

117. Goodman speaks of painting as a singular symbolic system. Cf. Goodman, *Ways of Worldmaking*, 48.

118. The criterion (G) is certainly a strong interpretation of Davidson's second-order criterion. However, below I will show that Davidson, inter alia, because of his rejection of unconscious intentional states, is forced to hold such a strong interpretation.

119. Kant, *The Critique of Pure Reason*, trans. W. S. Pluhar (Indianapolis: Hackett, 1999), 59, B 131–132.

120. It is clear that this interpretation imputes Davidson with a strong interpretation of the second-order criterion. However, because Davidson understands mental states as theoretical entities of rationalizations of action, that is, of interpretations, and he holds a strict antirealistic interpretation of intentional states, the interpretation by no means seems to me to be too strong. Davidson's rejection of unconscious intentional states also seems to point in a very similar direction. For the "existence" of such necessarily uninterpreted states (interpretation is connected to consciousness) would be irreconcilable with the doctrine that interpretation is the only content-individuating mechanism.

121. Cf. Wilfried Hinsch, *Erfahrung und Selbstbewusstsein: Zur Kategoriendeduktion bei Kant* (Hamburg: Meiner, 1986), 20–31.

122. I investigate the perspective of this criterion in more detail in section 3.2.3. Cf. pp. 220–233.

123. Cf. p. 216.

124. In this way, Brandom views noninferential observation reports as "language entry transitions" (cf. Brandom, *Making It Explicit*, chap. 4).

125. In chapter 4 I will again take up these reflections, which form a basis for determining the relationship between media and rationality.

126. It should be clear that (H2) does not preclude that artists might follow ideas, maxims, programs, social goals or the like that are present as propositions. The suggestion that is being made here should rather prepare a kernel of artistic action that is as independent of such propositional attitudes as possible. The reconstruction suggestion, which refers, in the present context, to artistic action primarily in the sense of an example of a form of action that eludes complete propositional reconstructions, has the advantage, in an aesthetic perspective, of being open to a number of conceptions of art. But it has no ambitions to be the centerpiece of an ad hoc aesthetic. Admittedly, the reconstruction seems to me to be able to accommodate some important intuitions of widespread concepts of art, for example, also the widespread view that interpretations of works of art are characterized by their principal openness. In addition, according to (H2), the production of works of art is not to be understood as the implementation of a plan that exists independently of and prior to the process of implementation. For (H2) does not preclude that P_1 individuates the B-intentional state $I_b(K)$ by producing the work of art K.

127. Cf. John Dewey, *Art as Experience* (New York: Perigree, 2005), 110.

128. See p. 100.

129. Joachim Schulte, "Nachwort," in *Der Mythos des Subjektiven: Philosophische Essays*, ed. Donald Davidson (Stuttgart: Reclam, 1993), 112.

130. Cf. Alana Donagan, *Choice: The Essential Element of Human Action* (London: Routledge, 1987).

131. The existence of a teaching practice here could be linked to the following criterion: (1) Under B_i, some B_L can be identified that produce complex medial performances. (2) Under B_i some B_S can be identified, who are mostly young and produce few or no complex medial performances. (3) Interactions between B_L and B_S can be observed for which it holds that (a) the B_L frequently negatively sanction the B_S if the B_S perform a type of activity such that this performance cannot be described as actualizing variations within the realm of possibilities of the assumed medium that makes the type identity of the performance of B_L plausible; (b) the B_L only seldom negatively sanction the B_S if the B_S perform a type of activity such that this performance can be described as actualizing variations within the realm of possibilities of the assumed medium that makes the type identity of the performance of B_L plausible, even if in this the B_S do not produce even remotely similarly complex performances to those of the B_L.

132. Cf. Føllesdal's criticism of Quine's theory of stimulus meaning and Davidson's theory of causation in Føllesdal, "The Status of Rationality Assumptions in Interpretation and in the Explanation of Action," in *Dialectica* 36 (1982): 301–316.

133. See pp. 183–234.

134. That should only mean that the consequences of the behavior that is performed in reference to the perception of the noise are relevant for an evaluation—which is realized in behavior—of the situation that arises through the interpretive behavior. In short, the interpretive behavior has consequences such that the situation that arises from this is one that will tend to be sought or to be avoided. The concept of preference-relative behavior is used to characterize a behavior that one could subsume under the concept of a sanction, which, however, in the context of the reflections here has normative implications that are far too strong.

135. Cf. p. 176.

136. By *emotion*, here I of course do not mean propositionally differentiated feelings, but states that have significance for the well-being of the animal, for example, that we would characterize as fear, contentment, sadness, etc.

137. Cf. p. 185.

138. Cf. Brandom, *Making It Explicit*, 34–46.

139. The level of linguistic behavior, which is supposed to be apprehended as rational, linguistic interacting, can, leaning on reflections of Jonathan Bennett, be linked to the criterion that, in a medial community, expressions occur that must be understood as negations of reasons for medial performances. Cf. Jonathan Bennett, *Rationality: An Essay Towards Analysis* (London: Routledge, 1971), 49–78.

140. Cf. Niklas Luhmann, *Social Systems*, trans. John Bednarz Jr. and Dirk Baecker (Stanford, CA: Stanford University Press, 1996), 12.

141. Cf. John R. Searle, *The Construction of Social Reality* (New York: Free Press, 1997), 1–5.

142. Cf. ibid., 6.

143. So, especially the step between the biological level and the level of intentionality can be reconstructed with the help of the distinction between simple and higher intentionality (cf. p. 178) so that, at the level of biological systems, a form of consciousness is possible that is subject to the limitations of A-intentionality, and the level of higher intentionality is only reached when the interpretationist presupposition is fulfilled, namely, when a social media interpretation practice or a linguistically supported interpretation practice exists. Nevertheless, independently of the ability to connect this ontology to interpretationist assumptions, Searle also must be interested in minimizing the dependency of his reflections on the rough ontology, especially when both the theory of materiality and the evolutionary theory are fallible natural scientific theories.

144. Cf. Searle, *Construction of Social Reality*, 9ff.

145. Ibid., 13. I have added the indexes.

146. Cf. ibid., 24.

147. Raimo Tuomela also suggests a detailed analysis that is individualistic in this sense. Cf. Raimo Tuomela, *The Importance of Us: A Philosophical Study of Basic Social Notions* (Stanford, CA: Stanford University Press, 1995), 145ff.

148. Here I will refrain from possible further refinements of this analysis.

149. Cf. John R. Searle, "What Is a Speech Act?" in *Readings in Language and Mind*, ed. H. Geirsson and Michael Losonsky (London: Blackwell, 1996), 110–120; and John Rawls, "Two Concepts of Rules," *Philosophical Review* 64 (1955): 24–25.

150. Cf. Searle, *Construction of Social Reality*, 26.

151. Cf. ibid., 39ff., 114ff.

152. See p. 155.

153. This does not, however, mean that we might not understand constitutive rules in the broader sense of explicit rules developed above. See p. 153.

154. Dewey, *Art as Experience*, 235.

155. Cf. Arthur C. Danto, *The Transfiguration of the Commonplace: A Philosophy of Art* (Cambridge, MA: Harvard University Press, 1981), 1–6.

156. This criterion is obviously weaker than Goodman's nearly unsatisfiable and counterintuitive criterion for fulfilling a score. Goodman writes: "Since complete compliance with the score is the only requirement for a genuine instance of a work,

the most miserable performance without actual mistakes does count as such an instance, while the most brilliant with a single wrong note does not" (*Languages of Art: An Approach to a Theory of Symbols* [Indianapolis: Hackett, 1967], 186). If we understand scores as directions for implementing a medial constellation, then such performances should serve as implementations that allow a complex thought to be identified with a compositional identity that is articulated by performances of differing quality. The fact that competent listeners could ignore the mistakes of a performance to the benefit of other qualities shows clearly that their structuring of the piece enables them to correct mistakes internally, just like charitable interpreters who are oriented on the (assumed) compositional identity of the articulated thoughts. It is possible for performance mistakes to prevent the thought from being replicated, but fortunately, this occurs rather rarely.

157. This failure is not linked to the fact that the target medium has a scope of action in which the relevant medial attributes of the source constellation cannot be articulated. Even when the target medium is richer and brings medial attributes into play that have nothing corresponding to them in the source constellation, the compositional identity of the work is endangered. In this case, performances of compositions for harpsichord that are played on piano would only be translations if it were guaranteed that all the strikes on the piano had the same volume.

158. So one could ask whether, for example, the concept of a translation ought to be connected to the condition that the source and target constellation must exist in different media. Werner Koller, for example, characterizes cases of interlingual and diachronic intralingual translations (in contrast to intralingual paraphrase) as genuine cases of translation (cf. Werner Koller, *Einführung in die Übersetzungswissenschaft* [Heidelberg: Quelle & Meyer, 1983], 108). Insofar as the case of diachronic intralingual translation is, however, only to be distinguished from paraphrasing by the fact that the source and target constellation are not in the *same* medium, it appears to me that the disparity is fundamental.

159. The difference that I have in mind here can be explained with a view to both sign language systems that are used in Germany. While the vocal-accompanying sign language (*lautbegleitende Gebärdensprache*—LGB) is in principle German translated into a sign language, the German sign language (*deutsche Gebärdensprache*—DGS) is an independent natural language that the deaf developed and that they generally prefer for communication among one another. German does not have a model function for DGS.

160. Or put in Brandomian terms, the uttering being is endowed with the same entitlements and commitments.

161. As an art form that is implemented by means of language, literature—especially lyric poetry—presents a special case. On the one hand, it is possible to translate sentences from one language into another. However, the fact that literature also has a level of untranslatability is clearly demonstrated by the fact that literature, as a medium to convey experience, uses associative contexts that cannot be secured across the boundaries of different languages.

162. The impression that money is a nonlinguistic medium may be based on the fact that by using money, one is in fact able, especially in supermarkets, to purchase things without speaking. But the fact that exchange acts based on money are also possible without speech, and thus can replace linguistic communication, has wide-reaching institutional prerequisites that provide the background for linguistically anchored routines.

163. Cf. chapter 2.

164. That of course also means that if there is a practice of physically implementing medial constellations that needs electric light, it *can* play the role of a medial tool.

4. THE CONSEQUENCES FOR A CONCEPT OF RATIONALITY

1. Cf. p. 71.

2. Of course, subsentential expression can have content; however, for both Davidson and Brandom this is theoretically derivative from the content of sentences.

3. Robert B. Brandom, *Making It Explicit* (Cambridge, MA: Harvard University Press, 1994), 5.

4. Cf. p. 190.

5. Cf. Fred Dretske, *Explaining Behavior: Reasons in a World of Causes* (Cambridge: Cambridge University Press, 1997), 54, where he writes of birdsong, tracks in the snow, and fingerprints, among other things: "These are what are sometimes called *natural signs*: events and conditions that derive their indicative power, not (as in the case of symbols) from us, from our *use* of them to indicate, but from the way they are objectively related to the conditions they signify."

6. Here it is beneficial to call to mind that Dewey characterized instinctive crying or laughing particularly as activities that need no medium (cf. p. 99). Without wanting to overstretch these thoughts, I would maintain that precisely this connection is responsible for the fact that an activity such as ripping paper, which is popular in some works of the "serious" music of the twentieth and twenty-first centuries, seldom are really well integrated into the musical material of a composition.

7. This of course holds only as long as the medial constellation is not placed in a rich context (such as the "artworld" in Danto's sense), which forms the background for arbitrarily complex linguistic interpretations, also of simple objects in this context.

8. Cf. pp. 46ff.

9. Cf. pp. 153–154.

10. If I am correct, this is Brandom's strategy; for Brandom determines (inferential) content precisely in line with normative relations that rest on sanction practices.

11. Cf. Føllesdal, "The Status of Rationality Assumptions in Interpretation and in the Explanation of Action," *Dialectica* 36 (1982): 301–316.

12. Cf. the marked reactions to affectual expressions in phase 1 of the communication development. See p. 184.

13. In particular, it is necessary to precisely examine whether this analysis threatens the possibility that students retain the ability to breach rules.

14. See p. 155.

15. See p. 218.

16. Ingeborg Bachmann, "Youth in an Austrian Town," in *The Thirtieth Year* (New York: Holmes & Meier, 1987), 10.

17. Ottfried Höffe, *Immanuel Kant* (Munich: Beck, 1992) (my emphasis).

18. Cf. Immanuel Kant, *The Critique of Judgment*, trans. John H. Bernard (New York: Cosimo, 2007), 16–17, B XXXVII–XXXVIII.

19. Cf. ibid., 19–20, B XLII–XLIV.

20. Cf. ibid., 22, B XLVIII.

4. THE CONSEQUENCES FOR A CONCEPT OF RATIONALITY / 339

21. Brigitte Scheer, *Einführung in die philosophische Ästhetik* (Darmstadt: Primus, 1997), 73–111, esp. 87.

22. Ibid., 90.

23. Kant's use of this expression is unfortunately wavering. Sometimes he uses the concept in order to refer to cognition (*Erkenntnisse*) in general (e.g., Immanuel Kant, *The Critique of Pure Reason*, trans. and ed. Paul Guyer and Allen Wood [Cambridge: Cambridge University Press, 1998], B XLVII, XXIX; B 28), sometimes as an expression for a certain mental state, that is a cognition generally (e.g., introduction to the first version, 37; B XLVIII; B 29, 30, 65).

24. Franz von Kutschera points to the tension between (a) and (b). Franz von Kutschera, *Ästhetik* (Berlin: De Gruyter, 1989), 72.

25. Cf. Kant, *The Critique of Pure Reason*, B 128 concerning (a); and Kant, *Critique of Judgment*, 27–28, 41, B 3–4, B 35 concerning (b); 20, 27, B XLIV, B 3 (footnote), 38, B 28 concerning (c); 117–118, B 193–194 concerning (d); and 22–23, B LI concerning (e).

26. Cf. Kant, *Critique of Judgment*, 17, B XXXVIII.

27. Ibid., 38, B 27.

28. Cf. ibid., 111, B 179.

29. Kant explains this as follows: "Such representations of the imagination we may call Ideas, partly because they at least strive after something which lies beyond the bounds of experience, to approximate to a presentation of concepts of reason (intellectual Ideas), thus giving to the latter the appearance of objective reality, but especially because no concept can be fully adequate to them as internal intuitions" (ibid., 118, B 193–194).

30. Ibid., 117–118, B 192–193.

31. Cf. ibid., 112, 118, B 181, 194.

32. Ibid., 112–113, B 182.

33. Ibid., 112, B 181.

34. In her article "The Enlightenment as Autonomy: Kant's Vindication of Reason" (in *The Enlightenment and Its Shadows*, ed. Peter Hulme and Ludmilla Jordanova [London: Routledge, 1990], 184–199), Onora O'Neill emphatically points out that, for Kant, only principles of reason come into consideration "that can secure the possibility of intersubjectivity" (194).

35. Cf. Georg Wilhelm Friedrich Hegel, *Aesthetics: Lectures on Fine Art*, 2 vols. (Oxford: Clarendon, 1988), 1:2. Following Hegel and Wittgenstein, Franz Koppe takes a similar step, albeit with different theoretical motifs; see Franz Koppe, *Grundbegriffe der Ästhetik* (Frankfurt: Suhrkamp, 1983), 184–185.

36. Kant, *Critique of Judgment*, 54, B 61.

37. Ibid., 23, B LII; cf. also 37, B 26.

38. Ibid., 112, B 181.

39. Ibid., 112, B 180.

40. Ibid., 112–113, B 181–182.

41. Cf. p. 161.

42. Kant, *Critique of Judgment*, 103, B 160–161.

43. We can here certainly also assume the elementary case that P, if P is familiar with a medium, can have a disposition to bring about a medial constellation as a reaction to X so that K need not even be a consciously used means.

44. See p. 197.

45. See p. 217.

46. If I am correct, this definition coincides with the fact that the experience of a medial constellation varies with the structuring that its recipients provide (through medial comprehension).

47. See p. 147.

48. See p. 274.

49. See pp. 183–184.

50. See p. 73.

51. See p. 15.

52. See pp. 198ff.

53. So one could, for example, also consider whether it is promising to formulate an interpretationist theory of emotions with media-theoretic means, which views medial expressions as intersubjectively accessible forms of constitutive reference to emotions and does not reduce them to evaluative attitudes or motivational components. Perhaps on the basis of the reference to experience of medial constellations, a connection between emotions and feelings can be reconstructed without relapsing into an introspectiohism.

54. If one follows Habermas, critique brings about "a translating activity of a unique kind": "It brings the experiential content of the work of art into normal language; the innovative potential of art and literature for the lifeworlds and life histories that reproduce themselves through everyday communicative practice can *only* be unleashed in this maieutic way" (Jürgen Habermas, *The Philosophical Discourse of Modernity*, trans. Frederick G. Lawrence [Cambridge, MA: MIT Press, 1987], 208) (my emphasis).

BIBLIOGRAPHY

Adorno, Theodor W. *Aesthetic Theory*. Translated by R. Hullot-Kentor. Minneapolis: University of Minnesota Press, 2004.
———. *Ästhetische Theorie*. Frankfurt: Suhrkamp, 1973.
———. *Gesammelte Schriften*. Vol. 16, *Musikalische Schriften I–III*. Frankfurt: Suhrkamp, 1978.
———. "Music and Language: A Fragment." In *Quasi una fantasia: Essays in Modern Music*, translated by Rodney Livingstone, 1–8. London: Verso, 2002.
———. *Negative Dialectics*. Translated by E. B. Ashton. London: Routledge, 2000.
———. "On Some Relationships Between Music and Painting." *Musical Quarterly* 79 (1995): 66–79.
Akademie der Künste Berlin, ed. *Der Traum der Vernunft. Vom Elend der Aufklärung*. Darmstadt: Luchterhand, 1985.
Anacker, Ulrich. "Vernunft." In *Handbuch philosophischer Grundbegriffe*, edited by H. Krings, H. M. Baumgartner, and C. Wild, 1597–1611. Munich: Kösel, 1974.
Apel, Karl-Otto. "Ist Intentionalität fundamentaler als sprachliche Bedeutung? Transzendentalpragmatische Argumente gegen die Rückkehr zum semantischen Intentionalismus der Bewußtseinsphilosophie." In *Intentionalität und Verstehen*, edited by Forum für Philosophie Bad Homburg, 13–54. Frankfurt: Suhrkamp, 1990.
———. "Rationalität und Rationalitätstypen: Versuch einer transzendentalpragmatischen Rekonstruktion des Unterschiedes zwischen Verstand und Vernunft." In *Pragmatische Rationalitätstheorien. Studies in Pragmatism, Idealism, and Philosophy of Mind*, 29–63. Würzburg: Königshausen & Neumann, 1995.
Apel, Karl-Otto, and Matthias Kettner, eds. *Die eine Vernunft und die vielen Rationalitäten*. Frankfurt: Suhrkamp, 1996.
Aristotle. "Analytica Posteriora." In *Werke in deutscher Übersetzung*. Vol. 3, *Zwei Halbbände*, translated by Wolfgang Detel. Berlin: Akademie, 1993.
Arnason, Johann P. "Das Andere der Vernunft und die Vernunft des Anderen." In *Zur Verteidigung der Vernunft gegen ihre Liebhaber und Verächter*, edited by Ch. Menke and M. Seel, 46–65. Frankfurt: Suhrkamp, 1993.

Aron, László. "Programme und Paradigmen." In *Computer, Kultur, Geschichte: Beiträge zur Philosophie des Informationszeitalters*, edited by D. Mersch and J. C. Nyíri, 127–132. Vienna: Passagen, 1991.

Ars Electronica, ed. *Im Netz der Systeme*. Berlin: Merve, 1990.

———. *Philosophien der neuen Technologie*. Berlin: Merve, 1989.

Assmann, Aleida. "Die Sprache der Dinge: Der lange Blick und die wilde Semiose." In *Materialität der Kommunikation*, edited by H. U. Gumbrecht and L. K. Pfeiffer, 237–251. Frankfurt: Suhrkamp, 1988.

Assmann, Aleida, and Jan Assmann. "Das Gestern im Heute: Medien und soziales Gedächtnis." In *Die Wirklichkeit der Medien. Eine Einführung in die Kommunikationswissenschaft*, edited by K. Merten, S. J. Schmidt, and S. Weischenberg, 115–140. Opladen: Westdeutscher, 1994.

Assmann, Jan. "Im Schatten junger Medienblüte: Ägypten und die Materialität des Zeichens." In *Materialität der Kommunikation*, edited by H. U. Gumbrecht and L. K. Pfeiffer, 141–160. Frankfurt: Suhrkamp, 1988.

Bachmann, Ingeborg. "Youth in an Austrian Town." In *The Thirtieth Year*, translated by Michael Bullock, 7–17. New York: Holmes & Meier, 1987.

Baier, Lothar. "Zeichen und Wunder: Eine semiologische Modenschau." *Kursbuch* 84 (1986): 17–33.

Baron-Cohen, Simon. *Mindblindness: An Essay on Autism and Theory of Mind*. Cambridge, MA: MIT Press, 1995.

Bataille, Georges. *The Accursed Share: An Essay on General Economy*. Translated by Robert Hurley. New York: Zone Books, 2007.

———. "The Psychological Structure of Fascism." In *The Bataille Reader*, edited by F. Botting and S. Wilson, 122–146. Oxford: Blackwell, 1997.

Baudrillard, Jean. *Die Agonie des Realen*. Berlin: Merve, 1978.

———. "Requiem for the Media." In *For a Critique of the Political Economy of the Sign*, translated by Charles Levin, 164–184. St. Louis: Telos, 1981.

———. *Symbolic Exchange and Death*. Translated by Mike Gane. London: Sage, 1993.

Becker, Alexander. *Verstehen und Bewusstsein*. Paderborn: Mentis, 2000.

Beckermann, Ansgar, ed. *Analytische Handlungstheorie Band: Handlungserklärungen*. Frankfurt: Suhrkamp, 1985.

———. "Handeln und Handlungserklärungen." In *Analytische Handlungstheorie Band 2: Handlungserklärungen*, edited by A. Beckermann, 7–84. Frankfurt: Suhrkamp, 1985.

Beniger, James R. *The Control Revolution: Technological and Economic Origins of the Information Society*. Cambridge, MA: Harvard University Press, 1997.

Benjamin, Walter. "Das Kunstwerk im Zeitalter seiner technischen Reproduzierbarkeit." In *Gesammelte Schriften*. Vol. 1/2, 471–508. Frankfurt: Suhrkamp, 1980.

Bennett, Jonathan. *Rationality: An Essay Towards Analysis*. London: Routledge, 1971.

Berger, Johannes. "Autopoiesis: Wie 'systemisch' ist die Theorie sozialer Systeme?" In *Sinn, Kommunikation und soziale Differenzierung: Beiträge zu Luhmanns Theorie sozialer Systeme*, edited by H. Haferkamp and M. Schmid, 129–152. Frankfurt: Suhrkamp, 1987.

Black, Max. "Why Should I Be Rational?" *Dialectica* 36 (1982): 147–168.

Böckelmann, Frank. *Theorie der Massenkommunikation: Das System hergestellter Öffentlichkeit, Wirkungsforschung und gesellschaftliche Kommunikationsverhältnisse*. Frankfurt: Suhrkamp, 1975.

Bodnár, István M. "Mündlichkeit und Schriftlichkeit im archaischen Griechenland." In *Computer, Kultur, Geschichte: Beiträge zur Philosophie des Informationszeitalters*, edited by D. Mersch and F. C. Nyíri, 79–86. Vienna: Passagen, 1991.
Bohn, Rainer, Eggo Müller, and Rainer Ruppert, eds. *Ansichten einer künftigen Medienwissenschaft*. Berlin: Sigma, 1988.
———. "Die Wirklichkeit im Zeitalter ihrer technischen Fingierbarkeit." In *Ansichten einer künftigen Medienwissenschaft*, 7–28. Berlin: Sigma, 1988.
Bohn, Volker, ed. *Romantik. Literatur und Philosophie*. Frankfurt: Suhrkamp, 1987.
Bolz, Norbert. "Neue Medien." *Information Philosophie* 1 (1994): 48–55.
———. *Theorie der neuen Medien*. Munich: Raben, 1990.
Bonß, Wolfgang, Helmut Dubiel, Gerhard Gamm, Heidrun Hesse, Axel Honneth, Christa Karpenstein-Eßbach, Gerd Kimmerle, Discussion leader: Christa Hackenesch. *Die Zukunft der Vernunft: Eine Auseinandersetzung*. Tübingen: Konkursbucherlag, 1985.
Brand, Stewart. *The Media Lab: Inventing the Future at MIT*. New York: Penguin, 1989.
Brandom, Robert B. *Articulating Reasons: An Introduction to Inferentialism*. Cambridge, MA: Harvard University Press, 2001.
———. *Making It Explicit*. Cambridge, MA: Harvard University Press, 1994.
Bratman, Michael E. "Shared Cooperative Activity." *Philosophical Review* 101, no. 2 (1992): 327–341.
Brecht, Bertold. "Radiotheorie 1927–1932." In *Gesammelte Werke*. Vol. 8, *Schriften zur Literatur und Kunst, Politik und Gesellschaft*, 117–137. Frankfurt: Suhrkamp, 1967.
Bredow, Wilfried von. "Auf dem Wege zu einem Analphabetismus für gehobene Ansprüche." In *Medien und Gesellschaft: Auf dem Weg zu einem Analphabetismus für gehobene Ansprüche?* 175–184. Stuttgart: Hirzel, 1990.
———, ed. *Medien und Gesellschaft: Auf dem Weg zu einem Analphabetismus für gehobene Ansprüche?* Stuttgart: Hirzel, 1990.
Bungard, Walter, and Hans Lenk, eds. *Technikbewertung: Philosophische und psychologische Perspektiven*. Frankfurt: Suhrkamp, 1988.
Burge, Tyler. "Reference and Proper Names." *Journal of Philosophy* 70 (1973): 425–439.
Bürger, Peter. "Kunst und Rationalität: Zur Dialektik von symbolischer und allegorischer Form." In *Zwischenbetrachtungen: Im Prozess der Aufklärung*, edited by A. Honneth, T. McCarthy, and C. Offe, 89–105. Frankfurt: Suhrkamp, 1989.
Carnap, Rudolf. *Logical Foundations of Probability*. Chicago: University of Chicago Press, 1951.
Cassirer, Ernst. *The Philosophy of Symbolic Forms*. 4 vols. Edited by J. M. Krois and D. P. Verene. New Haven, CT: Yale University Press, 1955.
Chalmers, David J. *The Conscious Mind: In Search of a Fundamental Theory*. New York: Oxford University Press, 1997.
Charlton, Michael. "Identität und Spiegelung an kulturellen Symbolen: Entwicklungschritte des Kindes bei der Symbolverwendung." In *Symbolische Formen—Medien—Identität*, edited by W. Raible, 235–248. Tübingen: Narr, 1991.
Cherniak, Christopher. *Minimal Rationality*. Cambridge, MA: MIT Press, 1992.
Chomsky, Noam. *Rules and Representations*. Oxford: Blackwell, 1982.
Cube, Felix von. *Kybernetische Grundlagen des Lernen und Lehrens*. Stuttgart: Klett-Cotta, 1982.
Culler, Jonathan. *On Deconstruction: Theory and Criticism After Structuralism*. Ithaca, NY: Cornell University Press, 1982.

D. G. "Medium (semiotisch)." In *Enzyklopädie Philosophie und Wissenschaftstheorie*, vol. 2, edited by J. Mittelstraß, 829–831. Stuttgart: Metzeler, 1984.

Dahlhaus, Carl. "Neue Musik und Wissenschaft." In *Wissenschaftliche und nichtwissenschaftliche Rationalität*, edited by K. Hübner and J. Vuillemin, 107–118. Stuttgart: Frommann, 1983.

Danielzyk, Rainer, and Fritz Rüdiger Volz, eds. *Parabel (no. 3): Vernunft der Moderne: Zu Habermas' Theorie des kommunikativen Handelns*. Münster: Liberación, 1986.

Danto, Arthur C. *The Transfiguration of the Commonplace: A Philosophy of Art*. Cambridge, MA: Harvard University Press, 1981.

Davidson, Donald. "Agency." In *Essays on Actions and Events*, 43–62. Oxford: Oxford University Press, 2001.

———. "Communication and Convention." In *Inquiries Into Truth and Interpretation*, 265–280. Oxford: Oxford University Press, 2001.

———. "The Conditions of Thought." In *The Mind of Donald Davidson*, edited by Johannes Brandl and Wolfgang L. Gombocz, 193–200. Amsterdam: Rodopi, 1989.

———. "Dialectic and Dialogue." In *Truth, Language, and History*, 251–261. Oxford: Oxford University Press, 2005.

———. *Expressing Evaluations (Lindley Lecture)*. Lawrence: University Press of Kansas, 1982.

———. "How Is Weakness of the Will Possible?" In *Essays on Actions and Events*, 21–42. New York: Oxford University Press, 2001.

———. "Incoherence and Irrationality." *Dialectica* 39 (1985): 345–354.

———. "Intending." In *Essays on Actions and Events*, 83–102. Oxford: Oxford University Press, 2001.

———. "Meaning, Truth, and Evidence." In *Truth, Language, and History*, 47–62. Oxford: Oxford University Press, 2005.

———. "The Myth of the Subjective." In *Subjective, Intersubjective, Objective*, 39–52. Oxford: Oxford University Press, 2001.

———. "A Nice Derangement of Epitaphs." In *The Essential Davidson*, 251–266. Oxford: Oxford University Press, 2006.

———. "On Saying That." In *Inquiries Into Truth and Interpretation*, 93–108. New York: Oxford University Press, 2001.

———. "On the Very Idea of a Conceptual Scheme." In *Inquiries Into Truth and Interpretation*. New York: Oxford University Press, 2001.

———. "Paradoxes of Irrationality." In *Philosophical Essays on Freud*, edited by R. Wohlheim and J. Hopkins, 289–305. New York: Cambridge University Press, 1982.

———. "Psychology as Philosophy." In *Essays on Actions and Events*, 229–238. Oxford: Oxford University Press, 2001.

———. "Quotation." In *Inquiries Into Truth and Interpretation*, 79–92. New York: Oxford University Press, 2001.

———. "Radical Interpretation." In *Inquiries Into Truth and Interpretation*, 125–140. New York: Oxford University Press, 2001.

———. "Rational Animals." *Dialectica* 36 (1982): 317–327.

———. "Thought and Talk." In *Inquiries Into Truth and Interpretation*, 155–170. New York: Oxford University Press, 2001.

———. "Three Varieties of Knowledge." In *Subjective, Intersubjective, Objective*, 205–220. Oxford: Oxford University Press, 2001.

———. "Truth and Meaning." In *Inquiries Into Truth and Interpretation*, 17–42. New York: Oxford University Press, 2001.

———. "Verbs of Action." In *Essays on Davidson: Actions and Events*, edited by B. Vermazen and J. Hintikka, 230–241. Oxford: Clarendon, 1985.
———. "What Metaphors Mean." In *The Essential Davidson*, 209–224. Oxford: Oxford University Press, 2006.
Davies, Stephen. *Musical Meaning and Expression*. Ithaca, NY: Cornell University Press, 1994.
Dennett, Daniel C. *The Intentional Stance*. Cambridge, MA: MIT Press, 1996.
———. "Intentional Systems." In *Brainstorms: Philosophical Essays on Mind and Psychology*, 3–22. Cambridge, MA: MIT Press, 1981.
Derrida, Jacques. *Of Grammatology*. Corrected edition, translated by Gayatri Chakravorty Spivak. Baltimore: Johns Hopkins University Press, 1998.
Detel, Wolfgang. "Foucault on Power and the Will to Knowledge." *European Journal of Philosophy* 3, no. 4 (1996): 296–327.
———. "Haben Frösche und Sumpfmenschen Gedanken? Einige Probleme der Teleosemantik." *Deutsche Zeitschrift für Philosophie* 49, no. 4 (2001): 601–626.
———. *Macht, Moral, Wissen. Foucault und die klassische Antike*. Frankfurt: Suhrkamp, 1998.
———. "Teleosemantik. Ein neuer Blick auf den Geist?" *Deutsche Zeitschrift für Philosophie* 49, no. 3 (2001): 465–491.
Dewey, John. *Art as Experience*. New York: Perigree, 2005.
———. *How We Think*. New York: Heath, 1910.
———. *On Experience, Nature and Freedom*. Indianapolis: Bobbs-Merrill, 1960.
Dietz, Simone. *Lebenswelt und System: Widerstreitende Ansätze in der Gesellschaftstheorie von Jürgen Habermas*. Würzburg: Königshausen & Neumann, 1993.
Dietz, Simone, Heiner Hastedt, Geert Keil, and Anke Thyen, eds. *Sich im Denken orientieren*. Frankfurt: Suhrkamp, 1996.
Donagan, Alana. *Choice: The Essential Element of Human Action*. London: Routledge, 1987.
Dorffner, Georg. *Konnektionismus*. Stuttgart: Teubner, 1991.
Dornes, Martin. *Der kompetente Säugling: Die präverbale Entwicklung des Menschen*. Frankfurt: Fischer, 1993.
———. *Die frühe Kindheit: Entwicklungspsychologie der ersten Lebensjahre*. Frankfurt: Suhrkamp, 1997.
Dornes, Michael. *Die emotionale Welt des Kindes*. Frankfurt: Suhrkamp, 2000.
Dretske, Fred. *Explaining Behavior: Reasons in a World of Causes*. Cambridge: Cambridge University Press, 1997.
Dreyfus, Hubert L. *Was Computer nicht können*. Frankfurt: Athenaeum, 1985.
Dreyfus, Hubert L., and Stuart E. Dreyfus. *Künstliche Intelligenz: Von der Denkmaschine und dem Wert der Intuition*. Reinbek: Rowohlt, 1991.
Duerr, Hans Peter, ed. *Der Wissenschaftler und das Irrationale*. Vol. 2, *Beiträge aus Philosophie und Psychologie*. Frankfurt: Syndikat, 1981.
Eco, Umberto. *Einführung in die Semiotik*. Munich: Fink, 1985.
Ekman, Paul. "Biological and Cultural Contributions to Body and Facial Movement in the Expression of Emotions." In *Explaining Emotions*, edited by A. O. Rorty, 73–102. Berkeley: University of California Press, 1980.
Elsner, Monika, Hans Ullrich Gumbrecht, Thomas Müller, et al. "Zur Kulturgeschichte der Medien." In *Die Wirklichkeit der Medien. Eine Einführung in die Kommunikationswissenschaft*, edited by K. Merten, S. J. Schmidt, and S. Weischenberg, 163–187. Opladen: Westdeutscher, 1994.

Elster, Jon. *Sour Grapes: Studies in the Subversion of Rationality*. Cambridge: Cambridge University Press, 1983.

Enzensberger, Hans Magnus. "Baukasten zu einer Theorie der Medien." *Kursbuch* 20 (1970): 159–186.

Evnine, Simon. *Donald Davidson*. Stanford, CA: Stanford University Press, 1991.

Faltin, Peter. "Ist Musik eine Sprache?" In *Die Zeichen: Neue Aspekte der musikalischen Ästhetik 2*, edited by H. W. Henze, 32–50. Frankfurt: Suhrkamp, 1981.

Faulstich, Werner, ed. *Kritische Stichwörter zur Medienwissenschaft*. Munich: Fink, 1979.

——. *Medientheorien: Einführung und Überblick*. Göttingen: Vandenhoeck & Ruprecht, 1991.

Feyerabend, Paul. "Irrationalität oder: Wer hat Angst vorm schwarzen Mann." In *Der Wissenschaftler und das Irrationale*. Vol. 2, *Beiträge aus Philosophie und Psychologie*, edited by H. P. Duerr, 37–59. Frankfurt: Syndikat, 1981.

Fischer, Ludwig. "Ansichten einer Wissenschaft der Zukunft? Unsystematische Gedanken von Nutz und Frommen der Medienwissenschaft." In *Ansichten einer künftigen Medienwissenschaft*, edited by R. Bohn, E. Müller, and R. Ruppert, 257–284. Berlin: Sigma, 1988.

Floros, Constantin. *Musik als Botschaft*. Wiesbaden: Breitkopf & Härtel, 1989.

Flusser, Vilém. *Die Schrift: Hat Schreiben Zukunft?* Göttingen: Immatrix, 1989.

——. "Digitaler Schein." In *Digitaler Schein: Ästhetik der elektronischen Medien*, edited by F. Rötzer, 147–159. Frankfurt: Suhrkamp, 1991.

Foerster, Heinz von. "Bemerkungen zur Epistemologie des Lebendigen." In *Wissen und Gewissen: Versuch einer Brücke*, 116–133. Frankfurt: Suhrkamp, 1993.

——. "Epistemologie der Kommunikation." In *Wissen und Gewissen: Versuch einer Brücke*, 269–281. Frankfurt: Suhrkamp, 1993.

——. "Kompetenz und Verantwortung." In *KybernEthik*, 161–173. Berlin: Merve, 1993.

——. "Über das Konstruieren von Wirklichkeiten." In *Wissen und Gewissen: Versuch einer Brücke*, 25–49. Frankfurt: Suhrkamp, 1993.

——. "Über selbstorganisierende Systeme und ihre Umwelten." In *Wissen und Gewissen: Versuch einer Brücke*, 211–232. Frankfurt: Suhrkamp, 1993.

——. "Unordnung und Ordnung: Entdeckung oder Erfindung?" In *Wissen und Gewissen: Versuch einer Brücke*, 134–148. Frankfurt: Suhrkamp, 1993.

——. "Verstehen verstehen." In *Wissen und Gewissen: Versuch einer Brücke*, 282–298. Frankfurt: Suhrkamp, 1993.

——. *Wissen und Gewissen: Versuch einer Brücke*. Frankfurt: Suhrkamp, 1993.

Føllesdal, Dagfinn. "The Status of Rationality Assumptions in Interpretation and in the Explanation of Action." *Dialectica* 36 (1982): 301–316.

Fonagy, Peter, and Mary Target. "Playing with Reality: I. Theory of Mind and the Normal Development of Psychic Reality." *International Journal of Psychoanalysis* 77 (1996): 217–233.

Forum für Philosophie Bad Homburg, ed. *Intentionalität und Verstehen*. Frankfurt: Suhrkamp, 1990.

Foucault, Michel. *The History of Sexuality: The Will to Knowledge I*. New York: Penguin, 2008.

——. "The Subject and Power." *Critical Inquiry* 8, no. 4 (1982): 777–795.

———. "What Is Critique?" Translated by Paul Geiman. In *What Is Enlightenment? Eighteenth-Century Answers and Twentieth-Century Questions*, edited by James Schmidt, 282–298. Berkeley: University of California Press, 1996.

———. "What Is Enlightenment?" In *The Foucault Reader*, edited by Paul Rabinow, 32–50. New York: Pantheon, 1984.

Frank, Manfred. *Die Grenzen der Verständigung: Ein Geistergespräch zwischen Lyotard und Habermas*. Frankfurt: Suhrkamp, 1988.

———. *Die Unhintergehbarkeit der Individualität*. Frankfurt: Suhrkamp, 1986.

———. "Two Centuries of Philosophical Critique of Reason and Its 'Postmodern' Radicalization." In *Reason and Its Other: Rationality in Modern German Philosophy and Culture*, edited by Dieter Freundlieb and Wayne Hudson, 67–86. Providence, RI: Berg, 1993.

Franke, Herbert W. "Der Monitor als Fenster in einen unbegrenzten Raum: Ein Gespräch." In *Digitaler Schein. Ästhetik der elektronischen Medien*, edited by F. Rötzer, 282–293. Frankfurt: Suhrkamp, 1991.

Gadamer, Hans-Georg. "Kultur und Medien." In *Zwischenbetrachtungen: Im Prozeß der Aufklärung*, edited by A. Honneth, T. McCarthy, C. Offe, and A. Wellmer, 713–732. Frankfurt: Suhrkamp, 1989.

———. "Rationalität im Wandel der Zeiten." In *Gesammelte Werke*. Vol. 4, *Neuere Philosophie II: Probleme—Gestalten*, 23–36. Tübingen: Mohr (Paul Siebeck), 1987.

———. *Truth and Method*. Translated by Joel Weinsheimer and Donald G. Marshall. London: Continuum, 2004.

Gehlen, Arnold. *Anthropologische Forschung*. Reinbek: Rowohlt, 1961.

———. "Der Mensch und die Technik." In *Anthropologische und Sozialpsychologische Untersuchungen*, 147–162. Reinbek: Rowohlt, 1986.

———. "Die Technik in der Sichtweise der Anthropologie." In *Anthropologische Forschung*, 93–103. Reinbek: Rowohlt, 1961.

———. "Man and Technique." In *Man in the Age of Technology*, translated by Patricia Lipscomb, 1–24. New York: Columbia University Press, 1980.

Gergely, György, and James Watson. "The Social Biofeedback Theory of Parental Affect-Mirroring: The Development of Emotional Self-Awareness and Self-Control in Infancy." *International Journal of Psychoanalysis* 77 (1996): 1181–1212.

Giedeon, Siegfried. *Die Herrschaft der Mechanisierung*. Frankfurt: Athenaeum, 1987.

Glasersfeld, Ernst von. "Siegener Gespräche über Radikalen Konstruktivismus." In *Der Diskurs des Radikalen Konstruktivismus*, edited by S. J. Schmidt, 401–440. Frankfurt: Suhrkamp, 1991.

———. *Wissen, Sprache und Wirklichkeit: Arbeiten zum radikalen Konstruktivismus*. Braunschweig: Vieweg, 1987.

Glucksmann, André. *Die Meisterdenker*. Reinbek: Rowohlt, 1978.

Goetsch, Paul. "Der Übergang von Mündlichkeit zu Schriftlichkeit: De kulturkritischen und ideologischen Implikationen der Theorien von McLuhan, Goody und Ong." In *Symbolische Formen—Medien—Identität*, edited by W. Raible, 113–129. Tübingen: Narr, 1991.

Goldmann, Lucien. *Cultural Creation in Modern Society*. Translated by William Mayrl. St. Louis: Telos, 1976.

Goodman, Nelson. "Art and Inquiry." In *Problems and Projects*, 103–119. New York: Bobbs-Merrill, 1972.

———. *Languages of Art: An Approach to a Theory of Symbols*. Indianapolis: Hackett, 1967.

———. *Ways of Worldmaking*. Indianapolis: Hackett, 1978.

Gosepath, Stefan. *Aufgeklärtes Eigeninteresse: Eine Theorie theoretischer und praktischer Rationalität*. Frankfurt: Suhrkamp, 1992.

Götschl, Johann. "Zur philosophischen Bedeutung des Paradigmas der Selbstorganisation für den Zusammenhang von Naturverständnis und Selbstverständnis." In *Selbstorganisation. Aspekte einer wissenschaftlichen Revolution*, edited by W. Krohn and G. Küppers, 181–199. Braunschweig: Vieweg, 1990.

Granet, Marcel. *Das chinesische Denken. (La pensée chinoise)*. Frankfurt: Suhrkamp, 1985.

Gumbrecht, Hans Ulrich, and K. Ludwig Pfeifer. *Materialität der Kommunikation*. Frankfurt: Suhrkamp, 1988.

Günther, Gotthard. *Das Bewusstsein der Maschinen*. Baden-Baden: Agis, 1963.

Habermas, Jürgen. "The Dialectics of Rationalization." In *Autonomy and Solidarity: Interviews with Jürgen Habermas*, edited by Peter Dews, 95–130. London: Verso, 1992.

———. *Die Philosophie als Platzhalter und Interpret*. Frankfurt: Suhrkamp, 1983.

———. "Discourse Ethics: Notes on a Program of Philosophical Justification." In *Moral Consciousness and Communicative Action*, translated by Christian Lenhardt and Shierry Weber Nicholsen, 43–115. Cambridge, MA: MIT Press, 1999.

———. "Erläuterungen zum Begriff des kommunikativen Handelns." In *Vorstudien und Ergänzungen zur Theorie des kommunikativen Handelns*, 571–606. Frankfurt: Suhrkamp, 1986.

———. *Faktizität und Geltung: Beiträge zur Diskurstheorie des Rechts und des demokratischen Rechtsstaates*. Frankfurt: Suhrkamp, 1992.

———. "Handlung und System: Bemerkungen zu Parsons' Medientheorie." In *Verhalten, Handeln und System*, edited by W. Schluchter, 68–105. Frankfurt: Suhrkamp, 1980.

———. "Intention, Konvention und sprachliche Interaktion." In *Vorstudien und Ergänzungen zur Theorie des kommunikativen Handelns*, 307–331. Frankfurt: Suhrkamp, 1986.

———. "Intentionalistische Semantik." In *Vorstudien und Ergänzungen zur Theorie des kommunikativen Handelns*, 332–349. Frankfurt: Suhrkamp, 1986.

———. "Modernity: An Incomplete Project." In *The Anti-Aesthetic: Essays in Postmodern Culture*, edited by Hal Foster, 3–15. Seattle: Bay Press, 1991.

———. *The Philosophical Discourse of Modernity*. Translated by Frederick G. Lawrence. Cambridge, MA: MIT Press, 1987.

———. *Rekonstruktion des historischen Materialismus*. Frankfurt: Suhrkamp, 1976.

———. "A Reply." In *Communicative Action: Essays on Jürgen Habermas's Theory of Communicative Action*, edited by Axel Honneth and Hans Joas, 214–264. Cambridge: Polity, 1991.

———. "Rortys pragmatische Wende." *Deutsche Zeitschrift für Philosophie* 5 (1996): 715–741.

———. *Strukturwandel der Öffentlichkeit. Untersuchungen zu einer Kategorie der bürgerlichen Gesellschaft*. Darmstadt: Luchterhand, 1979.

———. *Theory and Practice*. Translated by John Viertel. Cambridge: Polity, 1988.

———. *The Theory of Communicative Action*. Vol. 1, *Reason and the Rationalization of Society*. Translated by Thomas McCarthy. Boston: Beacon, 1984.

———. *The Theory of Communicative Action*. Vol. 2, *Lifeworld and System*. Translated by Thomas McCarthy. Boston: Beacon, 2000.

———. "The Unity of Reason in the Diversity of Its Voices." In *Postmetaphysical Thinking: Philosophical Essays*, translated by William Mark Hohengarten, 115–148. Cambridge, MA: MIT Press, 1992.

———. *Vorstudien und Ergänzungen zur Theorie des kommunikativen Handelns*. Frankfurt: Suhrkamp, 1986.

———. "What Is Universal Pragmatics?" In *On the Pragmatics of Communication*, edited by Maeve Cooke, 21–104. Cambridge, MA: MIT Press, 1998.

Habermas, Jürgen, and Niklas Luhmann. *Theorie der Gesellschaft oder Sozialtechnologie*. Frankfurt: Suhrkamp. 1976.

Hacking, Ian. "The Parody of Conversation." In *Truth and Interpretation: Perspectives on the Philosophy of Donald Davidson*, edited by E. LePore, 447–458. Oxford: Blackwell, 1986.

Haefner, Klaus. "Bildung und Kultur im 'Computerzeitalter'—Tradition und Perspektive." In *Computer, Kultur, Geschichte: Beiträge zur Philosophie des Informationszeitalters*, edited by D. Mersch and J. C. Nyíri, 21–39. Vienna: Passagen, 1991.

Haferkamp, Hans, and Michael Schmid, eds. *Sinn, Kommunikation und soziale Differenzierung: Beiträge zu Luhmanns Theorie sozialer Systeme*. Frankfurt: Suhrkamp, 1987.

Hahn, Alois. "Sinn und Sinnlosigkeit." In *Sinn, Kommunikation und soziale Differenzierung: Beiträge zu Luhmanns Theorie sozialer Systeme*, edited by H. Haferkamp and M. Schmid, 155–164. Frankfurt: Suhrkamp, 1987.

Hanslick, Eduard. *On the Musically Beautiful*. Translated by Geoffrey Payzant. New York: Liberal Arts Press, 1957.

Harding, Sandra. "Is Gender a Variable in Conceptions of Rationality? A Survey of Issues." *Dialectica* 36, no. 2–3 (1982): 225–242.

Hare, Richard M. *The Language of Morals*. Oxford: Oxford University Press, 1952.

Harman, Gilbert. "Moral Relativism Defended." *Philosophical Review* 84 (1975): 3–22.

Hassan, Ihab. "Postmoderne heute." In *Wege aus der Moderne: Schlüsseltexte der Postmoderne—Diskussion*, edited by W. Welsch, 47–56. Weinheim: VCH, 1988.

Haverkamp, Anselm, and Renate Lachmann, eds. *Gedächtniskunst: Raum—Bild—Schrift. Studien zur Mnemotechnik*. Frankfurt: Suhrkamp, 1991.

Hegel, Georg Wilhelm Friedrich. *Aesthetics: Lectures on Fine Art*. 2 vols. Translated by T. M. Knox. Oxford: Clarendon, 1988.

———. *Phenomenology of Spirit*. Translated by A. V. Miller. New Delhi: Shri Jainendra Press, 1998.

———. "Vorlesungen über die Philosophie der Geschichte." In *Werke in zwanzig Bänden*. Vol. 12. Frankfurt: Suhrkamp, 1970.

Heidegger, Martin. *Being and Time*. Translated by Blackwell Publishing Ltd. Oxford: Blackwell, 1962.

———. *Die Technik und die Kehre*. Pfullingen: Neske, 1991.

Heidelberger, Michael. "Selbstorganisation im 19. Jahrhundert." In *Selbstorganisation: Aspekte einer wissenschaftlichen Revolution*, edited by W. Krohn and G. Küppers, 67–104. Braunschweig: Vieweg, 1990.

Heider, Fritz. "Ding und Medium." *Symposium* 1 (1926): 108–157.

Hempel, Carl G. "Rational Action." *Proceedings and Addresses of the American Philosophical Association* 35 (1962): 5–24.

Henrich, Dieter. *Fluchtlinien: Philosophische Essays*. Frankfurt: Suhrkamp, 1982.

———. "Was ist Metaphysik—was Moderne?" In *Konzepte*, 11–43. Frankfurt: Suhrkamp, 1987.
Hentig, Hartmut von. "Die Erziehung des Menschengeschlechts: Ein Plädoyer für die Wiederherstellung der Aufklärung." In *Der Traum der Vernunft: Vom Elend der Aufklärung*, edited by Akademie der Künste Berlin, 105–124. Darmstadt: Luchterhand, 1985.
Henze, Hans Werner. "Die Folgen der Vereinsamung." *Die Zeit* 34 (1979): 31.
Herken, R., ed. *The Universal Turing Machine*. Berlin: Kammerer & Unverzagt, 1988.
Heuser, MarieLuise. "Wissenschaft und Metaphysik: Überlegung zu einer allgemeinen Selbstorganisationstheorie." In *Selbstorganisation: Aspekte einer wissenschaftlichen Revolution*, edited by W. Krohn and G. Küppers, 39–68. Braunschweig: Vieweg, 1990.
Hickethier, Knut. "Das 'Medium', die 'Medien' und die Medienwissenschaft." In *Ansichten einer künftigen Medienwissenschaft*, edited by R. Bohn, E. Müller, and R. Ruppert, 51–74. Berlin: Sigma, 1988.
Hinsch, Wilfried. *Erfahrung und Selbstbewusstsein: Zur Kategoriendeduktion bei Kant*. Hamburg: Meiner, 1986.
Hodges, Andrew. *Alan Turing: The Enigma*. New York: Simon & Schuster, 1983.
Höffe, Ottfried. *Immanuel Kant*. Munich: Beck, 1992.
Hollis, Martin. *Rationalität und soziales Verstehen*. Frankfurt: Suhrkamp, 1991.
Honneth, Axel, and Hans Joas, eds. *Communicative Action: Essays on Jürgen Habermas's Theory of Communicative Action*. Cambridge, MA: MIT Press, 1991.
Honneth, Axel, Thomas McCarthy, Claus Offe, and Albrecht Wellmer, eds. *Cultural-Political Interventions in the Unfinished Project of Enlightenment*. Cambridge, MA: MIT Press, 1992.
Hopcroft, John E., and Jeffrey Ullman. *Introduction to Automata Theory, Languages, and Computation*. Reading, MA: Addison-Wesley, 2007.
Horkheimer, Max, and Theodor W. Adorno. *Dialektik der Aufklärung*. Frankfurt: Fischer, 1982.
Hübner, Kurt. "Rationalität im mythischen Denken." In *Wissenschaftliche und nichtwissenschaftliche Rationalität*, edited by K. Hübner and J. Vuillemin, 49–68. Stuttgart: Frommann, 1983.
Hübner, Kurt, and Jules Vuillemin, eds. *Wissenschaftliche und nichtwissenschaftliche Rationalität*. Stuttgart: Frommann, 1983.
Hume, David. *A Treatise of Human Nature*. Oxford: Oxford University Press, 1978.
Hunziker, Peter. *Medien, Kommunikation und Gesellschaft. Einführung in die Soziologie der Massenkommunikation*. Darmstadt: Wissenschaftliche Buchgesellschaft, 1988.
Huyssen, Andreas, and Klaus R. Scherpe, eds. *Postmoderne: Zeichen eines kulturellen Wandels*. Reinbek: Rowohlt, 1986.
IBM Deutschland GmbH, ed. *Alles ist Information*. Stuttgart: IBM Deutschland, 1984.
———. *Technik und Gesellschaft: Innovation durch Information*. Stuttgart: IBM Deutschland, 1982.
Idensen, Heiko, and Matthias Krohn. "Kunst-Netzwerke: Ideen als Objekte." In *Digitaler Schein: Ästhetik der elektronischen Medien*, edited by F. Rötzer, 371–396. Frankfurt: Suhrkamp, 1991.
Jacobi, Klaus. "Möglichkeit." In *Handbuch philosophischer Grundbegriffe*. Vol. 4, edited by H. Krings, H. M. Baumgartner, and C. Wild, 930–947. Munich: Kösel, 1973.

Jameux, Dominique. "Musik und Rationalität." In *Wissenschaftliche und nichtwissenschaftliche Rationalität*, edited by K. Hübner and J. Vuillemin, 119–134. Stuttgart: Frommann, 1983.

Jensen, Stefan. "Einleitung." In *Zur Theorie der Interaktionsmedien*, by Talcott Parsons, 7–55. Opladen: Westdeutscher, 1980.

———. *Systemtheorie*. Stuttgart: Kohlhammer, 1983.

———. *Talcott Parsons: Eine Einführung*. Stuttgart: Teubner, 1980.

Joas, Hans. "Die unglückliche Ehe von Hermeneutik und Funktionalismus." In *Kommunikatives Handeln*, edited by A. Honneth and H. Joas, 144–176. Frankfurt: Suhrkamp, 1986.

Joerges, Bernward, ed. *Technik im Alltag*. Frankfurt: Suhrkamp, 1988.

Joly, Henri. "Die Rationalität im griechischen mythischen Denken." In *Wissenschaftliche und nichtwissenschaftliche Rationalität*, edited by K. Hübner and J. Vuillemin, 69–96. Stuttgart: Frommann. 1983.

Kambartel, Friedrich. "Begründungen und Lebensformen: Zur Kritik des ethischen Pluralismus." In *Philosophie der humanen Welt*, 44–58. Frankfurt: Suhrkamp, 1989.

———. "Die Vernunft und das Allgemeine: Zum Verständnis rationaler Sprache und Praxis." In *Die eine Vernunft und die vielen Rationalitäten*, edited by K.-O. Apel and M. Kettner, 58–72. Frankfurt: Suhrkamp, 1996.

———. *Philosophie der humanen Welt*. Frankfurt: Suhrkamp, 1989.

———. "Universalität als Lebensform: Zu den (unlösbaren) Schwierigkeiten, das gute und vernünftige Leben über formale Kriterien zu bestimmen." In *Philosophie der humanen Welt*, 15–26. Frankfurt: Suhrkamp, 1989.

———. "Vernunft: Kriterium oder Kultur? Zur Definierbarkeit des Vernünftigen." In *Philosophie der humanen Welt*. Frankfurt: Suhrkamp, 1989.

———. "Wittgensteins späte Philosophie: Zur Vollendung von Kants Kritik der wissenschaftlichen Aufklärung." In *Philosophie der humanen Welt*, 146–159. Frankfurt: Suhrkamp, 1989.

Kamper, Dietmar. "Der Januskopf der Medien: Ästhetisierung der Wirklichkeit, Entrüstung der Sinne." In *Digitaler Schein: Ästhetik der elektronischen Medien*, edited by F. Rötzer, 93–99. Frankfurt: Suhrkamp, 1991.

Kamper, Dietmar, and Willem van Reijen, eds. *Die vollendete Vernunft: Moderne versus Postmoderne*. Frankfurt: Suhrkamp, 1987.

Kandinsky, Wassily. *Punkt und Linie zu Fläche*. Bern: Benteli, 1973.

Kant, Immanuel. "Beantwortung der Frage: Was ist Aufklärung?" In *Werksausgabe*. Vol. 9, *Schriften zur Anthropologie, Geschichtsphilosophie, Politik und Pädagogik*, edited by W. Weischedel, 53–61. Darmstadt: Wissenschaftliche Buchgesellschaft, 1983.

———. *The Critique of Judgment*. Translated by John H. Bernard. New York: Cosimo, 2007.

———. *The Critique of Pure Reason*. Translated and edited by Paul Guyer and Allen Wood. Cambridge: Cambridge University Press, 2007.

Karl, Markus Michel, and Tilman Spengler, eds. *Kursbuch 75: Computerkultur*. Berlin: Kursbuch, 1984.

———. *Kursbuch 84: Sprachlose Intelligenz*. Berlin: Kursbuch, 1986.

———. *Kursbuch 90: Die Medien*. Berlin: Kursbuch, 1987.

———. *Kursbuch 98: Das Chaos*. Berlin: Kursbuch, 1989.

Kausch, Michael. *Kulturindustrie und Populärkultur: Kritische Theorie der Massenmedien.* Frankfurt: Suhrkamp, 1988.
Kerman, Joseph. "The State of Academic Music Criticism." In *On Criticizing Music: Five Philosophical Perspectives,* edited by Kingsley Price. Baltimore: Johns Hopkins University Press, 1981.
Kidder, Tracy. *The Soul of a New Machine.* Boston: Little, Brown, 1981.
Kittler, Friedrich. *Aufschreibesysteme 1800 1900.* Munich: Fink, 1987.
——. *Grammophon. Film. Typewriter.* Berlin: Brinkmann & Bose, 1986.
——. "SignalRauschAbstand." In *Materialität der Kommunikation,* edited by H. U. Gumbrecht and L. K. Pfeiffer, 342–359. Frankfurt: Suhrkamp, 1988.
Kivy, Peter. "It's Only Music: So What's to Understand?" *Journal of Aesthetic Education* 20 (1986): 1–74.
Klaus, Georg. *Kybernetik und Gesellschaft.* Berlin: Rotdruck, 1964.
Klier, Peter, and Jean-Luc Evard, eds. *Mediendämmerung: Zur Archäologie der Medien.* Berlin: Edition Tiamat, 1989.
Klinger, Cornelia. *Flucht Trost Revolte: Die Moderne und ihre ästhetischen Gegenwelten.* Munich: Hanser, 1995.
——. "Modernisierungsorientiertes oder traditionsorientiertes Emanzipationskonzept? Zwei Befreiungsbewegungen—Ein Dilemma." In *Was Philosophinnen denken II,* edited by M. Andreas-Grisebach and B. Weisshaupt, 71–96. Zurich: Ammann, 1986.
Kloepfer, Rolf. "Medienästhetik: Polysensitivität, Semiotik und Ästhetik. Ein Versuch." In *Ansichten einer künftigen Medienwissenschaft,* edited by R. Bohn, E. Müller, and R. Ruppert, 75–90. Berlin: Sigma, 1988.
Kluxen, Wolfgang. "Über die Rationalität der religiösen Erfahrung." In *Wissenschaftliche und nichtwissenschaftliche Rationalität,* edited by K. Hübner and J. Vuillemin, 97–106. Stuttgart: Frommann, 1983.
Knilli, Friedrich. "Medium." In *Kritische Stichwörter zur Medienwissenschaft,* edited by W. Faulstich, 230–251. Munich: Fink, 1989.
Koller, Werner. *Einführung in die Übersetzungswissenschaft.* Heidelberg: Quelle & Meyer, 1983.
Koppe, Franz. *Grundbegriffe der Ästhetik.* Frankfurt: Suhrkamp, 1983.
Korean Overseas Information Service. *Hangul.* Seoul: Korean Overseas Information Service, 1973.
Koselleck, Reinhart. "Fortschritt und Beschleunigung." In *Der Traum der Vernunft: Vom Elend der Aufklärung,* edited by Akademie der Künste Berlin, 75–104. Darmstadt: Luchterhand, 1985.
Koslowski, Peter. *Die Prüfungen der Neuzeit.* Vienna: Passagen, 1989.
——, ed. *Supermoderne oder Postmoderne?* Vienna: Passagen, 1989.
Kracauer, Siegfried. *Theory of Film: The Redemption of Physical Reality.* Princeton, NJ: Princeton University Press, 1997.
Krämer, Sybille. "Das Medium als Spur und als Apparat." In *Medien, Computer, Realität,* 73–94. Frankfurt: Suhrkamp, 1998.
——, ed. *Medien, Computer, Realität.* Frankfurt: Suhrkamp, 1998.
——. "Was haben die Medien, der Computer und die Realität miteinander zu tun?" In *Medien, Computer, Realität,* 9–26. Frankfurt: Suhrkamp, 1998.
Krings, Hermann, Hans Michael Baumgartner, and Christoph Wild. *Handbuch philosophischer Grundbegriffe.* 6 vols. Munich: Kösel, 1974.

Krohn, Wolfgang, and Günther Küppers. "Wissenschaft als selbstorganisierendes System: Eine neue Sicht alter Probleme." In *Selbstorganisation: Aspekte einer wissenschaftlichen Revolution*, edited by W. Krohn and G. Küppers, 303–327. Braunschweig: Vieweg, 1990.

———. *Selbstorganisation: Aspekte einer wissenschaftlichen Revolution*. Braunschweig: Vieweg, 1990.

Krohn, Wolfgang, Günther Küppers, and Rainer Paslak. "Selbstorganisation: Zur Genese und Entwicklung einer wissenschaftlichen Revolution." In *Der Diskurs des radikalen Konstruktivismus*, edited by S. J. Schmidt, 466–474. Frankfurt: Suhrkamp, 1991.

Krüger, Hans Peter. "Das mehrdeutige Selbst: H. R. Maturanas Konzept philosophisch betrachtet." In *Selbstorganisation. Aspekte einer wissenschaftlichen Revolution*, edited by W. Krohn and G. Küppers, 193–166. Braunschweig: Vieweg, 1990.

Kübler, Hans-Dieter. "Auf dem Weg zur wissenschaftlichen Identität und methodologischen Kompetenz: Herausforderungen und Desiderate der Medienwissenschaft." In *Ansichten einer künftigen Medienwissenschaft*, edited by R. Bohn, E. Müller, and R. Ruppert, 29–50. Berlin: Sigma, 1988.

Kuhn, Thomas S. *The Structure of Scientific Revolutions*. Chicago: University of Chicago Press, 1962.

Künne, Wolfgang. "Prinzipien der wohlwollenden Interpretation." In *Intentionalität und Verstehen*, edited by Forum für Philosophie Bad Homburg, 211–237. Frankfurt: Suhrkamp, 1990.

———. "Wahrheit." In *Philosophie: Ein Grundkurs*, edited by E. Martens and H. Schnädelbach. Reinbek: Rowohlt, 1986.

Künzler, Jan. *Medien und Gesellschaft: Die Medienkonzepte von Talcott Parsons, Jürgen Habermas und Niklas Luhmann*. Stuttgart: Enke, 1989.

Kutschera, Franz von. *Ästhetik*. Berlin: De Gruyter, 1989.

Laermann, Klaus. "Lacancan und Derridada: Über die Frankolatrie in den Kulturwissenschaften." *Kursbuch* 84 (1986): 34–43.

Lakatos, Imre. "Falsification and Methodology of Scientific Research Programmes." In *Criticism and the Growth of Knowledge*, edited by Imre Lakatos and Alan Musgrave, 91–196. Cambridge: Cambridge University Press, 1970.

Langer, Susanne. *Philosophy in a New Key: A Study in the Symbolism of Reason, Rite, and Art*. New York: New American Library, 1954.

Ledyard, Gari Keith. *The Korean Language Reform of 1446: The Origin, Background, and Early History of the Korean Alphabet*. Ann Arbor, MI: University Microfilms, 1973.

Lerdahl, Fred, and Ray Jackendoff. *A Generative Theory of Tonal Music*. Cambridge, MA: MIT Press, 1983.

Leroi-Gourhan, André. *Gesture and Speech*. Translated by A. B. Berger. Cambridge, MA: MIT Press, 1993.

List, Elisabeth, and Herlinde Studer, eds. *Denkverhältnisse. Feminismus und Kritik*. Frankfurt: Suhrkamp, 1989.

Lübbe, Hermann. "Kulturelle und politische Folgen beschleunigter technischer Evolution." In *Computer, Kultur, Geschichte: Beiträge zur Philosophie des Informationszeitalters*, edited by D. Mersch and J. C. Nyíri, 41–62. Vienna: Passagen, 1991.

Luhmann, Niklas. *Archimedes und wir*. Berlin: Merve, 1987.

———. "Autopoiesis als soziologischer Begriff." In *Sinn, Kommunikation und soziale Differenzierung: Beiträge zu Luhmanns Theorie sozialer Systeme*, edited by H. Haferkamp and M. Schmid, 307–324. Frankfurt: Suhrkamp, 1987.

———. "Biographie, Attitüden, Zettelkasten." In *Archimedes und wir*, 125–155. Berlin: Merve, 1987.

———. "Codierung und Programmierung: Bildung und Selektion im Erwachsenensystem." In *Soziologische Aufklärung 4*, 182–201. Opladen: Westdeutscher, 1987.

———. "Der Wohlfahrtsstaat zwischen Evolution und Rationalität." In *Soziologische Aufklärung 4: Beiträge zur funktionalen Differenzierung der Gesellschaft*, 14–116. Opladen: Westdeutscher, 1987.

———. *Die Kunst der Gesellschaft*. Frankfurt: Suhrkamp, 1996.

———. "Die Unwahrscheinlichkeit der Kommunikation." In *Soziologische Aufklärung 3*, 25–34. Opladen: Westdeutscher, 1981.

———. "'Distinctions directrices': Über Codierung von Semantiken und Systemen." In *Soziologische Aufklärung 4*, 13–31. Opladen: Westdeutscher, 1987.

———. *Ecological Communication*. Translated by John Bednarz Jr. Cambridge: Polity, 1989.

———. "Einführende Bemerkungen zu einer Theorie symbolisch generalisierter Kommunikationsmedien." In *Soziologische Aufklärung 2*, 170–192. Opladen: Westdeutscher, 1975.

———. *Gesellschaftsstruktur und Semantik: Studien zur Wissenssoziologie der modernen Gesellschaft*. Frankfurt: Suhrkamp, 1993.

———. "Handlungstheorie und Systemtheorie." In *Soziologische Aufklärung 3*, 50–66. Opladen: Westdeutscher, 1981.

———. "Ist Kunst codierbar?" In *Soziologische Aufklärung 3*, 245–266. Opladen: Westdeutscher, 1981.

———. *Observations on Modernity*. Translated by William Whobrey. Stanford, CA: Stanford University Press, 1998.

———. *Social Systems*. Translated by John Bednarz Jr. and Dirk Baecker. Stanford, CA: Stanford University Press, 1996.

———. *Soziologische Aufklärung 2: Aufsätze zur Theorie der Gesellschaft*. Opladen: Westdeutscher, 1975.

———. *Soziologische Aufklärung 3: Soziales System, Gesellschaft, Organisation*. Opladen: Westdeutscher, 1981.

———. *Soziologische Aufklärung 5: Konstruktivistische Perspektiven*. Opladen: Westdeutscher, 1990.

———. "Systemtheorie, Evolutionstheorie und Kommunikationstheorie." In *Soziologische Aufklärung 2*, 193–203. Opladen: Westdeutscher, 1975.

———. "Temporalstrukturen des Handlungssystems: Zum Zusammenhang von Handlungs- und Systemtheorie." In *Verhalten, Handeln und System*, edited by W. Schluchter, 32–67. Frankfurt: Suhrkamp, 1980.

———. *Trust and Power: Two Works*. Chichester, UK: Wiley, 1979.

———. "Über die Funktion der Negation in sinnkonstituierenden Systemen." In *Soziologische Aufklärung 3*, 35–49. Opladen: Westdeutscher, 1981.

———. "Veränderungen im System gesellschaftlicher Kommunikation und die Massenmedien." In *Soziologische Aufklärung 3*, 309–320. Opladen: Westdeutscher, 1981.

———. *Vertrauen: Ein Mechanismus der Reduktion sozialer Komplexität*. Stuttgart: Enke, 1973.

———. "Vorbemerkung zu einer Theorie sozialer Systeme." In *Soziologische Aufklärung 3*, 11–24. Opladen: Westdeutscher, 1981.

———. "Wie ist das Bewusstsein an Kommunikation beteiligt?" In *Materialität der Kommunikation*, edited by H. U. Gumbrecht and L. K. Pfeiffer, 884–905. Frankfurt: Suhrkamp, 1988.

———. *Zweckbegriff und Systemrationalität*. Frankfurt: Suhrkamp, 1991.

Lyotard, Jean-François. "Answering the Question: What Is the Postmodern?" In *The Postmodern Explained to Children*, translated by Don Berry et al., 1–16. Sydney: Power Publications, 1992.

———. *The Differend: Phrases in Dispute*. Translated by Georges Van Den Abbeele. Minneapolis: University of Minnesota Press, 1988.

———. *The Postmodern Condition: A Report on Knowledge*. Translated by Geoff Bennington and Brian Massumi. Minneapolis: University of Minnesota Press, 1985.

———. "Re-Writing Modernity." *SubStance* 16, no. 54 (1987): 3–9.

Lypp, Bernhard. "Über die Selbsterzeugung der Aufklärung." In *Der Traum der Vernunft: Vom Elend der Aufklärung*, edited by Akademie der Künste Berlin, 295–308. Darmstadt: Luchterhand, 1985.

Margolis, Joseph. "The Identity of a Work of Art." *Mind* 67 (1959): 34–50.

Marquard, Odo. *Die Erziehung des Menschengeschlechts: Eine Bilanz*. Darmstadt: Luchterhand, 1985.

Martens, Ekkehardt, and Herbert Schnädelbach. *Philosophie. Ein Grundkurs*. Reinbek: Rowohlt, 1986.

Marx, Karl. *Capital: A Critique of Political Economy*. 3 vols. Edited by Friedrich Engels. New York: Cosimo, 2007.

Marx, Karl, and Friedrich Engels. *The German Ideology*. Edited by C. J. Arthur. New York: International Publishers, 2004.

Mattheson, Johann. *Der vollkommene Kapellmeister*. Hamburg: Christian Herold, 1739.

Maturana, Humberto R. "Science and Daily Life: The Ontology of Scientific Explanations." In *Selforganization: Portrait of a Scientific Revolution*, edited by W. Krohn and G. Küppers, 12–35. Dordrecht: Kluwer, 1990.

Maturana, Humberto R., and Francisco J. Varela. *The Tree of Knowledge: The Biological Roots of Human Understanding*. Boston: Shambhala, 1987.

Maus, Ingeborg. "Verrechtlichung, Entrechtlichung und der Funktionswandel von Institutionen." In *Rechtstheorie und Politische Theorie im Industriekapitalismus*, 277–331. Munich: Fink, 1986.

McCarthy, Thomas. "Complexity and Democracy: Or The Seducements of Systems Theory." In *Communicative Action: Essays on Jürgen Habermas's Theory of Communicative Action*, edited by A. Honneth and H. Joas, translated by J. Gaines and D. Jones, 119–139. Cambridge: Polity, 1991.

———. *The Critical Theory of Jürgen Habermas*. London: Hutchinson, 1978.

McLuhan, Marshall. *The Gutenberg Galaxy*. Toronto: University of Toronto Press, 1992.

———. *Understanding Media: The Extensions of Man*. New York: McGraw-Hill, 1966.

McLuhan, Marshall, and Quentin Fiore. *The Medium Is the Massage: An Inventory of Effects*. New York: Bantam Books, 1967.

McLuhan, Marshall, and Eric McLuhan. *Laws of the Media: The New Science*. Toronto: University of Toronto Press, 1988.

Meggle, Georg, ed. *Analytische Handlungstheorie Band 1: Handlungsbeschreibungen*. Frankfurt: Suhrkamp, 1985.

Menke, Christoph, and Martin Seel, eds. *Zur Verteidigung der Vernunft gegen ihre Liebhaber und Verächter*. Frankfurt: Suhrkamp, 1993.

Menne, A. "Modalität des Urteils." In *Historisches Wörterbuch der Philosophie*. Vol. 6, edited by J. Ritter, 12–16. Basel: Schwabe, 1984.

Mersch, Dieter. "Digitalität und Nicht-Diskursives Denken." In *Computer, Kultur, Geschichte. Beiträge zur Philosophie des Informationszeitalters*, edited by D. Mersch and J. C. Nyíri, 109–126. Vienna: Passagen, 1991.

Mersch, Dieter, and J. C. Nyíri, eds. *Computer, Kultur, Geschichte. Beiträge zu Philosophie des Informationszeitalters*. Vienna: Passagen, 1991.

Merten, Klaus, Siegfried S. Schmidt, and Siegfried Weischenberg, eds. *Die Wirklichkeit der Medien. Eine Einführung in die Kommunikationswissenschaft*. Opladen: Westdeutscher, 1994.

Mezei, György Iván. "Wissensrepräsentation und philosophische Methodologie." In *Computer, Kultur, Geschichte. Beiträge zur Philosophie des Informationszeitalters*, edited by D. Mersch and J. C. Nyíri, 133–146. Vienna: Passagen, 1991.

Millikan, Ruth Garrett. *Language, Thought and Other Biological Categories: New Foundations for Realism*. Cambridge, MA: MIT Press, 1984.

Minsky, Marvin. *Mentopolis*. Stuttgart: Klett-Cotta, 1990.

Mittelstraß, Jürgen. *Der Flug der Eule*. Frankfurt: Suhrkamp, 1989.

——. "Von der Vernunft: Erwiderungen auf Friedrich Kambartel." In *Der Flug der Eule*, 120–141. Frankfurt: Suhrkamp, 1989.

Modick, Klaus. *Das Stellen der Schrift*. Siegen: Affholderbach & Strohmann, 1988.

Modick, Klaus, and Matthias-Johannes Fischer, eds. *Kabelhafte Perspektiven*. Hamburg: Nautilus/Nemo, 1984.

Moles, Abraham A. "Design and Immateriality: What of It in a Post Industrial Society?" *Design Issues* 4, no. 1–2 (1988): 25–32.

Moravec, Hans. *Mind Children: Der Wettlauf zwischen menschlicher und künstlicher Intelligenz*. Hamburg: Hoffmann & Campe, 1990.

Muck, Otto. "Verstand." In *Handbuch philosophischer Grundbegriffe*. Vol. 6, edited by H. Krings, H. M. Baumgartner, and C. Wild, 1613–1627. Munich: Kösel, 1974.

Müller, Jan Dirk. "Der Körper des Buchs: Zum Medienwechsel zwischen Handschrift und Druck." In *Materialität der Kommunikation*, edited by H. U. Gumbrecht and L. K. Pfeiffer, 203–217. Frankfurt: Suhrkamp, 1988.

Münch, Richard. "Talcott Parsons und die Theorie des Handelns I." *Soziale Welt* (1979): 385–409.

——. "Talcott Parsons und die Theorie des Handelns II." *Soziale Welt* (1980): 3–47.

——. "Von der Rationalisierung zur Verdinglichung der Lebenswelt?" *Soziologische Revue* (1982): 390–397.

Nagl, Ludwig. "Zeigt die Habermassche Kommunikationstheorie einen 'Ausweg aus der Subjektphilosophie'?" In *Die Frage nach dem Subjekt*, edited by M. Frank, G. Raulet, and W. van Reijen, 346–373. Frankfurt: Suhrkamp, 1988.

Nagl-Docekal, Herta. "Feministische Vernunftkritik." In *Die eine Vernunft und die vielen Rationalitäten*, edited by K.-O. Apel and M. Kettner, 166–205. Frankfurt: Suhrkamp, 1996.

Needham, Joseph. *Science and Civilization in China*. Cambridge: Cambridge University Press, 2000.

——. *Wissenschaftlicher Universalismus: Über Bedeutung und Besonderheit der chinesischen Wissenschaft*. Frankfurt: Suhrkamp, 1979.

Negt, Oskar. "Zur Dialektik der Vergesellschaftung des Menschen: Sechs Thesen über die Notwendigkeit der Selbstaufklärung der Aufklärung." In *Der Traum der Vernunft. Vom Elend der Aufklärung*, edited by Akademie der Künste Berlin, 237–254. Darmstadt: Luchterhand, 1985.

Neumann, Klaus. "Aufwachsen im Medienzeitalter: Eine Fallstudie." In *Symbolische Formen—Medien—Identität*, edited by W. Raible, 249–270. Tübingen: Narr, 1991.

Newman, William S. "Sonate." In *Musik in Geschichte und Gegenwart*. Munich: Deutscher Taschenbuch/Bärenreiter, 1965, vol. 12.

Nyíri, J. C. "Historisches Bewusstsein im Informationszeitalter." In *Computer, Kultur, Geschichte. Beiträge zur Philosophie des Informationszeitalters*, edited by D. Mersch and J. C. Nyíri, 63–78. Vienna: Passagen, 1991.

O'Neill, Onora. "The Enlightenment as Autonomy: Kant's Vindication of Reason." In *The Enlightenment and Its Shadows*, edited by Peter Hulme and Ludmilla Jordanova, 184–199. London: Routledge, 1990.

Ong, Walter J. *Orality and Literacy: The Technologizing of the World*. New York: Routledge, 2002.

Orazem, Vito. "Holographie und Gesellschaft—Über vier Aspekte der bildnerischen Holographie." In *Digitaler Schein. Ästhetik der elektronischen Medien*, edited by F. Rötzer, 294–304. Frankfurt: Suhrkamp, 1991.

Papert, Seymour. *Mindstorms: Children, Computers, and Powerful Ideas*. New York: Basic Books, 1980.

Parsons, Talcott. *Actor, Situation, and Normative Pattern*. Edited by Victor Lidz and Helmut Staubmann. Berlin: LIT, 2010.

——. "Die Stellung der Soziologie in den Sozialwissenschaften." In *Die Einheit der Sozialwissenschaften*, edited by W. Bernsdorf and G. Eisermann, 64–83. Stuttgart: F. Enke, 1955.

——. *Essays in Sociological Theory*. New York: Simon & Schuster, 1954.

——. "General Theory in Sociology." In *Sociology Today: Problems and Prospects*. Vol. 1, edited by Robert K. Merton, 3–38. New York: Harper & Row, 1965.

——. "A Note on Some Biological Analogies." In *Family, Socialization and Interaction Process*, edited by T. Parsons and R. F. Bales, 395–399. Glencoe, IL: Free Press, 1955.

——. "On Building Social Systems Theory: A Personal History." *Daedalus* 99, no. 4 (1970): 826–881.

——. "On the Concept of Influence." *Public Opinion Quarterly* 27, no. 1 (1963): 37–62.

——. "On the Concept of Political Power." *Proceedings of the American Philosophical Society* 107, no. 3 (1963): 232–262.

——. "On the Concept of Value Commitments." *Social Inquiry* 38 (1968): 135–160.

——. "An Outline of the Social System." In *Theories of Society*, edited by T. Parsons, 30–84. New York: Free Press, 1965.

——. "Pattern Variables Revisited: A Response to Robert Dubin." *American Sociological Review* 25 (1964): 467–483.

——. "The Point of View of the Author." In *The Social Theories of Talcott Parsons*, edited by M. Black, 311–363. Englewood Cliffs, NJ: Prentice Hall, 1961.

——. "The Present Position and Prospects of Systematic Theory in Sociology." In *Essays in Sociological Theory*, 212–237. New York: Free Press, 1954.

——. "The Present Status of 'Structural-Functional' Theory in Sociology." In *Social Systems and the Evolution of Action Theory*, 100–117. New York: Free Press, 1977.

———. "Social Interaction." In *Social Systems and the Evolution of Action Theory*, 145–153. New York: Free Press, 1977.

———. "Social Structure and the Symbolic Media of Interchange." In *Social Systems and the Evolution of Action Theory*, 204–228. New York: Free Press, 1977.

———. *The Social System*. Glencoe, IL: Free Press, 1951.

———. "Social Systems." In *Social Systems and the Evolution of Action Theory*. New York: Free Press, 1977.

———. *Social Systems and the Evolution of Action Theory*. New York: Free Press, 1977.

———. *Societies: Evolutionary and Comparative Perspectives*. Englewood Cliffs, NJ: Prentice Hall, 1966.

———. "Some Problems of General Theory in Sociology." In *Social Systems and the Evolution of Action Theory*, 229–269. New York: Free Press, 1977.

———. *The Structure of Social Action*. New York: Free Press, 1964.

———. "The Superego and the Theory of Social Systems." In *Working Papers in the Theory of Action*, edited by Talcott Parsons, Robert F. Bales, and Edward A. Shils, 13–29. New York: Free Press, 1953.

———. *The System of Modern Societies*. Englewood Cliffs, NJ: Prentice Hall, 1971.

———. *Zur Theorie der sozialen Interaktionsmedien*, edited by Stefan Jensen. Opladen: Westdeutscher, 1980.

———. *Zur Theorie sozialer Systeme*, edited by Stefan Jensen. Opladen: Westdeutscher, 1976.

Parsons, Talcott, and Charles Ackerman. "The Concept of 'Social System' as a Theoretical Device." In *Concepts, Theory, and Explanation in the Behavioral Sciences*, edited by G. J. Di Renzo, 19–40. New York: Random House, 1966.

Parsons, Talcott, and E. A. Shils, eds. *Toward a General Theory of Action*. Cambridge, MA: Harvard University Press, 1959.

Paslak, Rainer. "Selbstorganisation und neue soziale Bewegungen." In *Selbstorganisation: Aspekte einer wissenschaftlichen Revolution*, edited by W. Krohn and G. Küppers, 280–301. Braunschweig: Vieweg, 1990.

Pereda, Carlos. "Zwei Modelle aufgeklärter Vernunft." In *Zur Verteidigung der Vernunft gegen ihre Liebhaber und Verächter*, edited by Ch. Menke and M. Seel, 129–148. Frankfurt: Suhrkamp, 1993.

Peters, Bernhardt. *Rationalität, Recht und Gesellschaft*. Frankfurt: Suhrkamp, 1991.

Picardi, Eva, and Joachim Schulte. *Die Wahrheit der Interpretation: Beiträge zur Philosophie Donald Davidsons*. Frankfurt: Suhrkamp, 1990.

Plato. "Phaedrus." Translated by Alexander Nehamas and Paul Woodruff. In *Plato: Complete Works*, edited by J. M. Cooper, 506–556. Indianapolis: Hackett, 1997.

Poe, Edgar Allan. "The Philosophy of Composition." *Graham's Magazine* 28 (1846): 163–167.

Poser, Hans. "Homo compensator? Über Bildung im Computer-Zeitalter." In *Computer, Kultur, Geschichte. Beiträge zur Philosophie des Informationszeitalters*, edited by D. Mersch and J. C. Nyíri, 87–108. Vienna: Passagen, 1991.

Postman, Neil. *Technopoly: The Surrender of Culture to Technology*. New York: Vintage Books, 1993.

Procter, Ian. "Voluntarism and Structural-Functionalism in Parsons' Early Work." *Human Studies* 3 (1980): 331–346.

Prokop, Dieter, ed. *Medienforschung: Band 1 Konzerne Macher Kontrolleure*. Frankfurt: Fischer, 1985.

———. *Medienforschung: Band 2 Wünsche Zielgruppen Wirkungen.* Frankfurt: Fischer, 1985.
———. *Medienforschung: Band 3 Analysen Kritiken Ästhetik.* Frankfurt: Fischer, 1986.
Putnam, Hilary. "Minds and Machines." In *Mind, Language and Reality*, 362–385. Cambridge: Cambridge University Press, 1975.
———. *Reason, Truth, and History.* Cambridge: Cambridge University Press, 1981.
Quante, Michael. "Rationalität—Zement des Geistes: Die pragmatische Rettung des Mentalen bei D. C. Dennett." In *Pragmatische Rationalitätstheorien: Studies in Pragmatism, Idealism, and Philosophy of Mind*, 223–268. Würzburg: Königshausen & Neumann, 1995.
Quine, Willard van Orman. *Word and Object.* Cambridge, MA: MIT Press, 1960.
Raffman, Diana. *Language, Music and Mind.* Cambridge, MA: MIT Press, 1993.
Raible, Wolfgang, ed. *Symbolische Formen—Medien—Identität.* Tübingen: Narr, 1991.
Raulet, Gérard. "The New Utopia: Communication Technologies." *Telos* 87 (1991): 39–58.
Rawls, John. "Two Concepts of Rules." *Philosophical Review* 64 (1955): 3–32.
Rescher, Nicholas. "On the Characterization of Actions." In *The Nature of Human Action*, edited by Myles Brand, 215–220. Glenview, IL: Scott Foresman, 1970.
Riegas, Volker, and Christian Vetter. *Zur Biologie der Kognition.* Frankfurt: Suhrkamp, 1990.
Riethmüller, Albrecht. "Stoff der Musik ist Klang und Körperbewegung." In *Materialität der Kommunikation*, edited by H. U. Gumbrecht and L. K. Pfeiffer, 51–62. Frankfurt: Suhrkamp, 1988.
Rochat, Philippe. "Early Objectivation of the Self." In *The Self in Early Infancy: Theory and Research*, edited by P. Rochat, 53–71. Amsterdam: Elsevier, 1995.
Ropohl, Günter. *Die unvollkommene Technik.* Frankfurt: Suhrkamp, 1985.
———. *Technologische Aufklärung: Beiträge zur Technikphilosophie.* Frankfurt: Suhrkamp, 1991.
Rorty, Richard. *Objectivity, Relativism and Truth.* Cambridge: Cambridge University Press, 1991.
———. "The Priority of Democracy to Philosophy." In *Objectivity, Relativism and Truth*, 175–196. Cambridge: Cambridge University Press, 1991.
———. "Solidarity or Objectivity?" In *Objectivity, Relativism and Truth*, 21–34. Cambridge: Cambridge University Press, 1991.
Roth, Gerhardt. "Autopoiese und Kognition: Die Theorie H. R. Maturanas und die Notwendigkeit ihrer Weiterentwicklung." In *Der Diskurs des Radikalen Konstruktivismus*, edited by S. J. Schmidt, 256–287. Frankfurt: Suhrkamp, 1991.
———. "Erkenntnis und Realität: Das reale Gehirn und seine Wirklichkeit." In *Der Diskurs des Radikalen Konstruktivismus*, edited by S. J. Schmidt, 229–255. Frankfurt: Suhrkamp, 1991.
———. "Gehirn und Selbstorganisation." In *Selbstorganisation: Aspekte einer wissenschaftlichen Revolution*, edited by W. Krohn and G. Küppers, 167–180. Braunschweig: Vieweg, 1990.
Rötzer, Florian. *Die Telepolis: Urbanität im digitalen Zeitalter.* Mannheim: Bollmann, 1995.
———. *Digitaler Schein: Ästhetik der elektronischen Medien.* Frankfurt: Suhrkamp, 1991.
———. "Zerstreute Bemerkungen und Hinweise eines irritierten informationsverarbeitenden Systems." In *Digitaler Schein: Ästhetik der elektronischen Medien*, edited by F. Rötzer, 9–78. Frankfurt: Suhrkamp, 1991.

Rueger, Christoph, ed. *Die musikalische Hausapotheke: Audio CDs*. Geneva: Ariston, 1991.
Rusch, Gebhard. "Kommunikation und Verstehen." In *Die Wirklichkeit der Medien: Eine Einführung in die Kommunikationswissenschaft*, edited by K. Merten, S. J. Schmidt, and S. Weischenberg, 60–78. Opladen: Westdeutscher, 1994.
Ryle, Gilbert. *The Concept of Mind*. Chicago: University of Chicago Press, 2000.
Scheer, Brigitte. *Einführung in die philosophische Ästhetik*. Darmstadt: Primus, 1997.
Scherer, Wolfgang. "'Aus der Seele muss man spielen': Instrumentelle und technische Bedingungen der musikalischen Empfindsamkeit." In *Materialität der Kommunikation*, edited by H. U. Gumbrecht and L. K. Pfeiffer, 295–309. Frankfurt: Suhrkamp, 1988.
Schluchter, Wolfgang, ed. *Verhalten, Handeln und System: Talcott Parsons' Beitrag zur Entwicklung der Sozialwissenschaften*. Frankfurt: Suhrkamp, 1980.
Schmidt, Michael. "Autopoiesis und soziales System: Eine Standortbestimmung." In *Sinn, Kommunikation und soziale Differenzierung. Beiträge zu Luhmanns Theorie sozialer Systeme*, edited by H. Haferkamp and M. Schmid, 25–50. Frankfurt: Suhrkamp, 1987.
Schmidt, Siegfried J., ed. *Der Diskurs des radikalen Konstruktivismus*. Frankfurt: Suhrkamp, 1991.
——. "Der Radikale Konstruktivismus: Ein neues Paradigma im interdisziplinären Diskurs." In *Der Diskurs des radikalen Konstruktivismus*, 11–88. Frankfurt: Suhrkamp, 1991.
——. "Die Wirklichkeit des Beobachters." In *Die Wirklichkeit der Medien: Eine Einführung in die Kommunikationswissenschaft*, edited by K. Merten, S. J. Schmidt, and S. Weischenberg, 3–19. Opladen: Westdeutscher, 1994.
——. "Konstruktivismus in der Medienforschung: Konzepte, Kritiken, Konsequenzen." In *Die Wirklichkeit der Medien. Eine Einführung in die Kommunikationswissenschaft*, edited by K. Merten, S. J. Schmidt, and S. Weischenberg, 595–623. Opladen: Westdeutscher, 1994.
Schnädelbach, Herbert. "'. . . dass p': Über Intentionalität und Sprache." In *Philosophie in der modernen Kultur*, 204–255. Frankfurt: Suhrkamp, 2000.
——. "Observations on Rationality and Language." In *Reason and Its Other: Rationality in Modern German Philosophy and Culture*, edited by Dieter Freundlieb and Wayne Hudson, 49–66. Oxford: Berg, 1993.
——. "Philosophie als Theorie der Rationalität." In *Zur Rehabilitierung des* animal rationale*: Vorträge und Abhandlungen*. Vol. 2, 41–60. Frankfurt: Suhrkamp, 1992.
——, ed. *Rationalität*. Frankfurt: Suhrkamp, 1984.
——. "Rationalität und Begründung." In *Zur Rehabilitierung des* animal rationale*: Vorträge und Abhandlungen*. Vol. 2, 61–78. Frankfurt: Suhrkamp, 1992.
——. "Rationalität und Normativität." In *Zur Rehabilitierung des* animal rationale: *Vorträge und Abhandlungen*. Vol. 2, 79–103. Frankfurt: Suhrkamp, 1992.
——. "Rationalitätstypen." In *Philosophie in der modernen Kultur*, 256–281. Frankfurt: Suhrkamp, 2000.
——. "The Transformation of Critical Theory." In *Communicative Action: Essays on Jürgen Habermas's Theory of Communicative Action*, edited by Axel Honneth and Hans Joas, 7–22. Cambridge: Polity, 1991.
——. "Über die Vernünftigkeit der Geschichte und die Geschichtlichkeit der Vernunft." In *Vernunft und Geschichte*, 9–20. Frankfurt: Suhrkamp, 1987.
——. "Über historische Aufklärung." In *Vernunft und Geschichte*, 23–46. Frankfurt: Suhrkamp, 1987.

———. "Über Rationalismus und Irrationalismus." In *Der Wissenschaftler und das Irrationale.* Vol. 2, *Beiträge aus Philosophie und Psychologie,* edited by H. P. Duerr, 155–164. Frankfurt: Syndikat, 1981.

———. "Vernunft." In *Philosophie: Ein Grundkurs,* edited by E. Martens and H. Schnädelbach, 77–110. Reinbek: Rowohlt, 1986.

———. *Vernunft und Geschichte.* Frankfurt: Suhrkamp, 1987.

———. "Zur Rehabilitierung des *animal rationale.*" In *Zur Rehabilitierung des* animal rationale: *Vorträge und Abhandlungen.* Vol. 2, 13–37. Frankfurt: Suhrkamp, 1992.

———. *Zur Rehabilitierung des* animal rationale: *Vorträge und Abhandlungen.* Vol. 2. Frankfurt: Suhrkamp, 1992.

Schulte, Joachim. "Nachwort." In *Der Mythos des Subjektiven: Philosophische Essays,* edited by Donald Davidson, 109–117. Stuttgart: Reclam, 1993.

Schulte-Sasse, Jochen. "Von der schriftlichen zur elektronischen Kultur: Über neuere Wechselbeziehungen zwischen Mediengeschichte und Kulturgeschichte." In *Materialität der Kommunikation,* edited by H. U. Gumbrecht and L. K. Pfeiffer, 429–453. Frankfurt: Suhrkamp, 1988.

Schuster, Thomas. *Staat und Medien: Über die elektronische Konditionierung der Wirklichkeit.* Frankfurt: Fischer, 1995.

Schwegler, Helmut. "Autopoiese aus physikalischer Sicht." In *Zur Biologie der Kognition,* edited by V. Riegas and C. Vetter, 91–98. Frankfurt: Suhrkamp, 1990.

Schwemmer, Oswald. "Glanz und Elend der Medienkultur." In *Medien und Gesellschaft,* edited by W. von Bredow, 15–39. Stuttgart: Hirzel, 1990.

Searle, John R. *The Construction of Social Reality.* New York: Free Press, 1995.

———. *Intentionality: An Essay in the Philosophy of Mind.* Cambridge: Cambridge University Press, 1983.

———. *Minds, Brains and Science.* Cambridge, MA: Harvard University Press, 1984.

———. "What Is a Speech Act?" In *Readings in Language and Mind,* edited by H. Geirsson and Michael Losonsky, 110–120. London: Blackwell, 1996.

Seel, Martin. "Bestimmen und Bestimmenlassen: Anfänge einer medialen Erkenntnistheorie." *Deutsche Zeitschrift für Philosophie* 3 (1998): 351–365.

———. *Die Kunst der Entzweiung: Zum Begriff der ästhetischen Rationalität.* Frankfurt: Suhrkamp, 1985.

———. "Die zwei Bedeutungen 'kommunikativer' Rationalität." In *Kommunikatives Handeln,* edited by A. Honneth and H. Joas, 53–72. Frankfurt: Suhrkamp, 1986.

———. "Medien der Realität und Realität der Medien." In *Medien, Computer, Realität,* edited by S. Krämer, 244–268. Frankfurt: Suhrkamp, 1998.

Shannon, Claude E., and Warren Weaver. *The Mathematical Theory of Communication.* Urbana: University of Illinois Press, 1963.

Silbermann, Alphons, and Udo Michael Krüger. *Soziologie der Massenkommunikation.* Stuttgart: Kohlhammer, 1973.

Simon, H. A. *Die Wissenschaften vom Künstlichen.* Berlin: Kammerer & Unverzagt, 1990.

Specht, R. "Modalität." In *Historisches Wörterbuch der Philosophie.* Vol. 6, edited by J. Ritter, 9–12. Basel: Schwabe 1984.

Spengler, Tilmann. "Die Entdeckung der chinesischen Wissenschafts- und Technikgeschichte." In *Wissenschaftlicher Universalismus: Über die Besonderheit der chinesischen Wissenschaft,* edited by J. Needham, 7–52. Frankfurt: Suhrkamp, 1979.

Spitzley, Thomas. "Zur Rationalitätsannahme bei Davidson." In *Pragmatische Rationalitätstheorien: Studies in Pragmatism, Idealism, and Philosophy of Mind,* edited by A. Wüstehube, 205–221. Würzburg: Königshausen & Neumann, 1995.

Stegmüller, Wilhelm. "Die zweite industrielle Revolution hat eben begonnen." *Kursbuch* 66 (1981): 152–188.
Stegmüller, Wolfgang. *Kripkes Deutung der Spätphilosophie Wittgensteins: Kommentarversuch über einen versuchten Kommentar.* Stuttgart: Kröner, 1986.
Stichweh, Rudolf. "Rationalität bei Parsons." *Zeitschrift für Soziologie* 1 (1980): 54–78.
——. "Selbstorganisation in der Entstehung des modernen Wissenschaftssystems." In *Selbstorganisation: Aspekte einer wissenschaftlichen Revolution*, edited by W. Krohn and G. Küppers, 265–277. Braunschweig: Vieweg, 1990.
Stonier, Tom. *Information and the Internal Structure of the Universe.* London: Springer, 1990.
Tallár, Ferenc. "Worüber sprechen wir?" In *Zur Verteidigung der Vernunft gegen ihre Liebhaber und Verächter*, edited by Ch. Menke and M. Seel, 15–25. Frankfurt: Suhrkamp, 1993.
Taube, Mortimer. *Computers and Common Sense: The Myth of Thinking Machines.* New York: Columbia University Press, 1961.
Teubner, Gunther. "Hyperzyklus in Recht und Organisation: Zum Verhältnis von Selbstbeobachtung, Selbstkonstitution und Autopoiese." In *Selbstorganisation: Aspekte einer wissenschaftlichen Revolution*, edited by W. Krohn and G. Küppers, 231–263. Braunschweig: Vieweg, 1990.
Tietz, Udo. "Die Rationalität des Verstehens." In *Die eine Vernunft und die vielen Rationalitäten*, edited by K.-O. Apel and M. Kettner, 373–403. Frankfurt: Suhrkamp, 1996.
——. "Vernunft und Verstehen: Bemerkungen zum Verhältnis von formaler und materialer Rationalität." In *Sichim Denken orientieren*, edited by Simone Dietz, Heiner Hastedt, Geert Keil, and Anke Thyen, 84–102. Frankfurt: Suhrkamp, 1997.
Tuomela, Raimo. *The Importance of Us: A Philosophical Study of Basic Social Notions.* Stanford, CA: Stanford University Press, 1995.
Tuomela, Raimo, and Kaarlo Miller. "WeIntentions." *Philosophical Studies* 53 (1988): 367–389.
Turing, Alan Mathison. *Collected Works of A. M. Turing: Mechanical Intelligence.* Edited by D. C. Ince. Amsterdam: Elsevier Science, 1992.
Turkle, Sherry. *The Second Self: Computers and the Human Spirit.* New York: Simon & Schuster, 1984.
Ulshöfer, Andrea. "Überlegungen zu den mesopotamischen Listen als Phänomene früher Verschriftlichung." In *Symbolische Formen—Medien—Identität*, edited by W. Raible, 147–169. Tübingen: Narr, 1991.
Unseld, Godela. *Maschinenintelligenz oder Menschenphantasie.* Frankfurt: Suhrkamp, 1992.
Vámos, Tibor. "Rechnerwissenschaft und Demokratie." In *Computer, Kultur, Geschichte: Beiträge zur Philosophie des Informationszeitalters*, edited by D. Mersch and J. C. Nyíri, 15–20. Vienna: Passagen, 1991.
Varela, Francisco J. *Kognitionswissenschaft-Kognitionstechnik: Eine Skizze aktueller Perspektiven.* Frankfurt: Suhrkamp, 1990.
Varela, Francisco, and Evan Thompson. *The Embodied Mind: Cognitive Science and Human Experience.* Cambridge, MA: MIT Press, 1991.
Vester, Heinz-Günther. *Die Thematisierung des Selbst in der postmodernen Gesellschaft.* Bonn: Bouvier, 1984.
Vief, Bernhardt. "Digitales Geld." In *Digitaler Schein: Ästhetik der elektronischen Medien*, edited by F. Rötzer, 117–146. Frankfurt: Suhrkamp, 1991.

Virilio, Paul. *The Aesthetics of Disappearance*. New York: Semiotext(e), 1991.
———. *Speed and Politics: An Essay on Dromology*. New York: Semiotext(e), 1977.
———. *The Vision Machine*. Bloomington: Indiana University Press, 1994.
Vogel, Matthias. "Medien im Experiment der Demokratie." In *Demokratischer Experimentalismus*, edited by Hauke Brunkhorst, 104–143. Frankfurt: Suhrkamp, 1998.
Wallace, John. "Positive, Comparative, Superlative." *Journal of Philosophy* 69 (1972): 773–782.
Watzlawick, Paul. "Verschreiben statt Verstehen als Technik von Problemlösungen." In *Materialität der Kommunikation*, edited by H. U. Gumbrecht and L. K. Pfeiffer, 878–883. Frankfurt: Suhrkamp, 1988.
Weber, Max. "Die Wirtschaftsethik der Weltreligionen I." In *Gesammelte Aufsätze zur Religionssoziologie I*, 276–536. Tübingen: Mohr, 1988.
Webern, Anton. *The Path to the New Music*. Edited by Willi Reich. Bryn Mawr, PA: Presser, 1963.
Weidemann, H. "Modalanalyse." In *Historisches Wörterbuch der Philosophie*. Vol. 6, edited by J. Ritter, 3–7. Basel: Schwabe, 1984.
Weingarten, Rüdiger. *Die Verkabelung der Sprache: Grenzen der Technisierung von Kommunikation*. Frankfurt: Fischer, 1989.
———, ed. *Information ohne Kommunikation? Die Loslösung der Sprache vom Sprecher*. Frankfurt: Fischer, 1990.
Weizenbaum, Joseph. *Die Macht der Computer und die Ohnmacht der Vernunft*. Frankfurt: Suhrkamp, 1978.
———. *Kurs auf den Eisberg: Oder nur das Wunder wird uns retten, sagt der Computerexperte*. Zurich: Pendo, 1984.
Wellmer, Albrecht. "Was ist eine pragmatische Bedeutungstheorie? Variationen über den Satz 'Wir verstehen einen Sprechakt, wenn wir wissen, was ihn akzeptabel macht.'" In *Zwischenbetrachtungen: Im Prozess der Aufklärung*, edited by A. Honneth, T. McCarthy, C. Offe, and A. Wellmer, 318–372. Frankfurt: Suhrkamp, 1989.
Welsch, Wolfgang. *Ästhetisches Denken*. Stuttgart: Reclam, 1993.
———. "Die Geburt der postmodernen Philosophie aus den Geist der modernen Kunst." In *Ästhetisches Denken*, 79–113. Stuttgart: Reclam, 1993.
———. *Die zeitgenössische Vernunftkritik und das Konzept der transversalen Vernunft*. Frankfurt: Suhrkamp, 1995.
———. "Identität im Übergang." In *Ästhetisches Denken*, 168–200. Stuttgart: Reclam, 1993.
———. "Perspektiven für das Design der Zukunft." In *Ästhetisches Denken*, 201–218. Stuttgart: Reclam, 1993.
———. *Vernunft: Die zeitgenössische Vernunftkritik und das Konzept der transversalen Vernunft*. Frankfurt: Suhrkamp, 1996.
———. "Vernunft und Übergang: Zum Begriff der transversalen Vernunft." In *Die eine Vernunft und die vielen Rationalitäten*, edited by K.-O. Apel and M. Kettner, 139–205. Frankfurt: Suhrkamp, 1996.
———, ed. *Wege aus der Moderne: Schlüsseltexte der Postmoderne—Diskussion*. Weinheim: VCH, 1988.
Wenzel, Harald. "Einige Bemerkungen zu Parsons' Programm einer Theorie des Handelns." In *Aktor, Situation und normative Muster*, by T. Parsons, edited by H. Wenzel, 7–58. Frankfurt: Suhrkamp, 1994.

Wieland, Wolfgang. "Platons Schriftkritik und die Grenzen der Mitteilbarkeit." In *Romantik: Literatur und Philosophie*, edited by V. Bohn, 24–44. Frankfurt: Suhrkamp, 1987.

Wiener, Norbert. *Cybernetics: Or Control and Communication in the Animal and the Machine*. Cambridge, MA: MIT Press, 1965.

Wiener, Oswald. *Probleme der künstlichen Intelligenz*. Berlin: Merve, 1990.

Wiesenthal, Helmut. "Die Ratlosigkeit des homo oeconomicus." In Introduction to *Subversion der Rationalität*, by Jon Elster, 7–19. Frankfurt: Campus, 1987.

Wiggershaus, Rolf. "Zum Begriff der Regel in der Philosophie der Umgangssprache über Wittgenstein, Austin und Searle." PhD diss., Frankfurt, 1974.

Willke, Helmut. "Differenzierung und Integration in Luhmanns Theorie sozialer Systeme." In *Sinn, Kommunikation und soziale Differenzierung: Beiträge zu Luhmanns Theorie sozialer Systeme*, edited by H. Haferkamp and M. Schmid, 247–274. Frankfurt: Suhrkamp, 1987.

Winkler, Hartmut. *Docuverse: Zur Medientheorie der Computer*. N.p.: Klaus Boer, 1997.

Winograd, Terry, and Fernando Flores. *Understanding Computers and Cognition: A New Foundation for Design*. Reading, MA: Addison-Wesley, 1987.

Wüstenhube, Axel, ed. *Pragmatische Realitätstheorien: Studies in Pragmatism, Idealism, and Philosophy of Mind*. Würzburg: Königshausen & Neumann, 1995.

——. "Pragmatische Realitätstheorien: Zur Einführung." In *Pragmatische Realitätstheorien: Studies in Pragmatism, Idealism, and Philosophy of Mind*, 9–27. Würzburg: Königshausen & Neumann, 1995.

Youngblood, Gene. "Metadesign." In *Digitaler Schein: Ästhetik der elektronischen Medien*, edited by F. Rötzer, 305–322. Frankfurt: Suhrkamp, 1991.

Zahn, Manfred. "System." In *Handbuch philosophischer Grundbegriffe*. Vol. 3, edited by H. Krings, H. M. Baumgartner, and C. Wild, 1458–1475. Munich: Kösel, 1974.

Zanetti, Véronique. "Kann man ohne Körper denken? Über das Verhältnis von Leib und Bewusstsein bei Luhmann und Kant." In *Materialität der Kommunikation*, edited by H. U. Gumbrecht and L. K. Pfeiffer, 280–294. Frankfurt: Suhrkamp, 1988.

Zimmer, Dieter E. "Deus in machina. oder: Wieviel Geist steckt im Computer." *Die Zeit* 22 (1990): 54.

——. "Wie kommt der Geist in den Kopf." *Die Zeit* 29 (1990): 42.

Zimmerli, Walter Ch., ed. *Technologisches Zeitalter oder Postmoderne*. Munich: Fink, 1991.

Žižek, Slavoj. *The Ticklish Subject*. London: Verso, 2000.

Zuse, Konrad. *Der Computer mein Lebenswerk*. Berlin: Springer, 1990.

INDEX

Italic page numbers indicate material in tables or figures.

action-related functional assignments, 245
actions: coordination of, 36, 83–86, 89, 113; general system of, *82*, 86, 95–96; intentional vs. nonintentional, 99–102; rationality of, 46–49, 277; rationalization of, 217–218; status of, 227–228, 302; types of, 147, 300. *See also* artistic action
action-theoretic conception of media, 96–99, 115, 123–124
Adorno, Theodor W., 1–2, 120–121
aesthetic attitude, 302
aesthetic communication, 109–111, 192, 219–220, 267–268, 290, 305
aesthetic experience, 98, 283–286, 291–292
aesthetic idea, 287–288, 291
affect-centered communication, 180, 183–187, *187*
A-intentional states, 130–136, 167, *208*; as biological phenomena, 187; and conditions of satisfaction, 175–176; connecting causal reconstruction and reason, 133; content of, 132; distinguishing from thoughts, 132, 206; intrinsically intentional, 131–132, 206–207; lack of constraint of, 296–297; preliminary criterion for, 131, 175, 303
Alex the parrot, 171–172

alternatives *for*, 50, 132, 225–228, 297, 302
animals: behavioral options of, 225–226; birds, 226, 338n5; disposition to expressive behavior, 237–238; hunting of, 247; nonspeaking, 126–127; play among, 238–239
anthropological openness, 16, 18–19
antirealistic theory of meaning, 59
Apel, Karl-Otto, 42
apprehending comprehension, 298
argumentative discourse as final authority, 14
art: explaining rejection of, 112; as freest form of communication, 107, 109; and linguistic paradigm, ix; understanding, 137–143, 155. *See also* music; painting; works of art
Art as Experience (Dewey), 97, 105, 110
articulation(s): acts of, 134–136; artistic, 104; of interests/emotional states, 83, 191, 277; optimizing, 193–194; of self-understanding, 305; vs. thoughts, 173
artifacts as words, 95
artificial actions, 217–218
artistic action, 97; vs. artistic activity, 140–141; instrumentalist analysis of, 123; and intrinsic intentionality, 132; understanding, 139
art lessons, 156–157

art sketches and studies, purpose of, 300–301
ASCII, 263
ascription of nonintrinsic features, 243–244
assignment of a function, 244
assimilationist strategies, 203
associative learning, 238
Aufgeklärtes Eigeninteresse (Gosepath), 45
Austin, John, 36–37, 59
authority(ies): argumentative discourse as, 14; and autonomy, 51–52; external to reason, 28–29; narrative as, 4; for rightness, 161
autodestructive self-reference, 17
autonomy and rationality, 51–52

Bachmann, Ingeborg, 283
background, redundant, 298
back-scratching primate example, 233–240
basal rationality, 73–74, 141–142, 297, 301–302
Baudelaire, Charles, 254
Baudrillard, Jean, 114
beauty, concept of, 288–289
Becker, Alexander, 70
behavior as action, 116
belief, 127; formation of, 47–48; required for thoughts, 167–168
"billion pesetas" and relational identity, 171
binary schematism, 92
B-intentional states, *208*; content of, 216–217, 273–274; development of, 190–198, *198*; distinguished from A- and C-intentionality, 200, 206–207; and "I think" requirement, 213; linguistic beliefs about, 210–211, 213, 215; as medial thoughts, 280–281; transindividual individuation of, 301
biofeedback and mirroring emotion, 184–185
biological phenomena: consciousness and, 242–243; and evolutionary theory, 44; intentionality states as, 133, 178, 187, 241, 245–247
biologism, 95
birdsongs, 226, 338n5
Bleu de Ciel (Kandinsky) reproduction, 254–255
Brandom, Robert B., 106, 203, 273, 279
bricks-and-mortar example, 101

cameras, 264
Cassirer, Ernst, 112
cathode ray tubes, 264
cat on mat example, 139
causal reference theory, 65, 99, 107, 278
chess, 159–160
children: becoming producers, 193–194; under Davidson's theory of mind, 182; intentional states of, 130–134; mental development of, 178; painting by, 276; reaching toward object, 130–131, 133–136. *See also* phase model of child development
Chomsky, Noam, 43–44, 122
chosen activities, 166. *See also* alternatives *for*
Christianity, 25
C-intentional states, 198–203, *208*, 259, *265*, 265–266
circle of self-sufficient self-justification, 28
circularity pitfalls, 52–57, 69, 88, 106
citation, 209–210
code concept, 80–82, 84, 90–91, 263
cognition generally, 284–286, 291
cognitive faculties, 291
cognitive instrumental reason, 34
cognitive rule implementation, 150
cognitive starting point, 47
collective experience, 112
collective intentionality, 244, 245–248
colors: as the painting, 101; substitutability of, 252, 255
communication: and aesthetic experiences, 286–290; art as freest form of, 107–108; as coordinated selections, 89; by example, 156–158; medium always a mode of, 102–104
communicative action, 38
communicative competence, 42–43
communicative intentions, 59, 61
communicative reason, 34
communicative rule competence, 35
communicative sociation, 13
community-shaping processes, 112
competency: competencies for understanding, 57, 282–283; multiplication as a, 152; rationality as a, 34, 42, 50
competition and rational standards, 48
"completely other," 23
composed unity, 145
compositional identity: of an expression (CI_0, CIE_1, CIE_2), 165–166, 171–173;

and B-intentional states, 207; in child development, 196, 199–200; and nonlinguistic thought, 169, 215; and substitutability, 253; of a work of art, 145–147
compositionality of language, 202–203
comprehensibility of sensory objects, 286
concepts: of belief/thought, 127, 207, 210; of meaning and of desire, 133; as necessary conditions for aesthetic experiences, 285
conditionality analysis, 195, 238–239
conditions for the possibility of choice, 51
conditions of satisfaction, 129, 175–177, *190*, 191
congruous methodic relativism, 22
connecting actions/behavior, 202, 238–239
consciousness: of B-intentional state optionality, 213–215; and biological phenomena, 242–243; of conditions of satisfaction, 175–176; content and, 212; evolution and ontology of, 242; interactionism and emergence of, 178–179; systems and ontology of, 242
consensus in the lifeworld, 86
conservation principle, 69–70
constitutive rules, 105–107, 244, 248, 250
Construction of Social Reality, The (Searle), 241
constructive vote of distrust, 24
content: acquiring, 181, 197; of an intentional state, 176, 206–208; and contentful states, 167–168; and content-unspecified assumption, 65; for interpreter only, 206; of media, 95, 211, 273–275; mental states with, 205–207, 273–275; of nonlinguistic artistic thoughts, 215; of nonlinguistic expressions, 274; for performer, 206–207
contextualist relativism, 21–22
contextually accessible attributes, 299
continence principle, 69–70
contingency concept, 90
contingent rule-following, 153
cooking, art of, 111
cool media, 94
coordinated selections, 89

correlations based on understanding, 299
correlations in interpretation (C1, C2), 292–293
creativity vs. rule breaking, 153
criteria of optional rationality, 302–303
criterion of development, 33
criticism, mutual, 39
critique: as form of Enlightenment, 13, 17; nonlinguistic, 280; reason as medium of, 26, 31
Critique of Judgment (Kant), 283, 291
Critique of Pure Reason (Kant), 285
crying, 100
cultural fiduciary system (L), 81, *82*
cultural imperialism, 20
cultural invariances, 48
culturalist concept of rationality, 12, 31

dance, 158, 164, 212
Dante, 254–257
Dante Symphonie (Liszt) substitution, 254–257
Danto, Arthur C., 252
Davidson, Donald, xi; on criteria for thoughts, 167–169, 181, 205, 207–208, 213; and intentionality, 131–132; on "I think" requirement for thought, 213; on language as a behavioral pattern, 126–128; and radical interpretation, 106; triangulation model of, 66–67, 181–182, 278; on truth semantics, 35–36, 168, 181; and understanding, 58–71
Davies, Stephen, 146–147
decentering of reason, 25–26, 28
decision theory principles, 69
deficient language, music as, 121
deictic practice, 64, 161, 162, 278–279
demasking critique, 2–3, 26
demonstrative rules, 250, 277–280, 290
demonstrative structuring, 158
demythologizing history of reason, 27
Dennett, Daniel C., 286
Descartes, René, 25
design stance, 286
determinant judgment, 284
Dewey, John, 96–113; action-theoretic conception of, 96–99, 115; and aesthetic communication, 108–111, 192, 219–220; bricks-and-mortar analogy of, 101; on distinguishing media, 251;

Dewey, John (*continued*)
  on media as established means, 103–106; on media as mode of language, 102–103; on media incorporation into product, 100; normative component of views of, 113; optimism of, 107, 111–112
diagnosis of convergence. *See* media convergence thesis
direct citation, 209
directions of fit, 74, 129, 134, 138, 175
distanced observer perspective, 8–9
distribution media, 90, 92
Divina Commedia, La (Dante), substitution, 254–257
Divine Comedy, The (Dante), substitution, 254–257
divisions of labor, 153, 178–179
"do it like this" training, 155–158
downward compatibility, 32
Dretske, Fred, 132
Dummett, Michael, 35–36
duplication rules, 91–92

economic system (A), 81, *82*, 86
economy of attention, 297–298, 302
economy of individuation, 302
educational processes, 302, 305
elementary media operations, 252–266
elucidative rationality, 279
emancipation from reason, 9
emphatic normative theories, 25
English Garden in Munich example, 172
Enlightenment: achieving the, 15–24; crisis of the, 1–4, 6; defining, viii, 8–14; and Enlightenment idea of reason, 13; media of the, 303–305; minimal conception of (A2), 16; normative foundation of, 17, 24; as a process (A1), 15, 75, 303
epistemic states, 180–181
errors and mistakes, 53
essential difference, 22
established means, media as, 103
ethnocentricity, 20
evolution: and action coordination, 85–86; and language, 128; and ontology of consciousness, 242; and rule concept, 44; and transition to speaking, 233–240
exaggeration in teaching, 158, 184
exceptionalist strategies, 203
exchange model, 81, 84–85, 90

existential philosophy, 26
experiences remembered as unities, 97
explicitness, 279–281
explicit vs. implicit rules, 149–151
expressions: goals vs. means of, 139–140; internal expression of thoughts, 174; propositional, 170; semantically intrinsically empty, 274–275, 297
expressive actions, 59; choices of, 189–190; connecting, 238–239, 274; self-presentations, 34; understanding as works of art, 137–138; varying the performance of, 238
extensional theory of meaning, 63
externalist theories of mind, 182–183, 186

false substantiation, 251
feedback processes, 53
film, 264
financial transactions as conversation, 84
finger-positioning medium, 232
fingerprints as natural signs, 338n5
finite axiomatization, 63
first-order media, 259–260, 262
"fitting" into nature, 286
Fleurs du Mal, Les (Baudelaire), substitution, 254, 257
folk psychological competencies, 179, 188
Føllesdal, Dagfinn, 278
formal reasons, 54
formal semantics, 60
forms of rightness (R1, R2), 161, 290
four-function schema (AGIL), 81–83
four-phase schema: assumptions of, 179–180, 234; (phase 1) affect-centered communication, 183–187, *187*, 216, 297; (phase 2) instrumental communication, 187–190, *190*; (phase 3) medial communication, 190–198, *198*, 276; (phase 4) linguistic communication, 198–203
Frankfurt School, 40
freedom, individual, 50–51, 82–83
Frege, Gottlob, 60, 202–203, 221
Freud, Sigmund, 53
functional assignments, 244–246
functionalism, 29, 226

Gadamer, Hans-Georg, 93
game, musical practice as a, 148, 224–225

Gehlen, Arnold, 53
generalization procedure, 84, 88–89
general reasonableness, criterion of, 32–33
general system of action, *82*
general validity of taste judgments, 288–289
genetic dispositions, 183, 186, 192, 237–238
geniuses and rules, 156
Gergely, György, 184–185
goals: as anthropological constancy, 47–48; and choice of means, 53; as contingent, 9; differentiating tools from media via, 100–101; media in intrinsic relationship to, 101–102, 110, 141
Goodman, Nelson, 209–210
Gosepath, Stefan, 45–52, 55
grammatical network of culture, 31
Grice, H. Paul, 59, 61

Habermas, Jürgen, xi, *29*; on argumentative justification and sincerity, 41–42; on consensus through discussion, 6; and double function of media, 241; on Enlightenment as incomplete, 3; Luhmann on, 10; on meaning and validity, 33, 36, 40–42; on media, 85–89, *88*; on normative construction of Enlightenment, 13–14; on philosophy, 6, 24–25; problem of regress in, 43; rationality construct of, 33–45; and rule concept, 43–45; and theory of communicative reason, 27; truth-analogous validity claim of, 141; types of action proposed by, *39*
habits, 151–152
habitual rationality, 74–75, 302
Hanslick, Eduard, 121
Hegel, Georg Wilhelm Friedrich, 2, 25, *29*, 102
heuristic hypothesis, 245
higher-level intentionality: artistic action and, 141; and child development, 134, 179–183; C-intentional states and, 198–203, *208*, *259*, *265*, 265–266; and dependence on social media, 136; and nonlinguistic thoughts, 132–136, 143, 174–175, 196, 197; (HI) schema, 133; and truth predicate, 168–169. *See also* B-intentional states
higher-order media, 262–263

historical competence criterion, 16, 19
historical materialism, 93, 95
Höffe, Ottfried, 283
holism, 64
homogenizing universalism, 20–21
horoscopes, 31
hot media, 94
hunting of animals, 247
hypothetical media, 224, 294
hypothetical-universalistic standards, 24

illocutionary speech acts, 36–37, *37*
Imagination and Understanding, 290
implicit vs. explicit rules, 149–151
indirect citation, 209
individual freedom, 50–51, 82–83
individuation: of A-intentional states, 176; of content, 275, 278; of higher-level intentional states, 272, 302; of nonlinguistic thoughts, 169–179; Searle on problem of, 129; of thoughts, 57, 168–169
influence, media of, 83–84
information science, 84
inherent rationality of media practices, 295–296
inhibition of expression: in child development, 196; inhibited performance as object of experience, 216–217; and obtaining content in social interaction, 275; and thinking as inhibited speaking, 174, 203, 204–205, 218
institutional facts, 248–249
institutionalization of media, 83, 88, 119, 249–250, 261–262
instrumental action, *39*, 122–123
instrumental communication, 187–190, *190*, 199
instrumental rationality, 11, 34, 50
instrumental work, viii–ix
instruments of reason, media as, 141, 269–272
intellectualist legend, 151, 153
intelligent capacities, 151
intelligible variation, 226
intensional springs, 62
intentionality: apart from language, 125; as basis of language, 128–130, 132; as biological phenomenon, 241; and choosing intentional states, 131; and C-intentional states, 198–203, *208*, *259*, *265*, 265–266; and individuation of states, 131; and intentional

intentionality (*continued*)
  stance, 180; intentional vs. nonintentional action, 99–102, 195–196; intrinsic, 175; language as condition for, 125–128, 219; prelinguistic nature of, 128; and rules of art-making, 157; and theory of meaning, 62; transitioning between states of, 136; we- vs. I-intentionality, 245. *See also* A-intentional states; B-intentional states; higher-level intentionality
Intentionality (Searle), 128
interactionist theory, 178
intermedial tools, 266
internalist thesis, 45, 50
interpersonal action coordination model, 84
interpreters/interpretationism, 178; charitable, 223; and child development, 133–134, 179–183; and compositional identity, 173, 298; conditions for success of, 298; development of competence of, 233–240; expanded by media theory, 119–126; and habitual rationality, 302; internalization of, 237; and language, 126–127, 141, 199–200, 304; and media typology, 258; and metalanguage, 120; of (possibly) nonlinguistic expressions, 221–230, 274; principles for judging, 304; radical interpretation, 58; rationality standards of, 140; reconstructing compositional identity, 298; and Searle's ontology, 243; transpositions as, 257
intersubjective truth, 167
intrinsically empty behavior/expressions, 239, 274–275, 297
intrinsic intentionality, 175; and A-intentional states, 131–132, 206–207; and nonlinguistic intentionality, 142–143; precluding reference to other states, 236–237
intrinsic satisfiers, 83
intrinsic vs. observer-relative features, 243–246
intuition, 120–122; Kant and, 284, 288, 290; of language analogy (I_1), 122, 132; of special form of intentionality (I_2), 123–124, 132, 148
inventive people, 156
irrationality, explaining, 54, 68, 70–71, 75
"I think," the, 213

justification procedures, 11; and argumentative justification, 41; and criterion of development, 33; and pre-understanding, 53, 56; and rationality, 26, 34, 42, 45, 51–57; and relativism, 21

Kambartel, Friedrich, 30–31, 33
Kandinsky, Wassily, 254–255
Kant, Immanuel, 25, *29*, 97, 104; and intuition, 284, 288, 290; on music and art lessons, 156–157; on presentations requiring "I think," 213; on rules in art, 289–290; on works of art, 287–288
Kerman, Joseph, 155–156
know-how vs. rules, 158–159
knowledge: as contingent, 9; fallible knowledge, 34; finite knowledge, 60, 63; narrative forms of, 4–5; postmodern knowledge, 7; pre-theoretical knowledge, 35; rationality and, 34; of rules, 67, 148, 154, 250, 256, 314n144; scientific knowledge, 4–5
Künzler, Jan, 78, 93

Langer, Susanne, 112
language(s): ascription of reasons presupposing, 225; as behavioral pattern, 126; compositionality of, 202–203; as condition for intentionality, 126–128, 219; Dewey and, 103; and individuation of truth-apt thoughts, 259; as late product of evolution, 128; media with institutional attributes dependent on, 249; as medium for giving/asking for reasons, 275; money as, 84–85, 261–262; moving rationality beyond, 125; music as, 120–122, 221–230; natural languages, 63–64; negation potential of, 91–92; as one medium among others, x; original mode of, 36; Parsons's model of, 87, 103; private languages, 111; propositional attitudes as, 259; and radical interpretation situation, 58; rationality moving beyond, 125; reducing improbability of understanding, 89; relationship of reason and, 272; role of, 275, 304; and sentences, 66, 69, 272–273; as species criterion, 18; and speech acts, 36–38, 137–138; thinking without,

117, 167–179. *See also* linguistic communication
latent universalism, 22
Laws of Media (McLuhan), 93, 95
learning process, viii
lessons, 155–159
levity, 15
lifeworld, 86–87
light-mindedness, 11
linguistic action, 13, 36, 42, 67, 115
linguistic citations, 209–210
linguistic communication, 198–203; vs. aesthetic communication, 108; and linguistic competence, 42; pretheoretical knowledge and, 35; relating expressive actions and circumstances, 200–201; thinking as inhibited speaking, 174. *See also* language(s)
linguistic paradigm, ix–x
linguistic turn, 124–125, 292
linguistification of the sacred, 13
Liszt, Franz, 254
locutionary speech acts, 36–37, *37*
logic: music and, 121; relativism and laws of, 47; of sentence structure, 69; systems logic, 86, 89
logical network of thoughts, 68, 168
logos, 25
Luhmann, Niklas, *29*; on Enlightenment as bankrupt, 3; on Habermas, 10; on technology and emancipation, 9; theory of social systems of, 89–93, 241; on virtue of the postmodern, 7
Lyotard, Jean-François, 3, 5, 7

marking, 185, 297
Marquard, Odo, 8–9
mass media, 87
material as medium, 102–105, 112, 146–149
materialism, historical, 93, 95
materially identical doubles, 252
material reasons, 54–55
maximization demand, 299–302
McLuhan, Marshall: on effects of media on users, 93–95; on media as extensions of man, 79, 94–95; and media tools, 263–264; on reliance on media-dependent possibilities, 115; three-phase development process of, 94
meaning: antirealistic theory of, 59; concepts of, 133; extensional theory of, 63; Habermas on, 33, 36, 40–42; intentionalist theory of, 62; Searle on, 129, 202; theory of (TM), 61–63; verificationist theory of, 129; of works of art, 119–123
means as medium, 100–103
means incorporated into outcome, 100–101
media convergence thesis: (M1), 116, 162; (M2), 147, 162, 297; (M3, M3.1), 162–163; (M4), 163; (M5, M5.1), 164; (M6), 164; (M7), 216; (M8), 217, 295; (M9), 217, 295; (M10), 241, 249; (M11), 250; (M12), 295; (M13), 296–297; (M14), 297; and compositional identity, 172; using to identify media, 251, 295
media effects on users/recipients: aesthetic communication and, 98–99, 108–109, 192–194; anticipating the, 205; and judging success of translation/reproduction, 218, 253–257; Kant on, 157; McLuhan on, 93–95; protomedial expressions and, 239; social context and, 197, 274
medial communication: and development of B-intentionality, 190–198, *198*; and expressions acquiring new roles, 199–200, 216; function of, 216
medial constellations: content of, 217, 275, 295; distinguished from medial tools, 264–265; and explicitness, 280; in first-order media, 263; interpretation of, 292–295; obtaining independence, 300–301; production of, 276–277; reconstructed and reproduced, 297; relationships between, 252; structure of, 299–300
media/medium, 216–217; articulation of, 189, 191–192, 216; attributes of, 227; and codes, 263; concept and role of, 116; concept of, x, 78; as conditions of reason, 273–282; dualism of, 87–89; elements and attributes of, 162–165, 262, 299; and expressive, communicatory intention, 102; and forms of reference, 210–211; of generalized communication, 87; hot and cool media, 94; of influence, 83–84; with institutional attributes, 249–250; as instruments of reason, 141, 269–272; means as, 100–103; as mediator, 98; as message, 94;

media/medium (*continued*)
as motivationally effective mechanisms, 83; performative proliferation of, 103–105, 112; as schema, 99; as social entities, 250; structure of, 217, 294; as subsystem exchanges, 81–85; tools of, 263–266; typology of, 251, 258–266, *265*

media theory: concepts ascribed to, 78–79; elementary concepts for, 115–119; media-theoretic interpreters, 166, 230, 233; and ontology, 240–250; and theory of mind, 215–220, 230, 240; and theory of rationality, 75–77, 269, 275, 298; vocabulary of, 162–166

"mental organs," 44
mental states, externalizing, 108
metalanguage, 61, 67, 208, 222–223
meta-medial applications, 209
metaphysics of the irrational, 25–26
métarécit, 7
methodological individualism, 246
microphones, 264
Millikan, Ruth Garrett, 132
mimetic responses, 184
minimization demand, 300–301
mirroring of affect, 184–185, 191
Mittelstraß, Jürgen, 12–14, 31–33
modus ponens as universal principle, 70
money: aiming at situation not intention, 83; as institutionalized medium, 83, 87, *265*; as language, 84–85, 261–262; measurability of, 88
motivationally effective mechanisms, media as, 83
Mozart, Amadeus, 148–150, 154–155, 157
Mulang people, 221–230
multiplication competency, 152–154, 160
music: autonomy of, 120–121; citation of, 210; content of, 273; and discussing a concert, 143–155, 165; and European pitch shifts, 227; inner state as reason for expression of, 228–229; and interpreting a song, 293–294; as language, 120–122, 221–230; physical properties vs. musical properties, *146*; and rules, 148, 159–165; sonata form of, 148–150, 154–155; as thought, 213; tones as, 101; translatability of, 121–122, 140; transmission of knowledge of, 155–167, 174; and truth, 142

Nagl, Ludwig, 308n20
nail-chewing habit, 151
narrative as authority for Enlightenment, 4
natural beauty and artifacts, 288–289
naturalism, 26, 128–130, 136–137, 167
natural law, 275
natural signs, 274, 338n5
nature as rule-providing power, 156–157, 287–288
neo-Kantianism, 26
network: of beliefs/desires, 141; of expectations, 239; of thoughts, 168–169
Nietzsche, Friedrich, 2, 26, *29*
nominalism, 61–62
nonconceptual rational competencies, 283
nonlinguistic desire, 175, 188
nonlinguistic media: and common action, 142; and competencies for understanding, 282–283; and content, 208–209, 280; and experience, 276, 295, 304; and higher-level intentionality, 205, 295–296; instantiating rightness, 279; and intentional states, xi, 142–143, 219; interpretations of, 274; as means for communicative intentions, 271; means for nonlinguistic thinking, 303; and meta-medial application, 209–210; production process and, 219, 276; reason and, 271–273, 280; as subset of first-order media, 259–260; translatability of, 275
nonlinguistic thoughts, ix–x; common characteristics with linguistic understanding, x; and explicitness, 279; and Habermas, 41–42; identity principle for, 169–179, 215; self-ascription and, 212–214
nonspeaking animals, 126–127
normatively disinterested theories, 25
normativity, 12–13; consistency of, 16–18; foundations of, 17; loss of potency of, 27; and regulated actions, 34
notes as music, 101

objective subjectivizing, 25
observable condition, necessity of, 103–104
observation, Enlightenment as, 10

observer-relative attributes, 147, 243–246
occasion sentences, 66
onomatopoeic statements, 200
ontology of media, 240–250
open sentences, 63
optional rationality, 75, 302
orderly thinking, 149

painting: *Bleu de Ciel* (Kandinsky) reproduction, 254–255; by children, 276; and correlation of nonlinguistic thoughts, 212; and possibility of citation, 209–210
paraphrase, lack of musical, 210
Parsons, Talcott, 80–85, 87, 103, 241
Peasant Shoes (van Gogh), 280
perceptions vs. thoughts, 132
performative proliferation of media, 103–105, 112
perlocutionary speech acts, 36–38, *37*
phase model of child development: assumptions of, 179–180, 234; (phase 1) affect-centered communication, 183–187, *187*, 216, 297; (phase 2) instrumental communication, 187–190, *190*; (phase 3) medial communication, 190–198, *198*, 276; (phase 4) linguistic communication, 198–203
philosophy of mind: and identity principle for nonlinguistic thoughts, 169–179; intermediate step in, 240; and thinking without language, 167–169
phonemes, 262–263
phonetic transcripts, 263
photocopies, substitutability of, 253
photography, 264
pitch: vs. frequency, *146*, 163–164, 227; in language and music, 221–222
planned labor, 18
play among higher animals, 238–239
pointing behavior, 189, 199, 201, 278
political system (G), 81, *82*
Popper, Karl, 53, 94
positive law, 87
postmodernism, mistakes of, 5–8
power, 83, 87–88
practical comprehension, 294
practical rationality, rule principle of, 46–48
practices and rule-conforming action, 151

pragmatism, 61, 96
preference coding, 92
preference relevance, 236–237
prelinguistic thought, 214
presuppositions as explanatory claims, 4
pre-understanding, 53, 56
primates, 233–240
principle of charity, 58, 65–66, 223, 298, 301
principle of coherence, 66
principle of correspondence, 66
principle of medial understanding, 299–303
procedural concepts of reason, 26–27
process of Enlightenment, 10–11, 13; minimal conception of, 16–24; social process thesis, 15
producers: adult caregivers as, 192; aesthetic experience of, 98–99; children as, 192–194; of medial constellations, 293–295, 300; nonlinguistic expressions of, 117; and productive constraint, 296–297; self-relationships of, 276–277; and sharing experience through media, 216–217, 274
production history, 163
production process, 219
program distinguished from code, 92
progressiveness criterion, 16, 19
propositional attitudes: actions and, 124–125, 128, 141; complexity of, 168; and consciousness, 212; and dependence on network, 67–68, 126–128, 223, 273; identity criterion of, 215; and intentional states, 199, *208*, 212, 218, 219; in interpretation theory, 325n13; as languages, 259; and rationality, 67–68, 70–71, 127, 174; truth aptness of, 141–142, 169
protobeliefs, 180
protodesires, 188
protomedial expression, 239
purposiveness, 288–290

quasi-economic principles, 297
Quine, Willard van Orman, 58

radical interpretation, 58, 64–69, 106, 117, 221, 299
radically objective and subjective variation, 47–48
radio dramas, 264
rational competencies, 295

"Rationalität und Begründung" (Schnädelbach), 53
rationality: aesthetic communication and development of, 305; as confined to linguistic beings, 272; criteria for, 69; and criticizable speech acts, 39; and justification, 52–57; moving beyond language, 125; norms of, 303; theories of, 16, 24–27; and understanding, 58–71
rationalization of artificial actions (H1), 124, 215; (H1.1), 137–140; (H1.2), 138; (H2), 217–219, 280
Rawls, John, 105
reactive actions, 201
reading silently, 196
reality testing, 53
reason: competencies for understanding not characterized by, 57; as concrete human capability, 27; defined by function, 26; as form of resistance, 12; as generated and changing, 28; as ideas, 13, 32–33; implemented by nonlinguistic means, 280–281; and just why-questions, 53; in language and music, 228–229, 271–272; as media and standards of critique, 26–27, 31; media as conditions of, 273–282; as relationship attributes, 31; as self-regulated machines, 28; as subordinate tools of will, 26
reception aesthetics, 97
recipients, aesthetic experience of, 98
recursive definition method, 63
reflected smartness, 45–52
reflection, 292
reflective judgment, 284
reflective subjective variation, 47
regress problem, 43, 150, 178
regulative rules, 105, 248
relational identity of expressions (RIE_1), 170–171
relational identity of thoughts (RIT_1, RIT_2), 169–171
relativism, 21, 47
reproductions, 253–254, 257
requirement of total evidence principle, 69
rightness, forms of (R1, R2), 161, 290
ritual, 112
Rorty, Richard: on Enlightenment as process, 10–11; on foundationalist demands of Enlightenment, 3; on "overstretched" relativism, 21
routines as rule-following, 150
rules, 43, 45–47, 67; of beautiful art, 156; and causality, 154; in context of aesthetic experience, 289–290; Dewey and, 104–107; and forms of rightness (R1, R2), 161, 290; implicit rules, 106, 149–150; intuitive rule consciousness, 314n144; knowledge of, 67, 148, 154, 250, 256; and language, 272, 277–279; music lessons without, 158–159; of practice, 105; and rational action, 277; and rule-conforming behavior, 150–154; socially shared, 107; for sonata form, 148–149; unconscious following of, 242, 250
Ryle, Gilbert, 151–153, 155, 159

sanctioning practices, 106, 152–155, 278
Scheer, Brigitte, 284–285
Schnädelbach, Herbert, 25–27; on circularity of justification model, 53–57; critique of Habermas, 42; on development of concepts of rationality, 28–29, *29*
Schopenhauer, Arthur, 26, *29*
scientific objectivity, 26
scientist view of reason, 53
scope of possibilities, 113, 127, 164–165
scope of self-conception, 18
scopes of action/behavior, 115
Searle, John, 128–130, 137; on constitutive and regulative rules, 105, 250; and intentionality, 176–177, 181; on language deriving from intentionality, 128–129, 136; and meaning, 129, 202; and ontology of media, 241–250; and structure of social facts, 244–246; types of features, 243–244, *244*
second nature, 159
second-order beliefs/intentional states, 127, 132–133, 205–206, 302
second-order media, 263
selection and organization processes, 104
self-ascription, 213–215
self-control principle, 69
self-fulfilling intentions, 138
self-interpretation of mental states, 207–212

self-reference, 4–5, 186
self-relationship, 272, 276–277
self-sufficiency problem, 28
semantically intrinsically empty expressions, 274–275, 297
sensory objects and comprehensibility, 286
sensory specialization, 94
sentence(s): occasion sentences, 66; as smallest unity of reason, 273; structure logic of, 69; thought as inner articulation of, 272
shared behavior patterns, 116
shared intentionality vs. we-intentionality, 247–248
shared medial competencies, 291
shared practice, 105–109
signs and selections, 92
sincerity as validity claim, 141
smartness rules, 46–49
sneezing, 100
sobriety, stance of, 9
soccer, 245, 246
social action contexts, 59
social facts, 244–246, 248–249
social interaction analysis, 80, 116
social interpretation, 67, 205, 258–259, 274
socially shared rules, 107
social media, 136
society: open vs. closed, 94; as social system, 81; and societal community system (I), 81–82, *82*; and sociologizing, 26
sociological theories of media, 80, 95–96; and first-order media, 260–262; of Jürgen Habermas, 85–89; of Niklas Luhmann, 89–93; of Talcott Parsons, 80–85, 87
soft relations, 140
something-as-something identification, 172
sonata form of music, 148–149, 154–155
special languages model, 82, 87, 103
specifications or substitutions, 115
speech acts: acceptability of, 36; expressive, 138; locutionary, illocutionary, and perlocutionary, 36–38, *37*, *137*. *See also* language(s)
speech content, 95
stamps on paper, function of, 245

standards, sets of, 23
standards of value, 85
status-assigning function, 250
steering media, 85–88, *88*, 131, 139, 185, 196
storytelling and substitutability, 253
structured replication, medially, 294
structure of social facts, 244–246
structuring competencies, 290
structuring function of media, 83
subjective belief vs. objective truth, 127, 167
subjective subjectivizing, 25
subnets, 71
substantialist-procedural interpretation, 27–29
substitutability of medial constellations, 252–256
subsystems, 81, *82*, 86
symbolically generalized media, 87, 90
systematic medial expressions, 195
system theory: derivative nature of, 95; integrating with action theory, 85–89; and ontology, 242–243; Parsons and, 80–85

taboo proscriptions, 105
talents, 104, 287
Tarski, Alfred, 60, 63
taste, 291
tautologies, 140
technology, 9, 93–96, 264
teleology, 89, 286
television, 264
theoretical rationality, rule principle of, 46
theory and self-reference, 3
theory and violence, 3–4
Theory of Communicative Action (Habermas), 87
thoughts/thinking: "aboutness" of, 215–216; and concept of thought, 127; content of, 273–275; defined, 205; as inhibited speaking, 174; as inner articulations of language, 272; vs. perceptions, 132–133; prelinguistic, 214; social conditions for, 67. *See also* higher-level intentionality
tokens, 195, 259
tools: in concepts of rationality, 29; and media, 100–102, 263–266, *265*; of the will, 26, *29*; vs. words, 243

tracks in snow as natural signs, 338n5
tradition, 16
translation(s): of literary texts, 254–255, 257; and music, 121; of nonlinguistic media, 260, 275
transpositions, 256–258, 260
triangulation model, 66–67, 181–182, 278
truth-apt and non-truth-apt thoughts, 259
truth-conditional propositional attitudes, 141–142
truth functionality, 221, 228–230
truth predicate, 63–64, 168
truth semantics, 35–36
T-theorems, 64–65, 117, 221–223
type-token differentiation, 226

understanding: ability of, 15–16; conditions for, 70–71; decreasing improbability of, 89–92; of music without language, 143–148, 167; and principle of medial understanding, 299–303; and rationality, 58–71; and relativity, 23; theories of, ix, 65–66, 122–123, 299–303
Understanding Media (McLuhan), 94
unity: experience remembered as, 97; in perception, 300; of reason, 32; work of art as a, 143–144
universalism, 22–23
universality, 16, 19–24

universal pragmatics, 35–43
untranslatability, 121–122, 275
utterances, successful, 35

validity claims for speech acts, 34–42
value commitment, 83
value disjunctions, 93
van Gogh, Vincent, 280
verificationist theory of meaning, 129
Vernünftigkeit, 18
vinaigrette, 102
voluntary states, 180–181

Watson, James, 184–185, 238
weak concept of universalism, 22–23
Weber, Max, 53
Webern, Anton, 120
we-intentionality, 244, 245–248
well-groundedness of rationality, 45–46, 52
will to power, 2, 3
winking, 100
Wittgenstein, Ludwig, 12, 59
Word and Object (Quine), 58
works of art: ability to identify individual, 143–144; compositional identity of, 255; meaning of understanding of, 119–123; production of, 119, 219; as products, 122–126, 137, 142; referring to as specific unities, 143–144; translatability of, 142, 215, 218, 254–255